Working Together

Working Together

COLLECTIVE ACTION, THE COMMONS, AND MULTIPLE METHODS IN PRACTICE

Amy R. Poteete
Marco A. Janssen
Elinor Ostrom

PRINCETON UNIVERSITY PRESS
PRINCETON AND OXFORD

Copyright © 2010 by Princeton University Press

Published by Princeton University Press, 41 William Street, Princeton, New Jersey 08540
In the United Kingdom: Princeton University Press, 6 Oxford Street, Woodstock,
Oxfordshire OX20 1TW
press.princeton.edu

Library of Congress Cataloging-in-Publication Data

Poteete, Amy R., 1968–
    Working together : collective action, the commons, and multiple methods in practice /
Amy R. Poteete, Marco A. Janssen, and Elinor Ostrom.
        p. cm.
    Includes bibliographical references and index.
    ISBN 978-0-691-14603-4 (hardcover : alk. paper) — ISBN 978-0-691-14604-1
(pbk. : alk. paper) 1. Commons—Management—Methodology. 2. Global commons—
Management—Methodology. 3. Natural resources, Communal—Management—
Methodology. I. Janssen, Marco, 1969– II. Ostrom, Elinor. III. Title.
    HD1286.P75 2010
    333.2—dc22

                                                                    2009046702

British Library Cataloging-in-Publication Data is available

This book has been composed in Sabon

Printed on acid-free paper. ∞

Printed in the United States of America

10 9 8 7 6 5 4 3 2 1

The authors thank many colleagues from all parts of the world who have actively participated in the research efforts described herein. This book would not have been possible without their thoughtful challenges, hard work, and insightful analyses.

Contents

Part Three: *Models and Experiments in the Laboratory and the Field*

Chapter Six
Experiments in the Laboratory and the Field

Chapter Seven
Agent-Based Models of Collective Action

Illustrations

Tables

Acknowledgments

THIS VOLUME DRAWS UPON and is greatly enriched by the authors' involvement in a number of research programs over a period of several decades. The book highlights our experiences with the Common-Pool Resource (CPR) research program, the Nepal Irrigation Institutions and Systems (NIIS) research program, the International Forestry Resources and Institutions (IFRI) research program, and broader research projects undertaken at the Workshop in Political Theory and Policy Analysis and the Center for the Study of Institutions, Population, and Environmental Change at Indiana University and the Center for the Study of Institutional Diversity at Arizona State University. We have also benefited from participating in interdisciplinary projects granted through the Biocomplexity and Human and Social Dynamics programs of the National Science Foundation. A number of funding agencies have supported these programs, including the Food and Agriculture Organization of the United Nations, the Ford Foundation, the MacArthur Foundation, and the National Science Foundation.

We have benefited from the research assistance of several diligent graduate assistants. Agnes K. Koós compiled the articles included in our meta-analysis of methodological practices between 1990 and 2004. Chris Fay provided bibliographic support. We deeply appreciate the superb organizational and editorial support provided by Patty Lezotte and database stewardship of Julie England and Robin Humphrey. We thank Christopher Bartlett for preparing the index for this book. Chuck Myers at Princeton University Press has been extremely helpful through the process of developing the organization of this book, managing the publication process, and arranging for excellent peer-review assessments for which we also thank the reviewers. We thank Lauren Lepow at Princeton University Press for her careful editing of the manuscript.

Colleagues who kindly shared their reactions to chapter drafts include Lee Alston, Marty Anderies, Kenneth Arrow, Robert Axtell, Xavier Basurto, Daniel Castillo, Cheryl Eavey, James Granato, Anirudh Krishna, Maria Claudia Lopez Perez, Olivier Petit, Armando Razo, Filippo Sabetti, Michael Schoon, Jamie Thomson, Arild Vatn, James Walker, and Abby York and the Experimental Reading Group at the Workshop. We also received feedback from graduate students, including Jeremy Speight, Joannie Tremblay-Boire, and participants in Edella Schlager's graduate seminar held at the University of Arizona during the spring of 2009, including Jeb Beagles, Tiffany Harper, Robin Lemaire, Janet McCaskill, and David Tecklin.

Although we have drawn upon a variety of publications and working papers, we have reworked the material thoroughly. Arguments voiced in previous papers certainly echo throughout the book. And, certainly, feedback on earlier papers received from Martin Johnson, Achim Schlueter, Stephen Voss, and participants in the CAPRi Workshop on Methods for Studying Collective Action held in Nyeri, Kenya (2002); the Empirically-Based Agent-Based Modeling workshop held in Bloomington, Indiana (2005); and the Workshop on Lab and Field Experiments on Commons Dilemmas held in Tempe, Arizona (2009), greatly helped us. At the same time, the process of repeated revision and reorganization has left little resemblance to the actual wording of earlier working papers and published articles.

Amy Poteete gave presentations related to this book at the CAPRi Workshop on Methods for Studying Collective Action, Nyeri, Kenya, in February 2002; the 100th annual meeting of the American Political Science Association, Chicago, Illinois, in September 2004; the annual meeting of the Southern Political Science Association, Atlanta, Georgia, in January 2006; the 101st annual meeting of the American Political Science Association, Washington, DC, in September 2005; and an International Political Science Association conference titled "International Political Science: New Theoretical and Regional Perspectives/La science politique dans le monde: Nouvelles perspectives théoriques et régionales," Montreal, in April 2008.

Marco Janssen gave presentations related to this book at the Workshop on Agent-Based Computational Economics Handbook, University of Michigan, Ann Arbor, in May 2004; the 3rd International Model-to-Model Workshop, Marseille, France, in March 2007; the 2007 Amsterdam Conference on the Human Dimensions of Global Environmental Change, Amsterdam, the Netherlands, in May 2007; the 4th annual meeting of the European Social Simulation Association, Toulouse, France, in September 2007; the 8th biannual conference of the European Society for Ecological Economics, Ljubljana, Slovenia, in June 2009; and the Socio-Ecological Theory and Empirical Research lectures, Montpellier, France, in July 2009.

Elinor Ostrom gave presentations directly related to the development of this book at the American Political Science Association, Philadelphia, in August 2006 and August 2007; a symposium titled "To Trust or Not to Trust? That Is the Question" at Princeton University in October 2007; the Public Choice Society annual meeting, San Antonio, Texas, in March 2008; the Adrian College Policy Institute on the 40th Anniversary of Garrett Hardin's "Tragedy of the Commons," Adrian, Michigan, in

November 2008; the Workshop on Lab and Field Experiments on Social Dilemmas, Arizona State University, Tempe, in January 2009; and a James S. McDonnell Foundation–sponsored workshop, Reconsidering the Good Life: Environmental Impact and Social Norms, Newport Beach, California, in January 2009. Ostrom was asked to give several lectures during the summer of 2009 where she explored in more detail the key topics in this book; among these lectures were one at the Frankfurt School of Finance and Management on June 19, where Hartmut Kliemt and Werner Güth gave very useful comments, and the Wittgenstein Lectures at Bayreuth University, June 22–26, where she received good comments from faculty and students, including Eckart Arnold, Marie Halbach, Rainer Hegelsmann, Benjamin Huppert, and Maximillan Schweifer.

Amy Poteete is deeply indebted to Enrico Schaar, who repeatedly took on more than his share of child-care responsibilities without complaint. And she thanks Celia Schaar, both for her patience with her mother's writing schedule and for insisting that time be set aside for play.

Prologue

As is increasingly recognized, reliance on one or two methods hinders theoretical development and the accumulation of knowledge within a research program. Calls for the use of multiple methods have proliferated, and mixed-methods research is now considered to be the best practice. For the most part, methodological choices are presented as a matter of matching theoretical and methodological assumptions. Methodological debates largely ignore how mundane considerations influence methodological practices.

This volume focuses on methods in *practice*. It reflects our experiences, both positive and negative, with a variety of research methods, with multimethod research, and with collaborative research related to collective action and the commons. This stream of research encompasses a variety of important contemporary challenges, including the management of ocean fisheries, protection of forests and wildlife, and efforts to ameliorate climate change. The challenges in conducting research on collective action related to common-pool natural resources are typical of research on topics for which reliable data are not readily available. We highlight four themes: (1) the interlinking of methodological debates with theoretical development, (2) the advantages and limitations of multimethod and collaborative research, (3) practical constraints on methodological choices, and (4) the often problematic influence of career incentives on methodological practice.

This volume discusses a variety of particular methods: case study research, meta-analysis, collaborative field-based research programs, laboratory experiments, agent-based models, and studies that combine agent-based models with experiments. We are not covering all relevant methods, but we are drawing upon those methods with which we are most familiar from our own experiences. Two of us (Poteete and Ostrom) began with qualitative case study research. The third (Janssen) comes from applied mathematics. All three of us have learned a variety of new methods in response to theoretical and empirical puzzles. We have also engaged in collaborative research with scholars who brought different methodological skills and disciplinary perspectives to our projects. These methods reflect a range of approaches actually used in research on collective action and the commons—and more widely in the social sciences.

We have seen the tremendous value to be gained from multiple methods and collaboration. Several important theoretical breakthroughs have occurred when scholars combined a variety of methods in their research, either across a series of studies or through collaboration. The establishment of the Panel on Common Property Resource Management at the National Research Council (NRC) in 1985, for example, drew attention to the very large number of case studies—from diverse regions, resource systems, and disciplinary perspectives—in which people did *not* overharvest shared resources. The realization that the "tragedy of the commons" (G. Hardin 1968) could be avoided raised questions about the conditions that favored successful collective action. These questions have been addressed in subsequent case studies, but also through more broadly comparative research, including meta-analyses of case studies and large-N field studies. Processes suggested by field-based research have been evaluated in laboratory experiments and agent-based models, and, more recently, field experiments and empirically grounded agent-based models. The vitality of research on collective action and the commons can be attributed, at least in part, to cross-fertilization across methodological and disciplinary traditions.

Although the plethora of cases of successful collective action on the commons uncovered by the NRC panel inspired a number of important comparative studies, most field-based research on collective action and the commons continues to rely on case studies and small-N comparisons. The use of multiple methods within a single research project remains rare as well. The ongoing prevalence of small-N and single-method studies is surprising in light of the broad interest in identifying general conditions that influence collective action for the management of shared natural resources.

Our own experiences drew attention to a variety of practical constraints. It is often difficult to acquire data relevant for the study of collective action, and the costs of field research are significant. Scholars are also constrained by the costs of mastering multiple methods. Collaboration facilitates both comparative research and the incorporation of multiple methods, but presents its own challenges. We are particularly troubled by professional norms and career incentives that discourage collaboration and multimethod research and fail to acknowledge the practical challenges that affect methodological practices.

We recognize that our concern with practical constraints on methodological practices departs somewhat from those of most recent publications on research design. This is not a methods textbook; that is, it does not offer advice on how to apply particular methods. It is not a volume on the philosophy of science. This is a book on methodological practices. Thus chapter 1 explains why methodological practices matter. As many others have argued, scholars *should* start with a research question and then select methods that match their research goals and their ontological assumptions about causality. Mismatches between ideal and actual methodological practices occur, however, and not always or only because scholars are ignoring the principles of research design or disagree with a positivist model of scientific research. Practical considerations often make it difficult-to-impossible to implement the ideal research design, even when scholars are very aware of what they should do. If debates about methods ignore these practical constraints, the scholarly community is not likely to recognize the importance of addressing them. We have written this book to draw attention to these practical considerations and to encourage efforts to address them.

PART ONE

Introduction

CHAPTER ONE

Overcoming Methodological Challenges

QUESTIONS ABOUT the relative merits of alternative research strategies pervade the social sciences. What counts as an adequate explanation for social phenomena? How can we evaluate competing explanations? What standards should we apply when weighing evidence? How much and what types of evidence are convincing? Can social phenomena related to policy areas be studied scientifically? Some eminent scholars appear to agree on broad methodological goals or criteria (Brady and Collier 2004; Gerring 2001; Lieberman 2005). Explanations should be general yet precise, accurate, and well-specified. Evidence should be theoretically relevant and should identify mechanisms linking explanations to outcomes. Abundant evidence, if theoretically relevant, is valued because it enhances confidence in findings.

Despite the apparent common ground underlying the work of many scholars, methodological divides within the social sciences also run deep. As lamented by Mahoney and Goertz (2006) and E. Ostrom (2006), rival camps often cast aspersions on each other's work rather than engage in constructive dialogue. The acrimony has several sources. The disagreements have been provoked in part by battles over induction versus deduction, poor methodological practice by some scholars, and a lack of sensitivity to diverse research goals. The stakes of the methodological debate are increased by the intertwining of methodological choice with ontological, normative, and theoretical positions, and with competition for professional status and resources (Moses and Knutsen 2007). These dynamics encourage intense and sometimes grossly unfair critiques.

The substantive focus of this book is on collective action and the commons. It is a field of research that utilizes multiple methods extensively, as well as being the one most familiar to the authors of this book. We believe that the discussion of the use of multiple methods in this research field, and the lessons we draw from our practical experiences, apply more broadly to social science in general. Therefore, we start this first chapter with a broader discussion on the methodological challenges in the social sciences.

Examples of poor methodological practice pervade social science research. Often, scholars follow "the rule of the hammer" and apply a single method indiscriminately, regardless of its suitability for a given research project. Harmonization of research goals, theory, data, and method does not, however, guarantee sound practice. One can find qualitative studies that overstate either the uniqueness or the generality of particular cases, fail to utilize relevant concepts and theories in the literature, or work with concepts that conflate multiple dimensions (Sartori 1991; compare Goldthorpe 1997). Quantitative studies sometimes use inadequate data and do not always use appropriate diagnostic checks and technical fixes (Jackman 1985; Scruggs 2007; Shalev 2007). Formal models often work with unrealistic assumptions without addressing the gap between assumptions and reality (Bendor 1988; Green and Shapiro 1994). No method is immune to poor applications.

Critics sometimes conflate methodological practice with the method itself, arguing that examples of poor application discredit the method. A method need not be abandoned because it has been poorly utilized; it makes more sense to encourage greater methodological awareness and better practices (Geddes 2003; Jackman 1985; King, Keohane, and Verba 1994; Scruggs 2007). Others fail to appreciate that research goals are varied and require diverse methods. More than three decades ago Robert Clark (1977, 10; emphasis in original) strongly warned against reliance on a single method:

> A first rule should be to beware of one researcher, one method, *or* one instrument. The point is not to prove that the hypothesis is *correct*, but to *find out* something. To rely on a single approach is to be shackled.

Indiscriminate application of a method makes little sense, but complete rejection of a method because it is inappropriate in a particular setting or for a particular purpose is not more sensible. It is important for social scientists to recognize that all methods generate results that contain some level of uncertainty. While multiple scientific goals and trade-offs in achieving those goals are widely acknowledged (Coppedge 1999; Gerring 2001), little consensus exists on the relative importance of particular goals. Some scholars prioritize one or a few goals to such an extent that they dismiss as unscientific research that prioritizes other goals. For example, Goldthorpe (1997) includes generality as the most important criterion in his definition of causal explanation, rather than as one of several criteria (compare Gerring 2001). Consequently, he sees unique events and contingency as marking the limits of scientific inquiry. By this definition, analyses of such events are not scientific and cannot support causal inferences. Proponents of path-dependent explanations, analytic narratives, interpretive methods, and other approaches strongly disagree (Bates et al. 1998; Bennett and Elman 2006; Rogowski 2004; R. Smith 2004). As in this example, and as discussed further below, methodological controversies often reflect competition between research traditions.

Fortunately, social scientists increasingly recognize trade-offs across methods (Bates 2007; Brady and Collier 2004; Gerring 2001).[1] King, Keohane, and Verba (1994), for example, point out that all methodologies have limitations; scholars should be more aware of these limits and more transparent about the limits as well as the solid contributions of their work. To overcome the limits of any one method, one needs to draw on multiple methods (Bates et al. 1998; Coppedge 1999; Granato and Scioli 2004; Jackman 1985; King, Keohane, and Verba 1994; Laitin 2003; Lieberman 2005; Scharpf 2000; Tarrow 2004). If social scientists have shared standards, no single method fully addresses all standards. Methods offer different strengths and weaknesses. Rigorous research that combines complementary methods will be superior to research that relies on any single method (Gray et al. 2007).

The pragmatism and respect for diverse methodological traditions in these reflections are welcome. Too often, however, the challenges involved in using multiple methods are themselves overlooked. Proponents of mixed methods justify their preferred combination in logical terms and illustrate the approach with a few examples. With some exceptions (Lieberman 2005; Scharpf 2000), this literature offers few specific practical suggestions.

Practical challenges can be formidable. Not all methods are equally feasible or even appropriate for all research topics (Bennett and Elman 2006; Poteete and Ostrom 2008). Lieberman's (2005) nested analysis, for example, involves large-N analysis *prior* to any case study work. There are many important topics for which broadly comparative data are scarce, difficult to access, or of dubious quality. Lieberman, however, does not address these challenges. Even if data availability is not a problem, the value of a multimethod approach requires sufficient command of multiple methods. Yet considerable investment is required to gain competency in any methodology, and the benefits of methodological specialization are substantial. While these challenges are sometimes acknowledged, few social scientists make practical suggestions to address them.

This book focuses on the practical challenges that influence methodological choice. We are particularly concerned with research on topics for which data are scarce, difficult to collect, and not readily comparable. These conditions affect research on a wide variety of topics, including those concerned with informal institutions, subnational organizations, and nonelite populations. We focus on collective action for the management of natural resources, an area of research in which all of these conditions apply. For such topics, data for large-N analysis are neither available nor readily accessible, and field research is unavoidable. Researchers often need considerable contextual knowledge even to recognize the phenomenon of interest. The need to conduct intensive fieldwork limits the potential for collecting enough data to support broadly comparative analysis.

We have become strongly aware of these challenges through our own work on collective action and natural resource management. We feel that the practical challenges of conducting rigorous social science research on topics for which data are scarce, or difficult to access or to interpret, have not received adequate attention in discussions about social science research. We have seen the benefits of collaboration and the combination of multiple methods in our research. We also have firsthand experience of the challenges involved in such research, and we will discuss these throughout this book.

In this chapter, we introduce four themes that recur through the book: (1) the interlinking of methodological debates with theoretical development, (2) the advantages and limitations of multiple methods and collaborative research, (3) practical constraints on methodological choices, and (4) the often problematic influence of career incentives on methodological practice. In this book, we explicitly acknowledge the practical challenges that affect methodological choices, evaluate several strategies for addressing these challenges, and direct attention to the influence of career incentives on methodological choices in social science research. We discuss a range of options for balancing competing methodological demands under the inevitable conditions of limited resources, including a variety of techniques that we feel have been underutilized in the social sciences. We discuss the merits and limits of each method, as well as the possibilities for and constraints on combining various methods. In our discussion of constraints on methodological choice, we hope to stimulate a debate about professional incentives and other structural aspects of academia that influence how research is conducted.

This book is more about methodological practice than about methodological ideals. We thus begin this chapter with a historical overview of methodological debates, highlighting interactions among methodological practices, changing theoretical orientations, and competition for professional status and resources. We then look more closely at issues surrounding research that uses multiple methods, an approach that has gained in acceptance in recent years. This leads to a discussion of constraints on methodological choice, both practical and professional. We then explain how our substantive focus—the study of collective action in natural resource management—helps us address our four thematic concerns. The chapter concludes with an outline of the rest of the book.

SOCIAL SCIENCE DEBATES OVER THE SUPERIORITY OF
PARTICULAR METHODS

The history of the social sciences can be recounted with reference to major methodological shifts. An initial reliance on qualitative analysis gave way dramatically to quantification in the early to mid-twentieth century. When this transformation began, quantification largely meant statistical analysis of large-N data sets of public opinion surveys. The last third of the twentieth century saw a surge in the use of formal models as well. Debates about the relative merits of qualitative, statistical, and formal methods contributed to several developments in the late twentieth and early twenty-first centuries: refinements of quantitative methods that attempt to better match social conditions; the rise of formal models; greater appreciation for combining multiple methods; and the spread of post-positivist methods such as discourse analysis.

The qualitative orientation of the early social sciences can be seen in the emphasis on case studies and participant observation in sociology, ethnographic field-based research in anthropology, and descriptive and normative analyses of formal legal arrangements. In the early decades of the twentieth century, many scholars embraced quantitative methods as part of a drive to make the social sciences more scientific.[2] Quantitative methods began to gain currency across the social sciences in the 1920s and 1930s. The adoption of these methods accelerated at midcentury, as conveyed by references to the behavioral revolution.

The branches of the social sciences differed in their timing, pace, and preferred forms of quantification. Nonetheless, the methodological shift from qualitative to quantitative methods in the social sciences was dramatic. Psychology rapidly adopted experimental and statistical methods. Quantitative methods in economics encompassed formal models as well as experiments and statistics. For sociology, research activities during World War II marked the ascendance of survey research, experiments, and statistical forms of analysis (Platt 1986). Postwar political science shared the enthusiasm for survey research and statistical analysis, but formal modeling became widespread only in the 1980s and 1990s. In sociocultural anthropology, some interest was expressed in mathematical models in the early postwar period, but multivariate statistical analyses remained relatively rare until the 1970s (Chibnik 1985).

The role of quantitative methods in the social sciences has always been contentious. Current methodological debates echo those of a century ago, even if framed in somewhat different terms.[3] Scholars concerned with methods have disagreed over (1) the goals of social research, (2) philosophical and theoretical issues, and (3) practical considerations, especially related to data quality. Methodological choices should be driven by theoretical and ontological assumptions (Hall 2003), but they also reflect underlying values and beliefs (Mahoney and Goertz 2006) and practical considerations (Platt 1986). The ontological and normative dimensions of methodological choices are not widely recognized (Mahoney and Goertz 2006). As a result, social science debates about methods involve frequent misunderstandings, with proponents of different approaches talking past each other (E. Ostrom 2006). Furthermore, because methodological discussions rarely acknowledge practical and professional considerations, they offer little guidance on how to address these constraints. In this section, we discuss controversies over the goals of social research, and how philosophical and theoretical issues interact with professional competition. We expand our treatment of practical and professional considerations in subsequent sections.

During the 1920s and 1930s, the social sciences became more institutionalized in North America. The social sciences sought recognition as sciences, and each discipline developed a more or less distinct professional identity (Guy 2003; Platt 1986). This process of institutionalization influenced methodological debates. During the prewar period, disagreements focused on the goals of social research. Should sociological research support social work to improve social conditions, seek subjective understanding of life experiences, or attempt to identify general patterns (Platt 1986)? Should the study of politics provide normative and practical guidance for administrators or objective understanding of political phenomena (Guy 2003; Lasswell 1951)? As universities set up schools of social work, public administration, and business administration alongside departments of sociology, political science, and economics, differences over goals were alleviated—but not really addressed—through the institutionalization of more focused programs of study.

Yet differences over the relative importance of theory and praxis cannot fully account for methodological debates. Scholars with common goals disagree over methods, and scholars draw on the same methods to pursue divergent goals. A lack of consensus on fundamental philosophical issues contributes to disagreements over methods. What counts as science? What model or models of causality and explanation make sense for social phenomena? In particular, do models of science and explanation developed in the natural, and especially the physical, sciences make sense for the social sciences?

Over the past century, some have embraced deductive models of science inspired by the natural sciences as a way to gain more reliable insights about social processes (King, Keohane, and Verba 1994; Przeworski and Teune 1970). Deduction involves the logical derivation of universalistic, lawlike statements of the sets of conditions associated with the outcome of interest from theoretical assumptions. Lawlike statements may be derived from formal or mathematical models, as in rational-choice approaches, or logical analysis, as in some qualitative studies. Empirical evaluations rely on the analysis of correlation, as in behavioral research or paired comparisons.[4] The journal *Public Choice* devoted a special issue in December 2008 to the topic "Homo Economicus and Homo Politicus" (edited by Geoffrey Brennan and Michael Gillespie) with nine articles addressing the question of how to reconcile the basic differences between theories of human behavior in economics and political science. In the introduction, Brennan (2008, 431) reflects that

> the ambition to find common ground on which public choice scholars and "political theorists" of a more traditional kind might have profitable exchange is not a trivial one: we start from very different conceptions of what counts as theory—even of what counts as worthwhile scholarship—and from rather different disciplinary presuppositions as to how differences in approach can most profitably be engaged and resolved.

Critics, however, argue that deductive methods do not allow for human agency and reflexivity, the influence of meaning and interpretation, or contingent relationships (Almond and Genco 1977; Hall 2003; Ragin 1987; see review in Platt 1986). If agency is taken seriously, we must allow for both creativity and differences in perspectives. But creativity and differences in interpretation mean that lawlike social patterns are unlikely to arise. Contingent relationships are possible even if questions of agency are put aside. These differences over the nature of causality have fueled heated methodological debates. In political science, both the behavioral revolution of the early postwar period and the rise of rational-choice theory in the 1980s and 1990s assumed the value of deductive-nomological reasoning. Scholars who used methods that reflected alternative ontological assumptions had difficulty gaining recognition for their work. Their frustration gave rise to the recent perestroika movement, in which constructivists and others challenged both the universality of social patterns assumed by rational choice and behavioral theories, and the dominance of statistical and formal methods associated with these approaches in the profession (Monroe 2005). Within economics, the concern that narrow rational-choice models have come to dominate much of economic scholarship is regularly expressed in the online journal *Real-World Economics Review*.[5]

Deductive-nomological reasoning suggests a mechanical view of the world, in which the same stimulus produces the same effect, ceteris paribus. Theories that view social phenomena as products of either evolutionary processes or intentional action challenge this mechanical view. Both evolutionary and intentional theories assume that individuals and organizations adjust their responses to social conditions (Alchian 1950; Brady 2004; E. Ostrom 2000; Thelen 2003). Intentional theories of human behavior assume that adaptation occurs as people struggle to solve puzzles related to the pursuit of their goals (Almond and Genco 1977; Elster 1983; Knight 1992). While some intentional theories emphasize routines and heuristics, there is always a possibility for creativity and innovation (March and Olsen 1984; Simon 1955). Evolutionary theories do not require intentionality but do require some sort of selection mechanism, such as market or electoral competition, to drive adaptation. Both forms of adaptation imply that the same circumstances will generate diverse responses across actors and changes in individual behavior over time, but that adaptations will reflect historical trajectories. Thus the same stimulus will *not* produce the same effect on average, and constant effects cannot be assumed. Both perspectives raise questions about the suitability of research methods that assume constant effects (Elster 1998; Hall 2003; Ragin 1987, 2000).

The choice of method tends to signal one's theoretical perspective, as does the nature of methodological critique. Those who discount qualitative methods as incapable of evaluating general relationships signal a belief in both lawlike social relations and the relative unimportance of factors such as agency, history, and informal context. Not surprisingly, critiques of quantitative methods often charge that they do not capture the most important aspects of social conditions. Likewise, those wary of formal models worry about the level of abstraction. How can formal models adequately represent the dense networks of formal and informal institutions and cultural understandings in which human action occurs? None of these critiques really concerns the method as method; rather, they target the theoretical assumptions as reflected in methodological choices. What variables are important? What is the relative importance of formal institutions, culture, social structure, or informal institutions? How important are mass beliefs and behavior, or individual interests, beliefs, and strategic action? How are those variables related? While the behavioral revolution during the mid-twentieth century certainly fostered the rapid spread of quantitative analysis, it also redirected theoretical emphasis from formal institutions to the behavior and attitudes of individuals interacting within both formal and informal institutions. Likewise, rational-choice analysis often relies on game theory and other varieties of formal modeling, but is defined by assumptions of methodological individualism and intentional action.

Yet the influence of theory—and the implied influence of ontology—on methodological practice cannot be assumed and should not be overstated.[6] Theoretical changes can and do occur independently of changes in methodological practice (Hall 2003; Platt 1986). Sometimes, methodological challenges seem to drive theoretical arguments rather than the other way around (Lieberson 1991, 318). Indeed, sophisticated methods sometimes crowd out theory altogether (Achen 2002, 2005). We argue that methodological choices are often driven as much by data availability or career incentives. When career survival is at stake, practical considerations can squeeze out concerns about matching theory and method. The link between methods and career prospects can, however, be expected to influence the tenor of methodological—and theoretical—debates.

Sometimes, methodological and theoretical debates take on existential overtones. When a particular theory and associated methods become extremely widespread, for example, proponents of alternative approaches may worry about their own academic survival. Proponents of new theories—and associated methods—also face an existential fight for recognition and survival. The degree of (perceived) existential threat depends on the extent to which fellowships, job opportunities, publishing outlets, and research grants are open (or closed) to diverse theories and methods. The recent perestroika movement in political science, for example, presented itself as defending against methodological hegemony, conjuring images of political scientists conspiring to control journal outlets and professional associations.[7] This was not simply a methodological critique but a call to action against presumed tyranny. While the inflammatory public language associated with the perestroika movement may be unusual, the layering of methodological debates with value judgments and competition for professional recognition and resources is commonplace.

Despite references to "revolutions" and paradigm shifts, new social science theories and methods have not fully displaced their predecessors. Rather, each new theory and method has added another strand. Constructivists, institutionalists, and postmodernists coexist with behavioralists and structuralists. Despite the history of theoretical and methodological competition and critique, scholars also engage in creative synthesis. The current appreciation for methodological pluralism may be interpreted as a product of the survival and adaptation of approaches that were once perceived to be under existential threat. Promotion of methodological pluralism favors a theoretical eclecticism that should decrease concerns about existential threats to particular approaches, and should thus decrease the intensity of methodological debates.

Multiple Methods: Promises and Challenges

There are many reasons for social scientists to welcome methodological pluralism and greater use of mixed methods. No single method overcomes all challenges. Case studies and small-N comparative research designs offer advantages for concept and theory development as well as evaluation of hypothesized causal sequences and mechanisms (Bates 2008; Bates et al. 1998; Collier, Brady, and Seawright 2004; Coppedge 1999; Lieberman 2005). Rich explanations of particular cases are often valuable substantively and theoretically (Mahoney and Goertz 2006; Rogowski 2004). Yet, as is widely recognized, small-N studies offer an uncertain foundation for positing or evaluating general relationships.

Formal methods seek to build logically coherent models and discern their logical implications. Their emphasis on logical consistency facilitates the distillation of parsimonious yet general hypotheses and guides the choice of statistical techniques (Achen 2002, 2005; Bates et al. 1998; Granato and Scioli 2004).[8] The high level of abstraction in formal models, however, raises questions about their empirical applicability (Green and Shapiro 1994). The controlled conditions in experimental research provide greater confidence in the internal validity of observed relationships. The external validity of general relationships can best be evaluated, however, through analysis of a large number of nonexperimental observations (Goldthorpe 1997; King, Keohane, and Verba 1994) as well as through field experiments (see Cardenas 2003; Cardenas, Stranlund, and Willis 2000; Henrich et al. 2004; List 2004).

Small-N qualitative studies can suggest the plausibility of formal models but provide little leverage in assessing the generality of relationships. The broad comparisons required to evaluate the generality of hypothesized relationships demand some form of quantitative analysis. Where quantitative analysis once meant regression-based analysis, options for quantitative analysis of empirical social science data now include Qualitative Comparative Analysis (QCA) and fuzzy-set Qualitative Comparative Analysis (fs/QCA) (Ragin 1987, 2000) as well as probabilistic, likelihood-based, and Bayesian statistics (Gill 2004).[9] This methodological menu includes options for scholars who hold varied ontological assumptions about the social world.

Mixed methods take a variety of forms. A researcher might use different methods to address different research questions or contexts. Or different methods might guide different stages of a research program (Lieberman 2005). Increasingly, scholars strive to use two or more methods at each stage of research. Those concerned with general causal patterns draw on quantitative and qualitative methods (Coppedge 1999; Lieberman 2005; Tarrow 2004). Combinations of formal and qualitative methods address concerns about logical coherence and causal processes in contingent relationships where there is no expectation of generality (Bates et al. 1998). Others contend that scholars should seek logical coherence and evidence for causal processes, and should test for the generality of relations by drawing on formal, qualitative, and quantitative methods (Granato and

Scioli 2004; Laitin 2003). Scholars who develop agent-based models use role games and experiments to collect data as well as involving stakeholders in the validation of their models (Barreteau, Le Page, and Aquino 2003; Bousquet et al. 2002; Gurung, Bousquet, and Trébuil 2006). Other scholars combine their formal models with ethnographic observations (Bharwani et al. 2005; Huigen, Overmars, and de Groot 2006).

The use of multiple methods, however, does not guarantee methodologically superior social science research. Some question the extent to which formal, qualitative, and quantitative research methods are actually complementary. Several recent publications have argued that different methods reflect different assumptions about the nature of causality, and have called for greater care in matching methods to ontological assumptions (Bennett and Elman 2006; Clark, Gilligan, and Golder 2006; Hall 2003; Mahoney 2003; Ragin 1987, 2000).

There are also limits to the feasibility of multimethod research. Hypotheses about complex causal relationships imply complex statistical models that stretch the limits of available data. Statistical analyses often add interaction terms or dummy variables to model contingent effects and multiple causal paths (Clark, Gilligan, and Golder 2006; Pontusson 2007), but these additional variables consume degrees of freedom in a context of limited data availability (Shalev 2007). Other techniques developed to address causal complexity, such as the analysis of time-series-cross-sectional data and hierarchical models, may strain the technical skills of both the researcher and the audience (Shalev 2007).

Mahoney and Goertz (2006) contend that interaction effects, dummy variables, hierarchical models, and other similar statistical fixes do not accurately reflect the relationships posited in the underlying theories. The assumption that observations are independent, for example, is called into question by globalization, diffusion effects, and actor-centered theories that emphasize strategic interactions. Even some quantitatively oriented scholars question the appropriateness of standard statistical techniques. In recent years, new techniques have been proposed to incorporate interdependence (Signorino 1999), Bayesian statistics (Dion 1998; Gill 2004), and Boolean logic (Braumoeller 2003; Ragin 1987, 2000). The verdict is still out on whether these new techniques match underlying assumptions better than does regression-based statistics.

Too often, the development of ever-more sophisticated techniques seems to be an end in itself. The latest techniques are sometimes adopted with little reference to theoretical considerations or understanding of the underlying assumptions. But methodological sophistication cannot substitute for theory. Achen (2002, 2005) warns that quantitative analyses that are not supported by theoretical microfoundations or careful exploration of the data yield unreliable results and should not be trusted.

Scholars must do more to develop explicit theoretical arguments and ensure that their methods match their underlying assumptions about causality, ontology, and epistemology (Achen 2002, 2005; Brady and Collier 2004; Hall 2003).

Neither theory nor methodological techniques substitute for a thorough familiarity with the data, gained from diagnostic tests and data exploration. Visualization techniques such as graphical analysis and simple statistical techniques such as cross-tabulations bring empirical regularities and patterned variation into focus (Achen 2002, 2005; Shalev 2007). Data exploration draws attention to potential causal heterogeneity, nonlinear relationships, interaction effects, and other aspects of the data that are obscured by more sophisticated multivariate techniques. Thus thorough data exploration contributes to theory testing and development by complementing more sophisticated forms of data analysis and drawing attention to empirical patterns that call out for theoretical explanation (Achen 2002, 2005).

Even if causal, epistemological, and ontological assumptions pose no barrier, practical considerations complicate methodological choice. These practical challenges, largely overlooked in the exchanges regarding the relative merits of alternative and multiple methods, stand at the center of our analysis. The groundswell of interest in multiple methods demands more intensive and diversified forms of technical skill-development. Yet individual researchers rarely master more than a couple of methodologies. Even within a single research tradition, technical language and efforts to solve technical problems threaten to obscure or overshadow substantive issues (Beck and Katz 1996; Green and Shapiro 1994; Shalev 2007). If there are limits to the methods any individual researcher can master, what are the implications for multimethod research? The next two sections elaborate on some of the practical and career-related constraints on methodological practice.

PRACTICAL CHALLENGES AND METHODOLOGICAL TRADE-OFFS

Methodological debates in the social sciences have had at least three positive effects. First, sterile debates over the superiority of alternative methods have given way to an appreciation of trade-offs and complementarities between approaches. Second, the goals of qualitative research and associated methods are receiving more explicit elaboration in response to a feeling that they were widely misunderstood (Brady and Collier 2004; Coppedge 1999; Gerring 2001, 2004; Goodwin and Horowitz 2002; Mahoney and Rueschemeyer 2003).[10] Third, more constructive critiques have stimulated considerable innovation in techniques within specific methodological traditions and in strategies for combining multiple methods in research (Bates et al. 1998; Braumoeller 2003, 2004; Gill 2004; Lieberman 2005; Ragin 1987, 2000).

Nonetheless, scholars often struggle to make full and appropriate use of available research methods. As each methodological tradition becomes more sophisticated, the task of mastering multiple methods also becomes more challenging. When research demands intensive fieldwork and substantial local knowledge, unavoidably large investments in data collection present additional obstacles. All too often, methodological discussions overlook these practical constraints on methodological choice.

We promote collaborative research as a way to expand the potential for using multiple methods well in the analysis of broadly comparative research. Collaboration can bring scholars from multiple disciplines together on the same research team with strengths in complementary methods, increasing confidence that each method is applied rigorously. Likewise, collaboration that brings together expertise about different countries can expand the scope of comparison. In this book, we will discuss a variety of strategies for collaborative research and analyze obstacles to collaborative and broadly comparative research. But first, we outline some practical constraints on multimethod and collaborative research.

Technological Development and the Costs of Border Crossing

Contemporary social science features tremendous innovation within each methodological tradition. Innovation indicates vitality but also increases the costs of competency in a particular method. Higher entry costs raise the barriers to methodological border crossing. And yet the benefits of multimethod research depend on competent application of each method. Otherwise, the use of multiple methods weakens rather than strengthens confidence in the research. To better illustrate the challenges, let us consider what is required for a researcher to gain competency in several methods: formal, quantitative, experimental, and qualitative.

The technical demands of formal modeling were evident even as this approach spread across the social sciences. Formal modeling requires a command of set theory and mathematical logic, optimization, and other techniques from economics, game theory, and complexity theory. Computational modelers require skills in programming and algorithmic design. Formal theorists devote considerable energy to the development of new modeling techniques and solution concepts.

Increasingly, similar conditions prevail in quantitative methodology. As recently as the 1980s, many social scientists equated quantitative research with ordinary least squares regression. The assumptions for multivariate regression rarely hold for social phenomena, however, and more suitable statistical techniques exist. "Standard" quantitative techniques now encompass maximum likelihood techniques, analysis of cross-national-time-series data, and analyses of event histories. A variety of other techniques, including Bayesian statistics and Boolean-based methods, are also becoming more common. Computational power and statistical software make it very easy to apply advanced statistical techniques, but do not guarantee appropriate application. Each technique involves a particular set of assumptions, diagnostic checks, and ongoing debates about technological fixes. As with formal methods, a large investment is required of the researcher seeking to gain and maintain competency in even a subset of quantitative methods.

If researchers are to perform experiments, it is crucial that they learn the practice of experimental design in order to measure the relevant attributes of different experimental treatments. This requires the development of hypotheses related to outcomes expected from different treatments based on formal models, and statistical analysis on the data collected from the experiments to test the significance of differences found across treatments. Someone on an experimental team will also need programming skills to enter and analyze the data, and to enter the experimental instructions and response categories for experiments run in computer laboratories.

The menu of qualitative methods of data collection techniques includes ethnography, participant observation, interviews, oral histories, and archival research. Each technique involves a set of issues that researchers must understand and address to apply the method well (e.g., Burawoy 1998; Lustick 1996; Rocheleau 1995). Many of these techniques require a substantial period of fieldwork, keen observational skills, thorough record keeping, and a high degree of self-awareness and ethical management of social relations.[11] For fieldwork, researchers must have appropriate language skills and sufficient understanding of the local context to gain access, recognize informal institutions, and accurately interpret culturally coded observations.

Fieldwork yields voluminous data, but the data generally take forms that are not easily processed (H. Becker 1996). Thus the value of a qualitative study hinges on disciplined data analysis related to theoretical questions (Campbell 1975; Lijphart 1971). Qualitative researchers have developed a variety of techniques to structure data analysis, such as counterfactual analysis, process tracing, structured comparisons, and analysis of deviant cases (Bennett and Elman 2006; Fearon 1991; Goldstone 1997; Tarrow 2004). The development of software for Computer-Assisted Qualitative Data Analysis (CAQDAS) expands options for data management. There is considerable confusion, however, about what these programs do, the differences among them, how to match programs and theoretical approaches, and even whether CAQDAS makes sense for a particular study or approach (MacMillan and Koenig 2004). As in quantitative research, the increase in computational tools can facilitate rigorous data analysis, but it can also produce misleading results if applied inappropriately.

Thus each method encompasses several sophisticated techniques. Whether a method yields analytical insights or misleading findings depends on competency in recognizing appropriate techniques, implementing them well, and making sense of the data. A large and ongoing investment is necessary for the researcher to gain and maintain competency in a given method. The investment required to master any single method is not excessive, but it limits the number of methods in which any individual can be expected to gain and maintain competency. While scholars should utilize diverse methods as possible and appropriate, methodological specialization and multimethod research designs present a dilemma. Collaboration offers a potential solution. Scholars with strengths in complementary methods can work together with increased confidence that each method is applied rigorously.

Availability and Accessibility of Data

Depending on the period, country, and scale of analysis, data might be abundant and readily available or virtually nonexistent. Different methods require different kinds and quantities of data. Data compiled by national and international agencies do not address many issues at the subnational level and are often blind to both informal institutions and nonelite actors. Even in industrialized democracies, data availability and quality vary considerably across states, provinces, cities, and other subnational jurisdictions. Reliable and comprehensive data sources often do not exist for nongovernmental organizations, informal institutions, or collective action. In part, the lack of readily available data on informal institutions, subnational phenomena, nonelite actors, and other similar topics reflects the difficulty of data collection. Informality and nonelite status imply a need for local knowledge and trust. In the absence of trust, local actors may hesitate to provide accurate information about themselves, their practices, or other informal institutions.

As the costs of data collection increase, so do the restrictions on methodological choice. Recommendations that qualitative researchers should gather more data (Goldthorpe 1997; King, Keohane, and Verba 1994; Lijphart 1971) ignore the difficulty of recognizing some types of phenomena in field settings, the costs of collecting qualitative data, and the voluminous yet difficult-to-process data yielded by qualitative research (H. Becker 1996; Poteete and Ostrom 2004b). These conditions make it more difficult to build large databases for quantitative analysis, even if quantitative analysis makes sense for a given theoretical approach.

Data problems also vary in severity. If data availability and access were unproblematic, then scholars could choose methodologies that matched their causal and epistemological assumptions. Scholars have to choose from a subset of less appropriate methods, however, when data are not readily available. As a result, the capacity to engage in quantitative analysis and broad comparison is higher for research on formal institutions, some types of international and national phenomena, and elites. Because data on informal institutions, subnational issues, and historically disadvantaged populations are less readily available, it is quite a challenge to engage in broadly comparative and quantitative social research on these topics.

At least in principle, collaborative research enhances a more general comparative analysis without sacrificing data quality. Collaborative research offers the potential to collect larger quantities of data, engage in more broadly comparative research, and utilize a broader array of methods competently. Unlike an individual researcher who is expected to do it all, collaborators can pool their data and draw on complementary methodological skills. Using formal models, Scott Page (2007) found that groups with a higher diversity of problem-solving approaches are more effective in overcoming difficult problems. This gives us even more confidence in strongly recommending collaboration across methods as an important foundation for the future development of the social sciences.

In practice, collaborative research is itself challenging. Collaboration is generally limited by divergent research interests and theoretical orientations. Inconsistency in conceptualization and measurement can be a problem as well (Poteete and Ostrom 2004b), especially for qualitative researchers who work hard to develop contextually suitable measures. Yet these challenges are not insurmountable. Colleagues with shared interests and theoretical perspectives can collaborate on the full research process, from conceptualization through analysis. As discussed below, however, the social sciences still reward individual research more than they do collaborative research. Scholars concerned about their careers recognize these incentives and limit their participation in collaborative efforts.

CAREER INCENTIVES AS METHODOLOGICAL CONSTRAINTS

Ideally, training in the social sciences should encourage scholars to develop competency in a variety of methods and engage in collaborations that further extend their methodological range. Universities should foster multi-method and collaborative research by encouraging cross-appointments, and by creating and sustaining thematic research centers and initiatives. Funding agencies should offer longer-term grants to support the longer time frame required for multimethod and collaborative research. In reality, academia rewards specialization and individual projects, especially in early career stages. Although collaborative and multimethod research can yield better knowledge, individual accomplishments do more to advance careers. The tenure clock also generates more stimulus for rapid research output than for the development of longer-term research programs. And funding agencies rarely provide long-term support.

Training

Graduate program curricula and programs for intensive methodological training provide an indication of disciplinary support for multimethod and collaborative research. Training in quantitative methods has been a standard component of graduate programs in economics, political science, and sociology throughout the postwar period. Likewise, opportunities to supplement in-house courses with intensive training in more specialized quantitative methods have been available for decades. Probably the best-known source of specialized quantitative training for social scientists, the Interuniversity Consortium for Political and Social Research (ICPSR) at the University of Michigan, has offered an annual summer institute in research methods since the 1960s.

By comparison, options for training in qualitative methods were rare until recently. Before the turn of the (current) century, most social science departments offered no graduate training in qualitative methods beyond a course in research design. Opportunities for intensive training in other qualitative methods and in multimethod research have expanded over the past decade. The Consortium on Qualitative Research Methods holds an annual intensive Institute in Qualitative and Multi-Method Research.[12] The (U.S.) National Science Foundation has supported methodological training programs for the social sciences, including month-long summer institutes on multimethod research beginning with the Empirical Implications of Theoretical Models (EITM) program, the Summer Institute on Research Design in Cultural Anthropology, Short Courses on Research Methods in Cultural Anthropology, and Field Training in Methods of Data Collection in Cultural Anthropology.[13] Even with these new opportunities, social science graduate students interested in multimethod research find it difficult to gain adequate training in nonquantitative methods (Siegel et al. 2007).

Career Incentives and Specialization

Susanne Lohmann (2007) argues forcefully that the procedures for reviewing manuscripts, grant applications, and applications for academic positions and promotions strongly favor specialization. All of these forms of evaluation rely on peer review. As Lohmann notes, peer review generally means review by specialists. The work of a specialist will be reviewed by other specialists in the same method, with the same area expertise, and/or with the same or similar substantive concerns. Scholars with the same specialization share a common understanding of their area, assume its value, and are familiar with practical challenges faced by their favored approach.

Scholars who engage multiple methods or disciplines, on the other hand, will most likely be evaluated by disciplinary specialists rather than other practitioners of multimethod or interdisciplinary research. The reviewers are not likely to fully understand all of the methods, the rationale for mixing methods, or the challenges involved in multimethod research. Specialists tend to discount the results of unfamiliar methods, references to works in other fields, publications in journals outside their own discipline, and interdisciplinary publications. Thus scholars who use multiple methods and draw on multiple disciplines tend to get less enthusiastic and more contradictory evaluations. Only the best scholars survive this process. As a result, Lohmann argues, a small proportion of social scientists are top-notch scholars who use diverse methods and cross subfield and disciplinary boundaries, but specialists dominate the field numerically. Despite increased interest in multimethod research, hiring committees still prefer candidates who have a strong command of a single method over candidates with more superficial competency in multiple methods (Siegel et al. 2007).

Similar dynamics associated with career incentives constrain collaborative research. Historically, as a profession, the social sciences have rewarded individual innovation and individual accomplishments more than they have collaborative research. Committees charged with hiring and promotion typically give more weight to single-authored publications than to multiauthored publications (Rothgeb and Burger 2009). Multiauthored publications are viewed with skepticism in part because it is impossible to discern the individual contribution of each author. Scholars are well aware of these issues and respond to them when making decisions about how to pursue their research agendas. Collaborative social science research has become more common, but publications rarely have more than three authors.[14] This contrasts sharply with the natural sciences, where publications often include the names of all of the researchers working in a laboratory.

Funding opportunities and career incentives that privilege particular methods also privilege research on topics for which those methods are possible (Lohmann 2007). One might imagine that relative scarcity of data and greater practical difficulties in collecting comparable data would merit higher levels of funding and institutional support for socially important topics. Often, however, this is not the case. Scholars who study data-scarce topics contend with practical challenges in data collection and analysis that limit their methodological options; but then, their methodological choices often limit their ability to compete for funding and gain critical appreciation for their work, as discussed above.

Funding agencies encourage fieldwork, collaboration, and multimethod social science research to some extent.[15] The prevalence of intensive fieldwork has waxed and waned, reflecting variable financial and institutional support for language training and extended periods of field-based research, as well as fluctuating professional appreciation for such research. In the United States, field-based research was encouraged during the period immediately following the world wars. As financial support for area studies declined, however, extended field-based research became less common. Theoretical and methodological trends favored broadly comparative analysis, which dampened interest in extended field-based research. Even when donors do support the sort of research required for the study of data-scarce topics, they rarely provide long-term support. Yet, for research on topics where data are relatively scarce and difficult to collect, long-term support may be required to fully overcome practical obstacles to broadly comparative research. Long-term support could also help overcome collective-action problems among scholars.

Career incentives *discourage* broad collaboration and multimethod research in the social sciences, especially for junior faculty, and exacerbate collective-action problems. The influence of career incentives on methodological choices appears as a leitmotif in this book.[16] Given the unavoidable influence of professional incentives and the other features of the academic world, this book considers how funding agencies, professional associations, universities, and academic departments and programs could better encourage innovative efforts to tackle practical challenges that influence methodological choices, and thus influence substantive emphases in social science research.

OUR SUBSTANTIVE FOCUS

We illustrate the challenges, advantages, and disadvantages associated with particular methods with reference to research on collective action for the regulation of natural resources. In its contemporary form, research on collective action for the management of natural resources responds to H. Scott Gordon (1954) and Garrett Hardin (1968), both of whom emphasized the difficulty of managing shared natural resources. Over the subsequent half century, scholars from across the social and natural sciences have used a wide variety of research techniques to establish the possibility of collective action for natural resource management, identify conditions associated with the emergence and durability of collective action, and assess whether and when collective action contributes to *sustainable* management of the resource base.

Although we could have drawn on examples related to diverse research agendas, focusing on a single well-defined research stream allows us to trace the interactions between theory, methods, and results, both in terms of how theory guides methodological choices and how various methods contribute to theoretical development. Collective-action problems are pervasive and important. They occur in families, the workplace, legislatures, and international relations. They affect the provision of public goods like infrastructure and social mobilization of groups with shared political agendas. Problems of collective action have contributed to the collapse of fisheries, deforestation, and climate change. Further, the co-authors of this volume have themselves undertaken extensive research, using multiple methods, on collective action for the management of natural resources. Thus we can speak from experience as well as drawing on the work of others.

In approaching natural resource management as a question of collective action, we are making a number of ontological assumptions. In our view, theoretical explanation must identify causal mechanisms. The theory of collective action assumes that individual behavior has a critical influence on collective outcomes. We are well aware of the limits of rationality, however, and favor a behavioral theory of individual action that allows for limited information, attention, and cognitive processing. We also assume that individual behavior is structured by context. For natural resources, relevant contextual conditions include the ecological structure of the resource system, the sociopolitical and economic structure, and an array of institutional arrangements. Perhaps most importantly for this volume, we assume that comparison is valuable, but that there is rarely a single or linear pattern. We expect causal heterogeneity; there is more than one route to the same outcome.

These assumptions and concerns have influenced the theoretical puzzles that we chose to highlight, the literature reviewed, and the methods examined. Our ontological assumptions are shared by many social scientists, but not all. Structuralists, interpretivists, and those who believe in lawlike social patterns may reject one or more of our assumptions. We hope that these scholars will nonetheless benefit from thinking about the potential theoretical contributions of a variety of methods and the practical challenges that affect methodological practices.

The research tradition on collective action for natural resource management offers a good point of reference for discussing (1) the interactions between methodology and theory development, (2) multiple methods and collaborative research, (3) practical constraints on methodological choices, and (4) the influence of career incentives on methodological practice.

Interactions between Theory and Methods

Scholarship on collective management of natural resources draws on a wide variety of research methods, including innovative strategies for addressing practical methodological constraints. We will show how different methods—abstract formal models, case studies, meta-analyses, cross-national comparisons, and laboratory and field experiments—have contributed at different points and in different ways to the development of this research agenda.

Multiple Methods and Collaborative Research

Puzzles related to collective management of natural resources span the social and natural sciences, and interdisciplinary research is prominent. This research tradition features several innovative efforts to overcome practical challenges and enable more broadly comparative, quantitative, and multimethod research. Yet, as we will document in chapter 5, collaborative research remains relatively uncommon. We draw upon our own experiences as well as the literature to highlight both the possibilities and the challenges of collaborative and multimethod research.[17]

Practical Constraints on Methodological Choices

Problems with scarce and difficult-to-access data are rampant in this research tradition. Collective management of many natural resources occurs on a subnational scale, and often entails the development of informal rules for resource use with little to no government involvement. Participants in the development and enforcement of these arrangements may include local, but not necessarily national, elites. Many examples of collective action for natural resource management—or its absence—involve ordinary or historically disadvantaged people. Because informal institutions can be difficult for outsiders to recognize, data on these efforts are scarce and not readily accessible. Qualitative field-based research is necessary to simply identify relevant cases for analysis. The practical challenges of such research are typical of work on topics for which data are scarce and difficult to acquire.

Career Incentives and Methodological Practice

Analysis of collective management of natural resources requires a firm understanding of the natural system, institutional arrangements, and human behavior. Arguably, research on this topic is inherently interdisciplinary and requires multiple methods. A patchwork of projects and research centers provides institutional and financial support that, to some extent, lowers the risks of interdisciplinary and multimethod research, but these do not fully compensate for systemwide career incentives. In general, career incentives encourage either specialization or relatively narrow forms of multimethod research. We draw upon our own experiences working with interdisciplinary and multimethod research centers that enjoyed strong institutional support, as well as in "ordinary" discipline-based settings.

OUTLINE OF THE BOOK

We welcome the recent turn away from recurring debates over the superiority of particular methods in the social sciences. We connect methodological debates to differences over theory and ontology, emphasize variation in the capacity to engage in ascendant methods, and draw out the implications for competition for career-related resources for several periods of intense methodological conflict across the social sciences. We agree that the use of multiple methods can improve research in many situations, but also stress that it is not always appropriate or feasible. That practical considerations constrain methodological choices is a central point. Even when scholars are aware of and open to diverse methods, methodological choices are constrained by specialized training, data scarcity, and problems of data accessibility. Career incentives within academia, unfortunately, by encouraging specialization and doing little to facilitate collaboration, make it more difficult for scholars to overcome practical obstacles.

In this introductory chapter, we have laid out our methodological and practical concerns, and have indicated that we will illustrate our points with reference to research on collective action and the commons. Parts II and III examine several strategies utilized in research on collective action related to natural resources. For each research strategy,

1. we provide a broad overview of the method;
2. we review the contributions of the method to the study of collective action on the commons; and
3. we discuss the method's strengths and weaknesses, when a method is particularly valuable; and refer to complementary methods.

We also discuss (in chapter 8) some relatively new research approaches that combine formal theoretical methods with data derived from case studies, participatory research, and experimental research so as to directly assess the capability of the formal model to generate similar patterns of outcomes.

Thus we will address some of the basic concerns related to the use of a particular method, including the following: the assumptions used; the analytical strategy; whether the method has internal or external validity and can be replicated; the potential contributions of this method to theory development; and some practical considerations (see table 1.1 for an overview of these concerns). We provide references to texts on particular methods and methodological issues, and we discuss pragmatic considerations that influence methodological practices, but we do not outline how to apply any specific method. In other words, this book is not a "methods textbook." Instead, we focus on what has been learned in a broad research program through the use of a diversity of methods. The underlying issues are discussed in general terms; examples are drawn primarily from work on collective action for natural resource management.

Part II looks more closely at methods used in empirical research related to natural resources, including case studies, meta-analyses of case studies, and large-N and collaborative field-based empirical research. In chapter 2, we first provide a brief overview of the conventional theory of the commons and then evaluate the contributions of case studies to theories of collective action and discuss their limitations. Chapter 3 reveals that, despite important broadly comparative and synthetic publications on collective action for natural resource management, case studies and small-N studies dominated articles published on this topic between 1990 and 2004. Most large-N studies published during this period analyzed survey data drawn from a single country or even a single subnational region. Consequently, these large-N studies offer scant improvement in external validity and are not well suited for research related to the prospects for collective action. As discussed in chapter 4, meta-analysis allows for more broadly comparative analysis by making structured comparisons based on a large number of existing studies. Meta-analysis is constrained by the body of existing empirical research, however, and cannot substitute for broadly comparative field-based research. Chapter 5 considers

TABLE 1.1
Methodological concerns and strategies

Methodological concerns	Research strategies
Assumptions	Single or multiple causal paths to outcome Deterministic or probabilistic relationships Universal or contingent relationships Comparability of cases (unit homogeneity) Independent or interdependent observations Random assignment or representative sample
Analytical strategy (evidence of causality)	Controlled design or statistical control Process tracing Correlations and analysis of variation
Form of validity and replicability	Internal or external validity Ease of replicability of findings
Potential contributions to theory development	Concept development Deductive or inductive theory development
Practical considerations	Data issues: access; availability of large data sets; gaps in source material (missing data); data quality—consistency, accuracy Costs: travel—costs, ease/difficulty of movement, field expenses; lab—availability, cost to run; payoffs; high-end computer Recognition and/or interpretation of data (e.g., potential unit of collective action) Skills: language skills; local (case-specific) knowledge; analytical skills (including QCA or Computer-Assisted Qualitative Data Analysis [CAQDAS]); programming skills; statistical skills Attributes of researchers: size of research team, composition, multiple disciplines

collaboration as a strategy for broadly comparative field-based research. There was relatively limited evidence of collaborative research in articles published from 1990 to 2004, and collaborative research was not more broadly comparative than single-authored research was. We examine several examples of collaboration, highlighting strategies developed to overcome practical constraints, and theoretical contributions to the study of collective action for natural resource management.

Part III discusses experimental research, field laboratories, and formal modeling approaches. Game theory has been the formal approach for the study of collective action in the past, and will remain an important method for the years to come. Chapter 6 focuses on experiments to study how small groups make decisions in collective-action settings. Early experiments showed that predictions from game theory were not confirmed in many social dilemma experiments. Later experiments have stimulated the development of an updated theory of collective action. Chapters 7 and 8 discuss the emerging use of agent-based modeling (ABM) as an alternative formal modeling approach for collective action (Miller and Page 2007; Tesfatsion and Judd 2006). The basic premise of agent-based modeling is that the macrolevel consequences of many microlevel interactions can be investigated. It puts more emphasis on heterogeneity among the actors, cognitive constraints, and the topology of interaction. The first generation of agent-based models focused on big questions in a theoretical perspective, such as "How does segregation emerge?" and "When do egoists cooperate?" (Axelrod 1984; Schelling 1978). Although most models of the first generation have been inspired by observation of real biological and social systems, the majority of these models are not rigorously tested on empirical data. In fact, the founding agent-based modeling efforts do not go beyond a "proof of concept." However, this is changing since an increasing number of scholars are starting to confront their models with empirical observation in more rigorous ways. We discuss these developments, especially how they are combined with human subject experiments and participatory processes.

Part IV offers a synthesis. Chapter 9 distills lessons about collective action related to natural resources. We provide a theoretical framework of collective action and the commons based on the findings over recent decades of empirical and theoretical research. In chapter 10, we elaborate on the practical implications for social science research using multiple methods.

This book confirms that each method can make valuable contributions if applied appropriately, but also underlines the limits of relying on any single method. Many advantages exist to multimethod research, particularly as research moves through successive stages. Yet practical challenges are significant. Thus the final chapter returns to the structural features of academia that influence methodological choices. We identify areas where incentives could be changed to foster more multimethod and collaborative research, as well as the sort of interdisciplinary research that is so valuable for studying the management of natural resources and many other policy-relevant topics. Ultimately, then, we hope this book will draw attention to practical constraints on research methods, identify strategies for overcoming these constraints, and stimulate discussions about how to encourage their adoption.

PART TWO

Field Methods

CHAPTER TWO

Small-N Case Studies:
Putting the Commons under a Magnifying Glass

THE CONVENTIONAL THEORY OF THE COMMONS

The theories of collective action, property rights, and the commons that developed in the middle of the twentieth century emphasized the difficulty of collective action (Sandler 1992), suggested that overexploitation of shared natural resources is inevitable, and presented privatization or state management as the only viable solutions. None of these approaches recognized the possibility that resource users might hold property rights collectively and manage resources sustainably. These arguments appeared so reasonable to many scholars and public officials that they became the conventional wisdom.

The tragedy of the commons deals explicitly with the challenges of avoiding overexploitation and degradation of a shared natural resource. Garrett Hardin (1968) envisioned a pasture open to all, in which each herder received an individual benefit from adding animals to graze on the pasture and suffered only delayed costs (with his fellow herders) from overgrazing. He assumed that there were no property rights to the land and no specified rights or duties related to grazing on the land. Hardin concluded:

> Therein is the tragedy. Each man is locked into a system that compels him to increase his herd without limit—in a world that is limited. Ruin is the destination toward which all men rush, each pursuing his own best interest in a society that believes in the freedom of the commons. (1968, 1244)

Hardin's logic was broadly similar to that of the distinguished economists H. Scott Gordon (1954) and Anthony Scott (1955), who had drawn similar conclusions about deep-sea fisheries. In Gordon's view, "The fish in the sea are valueless to the fisherman, because there is no assurance that they will be there for him tomorrow if they are left behind today" (1954, 125). The tragedy of the commons was also consistent with the mainstream economic theory of property rights. The property-rights school equated communal property with the absence of exclusive and effective rights and thus with an inability to capture returns from investments (Anderson and Hill [1977] 1998; Demsetz 1967; North and Thomas 1973).[1] From this perspective, inefficient use leading to degradation or depletion appeared inevitable for resources that remained communal property despite increasing value.

In the view of these scholars, the management of shared natural resources presents a social dilemma. In these situations, each individual hopes to limit his or her own costs while benefiting from the contributions of others, a practice Mancur Olson (1965) referred to as "free-riding." The socially optimal outcome could be achieved if everybody "cooperated." No one is independently motivated to cooperate, however, given the predicted lack of cooperation by others. Such situations are *dilemmas* because at least one outcome yields higher returns for *all* participants, but it is not predicted that participants will achieve this outcome (Liebrand, Messick, and Wilke 1992). Social dilemmas thus involve a conflict between individual rationality and optimal outcomes for a group (Lichbach 1996; Schelling 1978; Vatn 2005).

Case studies challenged the conventional wisdom and prompted theoretical refinements related to property rights and the prospects for collective action. These challenges and refinements, however, had limited initial effects. No single case study was conclusive; each could be dismissed as an anomaly. It was difficult to discern the big picture because these studies came from a variety of disciplines and were not coordinated. Case studies have contributed significantly to theoretical developments largely because scholars overcame their own collective-action problems. The organization of a variety of forums and networks improved the exchange of findings from case studies and facilitated cumulative learning. The adoption of a common framework for analysis made it easier to compare cases and discern patterns. Nonetheless, this success has been incomplete. The conventional wisdom still exercises considerable influence over policies related to natural resources and the provision of public goods despite subsequent theoretical revisions. Disciplinary divisions and specialization by resource type and region continue to restrict the dissemination of alternative theoretical approaches.

This chapter begins with an overview of the case study method, its analytical strengths and weaknesses, and practical considerations that affect both the adoption and theoretical contributions of case studies. The difficulty of synthesizing findings across case studies represents one of the most important practical challenges. The next section describes how the National Research Council (NRC) Panel on Common Property Resource Management and its promotion of the Institutional Analysis and Development (IAD) framework facilitated the accumulation of knowledge from case studies related to collective action and the commons. We then highlight theoretical contributions of the case study method, focusing on debates about property rights and the prospects for collective action that were central to the NRC panel. The chapter concludes with a recapitulation of the contributions and challenges associated with case study research.

THE CASE STUDY METHOD

The case study method refers to a research strategy of focusing intensively on individual cases to draw insights about causal relationships in a broader population of cases. Close examination of individual cases offers opportunities to develop concepts and theory, identify the limits of general relationships and disprove deterministic hypotheses, control for confounding effects through within-case comparisons, and disentangle causal processes. The case study method is especially appealing in the effort to make sense of complex processes. It is the only option for empirical field-based research when cross-case data are not readily available. Key disadvantages relate to limited external validity, problems of indeterminacy, and the difficulty of replication. Synthesis of findings represents an immense practical challenge. The contribution of case studies to theoretical development hinges on the ability of scholars to overcome barriers to the exchange of findings that arise from disciplinary divisions and the imperatives of specialization.

Cases, Case Studies, and Case Study Research

There is no universally agreed-upon definition for a "case study" in the social sciences. Gerring (2004, 2007a), for example, found eight distinct yet widespread meanings for the term. Part of the confusion arises from the use of a single term to refer to several distinct concepts. Social scientists differ in (1) conceptualizing cases as empirical units or theoretical constructs and (2) understanding case categories as either generic or specific to a given study (Ragin 1992). Many methodologists treat cases as equivalent to units of observations and distinct from observations on each unit (Collier, Brady, and Seawright 2004; King, Keohane, and Verba 1994). For others, case studies elucidate the personal history of a subject; this tradition reflects historical links between the social sciences and social work, in which the term "cases" refers to clients (Platt 1986, 46). Since empirical data must be translated into theoretical categories, "cases" are inherently theoretical *and* empirical constructs (Lakatos 1970; compare Ragin 1992, 11).[2] It is helpful to identify the "case" with the unit of analysis because the unit of analysis offers an empirical interpretation of the theoretical subject of study.[3]

   A case study, then, is an intensive study of a relatively well-bounded phenomenon or class of events (Collier, Brady, and Seawright 2004;

Gerring 2004, 2007a). Case studies often involve many levels of analysis with distinct units of analysis, but each level of analysis relates to a central substantive or theoretical phenomenon. That focal issue defines the *main* unit of analysis, which in turn defines the most relevant "cases" for the study as a whole. For collective action on the commons, the main unit of analysis can be defined as either the potential participants in collective action or the central objects of collective action. Typical cases include natural resource systems (e.g., forest, pasture, watershed); policy units such as villages, districts, and states; and social groups defined by proximity to or engagement with a natural resource (e.g., user groups).[4] For some studies, the objects of collective action refer to particular types of tasks (e.g., participation in meetings, guarding the shared resource, maintaining shared infrastructure).

While this chapter focuses on field-based studies, case study research is not defined by field-based research or any particular technique for data collection or analysis. Case study research is associated with triangulation of methods. Data collection often entails a combination of interviews, focus groups, participant observation, and archival work. Not infrequently, case studies also involve survey research or other data collection techniques. Studies related to natural resource management may turn to aerial photos or satellite images for evidence of resource conditions (e.g., Fairhead and Leach 1996; Homewood et al. 2001; Nagendra, Karmacharya, and Karna 2005; E. Ostrom and Nagendra 2006). Case study research draws upon a similarly diverse set of analytical techniques. Common techniques include structured comparisons, tracing of processes and sequences, and interpretations of discourse and identity.[5] Most case studies of collective action related to natural resources rely on intensive field research to discern informal and undocumented arrangements for regulating natural resource use. We also note contributions of historical case studies based on archival work. The works surveyed in this chapter approximate the breadth of analytical techniques typical of case study research.

The distinction between case studies and large-N cross-case studies turns on the intensity of attention given to individual cases. In fact, because nonstatistical analysis of more than a handful of cases is cumbersome, few case studies include more than a dozen cases (Gerring 2007a, 21–22; see also chap. 3). Most of the examples discussed in this chapter analyze data related to a handful of cases.

Analytical Strengths and Weaknesses

Case study research is appropriate for both exploratory and evaluative research from a wide variety of theoretical perspectives (Achen and Snidal

1989; George and Bennett 2005; Gerring 2007a; Rueschemeyer 2003; Yin 2002). Scholars find case study research attractive because it requires relatively few assumptions about the nature of the data or the underlying causal relationships (Mahoney and Goertz 2006; Munck 2004).[6] The case study method treats unit homogeneity (i.e., the comparability of observations), the independence of observations, the number of causal paths, and other ontological issues as hypotheses rather than assumptions (Mahoney and Goertz 2006; Munck 2004).[7] This skepticism encourages an open-ended and investigative approach toward observations and the nature of the relationships that link them. Close examination of cases means looking for conceptually important distinctions, disentangling complex relationships, and tracing sequences of events. These fine-grained observations support conceptual refinements and theory development, and enhance internal validity, data quality, and concept validity (Coppedge 1999; George and Bennett 2005; Munck 2004).

Case studies also contribute to theory testing. The drive for general theories produces broad concepts and hypotheses that reflect the underlying social complexity inadequately. Case study research essentially puts complex relationships under a magnifying glass so that closely interwoven strands can be teased apart. In this manner, case study research leads to sharper distinctions between related yet distinct concepts and phenomena, greater appreciation of multidimensionality, and more conditional hypotheses (Coppedge 1999; Mahoney and Goertz 2006).[8]

Intensive investigation of cases often reveals anomalies, multistranded relationships, or unanticipated patterns that suggest the limits of general patterns and call simplistic relationships into question (Dion 1998; Geddes 1990; George and Bennett 2005; Gerring 2004, 2007b; Mahoney 2003; Rogowski 2004). Analysis of anomalous findings encourages refinement of key concepts and analytical frameworks, or the development of alternative hypotheses. Inconsistent observations also raise the possibility of causal heterogeneity, in which more than one set of factors can cause the same sort of outcome (Brady and Collier 2004; Mahoney and Goertz 2006). Close engagement with specific cases also facilitates the tracing of causal processes behind correlations. It can highlight variation obscured by the focus on average effects in quantitative studies (Brady and Collier 2004; George and Bennett 2005; Gerring 2007a, 2007b; Goldstone 1997; Mahoney and Goertz 2006). Case studies frequently involve within-case comparisons that mimic experimental controls and increase confidence in the validity of observed relationships (Gerring 2007a).

On the other hand, case study research offers less support for deductive analysis than do experiments and simulations based on formal models (Bates et al. 1998; Granato and Scioli 2004; Janssen and Ostrom 2006b).

Case studies also offer limited leverage in the analysis of cross-case variation (Achen and Snidal 1989; Geddes 1990; George and Bennett 2005; Lieberson 1991; Lijphart 1971). Because a small set of cases cannot fully represent the broader population, findings generated through case studies lack external validity. Furthermore, it can be difficult or impossible to replicate case studies to confirm their findings. Because of the lack of external validity, some scholars strongly criticize the use of case studies in a scientific program of study (Dogan and Pelassy 1990). In fact, theoretical development in a coherent research program involves an alternation between the development of hypotheses about general relationships and elaborations of the limits to general relationships (Campbell and Stanley 1966; Flyvbjerg 2006; Lieberman 2005). Case studies are also needed for the analysis of causal processes (Gerring 2004, 2007a; Lieberman 2005; Lijphart 1971).

Small samples present two serious limitations: selection bias and indeterminacy. A sample is biased if the cases observed do not represent variation on the dependent or independent variable accurately; selection bias can result in over- or underestimation of general relationships (Geddes 1990; George and Bennett 2005). Cases examining the failure of local communities to solve collective-action problems are probably underrepresented for two reasons: (1) many social scientists "prefer to write about successful resource management ventures rather than failures" (Acheson 2006, 118) and (2) failures are harder to locate and assess given that frequently they result from nonaction rather than the failure of an overt process.

An analysis is indeterminate when observations are consistent with more than one hypothesis. Case study research is often depicted as inherently indeterminate by virtue of a small-N or degrees-of-freedom problem (Achen and Snidal 1989; Jackman 1985; Lieberson 1991; Lijphart 1971).[9] A degrees-of-freedom problem arises in statistics when the number of independent variables plus one exceeds the number of observations. Under these conditions, the analysis will be indeterminate because statistical control is not possible. Since case study research generates a wealth of observations, lack of data is not the main source of indeterminacy (Campbell 1975; George and Bennett 2005; Gerring 2007a, 2007b). Rather, indeterminacy generally arises from the close correlation of conditions of interest.

While case studies often analyze voluminous within-case data, they offer limited cross-case variation by definition. There are reasons to expect limits to the generality of social patterns. Intentionality, adaptation, strategic interactions, and path dependency reduce the regularity of the social world (Almond and Genco 1977; Bennett and Elman 2006; Brady 2004; Elster 1983; McKeown 2004). Theories that emphasize interactions of strategic individuals and the influence of context predict contingent relationships and possibly multiple paths to the same outcome (equifinality) (Elster 1998; Hall 2003; Mahoney and Goertz 2006; Ragin 1987; Signorino 1999). Even in a world of contingent relationships, equifinality, and other forms of causal complexity, the relative prevalence of particular causal paths should be evaluated. It is possible to acknowledge the contingencies arising from strategic interaction and contextual adaptation without giving up on the search for broader patterns. McAdam, Tarrow, and Tilly (2001), for example, identify similarities in the mechanisms and processes of contentious politics that lead to highly contingent outcomes. Such analysis of cross-case correlations and variation is critical for the evaluation of general hypotheses.

The possibilities for replicating case study research depend upon the data and analytical methods used. It is easier to replicate case studies that involve statistical analysis of survey data, for example, than those based on interpretative analysis of participant observation. Full replication may not be possible for case studies based on qualitative analysis of personal observations, interviews conducted by the author, or difficult-to-access documents. Even so, greater clarity about data sources and strategies for analysis can raise confidence in qualitative findings (Campbell 1975; King, Keohane, and Verba 1994; Munck and Snyder 2007).

Practical Considerations

The most important practical issues that influence the adoption of case study methods concern the availability of data, data consistency, the ease (or difficulty) of fieldwork, and the need for place-specific knowledge and skills. Since the contributions of case study research depend on an intensive engagement with the case, researchers must develop competency with several data collection techniques, such as archival research, interviews, and participant observation, to acquire the necessary wealth of case-specific observations. The most important impediment to theoretical contributions, however, is the difficulty of synthesizing findings from case studies. Effective synthesis is required if the researcher is to recognize patterns across cases, communicate those patterns to a broad audience, and thereby advance theory testing and development.

The time and energy required to collect data about each case depend greatly on the existence and accessibility of previously collected data and the ease of collecting original data when necessary.[10] Published data sets exist for an increasing variety of topics, and the Internet continues to expand access to existing data sets and primary data. Nonetheless, data are not readily available for all topics of interest to social scientists. The availability of relevant, reliable, and comparable data is particularly limited for topics related to informal institutions, subnational populations, and nonelite populations. Governments and international organizations are often inattentive or even entirely blind to these phenomena, and thus less likely to collect and publish reliable data on them.[11] Nonelite actors may be wary about sharing information, especially if their practices and informal institutions are not legally recognized. Historical data of all sorts are also limited, often severely. In these situations, intensive field or archival research becomes necessary.

The costs of fieldwork depend on the need for language training and place-specific issues like the infrastructure for telecommunications and transportation, and the openness of the social and political climate. The nature of the research question influences the intensity of fieldwork that is required. The importance of local knowledge increases for variables that are informal and context-specific. Scholars can increase their efficiency in the field through the accumulation of local knowledge, but possibilities of transferring local knowledge across research settings are limited. As the costs of collecting original data increase, large-N cross-case research declines in feasibility, at least for any individual scholar. In subsequent chapters we discuss strategies for overcoming these constraints.

A scholar may pursue case study research in response to theoretical puzzles, ontological considerations, or limited data availability combined with practical constraints on the accumulation of data. Researchers must collect high-quality data, often including observations related to processes and/or interpersonal relationships, to realize the strengths of the case study research. The need for high-quality data encourages the use of multiple forms of data collection and efforts at triangulation. Theory-driven scholars engaged in case study research must balance the need for observations that make sense locally against the need for consistent concepts and measures to enable comparison across studies. The balance that each scholar strikes influences the prospects for replication and external validity.

In principle, case studies should support both theory testing and development. In practice, a lack of synthesis of findings across case studies limits their theoretical contributions. Disciplinary divides and specialization impede synthesis by limiting the dissemination of results. Faced with an overwhelming flow of new publications, scholars tend to focus on work in their own discipline about their own area of specialization. One can easily remain unaware of related research conducted in different disciplines, focusing on different geographic regions, or addressing different substantive issues. Even when scholars do encounter case studies from other disciplines and contexts, the difficulty of comparing studies within different disciplinary and theoretical traditions constrains synthetic learning. In the absence of synthesis, however, findings do not cumulate across studies, and debates are reiterated without progress, much less resolution.

Case studies have contributed significantly to theoretical developments on collective action and the commons in part because scholars within this research tradition have developed a variety of strategies that promote synthesis. Below, we discuss how the NRC Panel on Common Property Resource Management drew attention to the large number of case studies related to the commons, and how its adoption of the IAD framework facilitated comparisons across cases, and thus synthetic learning.[12]

Synthesizing Challenges and Coordinating New Research Efforts

During the early 1980s, some scholars who regularly engaged in field-based research and knew of empirical evidence that was not consistent with the conventional theory became concerned about the dominance of the conventional theory and the subsequent policies of privatization and nationalization that were so widely adopted. It was not the case that the tragedy of the commons occurred everywhere; rather, considerable variance in resource user behavior and outcomes existed. Case studies illustrated that some resource users did self-organize and succeeded in preventing severe overharvesting of resources they depended on (see, for example, Berkes 1985; Coward 1977; Davis 1984; McCloskey 1976; Netting 1972; Spoehr 1980). Scholars in diverse disciplines, however, were not exchanging research findings. Not only did disciplinary divides reduce communication; there were also serious divides related to the *region* that people studied, as well as to the kind of *resource* they studied. If studies dealing with pastoral systems in the Alpine regions of Switzerland written by an anthropologist (for example, Netting 1972) were read only by other students of Western Europe who were anthropologists and interested in pastures, scholars could not develop a general body of knowledge.

Several scholars, including David Feeny, Margaret McKean, Ronald Oakerson, and James Thomson, were able to stimulate an interest at the National Research Council (NRC) in creating an ad hoc steering committee to explore ways of achieving a better synthesis of empirical findings. The first meetings of the committee occurred in September 1983. The committee began to identify existing case studies and was surprised by the large number of studies that they quickly discovered. The cases provided evidence of resource users who succeeded or failed in efforts to organize local fisheries, irrigation systems, pastures, and forests. A barrier to the awareness of this substantial evidence was "that it comprised a diverse set of studies that had been conducted by scholars from different disciplines, working in different regions of the world, on a wide variety of resource systems" (Feeny 1986, 8).

With the support of the NRC, the committee was transformed into the Panel on Common Property Resource Management in the Board on Science and Technology for International Development. The panel began planning a major conference to bring together scholars in multiple disciplines to assess what had been learned about common-property arrangements in diverse parts of the world. In planning for the conference, they convened a series of workshops to bring small groups of case study authors together to discuss a framework written by Ronald Oakerson (1986) drawing on the IAD framework (Kiser and Ostrom 1982).

The IAD framework is best thought of as a metatheoretical, conceptual map (see figure 2.1) that identifies an action situation, patterns of interactions and outcomes, and an evaluation of these outcomes (see right half of figure 2.1). The action situation is where individuals interact, exchange goods and services, solve problems, dominate one another, or fight (among the many things that individuals do). An action situation is structured by seven broad attributes, including (1) the set of participants confronting a collective-action problem, (2) the sets of positions or roles participants fill in the context of this situation, (3) the set of allowable actions for participants in each role or position, (4) the level of control that an individual or group has over an action, (5) the potential outcomes associated with each possible combination of actions, (6) the amount of information available to actors, and (7) the costs and benefits associated with each possible action and outcome (see figure 2.2). These seven attributes of an action situation can be thought of as core microvariables that affect the preferences, information, strategies, and actions of participants. Each attribute can take multiple forms that affect how individuals deal with collective-action problems as we discuss throughout this book.

Action situations also include a set of actors. Each actor can be thought of as a single individual or as a group functioning as a corporate actor. Each actor in an action situation is characterized by four clusters of variables:

1. the way actors acquire, process, retain, and use information and knowledge about contingencies;
2. the preferences of an actor related to actions and outcomes;
3. the conscious or unconscious processes actors use for selection of particular courses of action; and
4. the resources that the actor brings to the situation.

The first three are the core working parts of any theory of human behavior, while the fourth is situation-dependent.

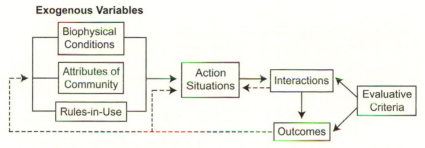

Fig. 2.1. A framework for institutional analysis. *Source*: Adapted from E. Ostrom 2005, 15.

A researcher can take two additional steps after making an effort to understand the initial structure of an action situation. One step inquires into the factors that affect the structure of an action situation. From this vantage point, the action situation is viewed as a set of variables dependent upon other contextual variables, including (1) the structure of the resource system involved (size, complexity, predictability), (2) the rules used by participants to order their relationships, and (3) the structure of the more general community within which any particular arena is placed.[13] Then a researcher can move outward from action situations to consider methods for explaining complex structures that link sequential and simultaneous action situations to one another (see the left side of figure 2.1).

Scholars at the Workshop in Political Theory and Policy Analysis at Indiana University initially developed the IAD framework to explain collective action in field settings of diverse structures—particularly the complex public economies of U.S. metropolitan areas. The NRC panel encouraged its adaptation for analysis of collective action related to natural resources to help authors of case studies from diverse disciplines and resource interests organize a presentation of their own cases in a manner that would increase the likelihood that an initial synthesis could be derived from the empirical studies.

The Conference on Common Property Resource Management was held in Annapolis in the spring of 1985. Nineteen empirical studies were presented related to fish and wildlife resources, water resources, agriculture land resources, and forest and bushland resources. The case studies presented at the NRC panel were particularly effective in focusing attention on conceptual problems related to property rights and empirical puzzles related to the prospects for collective action for the management of shared natural resources.

An initial effort at synthesis was presented at the concluding session. One of the first issues to be discussed concerned confusion in language use. The chair of the panel, Daniel Bromley, reflected on this problem in his remarks at the concluding session of the NRC conference:

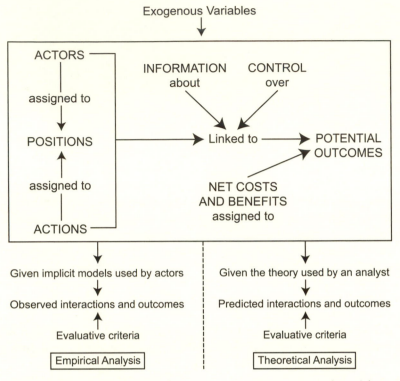

Fig. 2.2. The internal structure of an action situation. *Source*: Adapted from
E. Ostrom 2005, 33.

Through the week I have observed a persistent and potentially trouble-
some problem with language and concepts. I would start by asking
that we ought to be very careful in our use of the terms "common pool
resources" and "common property resources". . . . To talk of common property resources may leave the impression that there are certain
natural resources that are only controlled by common property arrangements. After all, do we ever talk of "private property resources"?
(Bromley 1986, 595)

Bromley was not the first to recognize that the standard terminology
conflated types of property rights with types of resources. More than a
decade earlier, Ciriacy-Wantrup and Bishop (1975) had argued forcefully
that "common property" should be used *only* to describe collectively
held rights to exclude others, and that situations characterized by the absence of rights to exclude should be referred to as "open access." Around
the same time, V. Ostrom and E. Ostrom (1977) had proposed a catego-

rization of economic goods based on the difficulty of exclusion and the subtractability of use that distinguishes four types of goods: (1) private goods for which one person's consumption subtracts from the availability of consumable benefits to others, but exclusion is relatively easy; (2) common-pool resources for which subtractability occurs and exclusion is difficult; (3) toll goods for which subtraction is relatively minimal and exclusion is easy; and (4) public goods for which consumption is not subtractable but exclusion is not possible either. These efforts had not resolved the conceptual confusion in part because disciplinary boundaries limited their dissemination and adoption. It did not help that scholars used the same initials, CPR, to refer to common-pool resources as well as to "common-property regimes." Consequently, conflation of these different phenomena continued. The NRC committee raised awareness of this lingering confusion and encouraged more widespread adoption of terminology that clearly distinguished between resources and property rights.

Elinor Ostrom was asked to develop an initial synthesis of the findings from the conference. She first observed that one of the major conclusions that could be drawn was that "more common property systems exist than central government and donor agency officials presume," and that some (but not all) of these systems performed very well (Ostrom 1986, 607). The empirical studies suggested the inductive hypothesis that, if local resource users were not prevented from developing their own user group organization, such organizations would be created whenever

- the user group is relatively small and has lived in close proximity and dependent upon a common-pool resource for a long time;
- the flow of use units is moderately scarce when compared with the demands that individuals within the user group make upon the common-pool resource; and
- the resource is subject to multiple users (simultaneous and sequential) and hence requires careful coordination and management of use. (Ostrom 1986, 608–9)

A further set of propositions tentatively derived from the empirical cases is shown in box 2.1. The papers and tentative conclusions were published one year later (NRC 1986) and became a major stimulus to the extensive research that is reported on in parts II and III of the current book. Since it had been presumed *impossible* that resource users could solve their own problems of overuse, it was an important accomplishment of the NRC panel that they found a very large number of cases where resource users succeeded.

The activities of the NRC panel stimulated a period of intensive empirical research and theoretical development because they raised awareness of empirical and theoretical challenges to the conventional theory,

Box 2.1
An initial synthesis of findings related to forming a user group organization
(UGO)

It is also possible to generalize further from our cases and discussion
about the relative difficulty or ease that diverse user groups may face in
attempting to create UGOs. The fewer difficulties that a user group faces,
the faster the group should form a UGO. . . . When scarcity of a common-
pool resource becomes apparent to user groups, the speed with which they
are able to organize is dependent upon the following:

1. Some heterogeneity of asset structure. Remember our discussion of
   the need for some entrepreneurship to get an organization started,
   though homogeneity may help later. . . .
2. Some prior or concurrent experience with other local organizations
   that provide an easy model to copy. Negotiating the constitution
   of a UGO from scratch is much costlier than borrowing the basic
   structure of a constitution from an extant organization. . . .
3. The availability of a general-purpose UGO that may be able to
   take on additional purposes. Many village organizations do several
   different activities, including the management of local common-pool
   resource systems.
4. The homogeneity in the community in terms of the uses made of the
   common-pool resource systems. The presence of two different groups
   who see their task as using the CPR in conflicting manners would
   make it more difficult for a UGO to develop.
5. The users' shared perceptions that the risks involved in continued
   open access arrangements may be reduced or better spread across the
   community by such an organization. The users' shared perception
   of the nature of their common situation may itself be enhanced by
   cultural homogeneity, value systems, and potentially the size of the
   group. Communication costs are much lower in a smaller group, and
   information about scarcity needs to be shared and discussed.
6. The physical unity of the user community. It is difficult for two
   fishing villages located on either side of a large lake to organize into
   one UGO. Two UGOs may develop with considerable intergroup
   conflict over the lake.

   The above propositions all need to be more carefully stated and to be
integrated into a more general theoretical framework. Right now, they are
simply an initial effort to summarize many of the relationships discussed at
this conference.

Source: E. Ostrom 1986, 609–10.

as well as existing conceptual and theoretical refinements, across disciplinary boundaries, and provided conceptual and analytical tools that facilitated new research. In particular, the NRC panel increased awareness of the prevalence of common property, of terminology that more clearly distinguishes between the characteristics of the natural resource and the system of property rights, and of the IAD framework for analyzing collective action for the development of institutions such as property rights. The rest of this chapter elaborates on the theoretical contributions of case studies to theoretical puzzles identified by the NRC panel on the relationship between property rights and the use of shared natural resources and conditions that influence collective action. Chapters 4 and 5 feature additional forms of research inspired, at least in part, by the NRC panel.

Contributions to the Study of the Commons

Case study research has thus been a significant source of contributions related to collective action for the management of common-pool resources. By challenging the conventional wisdom related to property rights and possibilities for collective action, case studies reset the terms of debate. Case studies contribute to theory building by directing attention to the complexity of relationships between social and ecological systems, and by facilitating efforts to disentangle these relationships. We address the contributions of case studies to three sets of issues highlighted by the NRC panel: (1) property rights and tenure security, (2) the implications of group characteristics for collective action, and (3) the implications of resource characteristics for collective action.

Property Rights and Tenure Security

As discussed above, Hardin's (1968) analysis of the tragedy of the commons reflected the conventional theory of property rights. The conventional theory distinguished among communal property, private property, and state property and equated communal property with the absence of exclusive rights (Anderson and Hill [1977] 1998; Demsetz 1967; North and Thomas 1973). Case studies challenged this conventional wisdom on three fronts. First, while failures were documented, numerous case studies demonstrated that, contrary to expectations, sustainable use of shared natural resources can occur in the absence of private individual or state property. Second, numerous case studies emphasized the importance of *security* of tenure and the ability of local resource users to *monitor and enforce* collective decisions. Third, case studies provided evidence that even well-defined and enforced property rights do not guarantee the sustainability of the commons. These studies contributed to the development of theory by identifying a variety of political, social, and economic factors—other than property rights—that influence the management of common-pool natural resources.

The deterministic formulation of Hardin's claim that sustainable resource use required either state or private property lent itself to rebuttal through case studies. The more lawlike and specific a theory, the more readily it can be tested through carefully selected case studies (Gerring 2007b). When a relationship is hypothesized to be invariant rather than probabilistic, evidence that it does not hold in even a single case provides grounds for dismissal or modification (Dion 1998; Gerring 2004, 2007a; Mahoney 2003).[14] Scholars identified numerous examples where a tragedy of the commons did not occur. Communities have cooperated in the management of fisheries (Acheson 2003; Berkes 1992; Schlager 1994; Singleton 1999), forests (McKean 1986; Schoonmaker Freudenberger 1993), grazing lands or pastures (Campbell et al. 2006; Gilles, Hammoudi, and Mahdi 1992; Netting 1981; Nugent and Sanchez 1999), groundwater and irrigation (Blomquist 1992; Grove 1993; Trawick 2001a, 2001b; van Steenbergen 1995), and wild plants and animals (Dyson-Hudson and Smith 1978; Eerkens 1999).[15] Case studies left little doubt that, contrary to theoretical expectations, collective action on the commons *is* possible and *not* merely a vestigial form (Feeny et al. 1998; McKean and Ostrom 1995).

Hardin argued for private rights for individuals or centralized regulation to avoid overexploitation. Case studies demonstrate that the management of natural resources does not correspond neatly with formal rights, and that neither private property nor state management guarantees sustainability. There are at least three possible reasons for the discrepancy: inadequately extensive rights, problems of enforcement, and low prioritization of sustainability.[16] Case studies directed attention to these variables and prompted conceptual and theoretical developments to incorporate them.

RECONCEPTUALIZING PROPERTY RIGHTS

Despite early recognition of property rights as bundles of rights that can be held in various combinations (Ciriacy-Wantrup and Bishop 1975), the conventional theory relied on a tripartite categorization of property rights (private, state, or communal) that does not fully reflect the possibilities for institutional diversity. Bundles of rights can vary both in extent across goods or products and in comprehensiveness related to any particular good or product. And the nature of the rights-holder can vary independently of the set of rights in a bundle. We address the extent of rights and the nature of the rights-holder in this subsection and then turn to the scope of rights.

Case studies challenged the equation of the commons with the absence of rights to exclude by documenting examples of collectively held rights of exclusion (Anderson and Simmons 1993; Bromley et al. 1992; Friedmann and Rangan 1993; McCay and Acheson 1987). Case studies also confirmed the critical importance of well-accepted and enforced rights of exclusion for the sustainability of shared natural resources. Conflict and environmental degradation generally *do* grow worse in the absence of effective rights of exclusion, even if users have formal rights of withdrawal or management (Agrawal 2000; Agrawal and Goyal 2001; Banana, Gombya-Ssembajjwe, and Bahati 2001; Twyman 2001). Although groups that enjoy rights of access, withdrawal, or exclusion often lack rights of alienation, the lack of "complete" rights does not prevent sustainable management. Comparisons of several forms of local natural resource management in India and Nepal suggest that effective management can occur in the absence of rights of alienation, as long as communities have enforceable rights of withdrawal, management, and exclusion (Agrawal and Ostrom 2001).[17]

Constraints on transfers are common in traditional rural societies (Berry 1992; Netting 1981; Wolf 1957). Even in contemporary intentionally formed communities in southern Indiana for which membership is voluntary, communities oversee changes in membership and generally limit rights of alienation of shared resources (Gibson and Koontz 1998; Poteete and Welch 2004). In both historical and contemporary settings, communities have sustained their shared resources despite limited or nonexistent rights of alienation. Indeed, limited rights of alienation may contribute to the success of collective management by reinforcing the cohesiveness of the communities (Gibson and Koontz 1998; Netting 1981).

In demonstrating the possibilities for successful collective management of natural resources and identifying examples of failures, case studies provided empirical support for two critical conceptual developments. First, collectively held rights to exclude others were distinguished from the absence of rights to exclude or open access (Ciriacy-Wantrup and Bishop 1975). Second, case studies made it apparent that the composition of a bundle of rights is analytically and empirically distinct from the attributes of the rights-holder (Edwards and Steins 1998; McKean 2000; V. Ostrom and E. Ostrom 1977). Case studies provided supporting evidence for conceptual developments that resulted in greater clarity about the distinctions between common property and open access, the possibilities for institutional diversity in bundles of property rights, and the distinctions between common-pool resources and common property; we discuss these conceptual developments in detail in chapter 4.

DEFINITION AND ENFORCEMENT OF RIGHTS TO MULTIPLE-USE
COMMON-POOL RESOURCES

Case studies illustrate the multiple and overlapping ways in which shared natural resources are used. In the Sahel, for example, different groups have historically held rights to the same land for grazing and the collection of gum arabic from acacia trees during different seasons (Schoonmaker Freudenberger 1993). In forested regions, groups differ in their reliance on forests for timber and construction materials, fodder and grazing, fuel, fruits and nuts, oils and resins, medicines, twine, and other nontimber products (e.g., Edwards and Steins 1998; Guha 1989; Kumar 2002).

Governments often promote spatially segregated packets of formal rights that prioritize a limited range of activities related to one or a few resources. These policies collide with a complex of spatially and temporally overlapping formal and informal rights to a variety of resources (Kipuri 1991; Poteete 2003a; Schoonmaker Freudenberger 1993). Indeed, as documented by numerous case studies, resource depletion often occurs because the state does not recognize or support informal common-property regimes and instead adopts schemes for privatization or centralization that undermine or destroy communal rights (e.g., Berkes 1992; Ghate 2004; Guha 1989; Malayang 1991; Ramnath 2001; Schoonmaker Freudenberger 1993; Tropp 2003; E. Young 2001).

On the other hand, an over-time case study in Mexico, using remote sensing, statistical analysis, and careful historical analysis, illustrates how a combination of institutional innovations and externally funded projects enabled the residents of the region to achieve long-term sustainable use of forests while most neighboring areas suffered substantial deforestation (Bray et al. 2004). Early governmental reforms establishing *ejidos* (collective land grants) during the 1930s, and later governmental programs with German technical assistance, helped to organize multilevel local institutions that could harvest forests sustainably and gain income for the local population.

Efforts to preserve biodiversity by creating protected areas in regions where local people had developed indigenous rights systems have frequently resulted in increased fragmentation, high conflict, and illegal uses. Liu et al. (2001) use remote sensing to demonstrate that the rate of habitat loss increased after the Wolong Nature Reserve was established in southwestern China. Robbins et al. (2007) also use remote sensing to examine the spatial distribution of land at the Kumbhalgarh Wildlife

Sanctuary in Rajasthan, India, for the ten years after its establishment. They find substantial intrusions near entry areas owing to ineffective enforcement by officials. An in-depth study by Riseth (2007) of the effect of the creation of national parks in areas of traditional use by the Sámi people in Norway describes the extensive conflict that has been engendered leading to boycotts and protests by activist groups. Twenty-three cases involving resistance by indigenous peoples to efforts by national governments to establish government policies that do not recognize their rights are brought together in a recent book edited by Cant, Goodall, and Inns (2005).

Policy interventions that threaten informal rights often generate considerable opposition. Such clashes may be more frequent with multiple-use resource systems, where governments tend to prioritize commercial uses while overlooking or discouraging subsistence use. African and Asian case studies, for example, document how centralization of forest management for timber production sparked a mix of sabotage and violent protests as people lost access to a variety of nontimber forest products (Agrawal and Ostrom 2001; Bryant 1996; Guha 1989; Hulme and Infield 2001; P. Scott 1998). Privatization of rangelands prioritizes commercial livestock production over a variety of subsistence uses in a similar manner. The victims of privatization of the range are often highly dispersed and marginalized, however; they face more substantial collective-action problems and generally respond with fewer and less sustained protests (Hitchcock 1980; Poteete 2003b).

Such conflicts underscore the difficulty of enforcing property rights. Too often, formal rights either are not enforced or conflict with informal rights in ways that create ambiguities and limit enforcement. Privatization through distribution of formal titles to individuals, for example, does not guarantee secure tenure (Barrows and Roth 1990; Bruce and Migot-Adholla 1994; Ducourtieux, Laffort, and Sacklokham 2005; Little and Brokensha 1987; Pinckney and Kimuyu 1994).[18] Access to the courts or other mechanisms of enforcement can be a substantial challenge. In Kenya, adjudication of land disputes weakens rather than enforces individual rights because it gives lineage members opportunities to block land transfers (Joireman 2008; Shipton 1988). Often, governments lack the capacity to enforce rights to common-pool resources. In the Philippines, for example, the government's ability to exercise rights of eminent domain over land depended on the relative effectiveness of physical force and harassment by the army and local residents defending de facto rights based on long-standing use (Malayang 1991). Likewise, forest conditions in two privately held forests and three communal forests in Guatemala corresponded more closely to indicators of effective enforcement by property owners than to formal property rights (Gibson,

Lehoucq, and Williams 2002). These and other case studies demonstrate the importance of tenure security. Indeed, case studies show that formal changes in property rights undermine the security of rights whenever they create competing systems of rights, increase uncertainty about institutional stability, undermine the legitimacy of rights, or exacerbate conflicts (e.g., Berry 1992; Klooster 2000a, 2000b; Kull 2002; Lund 2006; McDermott Hughes 2001; Tvedten 2002).

Where the property-rights school focused on economic incentives for evolutionary changes in property rights and the implications for efficiency, case studies reveal natural resource management as an intensely political matter. Rights to natural resources and the management of those resources are influenced by the social complexity of multiple-use resources, distributional conflicts surrounding rights to resources, and the difficulties of enforcing rights to resources. Property rights are not simply economic phenomena; they also reflect social patterns of economic organization, political dynamics of competition, and systems for collective decision making (Agrawal and Ostrom 2001; Berry 1992; Boone 1998, 2003, 2009).

THE LIMITS OF PROPERTY RIGHTS

Case studies make it clear that there are many alternative management goals and more than one point of reference for evaluating outcomes. Consequently, even secure tenure cannot guarantee efficient or sustainable management. In comparing four forests under individual tenure and two communal forests in Honduras, for example, Tucker (1999) found greater variation in forest conditions among the privately held forests than between forests under different tenure arrangements. Private forest owners had adopted diverse management strategies that reflected divergent assessments of the future value of their forest; when they expected higher returns from other forms of land use, they cleared their forests.

Case studies also demonstrate that communal management of natural resources may lead to better outcomes—in terms of efficiency, equity, conflict management, or risk spreading—than other options (Anderson and Simmons 1993; Derman and Hellum 2002; Hoffmann 2004; Lahiff 2000; Trawick 2003). The allocation of private rights over land-based resources to an individual often dispossesses people with overlapping rights to resources on the same parcel of land—including women and youth within the property owners' households as well as economically or politically marginal groups (Fleuret 1988; Hitchcock 1980; Joireman 2008; Kipuri 1991; Martin and Lemon 2001). In rural societies, especially in risky environments, limiting exposure to environmental perils often ranks higher than increasing average yields or sustaining the resource base (Abel and Blaikie 1989; Berry 1992; Halstead and O'Shea 1989;

Nugent and Sanchez 1999; J. Scott 1976; Shipton 1988; Western 1982). Risk may be reduced through mobility, diversification, exchange, or, if physically possible, storage (Halstead and O'Shea 1989). These strategies attempt to smooth consumption by either lowering dependence upon any single source or regulating consumption of the resource. Pastoralists, for example, often migrate and keep a mix of different animal species to manage risk (Western 1982).[19]

Formal property rights are not necessarily the best predictor of resource condition or management strategies. Nor are formal property rights necessarily the only or best indicator of collective action on the commons. Groups may overcome collective-action problems but pursue goals other than sustainability or efficiency. Further, some government policies have presumed that when formal rights and responsibilities are assigned to localities through national legislation, local participants will rapidly know about, utilize, and benefit from decentralization in a variety of forms. Case studies have illustrated that lack of information, skepticism of local users, lack of trust, and distress over losing the rights to develop their own rules have reduced the effectiveness of some formal "top-down" decentralization efforts (Andersson 2004; Andersson and Ostrom 2008; Banana et al. 2007; Ghate 2008; Marshall 2004; Namara 2006).

The conventional theory, focused on formal property rights, typically assumed that formal rights were enforced, and did not recognize common-property regimes. Many common-property regimes, however, consist of informal institutions that apply to a relatively small-scale locality, are easily overlooked, and may be actively opposed by the government. Case study research recognized these informal institutions because they drew upon intensive field research. Likewise, local actors are more likely to discuss practices that deviate from formal institutions or normative expectations, and may even be illegal, with researchers who are present for an extended period or return repeatedly over a period of years. Research based on official documents or elite interviews is less likely to appreciate the full extent of nonimplementation and enforcement, if it recognizes these problems at all. Thus case studies revealed issues of tenure security, enforcement of property rights, informal rights, and potentially divergent interests related to resource systems that the conventional theory had overlooked entirely. In drawing attention to these issues, case studies prompted conceptual refinements and the development of new hypotheses about property rights, collective action, and the commons.

Recognition that common property is a possibility, and that it does occur in some but not all field settings, raised new questions about the prospects for collective action. The NRC panel highlighted the importance of group characteristics and characteristics of the shared resource (see box 2.1). The next two sections look at the contributions of case studies to the development and testing of hypotheses about the implications for collective action of, first, group characteristics and, second, characteristics of the resource base.

Group Characteristics

Early formal models of collective action, such as those developed by Olson (1965), identified group size and heterogeneity as critical influences on the prospects for collective action. Numerous subsequent studies point to the importance of each attribute, giving rise to a broad consensus on their importance (see Baland and Platteau [1996] 2000; NRC 2002; E. Ostrom 1992, 1999). Since heterogeneity is commonly expected to be greater in larger groups, the effects of group size and heterogeneity are widely expected to interact with each other.[20] Empirical findings, however, have been inconsistent. Case studies have drawn attention to unexpected relationships related to group size and heterogeneity. In highlighting different forms of heterogeneity, case studies encourage the development of more precise concepts and more nuanced hypotheses. We first discuss group size and then heterogeneity.

GROUP SIZE

Olson (1965) hypothesized a negative association between group size and collective action based on three dynamics: (1) larger groups would be less likely to achieve collective action at all, (2) the overall level of collective provision would be lower for larger groups that did achieve collective action, and (3) the degree of suboptimality in collective provision would increase with group size. Case studies suggest a more complicated relationship. Activities related to the management of shared resources and investment in shared infrastructure differ, sometimes considerably, in the form and degree of collective action required for success. Case studies of diverse forms of collective action, sometimes within a single group, suggest that the influence of group size is both highly contextual and dependent upon the criteria for evaluating success.

Natural resource management involves more than the management of natural resource use. Resource mobilization can be important for the development of shared infrastructure (e.g., irrigation canals, drift fences), guarding, and maintenance activities. Very small communities in the Kumaon Hills of India, for example, protect their forests against rule violations by both community members and outsiders by hiring forest guards. To be effective, guarding must continue over a period of several months. The ability of a community to raise resources affects not only its capacity to hire a guard but also the duration of guarding. Agrawal and Yadama (1997) found that, overall, group size had a negligible effect on forest condition; although smaller groups placed less pressure on the forest, they also had less success in mobilizing the resources required to hire guards.

Further analysis of resource mobilization by forest communities in the Kumaon Hills suggests that not only does group size influence resource management and resource mobilization in different ways, but these relationships may be nonlinear and can differ across forms of resource mobilization. An analysis of data from 28 villages ranging in size from 10 to 175 households found a curvilinear relationship between group size and effective collective action for forest management (Agrawal and Goyal 2001). Medium-size groups proved more successful than smaller and larger groups in terms of total resources mobilized, per-household contributions, regularity of meetings, record maintenance, and rule enforcement. The most starkly curvilinear relationships concern resource mobilization. Both total budgets and per-household contributions are highest for village councils with 61 to 80 households. These figures drop off sharply for both smaller and larger villages.

Nagendra, Karmacharya, and Karna's (2005) comparison of forest conditions in two management systems in Nepal's *terai* suggests that group size may exert less influence on natural resource condition than do other factors, such as the availability of external sources of revenue. Buffer zones established around national parks attempt to provide protection to the forest but allow continued forest use by local residents within fairly tight guidelines. Community forestry is a more general program for handing over forests to user groups for management and use. Groups must develop management plans but face somewhat fewer restrictions. Nagendra and colleagues analyze satellite imagery for 23 forests from 1989 and 2000, before and after the formal introduction of community forestry and the creation of buffer zones in the early 1990s. The associated villages range in size from 75 to 1,237 households (450 to 8,000 individuals). The researchers found that forest conditions in buffer zones are improving more than those in community forests, and that loss of forest cover is greater in community forests. The differences do not correspond to differences in forest size, group size, or population density. Buffer zones benefit from higher monetary inputs, especially in terms of tourist revenues. In addition, buffer zones have a higher ratio of user group members to forest area.

Considered as a group, these case studies show that group size affects the prospects for collective action, but not in a straightforward manner. The nature of the relationship appears to depend on the goals of collective action and complex social interactions in particular contexts that are themselves the result of interactions among multiple variables. Case study research is more sensitive to this sort of causal heterogeneity precisely because it treats causal homogeneity as something to be established rather than assumed. When faced with evidence of causal heterogeneity, scholars face the challenge of discerning different causal patterns and mapping them conceptually to different types of observations. Case study research lends itself to this sort of exploratory analysis. The case studies summarized above suggest subtypes of collective action, within which causal homogeneity may exist. There is scope for further work in distinguishing and categorizing different forms of collective action. Case studies have an important and ongoing role to play in suggesting conceptual refinements and reformulations of received hypotheses about the relationship between group size and collective action.

HETEROGENEITY

As noted above, the heterogeneity of a group's membership is expected to influence the degree of common understanding about the existence and nature of a collective management problem, the commonality or divergence of interests and goals, and relative rates of participation in collective action. Nonetheless, diversity can take a number of different forms (Kurian and Dietz 2004). Case studies demonstrate that particular forms of heterogeneity shape the prospects for collective action in different ways, and suggest that the role played by a given form of heterogeneity depends on the situation. Case studies that emphasize social diversity also raise questions about how to conceptualize—and recognize in the field—the relevant set of people for analyzing collective action.

Discussions related to community-based natural resource management and other forms of decentralized resource management often assume (tacitly) that a territorially defined community is the relevant group for managing shared natural resources.[21] Evidence from field settings around the world makes this assumption untenable. The ubiquity of multiple-use resources implies that a single socially meaningful group of resource users may not exist. More or less distinct groups who may not interact regularly or identify with each other have been found to have a stake in many multiple-use commons (Agrawal and Gibson 1999, 2001; Edwards and Steins 1998; Guha 1989; Kumar 2002). Even within self-identified communities, several forms of heterogeneity exist. Collective action may require bargaining among distinct groups or subgroups as well as collective efforts to manage shared resources (Edwards and Steins 1998).

Many case studies on heterogeneity focus on economic inequality related to income, assets, or stability of income streams (Agrawal 1999; Bardhan 2000; Dayton-Johnson 1999, 2000; Kurian and Dietz 2004). Others examine heterogeneity in values (Gibson and Koontz 1998), of knowledge and skills (Johnson and Libecap 1982), of location (Mearns

1996; E. Ostrom 1996), or of interest in maintaining the resource (Ainslie 1999; Campbell et al. 2001). Social heterogeneity related to age, gender, ethnicity, status, or residence often translates into political and economic heterogeneity and is reflected in interests in shared resources (Ainslie 1999; Kipuri 1991).

Heterogeneity in interests often reflects other forms of heterogeneity that affect access to or benefits from natural resources. In southern India, interest in maintaining shared irrigation tanks (small dams that are linked to irrigation systems) declines with access to private tube wells as an alternative source of groundwater, which in turn reflects differences in wealth (Balasubramanian and Selvaraj 2003).[22] Lack of agreement on management goals constrains collective management of the commons in rural Zimbabwe; wealthier groups value the commons as a source of cattle feed, while the less wealthy rely on commercial harvesting of woodland products as a source of income (Campbell et al. 2001). In Nepal, where the costs of participation in management activities such as planting new trees or patrolling the forest depend on distance from the community forest, locational diversity is an important source of divergent interests (Chhetri and Pandey 1992; Chhetri, Tiwari, and Sigdel 1998). Benefits from fisheries reflect differences in knowledge about good fishing locations and fishing skills, as well as differences in equipment (Johnson and Libecap 1982). In the lower Amazon floodplain of Brazil, McGrath, Almeida, and Merry (2007) examine the implicit conflict within households and communities related to annual cropping on river levees, fishing in the lakes, and cattle ranching. Agreements reached at a community level have different impacts on household livelihood strategies depending on the relative importance of these activities. McGrath and coauthors argue that without recognizing the heterogeneity of uses of a resource by households within a community, scholars may miss important dynamics that affect the success of collective action.

Although different forms of heterogeneity often reinforce one another, the relationship between heterogeneity and collective action varies across forms of heterogeneity and collective action. Somanathan, Prabhakar, and Mehta (2002), for example, found that income inequality and caste heterogeneity had distinct effects on three measures of collective action in the Kumaon and Garhwal regions of northern India: the number of Van Panchayat (forest council) meetings held during the previous year, whether a community hired a watchman for their forest, and the extent of crown cover in forests managed by the village. The frequency of meetings increased modestly with income inequality but did not correlate significantly with caste heterogeneity. Neither measure of heterogeneity had an effect on the probability of a village's hiring a watchman or on the extent of crown cover.

In some situations, elite members of the community facilitate collective action. In other situations, reciprocity among groups with complementary resources buoys cooperation. Although pastoralists and crop producers sometimes clash violently when livestock destroys crops, these groups frequently cooperate to exchange access to crop residue for milk and manure (Agrawal 1999; Bassett 1988; Dafinger and Pelican 2006; Turner 1999). Cooperation on some activities tends to create interdependencies that constrain conflict (Dafinger and Pelican 2006), and can promote cooperation in other areas (Mearns 1996).

Case studies also demonstrate that institutional arrangements can moderate the effects of heterogeneity. Some villages in Nepal have compensated for locational differences by allowing more distant members to substitute the payment of fees for time spent in monitoring and maintenance work (Adhikari and Lovett 2006). In southern Indiana, most members of intentional communities with shared forest resources value their forested land primarily for nonconsumptive purposes while also enjoying limited consumption of mushrooms, firewood, berries, and other forest products for their own households. Serious conflicts can erupt when some members value consumptive over nonconsumptive uses, especially if some members want to use forest products as a source of income. In a comparison of two such communities, Gibson and Koontz (1998) found that one had developed institutions that effectively screened new members for shared values, reinforced common values through community activities, and managed conflicts arising from disagreements. A wariness of formal institutions left the other community more vulnerable to increases in value heterogeneity through the recruitment of new members, and less able to manage conflicts over forest management.[23] Thus institutions can dampen or exacerbate conflicts arising from heterogeneity.

Characteristics of a group, including its size and heterogeneity, do influence the ability of resource users to gain trust that others will not break rules and substantially overharvest. Without substantial trust in the reliability and reciprocity of members of a resource user community, it is very hard to establish cooperation in the management of a shared natural resource.

Case studies demonstrate that the effects of heterogeneity can be highly variable. The multiple dimensions of group characteristics and varied forms of collective action related to natural resource management result in a complex set of relationships. After documenting the diverse effects of different forms of heterogeneity in eight villages of Nepal, for example, Adhikari and Lovett (2006, 443) warn against presuming simple causes and simple remedies. Case studies helped tease apart these connections to reveal contingent relationships. In this manner, case studies have both tested the scope of prior hypotheses linking group size and heterogeneity to the success of collective action, and suggested modified hypotheses. As discussed above, case studies have built-in advantages in recognizing and responding to causal heterogeneity.

Resource Characteristics

We now turn to case studies that consider how the characteristics of natural resources affect interest in and collective action for the management of natural resources. First, case studies have identified various features of natural resources that influence the relative costs and benefits associated with the establishment and defense of property rights. Second, case studies underline variation in the complexity of natural resources and resource systems, which in turn influences the difficulty of the management problem, and the prospects for collective action.

RELEVANT CHARACTERISTICS

Scholars have long recognized that characteristics of a resource influence the feasibility and relative costs of alternative management strategies. Property-rights theory expected increases in demographic pressure and market demand to prompt interest in privatization (Alchian and Demsetz 1973; Demsetz 1967). Olson (1965) expected collective action to be particularly daunting when the costs of provision were borne privately while the noncontributors could not be excluded from enjoyment of the benefits.[24] Biological and physical differences influence both the response of the resource to human activity and the difficulty of establishing exclusive property rights (Gordon 1954). Even revisionist work on property rights and types of resources emphasized resource characteristics that influence the difficulty of exclusion (V. Ostrom and E. Ostrom 1977). Case studies drew attention to the multiple dimensions of resource characteristics that influence the value of the resource, and thus the level of interest in defending exclusive rights.

Case studies identified several features of natural resources that influenced the difficulty of exclusion and the expected value of defending exclusive rights. Several of these studies compared patterns of territoriality and property rights adopted by groups that used several natural resources, including land for crop production, fisheries, pastoral systems, and wild foods and game. Common-property systems of management seem to be more frequent for low-density resources and those characterized by patchiness, such as semiarid and arid grazing lands, possibly because the costs of defending more exclusive rights outweigh the likely benefits (Dyson-Hudson and Smith 1978; Netting 1981; Western 1982). The prospects for collective action are expected to be much lower for the management of migratory, mobile, or ephemeral resources, such as some types of fish, game, and wild plants, because no single group can regulate use of the resource, and the subsequent involvement of multiple groups raises the transaction costs of coordination (Dyson-Hudson and Smith 1978; O'Shea 1989). Defining flexible boundaries related to multiple resources in semiarid regions with high levels of uncertainty related to ecological conditions is particularly challenging (Quinn et al. 2007). For natural resources with these features, exclusive property rights often are not the best option. Preferred responses include storage, migration, diversification of resource use, and social exchange (Dyson-Hudson and Smith 1978; Halstead and O'Shea 1989; Netting 1981; Western 1982).

COMPLEXITY

Complexity refers to attributes of natural resources, ecological systems, and socioeconomic and political systems that affect the ability of resource users to recognize how their actions affect the condition of the resource. Complexity limits the ability of individuals to identify the full set of possible outcomes or assign probabilities to particular outcomes of specific actions. The complexity of particular natural resources and ecological systems can make it difficult to discern cause-effect relationships. Case studies of efforts to grapple with complexity have generated new hypotheses about the implications for collective action.

Many of the sources of variability discussed in the previous section raise the costs of management and of establishing exclusive property rights, but do not pose a cognitive problem. Complexity increases with the number of factors influencing resource condition, the period of time over which causal effects unfold, and interactions across social and ecological scales. Complexity related to an individual resource can present serious cognitive challenges; systemic forms of complexity are much more severe. Both ecological and social systems are complex, interdependent, and constantly changing. As James Wilson (2002, 2007) notes, these systems are characterized by causal relationships that are nonlinear, multivariate, and changing. The complexity of natural resource systems and their interaction with social, economic, and political systems can impede collective action when they obscure cause-effect relations, especially the connection between resource use and resource condition. Case studies suggest that the implications of the characteristics of particular natural resources for collective action depend on the extent to which complexity reduces predictability (Abel and Blaikie 1989; Poteete and Welch 2004; J. Wilson 2002, 2007). Unpredictable variation decreases the probability of any form of management (Halstead and O'Shea 1989). The cognitive problems are too severe, and the probability of reaping the benefits of management efforts is too low.

Over-time analyses of cases provide insights into the possibilities for overcoming these cognitive challenges through learning and adaptation.

Consider the initial lack of awareness of connections between forest and watershed management among residents of Loma Alta, Ecuador (C. Becker 1999, 2003; Gibson and Becker 2000). The forest covers a hilly terrain with altitudes ranging between 50 and 830 meters. Fog is prevalent at higher altitudes, where trees draw moisture into the watershed. Loss of trees thus decreases fog interception and the availability of water at lower elevations. Until the mid-1990s, residents of Loma Alta did not recognize that clearing forests at higher altitudes affected the aridity of the soil or the availability of water at lower altitudes (C. Becker 1999). In 1995, People Allied for Nature (PAN) measured fog interception at several locations in the forest. PAN shared evidence of sharp differences in the water intercepted in forests and pastures with the residents of Loma Alta and emphasized the implications for the erosion and drying of soils on pastureland, and for water supply in the village (C. Becker 1999). Even when presented with this evidence, some residents doubted the validity of such complex relationships and suspected that PAN wanted to trick them into giving up their land (C. Becker 1999). Only after several community meetings and considerable debate did the residents of Loma Alta vote to establish a community-managed forest reserve as a form of watershed management. Once an agreement to protect the forest had been reached, however, it was implemented rapidly (C. Becker 2003). In this case, systemic complexity initially obscured cause-effect relationships and later made it more difficult to achieve a common understanding about the nature of the management challenge.

Resource users can develop strategies to compensate for predictable variability in resource condition as long as they can perceive a connection between their actions and resource condition. A complex coastal fishery in Sri Lanka has functioned for more than 250 years, for example, as a result of the evolution of lottery rules assigning rotational rights to use stake-nets at agreed-upon fishing sites located on discrete channels. The institutional system enables the equitable sharing of substantial resource variability across time and space (Gunawardena and Steele 2008). Even if the residents of Loma Alta do not understand how fog interception works, most now understand that they can protect their water supply by limiting deforestation (C. Becker 2003). Communities around the world also cooperate in the management of nonmigratory fisheries (Berkes 1992; Cordell and McKean 1992; Schlager 1994; Singleton 1999; E. Young 2001) despite persistent uncertainty about the forces influencing fishing stocks (Gordon 1954; Wilson 2002). Successful community-based conservation is highly unlikely when local communities have little relevant information about the dynamics of the resource that others want them to conserve, as Altrichter (2008) found to be the case in an effort by a national government to urge community-based conservation of peccaries (Tayassuidae) in the Impenetrable Forest of northern Argentina.[25]

Resource complexity presents challenges for researchers as well as resource users. The large number of variables and the diverse forms of interactions among them make it difficult to isolate the effects of any one variable analytically. Case studies are particularly valuable in these situations because they offer opportunities for analytical control through structured comparisons, including within-case comparisons (Gerring 2007a; Snyder 2001). Within-case comparisons hold some variables constant and thus increase researchers' ability to trace relationships of interest. Which variables are held constant, such as a single group that uses several types of resources (Poteete and Welch 2004) or one resource system over time (C. Becker 1999, 2003; Gibson and Becker 2000; Gunawardena and Steele 2008), differ across within-case study comparisons. Over-time studies also enable process tracing, something that is not possible through cross-sectional comparisons. Case studies have taken advantage of these analytical strengths to demonstrate that resource complexity influences collective action independently of group characteristics, and that possibilities for learning and adaptation exist in response to complexity, at least as long as the links between action and resource conditions are recognized and perceived to be predictable.

CASE STUDIES AS A FOUNDATION

Case studies provided ample evidence of successful collective action by some resource users and raised new questions about sources of variation in achieving and sustaining collective action. Case studies debunked deterministic claims about the impossibility of collective action related to common-pool resources, but also illustrated failures, challenged overly general or simplistic hypotheses, teased apart distinct elements of tightly interwoven factors, and inspired conceptual refinements. Intensive case studies have informed the development of frameworks for analyzing property rights and increased appreciation of nonlinear and context-specific relationships between group characteristics and the prospects for collective action. Case studies have also facilitated ongoing efforts to disentangle interactions between complex social and ecological systems. These agenda-setting contributions built on the analytical strengths of the case study method, especially those related to concept and theory development, the ability to control for confounding effects via within-case comparisons, and process tracing. In this chapter, we reviewed a small fraction of the huge number of case studies about collective action in the context of natural resource management to illustrate the multifaceted contributions of case studies to the accumulation of knowledge.

As we have shown, case study research has contributed significantly to theory development and testing. Nonetheless, we acknowledge that the theoretical contributions of the case study method are constrained by the ongoing challenge of synthesis. The production of new case studies occurs on an immense scale and is uncoordinated. Most scholars prioritize work within their own discipline, theoretical perspective, and substantive areas of specialization. These rules of thumb or heuristics make the flood of new information more manageable, but they also impede cross-fertilization and synthetic learning. Synthesis would be challenging even in the absence of these divisions. Because scholarship is not coordinated, the sets of research questions posed and variables examined vary from study to study.

Case studies suggest many plausible hypothesized relationships. Above, we surveyed debates about property rights, characteristics of the group, and complexity. Other case studies have drawn attention to possible threats to the viability of institutions for managing common property, including demographic change (Harrison 1993; Singleton 1999), technological change (Anderson and Hill [1977] 1998; Cordell and McKean 1992; Schoonmaker Freudenberger 1993; van Steenbergen 1995), market pressures (Ensminger 1996; Gibson and Becker 2000; Parayil and Tong 1998), short-term economic considerations (Campbell et al. 2001), government policies and interventions (Bardhan 2000; Malayang 1991; Mwangi 2007b; Parayil and Tong 1998; Schoonmaker Freudenberger 1993; Western 1982; E. Young 2001), and macropolitical change (Klopp 2000; Mearns 1996; O'Hara and Hannan 1999). More than thirty factors are thought to influence the sustainability of common-pool resources (Agrawal 2001b). Case studies often present evidence of causal processes to demonstrate the influence of each condition, at least in a particular time and place and for a particular common-pool resource. In most situations, several factors influence collective action on the commons.

To some extent, the emphasis on different variables reflects alternative frameworks for analysis. In this book, we draw on the IAD framework and related approaches that direct attention to opportunities for and constraints on self-organization by resource users (Edwards and Steins 1998; Kiser and Ostrom 1982; Oakerson 1986). These approaches emphasize the importance of intentional human action and institutions, and are well-suited to the study of collective action on the commons. Other perspectives direct attention to somewhat different sets of variables. The political ecology framework, for example, gives greater emphasis to nonlocal structural and systemic factors (Bassett 1988; Bryant 1994; Schoonmaker Freudenberger 1993). From the perspective of cultural and interpretivist frameworks, cultural norms and efforts to generate meaning exert considerable influence over patterns of resource use; legitimacy and other symbolic implications sometimes rival economic value as a motivating force (Carney and Watts 1990; Derman and Hellum 2002; Klooster 2000a, 2000b; Kull 2002).

These distinctions should not be overstated. Many case studies approach natural resource use and management as a product of individual action; interactions of social, political, and economic structures at multiple scales; *and* the dynamics within social and ecological systems (e.g., Agrawal 1999; Agrawal and Ostrom 2001; Ainslie 1999; Kipuri 1991; Mearns 1996; Mwangi 2007a; Netting 1981; Nugent and Sanchez 1999; Poteete 2003b; Turner 1999). Likewise, many case studies highlight the entanglement of cultural and symbolic aspects of natural resource use with conflicts over authority and material benefits (e.g., Agrawal 2005; Berry 1992; Boone 1998, 2003; Carney and Watts 1990; Lund 2006; McDermott Hughes 2001; Poteete 2009; Ribot, Chhatre, and Lankina 2008; Tropp 2003; Tvedten 2002; Twyman 2001). On the other hand, scholars should not obscure analytical differences. Explicit evaluation of alternative frameworks helps advance theory development and analysis (Schlager 2007).

Case studies contribute to such assessments by enabling the tracing of processes at multiple levels as suggested by alternative frameworks. But case studies cannot evaluate the generality of alternative frameworks any more than they can evaluate the average effects of individual variables. Moreover, it is not always possible to identify "pathway cases" (Gerring 2007b) in which one independent variable is present while alternative explanatory variables are not. If case-based observations are consistent with more than one explanation, the analysis will be indeterminate.

This sort of diversity of perspectives is essential to the vitality of any research tradition, and yet it also presents challenges for the scientific community. While a common framework supports cumulative research within a particular tradition, the presence of alternative frameworks helps scholars guard against intellectual blind spots—if they are aware of work within related research traditions. The contributions of case study research to cumulative theory development and testing depend on widespread familiarity with a broad cross-section of case study research, complemented by synthetic learning. The practical impediments are severe: cognitive limitations on the volume of new studies that any individual can effectively process, career incentives that reward production of new studies over the "consumption" and processing of existing studies, and academic organization that rewards specialization and discourages broad reading.

And yet scholars recognize the value of synthesis and regularly act to achieve it. Well-written review essays often find a very broad audience. Smaller sets of scholars come together in workshops and research networks to exchange their findings and work through intellectual problems. Major foundations and other organizations sponsor medium-scale conferences along the lines of the NRC panel discussed in this chapter.

Synthesis can also occur through the collection of case studies in edited volumes or special journal issues. Several compendia of case studies related to collective action and the commons were published in the late 1980s and early 1990s (e.g., Anderson and Simmons 1993; Friedmann and Rangan 1993; McCay and Acheson 1987; NRC 1986). Some, including NRC (1986),[26] applied a common analytical framework to chapter-length case studies to enhance analytical leverage, while others synthesized lessons from case chapters in introductory and concluding chapters. Given the inevitably limited scope of edited volumes, these compilations cannot provide a thorough synthesis.[27]

As in other areas of collective activity, successful collective action among scholars concerned with cross-fertilization and synthesis is sporadic, partial, and rarely sustained.[28] Professional associations represent the most obvious vehicle for sustained cross-fertilization and synthesis. The International Association for the Study of the Commons, for example, has supported interdisciplinary and international exchanges related to collective action and the commons since 1989.[29] New interdisciplinary associations do not represent an easy solution to these problems. They must compete with disciplinary associations for participation, and are costly to create and maintain. University-based research centers can also facilitate both synthesis and exchange. This book features several research programs associated with the Workshop in Political Theory and Policy Analysis at Indiana University (see chapter 10).

In this chapter, we have shown how case studies can raise confidence about the validity of concepts, enable process tracing and multilevel analysis, and yield findings with high internal validity. But no method does everything. In particular, we have highlighted the challenge of synthesizing findings from case studies. The next three chapters focus on field-based empirical methods that offer greater external validity. Part III discusses formal methods that support deductive analysis and more controlled testing of hypothesized causal processes. Throughout, we retain our concern with the practical challenges that affect the choice of method, the synthesis of findings across studies, and the accumulation of scientific knowledge.

CHAPTER THREE

Broadly Comparative Field-Based Research

WHILE HYPOTHESIZED RELATIONSHIPS are often posited by case study authors, broadly comparative research is required to enable scholars to evaluate the generality of these relationships (Lijphart 1971). Even when theory predicts multiple causal paths, there is also an interest in identifying the set of conditions under which each causal process applies. Assessments of the generality of relationships and processes hinge on the breadth of comparison as well as on sample size.[1]

Some have suggested that the mix of methods used within a research tradition changes naturally with the accumulation of data and the development of theory. When data are scarce and theory is poorly developed, case study research is both recommended and unavoidable (Gerring 2007a; compare Achen 2002). Case studies suggest hypotheses about relationships and processes (Ragin and Becker 1992). As a line of research develops, a shift from case studies to synthetic analyses is expected (Gerring 2007a; Stern et al. 2002). Development of a set of hypotheses certainly increases the *value* of more synthetic and broadly comparative research designs, including large-N studies. But large-N comparative analysis also requires large and representative data sets. It is not obvious that theoretical development of a research program necessarily corresponds with improvements in data availability or accessibility.

As discussed in chapter 2, the Panel on Common Property Resource Management organized by the National Research Council (NRC) (NRC 1986) and a number of publications in the late 1980s and early 1990s (e.g., Anderson and Simmons 1993; Berkes et al. 1989; Friedmann and Rangan 1993; McCay and Acheson 1987; E. Ostrom 1990) offered synthetic analyses of large numbers of case studies, proposed a number of hypotheses about collective action and the commons, and helped define an agenda for ongoing research. These scholars called for more broadly comparative research on the management of common-pool resources. These calls for broadly comparative research have, however, largely been unanswered. This chapter documents the ongoing scarcity of cross-national research on collective action and the commons, and suggests that practical challenges to data collection place cross-national research beyond the reach of most individual researchers. We also discuss the advantages and disadvantages of meta-analysis as a strategy for using existing case studies to overcome these challenges.

The first section of the chapter presents an analysis of methodological practices represented in articles on collective action and the commons published between 1990 and 2004 and indexed in the Academic Search Premier database. We find that cross-national field-based research is extremely rare and has increased only modestly over time. Large-N research has increased, but mostly involves the analysis of survey data and is often limited to subnational samples. There was some growth in small-N cross-national comparisons, but we found that *no* large-N cross-national research was published during this period. Our analysis of methodological practices raises two questions. What are the constraints on large-N and cross-national research? And what options are available to scholars interested in pursuing broadly comparative field-based research?

Why did the considerable interest stimulated by the NRC and the other extensive case study research not yield more large-N research? Although new field research offers substantial control over research design and measurement, the collection of new data can be quite costly. We discuss a variety of practical challenges to accumulating the data required for broadly comparative research on collective action and the commons. Similar challenges affect research on a variety of topics concerned with informal institutions, subnational populations, or historically marginalized populations. In light of these practical challenges, it is not realistic to expect individual researchers to collect the data required for cross-national field-based research.

We argue that broadly comparative research is nonetheless possible. Collaborative research, which we discuss in chapter 5, is one option. In this chapter, we introduce another strategy for broadly comparative research: meta-analysis, or the "analysis of analyses" (Glass 1976, 3). This chapter highlights the methodological trade-offs between field-based research and meta-analysis; in chapter 4 we survey the contributions of meta-analysis to research on collective action for natural resource management. Meta-analysis avoids the costs of new field research by analyzing data gleaned from existing studies. This strategy puts cross-national analysis well within reach. Yet the pool of existing studies presents important limitations as well, ranging from problems of missing data to lack of control over the sample. Meta-analysis complements case studies and large-N field-based research but cannot replace either research strategy.

METHODOLOGICAL PRACTICES OVER FIFTEEN YEARS OF RESEARCH

To assess trends in methodological practices since the 1980s, we created a meta-database of articles concerned with collective action for the management of natural resources by users of those natural resources.[2] We surveyed articles published over a fifteen-year period, 1990–2004, to track trends in methodological practices following the calls for more broadly comparative research at the NRC panel and in the series of edited volumes in the late 1980s. A search of the Academic Search Premier bibliographic database (EBSCOhost Research Databases 2005)[3] retrieved thousands of scholarly articles with one or more of the following terms in the abstract or as keywords or subject terms: common-pool resource, commons, community management, community-based management, collective action, common resource management, forest management, irrigation, groundwater management, fishery management, management of fisheries, public land, grazing system, and pasture management.[4] The meta-database includes 172 articles that presented field-based empirical research related to collective action for natural resource management by users of those resources, and that included enough information for the analysis.[5]

Before the late 1980s, research on natural resource management rarely considered prospects for collective action. If collective action was considered at all, most studies assumed that people who shared natural resources were incapable of collective action (see chapter 2). Attention to the possibility and importance of collective action increased sharply over the fifteen-year period of our survey. The number of articles concerned with the role of and prospects for collective action for natural resource management increased from 8 articles published in 1990 through 1994 to 48 articles published 1995–99 and 116 articles published 2000–2004. In light of the initially limited but accelerating publication of research on the role of collective action in natural resource management, we compare methodological practices in the 56 peer-reviewed articles published 1990–99 with the 116 articles published 2000–2004. To assess the prevalence of methodological practices that support broadly comparative analysis, we consider the number of observations, their geographic scope, and whether the main unit of analysis allows analysis of the *prospects* for collective action.

Defining the Units of Analysis

Research often involves multiple types of observations at more than one scale of analysis. The presence of multiple types of observations within a study and inconsistent terminology in the literature contribute to confusion about the meaning of a "case study" (see chapter 2). Following Gerring (2004), we identify "cases" with the main unit of analysis. For each field-based empirical study, we determined the main unit of analysis based on data presentation: (1) policy units where the data were organized around the activities of natural resource users within countries, districts, or other political jurisdictions; (2) resource system or social units where data were organized around relevant resource systems (e.g., watershed, fishery) or groups defined by engagement with a natural resource (e.g., user groups); and (3) individual or household units when the organization of data focused on individual respondents or household surveys. Regardless of the unit of analysis, all articles are concerned with collective action by people who are using a shared natural resource. Studies that use policy units as the main unit of analysis, for example, present data about natural resource users *within* a policy unit (i.e., users within a certain jurisdiction); these are *not* studies of collective action by policymakers associated with a particular policy unit or jurisdiction.

When we speak of the number of cases in a study, we are referring to the number of observations on the main unit of analysis. If the main unit of analysis is a policy unit, then the number of cases or observations refers to the number of policy units for which data are presented. The number of cases does *not* refer to the number of observations *within* each unit of analysis (e.g., the number of people interviewed within the policy unit). Several articles present analysis related to several distinct questions, involving different units of analysis. To reflect our substantive concerns, we coded these articles based on the main unit of analysis in those analyses most related to the prospects for collective action.[6] Following the central limit theorem, we classified articles with thirty or more observations for the main unit of analysis as large-N studies.[7]

The choice of the unit of analysis influences the sorts of theoretical questions that a study can answer. Resource system or social units represent the most relevant unit of analysis for assessing *prospects* for collective action. Policy units can be relevant as well, if the boundaries of the resource system and the relevant groups of resource users fall within a single policy jurisdiction. The individual and household unit of analysis is the least relevant for the analysis of the *likelihood* of collective action. The very concept of a collective-action problem implies a disjuncture between individual preferences over outcomes, strategically rational individual behavior, and collectively desirable outcomes. Because they do not address the possibility that individual behavior may not correspond with individual preferences over outcomes, individual-level data have limited value for evaluating the *likelihood* of collective action. Analyses of individual- or household-level data are very appropriate for evaluations of *consequences* of the various arrangements of natural resource management. Indeed, most of the articles based on individual-level data are concerned with the implications of common property or community-based natural resource management for various outcomes at an individual or household level. These studies typically analyze patterns of natural resource utilization and variation in the contribution of natural resources to subsistence, document outcomes associated with institutional arrangements in particular settings, and measure expressed support for alternative institutional arrangements.

With the database we created, we can ask whether the synthetic and theoretical developments of the late 1980s started a move away from establishing the possibility of collective action on the commons and toward the development and testing of more general theory. If yes, we should find an increase in broadly comparative analyses of observations related to potential units of collective action in articles published after 1990. We will show that, although there has been a decrease in single case studies, it is associated largely with an increase in small-N comparisons. Furthermore, while there has been an increase in large-N studies, most of these studies analyze individual or household data and are more concerned with the consequences of current or past arrangements for natural resource management than with the prospects for collective action. Even if these patterns are interpreted as documenting initial steps toward more broadly comparative research, they also suggest that such changes in methodological practices are more difficult than is generally recognized.

Trading Geographic Scope for Numbers?

Only a relatively small subset of articles published between 1990 and 2004 engaged in broadly comparative research. Not only was the share of articles engaged in large-N analysis relatively small, but most large-N studies involved the analysis of individual- or household-level data collected from a limited geographic area. This pattern suggests that scholars may be making trade-offs between geographic scope and the number of observations. Very few articles published during this fifteen-year period made use of the sorts of research methods required to assess the generality of hypotheses concerning prospects for collective action for natural resource management.

Table 3.1 shows that barely more than one-fifth of the articles were large-N studies. Of 172 empirical field-based studies of natural resource management, 136 (79.1 percent) analyzed fewer than 30 observations of the main unit of analysis. There was a slight but statistically insignificant increase in large-N studies over time, from 16.1 percent of articles published in the 1990s to 23.3 percent of those published 2000–2004. Small-N studies tend to fall well below the 30-observation threshold. More than half (78 of 136 or 57.4 percent) of the small-N studies—and 45.3 percent of *all* articles—are presented as single case studies; an additional 16 articles analyzed two case studies. Fully 111 articles (64.5 percent of the total) relied on data for 5 or fewer cases.

TABLE 3.1
Frequency distributions of types of study

A. Small- and large-N studies: count and percentage by period

Sample size	1990–99	2000–2004	Total: 1990–2004
Small-N studies	47	89	136
(fewer than 30 observations)	83.9%	76.7%	79.1%
Large-N studies	9	27	36
(30 or more observations)	16.1%	23.3%	20.9%
Total	56	116	172

Pearson Chi-Square: 1.184   Statistical significance: 0.276
Eta (Sample size as dependent variable): 0.083
Eta (Period of publication as dependent variable): 0.083

B. Frequency of studies by number of observations: count and percentage by period

Number of observations	1990–99	2000–2004	Total: 1990–2004
1	33	45	78
	58.9%	38.8%	45.3%
2	4	12	16
	7.1%	10.3%	9.3%
3–5	4	13	17
	7.1%	11.2%	9.9%
6–10	3	8	11
	5.4%	6.9%	6.4%
11–29	3	11	14
	5.4%	9.5%	8.1%
30–39	4	10	14
	7.1%	8.6%	8.1%
100 or more	5	17	22
	8.9%	14.7%	12.8%
Total	56	116	172

Pearson Chi-Square: 6.423   Statistical significance: 0.377
Spearman Correlation: 0.174   Statistical significance: 0.022

There has been some movement, albeit modest, toward more large-N research related to collective action in natural resource management. We do see a decrease in single case studies, from 58.9 percent of the articles published in the 1990s to 38.8 percent of articles published 2000–2004, as well as a slight percentage increase in articles with 2 to 5 cases. Only 36 articles published over this 15-year period analyzed 30 or more observations, however, and can be considered large-N studies. Although large-N studies were rare, they generally analyzed far more than 30 observations; 22 reported findings based on 100 or more observations. Indeed, articles that analyzed 100 or more observations increased substantially, from 8.9 percent of all articles published 1990–99 to 14.7 percent of those published 2000–2004.

Articles published on collective action for natural research management generally have a limited geographic scope. The vast majority of articles (77.3 percent) published during the 1990–2004 period address natural resource management at the subnational level (see table 3.2). Almost all (97.2 percent) large-N empirical studies published during this period and more than two-thirds (72.1 percent) of the small-N empirical studies were subnational in scope. The focus on subnational studies has remained stable over time. Only 9 articles (5.2 percent) engaged in cross-national analysis, 2 in the 1990s and 7 between 2000 and 2004. In fact, geographic scope is strongly and inversely related to the number of observations. *All* cross-national studies and all except 1 national-level study involved small-N comparisons.[8]

TABLE 3.2
Type of study by geographic scope

A. Articles published 1990–99

| Type of study | Geographic scope | | | |
	Subnational	National	Cross-national	Total
Small-N	34	11	2	47
Column percent	79.1%	100%	100%	83.9%
Row percent	72.3%	23.4%	4.3%	
Large-N	9	0	0	9
Column percent	20.9%	0 %	0%	16.1%
Row percent	100%			
Total (N)	43	11	2	56
	76.8%	19.6%	3.6%	100%

Pearson Chi-Square: 3.242   Statistical significance: 0.198
Spearman Correlation: 0.240   Statistical significance: 0.075

B. 2000–2004

| Type of study | Geographic scope | | | |
	Subnational	National	Cross-national	Total
Small-N	64	18	7	89
Column percent	71.1%	94.7%	100%	76.7%
Row percent	71.9%	20.2%	7.9%	
Large-N	26	1	0	27
Column percent	28.9%	5.3%	0%	23.3%
Row percent	96.3%	3.7%		
Total (N)	90	19	7	116
	77.6%	16.4%	6.0%	100%

Pearson Chi-Square: 7.163   Statistical significance: 0.028
Spearman Correlation: 0.248   Statistical significance: 0.007

C. Total: 1990–2004

| Type of study | Geographic scope | | | |
	Subnational	National	Cross-national	Total
Small-N	98	29	9	136
Column percent	72.1%	21.3%	6.6%	79.1%
Row percent	73.7%	96.7%	100%	
Large-N	35	1	0	36
Column percent	97.2%	2.8 %	0%	20.9%
Row percent	26.3%	3.3%		
Total (N)	133	30	9	172
	77.3%	17.4%	5.2%	

Pearson Chi-Square: 10.326   Statistical significance: 0.006

The inverse relationship between the number of observations and geographic scope reflects the close correlation of the number of observations with the main unit of analysis. The small-N studies focus almost exclusively on either units of potential collective action, such as user groups and resource systems (78.7 percent of articles published 1990–99; 60.7 percent for 2000–2004; 66.9 percent overall), or policymaking units (21.3 percent for 1990–99; 38.2 percent for 2000–2004; 32.6 percent overall) (see table 3.3).[9] Likewise, almost all large-N studies (66.7 percent for 1990–99; 77.8 percent for 2000–2004; 75.0 percent overall) treat individual respondents as the main unit of analysis. If anything, this correspondence between the unit of analysis and the sample size has increased over time.

TABLE 3.3
Type of study by unit of analysis

A. 1990–99

Type of study	Unit of analysis			
	Individual or household respondents	Collective or resource system units (e.g., user group, forest)	Policy units	Total
Small-N study	0	37	10	47
Column percent	0%	92.5%	100%	
Row percent		78.7%	21.3%	83.9%
Large-N study	6	3	0	9
Column percent	100%	7.5%	0%	
Row percent	66.7%	33.3%		16.1%
Total (N)	6	40	10	56
Total (%)	10.7%	71.4%	17.9%	100%

Pearson Chi-Square: 35.427   Statistical significance: 0.000
Spearman Correlation: 0.592   Statistical significance: 0.000

B. 2000–2004

Type of study	Unit of analysis			
	Individual or household respondents	Collective or resource system units (e.g., user group, forest)	Policy units	Total
Small-N study	1	54	34	89
Column percent	4.5%	91.5%	97.1%	
Row percent	1.1%	60.7%	38.2%	76.6%
Large-N study	21	5	1	27
Column percent	95.5%	8.5%	2.9%	
Row percent	77.8%	18.5%	3.7%	23.3%
Total (N)	28	100	49	172
Total (%)	16.3%	58.1%	28.5%	100%

Pearson Chi-Square: 79.590   Statistical significance: 0.000
Spearman Correlation: 0.653   Statistical significance: 0.000

C. Total: 1990–2004

| Type of study | Unit of analysis | | | Total |
	Individual or household respondents	Collective or resource system units (e.g., user group, forest)	Policy units	
Small-N study	1	91	44	136
Column percent	3.6%	91.9%	97.8%	
Row percent	0.7%	66.9%	32.4%	79.1%
Large-N study	27	8	1	36
Column percent	96.4%	8.1%	2.2%	
Row percent	75.0%	22.2%	2.8%	20.9%
Total (N)	28	100	49	172
Total (%)	16.3%	58.1%	28.5%	100%

Large-N studies tend to be subnational studies because they mostly analyze survey or interview data, and almost all field-based studies informed by individual respondents (96.3 percent) draw on subnational samples. There is no evidence of change in this pattern over time. In general, large-N studies can contribute to assessments of both internal and external validity. An increase in the number of observations increases the capacity to address external validity, however, only if it expands the scope of population from which the sample is drawn. The inverse relationship between the number of observations and geographic scope means little if any increase in external validity has been gained.

Large-N surveys of individuals or households can be extremely helpful for assessing the relative importance of natural resources for a community, identifying variation in patterns of use and dependence across subpopulations, and the degree of support for alternative management regimes. All of these conditions either influence collective action or reflect outcomes associated with collective action. The unit of analysis for theories concerned with prospects for collective action, however, must be a unit of potential collective action. Unless individual-level data are analyzed relative to units of potential collective action and combined with observations related to those units of potential collective action, these studies have little to say about the generality of hypothesized influences on the emergence of collective action.

Theoretical Aspirations and Methodological Practices

If research methods were influenced primarily by theoretical developments, broadly comparative analyses should have become increasingly
prevalent in research published after 1990. The proportion of articles on
collective action for natural resource management that analyzed more
than 30 observations did increase, albeit modestly, from 16.1 percent in
the 1990s, to 23.3 percent between 2000 and 2004. A larger sample size
may be necessary for broadly comparative research, but it certainly does
not guarantee it. Our survey identified only 9 cross-national studies, none
of which compared more than 5 cases.[10] Most large-N studies analyzed
data from household surveys conducted within a single country.[11] To
the extent that scholars face a trade-off between sample size and geographic scope, increases in sample size will not increase external validity.
Methodological choices also influence the sorts of questions that can be
answered. Individual- and household-level responses are appropriate for
assessments of the *consequences of management strategies*, but do not
have obvious implications for the *prospects for collective action*. At least
through 2004, the call for more broadly comparative research on the
prospects for collective action for natural resource management was still
largely unanswered.

PRACTICAL CHALLENGES TO BROADLY COMPARATIVE FIELD-BASED RESEARCH

Why are broadly comparative field-based journal articles on collective action for natural resource management so rare despite theoretical developments and synthetic efforts in the late 1980s and early 1990s that set an
agenda for such research? The costs of field research related to collective
action for common-pool resources greatly constrain both the quantity of
data collected and their studies' geographic scope. The local knowledge,
financial resources, and time required to collect data on arrangements for
the management of local natural resources place the construction of large
cross-national data sets beyond the reach of most individual researchers.
Where even basic descriptive data are lacking, it is not always possible to
implement data collection methods that ensure a representative sample.
These challenges account for the relative scarcity of large-N studies of
resource system or policy units of analysis and the virtual nonexistence
of cross-national research on collective action related to common-pool
resources. Small-N comparative studies and intensively researched subnational analyses represent reasonable responses to the scarcity of readily
available data and the costliness of new data collection.

Costs of Data Collection

The costs of data collection depend on the nature of the data sought and their accessibility. The availability and accessibility of data related to common-pool natural resources are uneven. Some governments maintain lists of registered groups involved in natural resource management, such as irrigation systems in Mexico (Dayton-Johnson 1999, 2000) and Van Panchayats involved in forest management in India (Agrawal and Goyal 2001; Agrawal and Yadama 1997). For some places and periods, rich historical records document rules governing natural resource use and actual patterns of resource use and yields, as well as information about potential influences on collective action, such as demographic changes (De Moor, Shaw-Taylor, and Warde 2002; McKean 1986; Netting 1981). Often, however, written records related to collective management of shared resources do not exist, are not updated regularly, exclude groups that lack government recognition, reflect formal rules but not actual practices, or are known to be inaccurate for other reasons (Anderson and Simmons 1993; Berry 1992; Dayton-Johnson 1999; Meinzen-Dick, Raju, and Gulati 2002; M. Richards 1997). Even where fairly reliable records do exist, they generally concern a subset of natural resources within a single country.

Researchers have to overcome substantial challenges to collect enough data for large-N analysis related to subnational phenomena such as collective action for natural resource management. Research on collective action requires information about potential participants in collective action and evidence of collective action (or its absence). People do not present themselves to researchers in unambiguously demarcated groups, and collective action often involves informal institutions to regulate resource use and manage conflicts. Theory stresses the importance of institutional arrangements, especially informal institutions, and other contextual factors that require substantial local knowledge—of languages, culture, and practices. If the government does not recognize users' rights to a natural resource, collective action to manage the resource may be illegal. For these reasons, data collection generally requires extended periods of fieldwork to gain the trust of respondents and the local knowledge required to recognize and understand informal practices and institutions. In some situations, researchers may need to develop and maintain language skills. Local knowledge and language skills bring substantial advantages but are difficult to cultivate for more than a handful of locations.

Considering the physical limits to what any single researcher can accomplish, it is not surprising that relatively few scholars have compiled or analyzed large-N data sets on collective action for natural resource management by natural resource users across a number of localities. Quite simply, scholars have been hard-pressed to build databases for the study of common-pool resources large enough to analyze the many potential independent variables. Limits to the time and financing available for data collection force trade-offs between the number and type of variables measured and the number of cases for which data can be collected.

Research Design and Sampling

The limited availability of basic information about common-pool natural resources and the costs of collecting data related to collective action constrain research design. Small-N research designs often seek to mimic experimental design by selecting cases that hold confounding factors constant while making it possible to isolate the effects of alternative explanatory variables (George and Bennett 2005; Gerring 2007a). For large-N studies, a representative sample is required to achieve external validity. Both strategies are difficult or impossible to implement in the absence of basic descriptive data about the underlying population.

The relative merits of various strategies for selecting cases for small-N research are much debated (Campbell 1975; Collier and Mahoney 1996; Geddes 1990; Gerring 2007b; Lieberson 1991; Rogowski 2004; Rueschemeyer 2003). There is broad agreement that researchers should select cases to control the patterns of variation and comparability in ways that enhance analytical leverage. Recommendations diverge on the criteria for case selection, not on the goal of managing patterns of variation.[12] Implementation of these strategies depends on the availability of basic descriptive information about possible cases.

Three interrelated factors influence whether a large sample is representative: the nature of the underlying population, sample size, and the sampling technique. The central limit theorem posits that a sample of thirty observations drawn randomly from a population will be representative if the phenomenon of interest is normally distributed. A larger number of observations is required if a population is highly heterogeneous or features independent variables that are closely correlated with each other. Even a much larger sample may miss rare events, while relatively few observations are needed to adequately represent an extremely homogeneous population.

Randomization increases the likelihood that a large sample reflects the characteristics of the underlying population by avoiding assignment or selection based on the value of variables of interest. Randomization does not guarantee a representative sample, however, and is inefficient when the phenomenon of interest is not normally distributed or the full population is relatively small. Random sampling involves the use of a statistical randomization process to select observations from a complete list of possible observations. It is most common in the selection of individual or household respondents. Other sampling strategies have been developed to limit the risk of sample bias when randomization is either inappropriate or impossible. For a quota sample, for example, researchers select cases with an eye to matching the distribution of key characteristics in the world at large.

Since studies often involve several types of data collection, it is common to have purposive selection of some observations (e.g., sites) and random sampling of others (e.g., individual respondents) (e.g., Gillingham 1999). For example, in a study of organization and collective action related to irrigation systems in India, Meinzen-Dick, Raju, and Gulati (2002) purposefully selected two Indian states in which irrigation was a high priority, and, within each state, two irrigation systems that differed in terms of origins and organization (see also Meinzen-Dick 2007). They then used a stratified randomization procedure to select segments of each irrigation system for inclusion in their study.

Both random and purposive strategies for case selection assume the availability of basic descriptive information about the population of interest and its distribution. Such assumptions are often unmet for common-pool natural resources or the groups of people who use those resources. In our survey of articles published 1990–2004, 24 of the 36 large-N studies mentioned the use of random sampling.[13] Of these, 18 analyzed data from survey research. In nonsurvey research, random sampling occurs less frequently either because the population is relatively small (e.g., political jurisdictions) or because population lists do not exist or are highly biased.[14] Although Dayton-Johnson (1999, 2000) drew a random sample from a registry of irrigation systems developed by the Mexican state of Guanajuato to facilitate extension efforts, for example, the sample was not truly random because the state registry was incomplete and out of date. Whether sample bias is a problem depends on whether registration with the state correlates with characteristics of the irrigation systems featured in Dayton-Johnson's analysis. In other studies, problems of accessibility prevented the inclusion of some randomly selected observations (e.g., McCarthy and Vanderlinden 2004).

If a complete population list is not available but the distribution of key features of the population is well understood, the researcher can select cases to ensure the inclusion of a mix that reflects the underlying distribution. If the underlying population is not well understood, however, these techniques become impossible to implement. It may be possible to select cases in a structured manner to gain analytical leverage, but it is not possible to determine whether a sample is representative under such conditions. Thus the scarcity of descriptive data related to collective action for natural resource management further raises the costs of data collection by hindering the implementation of standard sampling techniques that enhance analytical leverage and ensure the generality of findings.

The Implications of Data Scarcity and Costliness

Given the scarcity of basic data about common-pool natural resources and the costs of collecting data related to collective action, the absence of large-N cross-national studies based on field research is perhaps predictable. Most field-based studies include cases from only one or two countries or, frequently, a single region within a single country. Our survey of methodological practices found only one large-N article that encompassed an entire country. No cross-national studies had more than five observations on the main unit of analysis.

The emphasis on subnational analysis may be specific to the study of shared natural resources, but the scarcity of cross-national research is not. A survey of three top-ranked comparative politics journals for the period 1989–2004 found similar patterns: single-country studies accounted for fully 45.7 percent of the articles surveyed, while only a quarter presented data for more than five countries (Munck and Snyder 2007). A historical survey of articles published in ten top-ranked political science journals found that between 25 percent and 39 percent of the articles published since 1975 involve case studies (Bennett, Barth, and Rutherford 2003, 374). The prevalence of small-N research in peer-reviewed journals suggests that data scarcity and high costs of data collection affect many topics of broadly comparative interest.

Geographically restricted samples make it impossible to evaluate the generality of relationships beyond the region or country from which data are drawn. Indeed, the theoretical value of broadly comparative research has long been recognized. The absence of a clear movement toward more broadly comparative field-based research reflects the difficulty of conducting such research. Arguably, the costs of data collection put large-N cross-national field-based research beyond the reach of individual researchers. We look at strategies for addressing these challenges through collaboration in chapter 5. The rest of this chapter introduces another option: meta-analysis of existing case studies.

META-ANALYSIS: AN INTRODUCTION

Compilation of a large database may involve the collection and coding of primary data from observations in field settings or archival research, or the compilation and coding of existing studies for meta-analysis (Glass 1976).[15] Meta-analysis is the "analysis of analyses" (Glass 1976, 3). It offers a strategy for systematically integrating large bodies of literature and making sense of contradictory findings that is more thorough and less vulnerable to reviewer bias than are narrative forms of research synthesis (Cooper and Hedges 1994; Glass 1976; Hunter and Schmidt 1990; Rosenthal et al. 2006; Rudel 2008).[16]

Since the early 1980s, meta-analysis has spread dramatically in medicine, psychology, and education (Chambers 2004; Rosenthal and DiMatteo 2001; Slavin 1986). In these fields, meta-analysis is generally used to calculate the average effect size for particular treatment variables from the data produced in experimental or quasi-experimental research. Most of the literature on meta-analysis addresses issues and techniques related to the quantitative analysis of data derived from quantitative analyses (e.g., Cooper and Hedges 1994; Hunter and Schmidt 1990; Lipsey and Wilson 2001). Indeed, some definitions restrict meta-analysis to "the quantitative synthesis of research" (Bangert-Drowns 1995, 305) or more specifically to the calculation of effect sizes from a body of experimental or quasi-experimental research (e.g., Lipsey and Wilson 2001). Many others, however, contend that the research design of the studies to be analyzed and the techniques used to analyze them should *not* be part of the definition of meta-analysis (Bangert-Drowns 1995; Rudel 2008; Shelby and Vaske 2008). As Bangert-Drowns argues, "it is better to think of meta-analysis as a perspective than as a method, a way of perceiving individual studies as data points" (1995, 306).

In this spirit, we define meta-analysis as a formally structured analysis of analyses that involves systematic coding of data and characteristics derived from existing studies. This definition makes the distinction between informal literature reviews and meta-analysis explicit. Yet it also encompasses a broad array of techniques for analyzing the data gleaned from existing studies and does not restrict the research design used in the studies to be analyzed.[17] With meta-analysis, as with other methods of analysis, the specific techniques used *should* vary to reflect the variable nature of the research to be synthesized (Bangert-Drowns 1995; Light and Pillemer 1984; Shelby and Vaske 2008; Slavin 1986).

While meta-analyses in the clinical sciences generally involve the calculation of average effects from quantitative studies, meta-analyses related to natural resources have synthesized findings from case studies (see chapter 4).[18] Meta-analysis of qualitative case studies obviously cannot support the calculation of quantitative measures of average effects. Instead, meta-analysts treat the case studies as sources of data relevant for the evaluation of a theoretically informed model. Rudel (2008) highlights the distinctiveness of these strategies of analysis by referring to them as variable-centered and model-centered. Where variable-centered analysis evaluates the explanatory value of individual variables, model-centered analysis evaluates the explanatory value of particular combinations of variables for particular subsets of cases. Variable-centered analysis makes sense only if variables are believed to have constant effects on outcomes of interest, regardless of other conditions. Model-centered analysis allows for both causal heterogeneity and conjunctural relationships, as discussed further below.

Rudel (2008) argues that Qualitative Comparative Analysis (QCA) is particularly well suited for meta-analysis of case studies related to global environment change. QCA was developed to address the possibility of multiple causation (Ragin 1987). Multiple causation occurs when more than one combination of conditions is associated with an outcome. In its simplest form, QCA requires the dichotomous coding of each variable as present or absent for each observation or case.[19] QCA generates a set of *all* conjunctures (combinations of conditions) that are observed when the outcome of interest is observed, including conjunctures that involve the absence of one or more conditions. QCA contrasts sharply with standard statistical techniques for multivariate analysis in that it directs attention to combinations of variables instead of individual variables, and to the presence or absence of conjunctures instead of their average effects. Although data may be generated from fieldwork, experiments, or meta-analysis, the technique does require a large data set. In fact, given its reliance on set theory, the application of QCA to a small or unrepresentative sample can yield misleading results. QCA allows empirical investigation of configurations of conditions associated with outcomes of interest. Early applications within sociology addressed questions related to the welfare state (Amenta, Carruthers, and Zylan 1992; Amenta and Poulsen 1996), social movements (Cress and Snow 2000), and unions (Brown and Boswell 1995; Dixon, Roscigno, and Hodson 2004; Ebbinghaus and Visser 1999). More recently, QCA has spread beyond sociology, to other areas of research including that related to natural resources and the environment (Basurto 2009; Hellström 1998, 2001; Lam and Ostrom 2009; Rudel 2005, 2008; Rudel and Roper 1996). QCA makes it possible to assess whether the conditions associated with collective action vary across cultural or political settings, or whether conditions associated with sustainable natural resource management differ across ecological zones.

Given the diverse practices found under the umbrella label of meta-analysis, scholars who use these techniques should specify both the type of research designs included in the meta-analysis and the analytical technique used.[20] We address issues that affect all forms of meta-analysis, but focus on issues and techniques that are particularly important for meta-analysis of case studies.

Weighing the Benefits and Costs of Meta-Analysis

The two main strategies for developing large databases—meta-analysis of existing studies and field-based studies—present trade-offs in the costs of data collection, the expected benefits from different analytical strategies, control over research design and the quality of data, and external validity. Whether the balance favors primary analysis or meta-analysis depends upon the nature of the research to be conducted and the state of the discipline at a particular time.

Meta-analysis keeps the costs of data collection down by tapping the wealth of data in existing case studies. Construction of a meta-database offers a cost-effective way to condense the depth and complexity of existing case studies in order to reveal general patterns and anomalies. Inclusion in a meta-database makes data from case studies more readily accessible to the broader scholarly community, thus increasing the (collective) return on investments in research (Rosenthal and DiMatteo 2001). Note, however, that the cost advantage of meta-analysis depends on the nature of the research question. Some types of data can be accessed or generated at relatively low cost, while the costs of meta-analysis increase with the volume and complexity of the studies to be included. Screening and coding of qualitative studies for model-centered meta-analysis can be demanding (Rudel 2008). Furthermore, the value of meta-analysis as a way of limiting expenses related to data collection must be weighed against decreased control over measurement and research design.[21]

Coding Strategies and Missing Data

The move from concept to data collection leaves ample room for differences in interpretation and measurement. Many concepts are multidimensional. The existence of multiple forms of heterogeneity, for instance, feeds ongoing debates about its relationship to collective action (Baland and Platteau [1996] 2000, 302–12; Poteete and Ostrom 2004a) (also see chapter 2). Scholars contest the meaning of other concepts. What counts as successful collective action, for instance, can be defined in terms of sustainability, efficiency, equity, risk spreading, or any number of other dimensions.

Strategies for building large databases differ in the control the researcher can exercise over what variables are measured and how they are measured. A scholar engaged in primary research can focus data collection on the set of variables relevant for a particular research program. Although the desire to address broader theoretical debates encourages the use of similar variables and conventional measures, theoretical considerations, lessons from empirical research, and local conditions can justify innovations. Different theoretical frameworks and disciplinary perspectives direct attention to somewhat different sets of variables. Concerns with theoretical precision and the validity of measures encourage a proliferation of measures. When building a large database from new observations in the field, the researcher decides how to balance consistency with conventional measures against innovations to reflect theoretical developments or local context.

Rigorous research design can promote consistency in conceptualization and measurement within a given study. While meta-analysis allows the use of clearly defined concepts and measures, the meta-analyst has to work with the concepts and measures as they are used in existing studies (Bangert-Drowns 1995; Yang 2002). Meta-analysis assumes that the essential elements of case studies are sufficiently similar that comparison makes sense (Rudel 2008). The ability to compare case studies depends on some consistency in the research questions addressed, the conceptualization of the unit of analysis, and the conceptualization and measurement of dependent and independent variables.

Case studies, no matter how well done, do not fully represent comparable data records, and even an exhaustive coding scheme cannot fully compensate for the different concerns and perspectives found in source materials. The need to produce tightly focused analyses for publication discourages the provision of descriptive details about variables that are not featured in a particular article or that are held constant. Disciplinary and theoretical differences create additional blind spots, so that variables of interest for comparative analysis may be overlooked or described in a cursory manner. Differences across studies in the variables included in the analysis and how they are measured, however, present serious challenges for meta-analysis.

Critics argue that meta-analysis often includes studies that differ so much in their interpretation and measurement of key concepts that the resulting analysis is meaningless (e.g., Slavin 1986). The literature on meta-analysis refers to this issue as part of a more general "apples and oranges" problem arising from heterogeneity in the research designs of studies included in the meta-analysis; that is, comparison of studies with diverse research designs is like comparing apples and oranges. There are at least three responses to heterogeneity in concepts and measures: (1) broad criteria for inclusion, (2) narrow criteria for inclusion at the cost of a smaller usable sample, and (3) iterative coding that involves a narrowing of coding criteria in each successive round.

The first strategy includes studies that define and measure key variables in diverse ways. This strategy results in fewer missing cases but also a greater level of abstraction. Analysis of broadly defined variables is often theoretically unsatisfactory as it fails to address distinctions in the literature. Furthermore, broadly defined measures may obscure internal heterogeneity. The researcher can assess the presence of internal heterogeneity by coding for major variants in conceptualization (or other dimensions of heterogeneity in research design) (Chambers 2004; Hunter and Schmidt 1990; Rosenthal and DiMatteo 2001; Rosenthal et al. 2006). This strategy makes it possible to evaluate whether the nature or strength of particular relationships changes substantially when measured in different ways. Recognition of different measures as a source of variation can prompt conceptual refinements and theoretical development (Bangert-Drowns 1995; Yang 2002).

The second strategy treats the challenges presented by different measurements in existing studies as comparable to those arising from open-ended interview responses or content analysis of texts. A well-specified coding scheme provides a mechanism for measuring variables of interest consistently for model-centered meta-analysis, even if those variables were measured inconsistently or were not emphasized in the source material. This strategy results in more missing data and so constricts the set of studies that can be included in the meta-analysis. If there are systemic patterns in the types of scholars attentive to particular variables, those patterns will introduce bias into the meta-analysis. These problems limit the possibilities for broadly comparative research based on model-centered meta-analysis.

This trade-off between conceptual precision and missing data can be moderated somewhat through the adoption of a strategy of iterative coding (Rudel 2008). Iterative coding begins with more general definitions that apply to more cases and result in more abstract findings. Subsequent rounds of recoding use more precise definitions that result in more missing cases but also enable assessments of relationships involving more specific variables. Since multiple rounds of coding require a considerable investment of time, this strategy becomes unmanageable for larger numbers of case studies (Rudel 2008).

Potential Sources of Sample Bias

The researcher engaged in meta-analysis confronts at least three potential sources of sampling bias: quality differences across existing studies, potential nonindependence of studies, and publication bias. Considerable debate exists about whether the quality of the research design should be among the criteria for inclusion in a meta-analysis. Glass (1976) argues that differences in the quality of research design do not seem to be related to the outcome of interest, and, at a minimum, any relationship should be evaluated empirically rather than assumed. Those concerned about quality differences in quantitative research designs equate quality with statistical significance to an extent that proponents of meta-analysis consider excessive (Glass 1976; Hunter and Schmidt 1990; Rosenthal and DiMatteo 2001). Since statistical significance is an artifact of sample size, sampling based on research quality disadvantages studies based on smaller samples. But exclusion of studies based on sample size and other aspects of research design may introduce bias if these features are correlated with variety in the underlying population. Proponents of inclusive sampling prefer to test statistically for bias associated with sample size and make corrections as necessary (Chambers 2004; Hunter and Schmidt 1990; Rosenthal and DiMatteo 2001; Sutton et al. 2000).[22] The inclusion of studies with demonstrably weak research designs, however, can undermine the validity of the analysis by introducing biased data. At a minimum, meta-analysts should exclude studies based on research designs that do not adequately address known sources of bias, and, at least for policy-relevant topics, studies with very low external validity (Slavin 1986).

Quantitative analysis of general patterns and sources of variation assumes the independence of each observation. Sometimes, there is reason to expect nonindependence of observations, as in panel surveys or repeated observations from the same set of political jurisdictions. Indeed, the research may seek to understand change over time, as in panel surveys, or other patterns of interaction across observations, such as globalization or learning. If patterns of nonindependence are suspected but not central to the research agenda, the analysts must seek to limit it or correct for it. In field-based research, careful research design can limit the risk that nonindependent observations are included in a sample inadvertently. Various statistical techniques exist to check for the presence of autocorrelation or nonindependence in a sample and, if necessary, correct for it.

Nonindependence of observations can be particularly problematic for meta-analysis if multiple observations based on the same data are included in the analysis. Researchers can try to avoid this problem by screening carefully for multiple reports related to the same observations and adopting strategies for data management to avoid duplication of the same observations (Chambers 2004; Rosenthal and DiMatteo 2001). This is not always so straightforward. Researchers quite commonly explore alternative conceptualizations and measurements, for example, by comparing multiple analyses of the same data that use alternative specifications. And, in clinical studies, the sample control group is commonly used for comparison with a number of different treatment groups (Gleser and Olkin 1994). These forms of nonindependence may present challenges for coding and analysis, but are at least transparent and can be addressed explicitly (Gleser and Olkin 1994). Sometimes, however, scholars analyze the same data in multiple reports without clearly signaling the duplication (Sutton et al. 2000); if the interdependence is not recognized, it cannot be addressed. Since case studies usually report place-names and the dates of fieldwork, meta-analysts can generally limit problems of nonindependence through careful screening and data management.

Publication bias, procedures for identifying published and unpublished reports, and the challenges of accessing unpublished (and some published) studies represent more general sources of potential bias. Inclusion of an empirical case in the body of literature does not reflect a random sample, a quota sample, a structured sample, or any other systematic sampling technique. Rather, it reflects the interests of a set of uncoordinated researchers and the ability of those authors to get their work published. There is evidence that, for experimental and quasi-experimental research, statistically significant findings are more likely to get published (Light and Pillemer 1984; Rosenthal and DiMatteo 2001; Sutton et al. 2000).

The processes of sampling through choice of research topic and publication are sources of bias to the extent that these processes are systematically associated with variables to be analyzed. The scholarly community typically reacts to new information in a Bayesian manner, such that evidence that challenges conventional expectations gets more attention than confirmatory evidence (McKeown 2004). The publication process thus selects for novelty, not representativeness. Novelty often takes the form of challenges to the conventional wisdom or innovations related to concepts and measures. Thus Garrett Hardin's (1968) argument about the "tragedy of the commons" prompted disproportionate attention to successful cases of collective action, in terms of both research interest and publication. The difficulty of recognizing and studying cases of unrealized or failed collective action only reinforced this neglect of failed cases. The types of cases that receive scholarly attention do change with intellectual developments, and there is a tendency to correct for overgeneralization over time. Nonetheless, there is no reason to expect that the dynamics of shifting interests within the scholarly community will produce a representative sample of case studies, especially over the short to medium term. Bias can also arise from differences in accessibility related either to the circulation of research in formal journals versus informal outlets (e.g., reports of NGOs) or to language. Researchers who are not native speakers of English tend to publish significant findings in English-language journals and nonsignificant findings in their local language (Sutton et al. 2000).

If a meta-analysis includes only articles in prominent journals, only research published in English, or even all published research, the sample will be biased. Meta-analysts cannot use random or intentionally structured selection to limit bias, but they can limit publication bias by aggressively seeking to identify *all* relevant studies, whether published or not, and regardless of the publication outlet. In practical terms, this means searching a variety of electronic databases; drawing upon bibliographies and reference lists for additional sources, including dissertations, conference papers, government reports, and reports from nongovernmental organizations; and requesting unpublished papers and additional citations from scholars working on the research topic (Dickersin 1994; Light and Pillemer 1984; Lipsey and Wilson 2001; Reed and Baxter 1994; Rosenthal 1994; White 1994).

Even when all of these strategies are pursued, no meta-analysis can include all possible studies (Bangert-Drowns 1995). Indexes and archives are incomplete. Scholars do not always respond to requests for unpublished papers; Chambers (2004), for example, reported a response rate of only 5 percent. Analysis of biased data can be useful *if* the researcher acknowledges the bias, restricts claims of generality accordingly, and suggests adjustments for known biases (King, Keohane, and Verba 1994, 66–74). A variety of statistical techniques have been developed to compensate for publication bias in meta-analyses of quantitative studies (Rosenthal and DiMatteo 2001). Sutton et al. (2000) note, however, that most of these techniques have not been widely applied, the most frequently used techniques rely on dubious assumptions, and the most realistic techniques are often quite complex. Of course, these statistical fixes are not appropriate for meta-analyses of case studies. In any case, even when statistical fixes are possible, narrative discussion of the implications of bias might be the most valuable response.

The Choice of Methodological Strategy: Weighing Costs against Control

Meta-analysis offers less control over measurement and sampling than does primary analysis, but it provides a valuable overview of patterns and sources of variation in the existing literature. For some types of research, meta-analysis is substantially less expensive than is the collection of new primary data. For some research questions, meta-analysis may be the only feasible strategy for broadly comparative research given limited data availability and accessibility. Ultimately, the relative importance of internal validity from rigorous measurement, external validity from a representative sample, the generation of new primary data, and synthesis of the existing studies depends upon the nature and state of a research tradition and the relative professional rewards expected from different analytical strategies.

For new fields of study in which relatively little research has been conducted, new primary analysis, whether qualitative or quantitative, must be conducted before meta-analysis even becomes possible. As a research tradition matures and the body of primary analyses grows, meta-analysis becomes possible and increasingly valuable. Even then, meta-analysis can assess only variables and theories that are represented well in the literature. Development and evaluation of new concepts, measures, and theories—including those suggested by meta-analysis—require ongoing primary research (Bangert-Drowns 1995; Yang 2002).

In the clinical sciences, the choice between primary and meta-analysis is a choice between two strategies for large-N analysis. Although historically the granting agencies and the profession have rewarded primary research more than they have meta-analysis (e.g., Glass 1976), the explosion of new primary analyses with contradictory findings decreased the value of any single new primary analysis. The surge of interest in meta-analysis in these disciplines since 1980 reflects this shift. The application of meta-analysis to social scientific research has spread more slowly. Many social scientists with a quantitative orientation have preferred to engage in secondary analysis of existing databases, when available. Research synthesis typically relies on narrative reviews. Yet the accumulation of primary analyses and contradictory findings are at least as much of a problem for the nonclinical social sciences. Meta-analysis offers a partial solution.

In many areas of social scientific research, however, meta-analysis of quantitative research is not an option, or will become an option only in the future. Heavy reliance on secondary analysis of existing data sets in quantitative analysis limits the possibilities for meta-analysis. Heavy reliance on standard governmental or nongovernmental sources for key variables in new data sets also represents a constraint. For many social scientific research traditions, little or no quantitative primary analysis has been conducted, even if a voluminous literature exists. In this context, meta-analysis represents a choice not only between primary analysis and meta-analysis, but also between small-N and large-N analysis. For research traditions that have relied heavily on case study research, meta-analysis becomes attractive *both* as a way of integrating a large number of studies with contradictory findings *and* as a way of approaching external validity.

Meta-analysis is a relatively inexpensive technique for synthetic analysis but presents two basic challenges. First, it is difficult to glean consistently measured concepts from source materials that reflect diverse local contexts, research questions, and theoretical perspectives. Second, the pool of available case studies does not constitute a representative sample.

Large-N studies based on new fieldwork offer greater control over measurement and sampling, but the need for fieldwork and the associated costs limit the possibilities for such research. For many social scientific issues, meta-analysis is much less expensive than new fieldwork. Furthermore, even if findings derived from meta-analysis are not entirely representative, they distinguish common patterns from correlations found in only a handful of cases. Systematic analysis of existing case studies through meta-analysis can in turn guide broadly comparative field-based research. Because meta-analysis suggests ways to improve the precision and focus of data collection, meta-analysis can reduce the costs and improve the analytical value gained from new fieldwork.

We began this chapter with evidence that most journal articles on collective action for the management of common-pool natural resources published through 2004 were not broadly comparative. The near nonexistence of cross-national field-based empirical research may not be surprising given the obstacles to large-scale data collection on subnational phenomena. Nonetheless, it limits theoretical development and should be cause for concern. We have introduced meta-analysis as a more feasible alternative to broadly comparative research based on field research. Chapter 4 surveys significant contributions of meta-analysis to theoretical developments in the study of collective action and the management of common-pool resources. Chapter 4 also shows that meta-analysis has real limitations and cannot substitute for broadly comparative field-based research. Chapter 5 thus considers another strategy for broadly comparative research based on fieldwork: collaboration.

CHAPTER FOUR

Meta-Analysis:
Getting the Big Picture through Synthesis

CHAPTER 3 DEMONSTRATED that broadly comparative research based on field research remains relatively rare. The accumulation of knowledge gleaned from small-N case studies hinges on regular and effective research synthesis. This chapter presents several examples of synthetic research. First, we consider meta-analysis as one strategy that builds on existing case studies. An in-depth discussion of the Common-Pool Resource (CPR) research program and the Nepal Irrigation Institutions and Systems (NIIS) research program illustrates the challenges associated with meta-analysis and strategies for their amelioration. Second, we briefly discuss other examples of meta-analysis, narrative synthesis, and collaborative research related to collective action for the management of natural resources. This overview indicates the diversity of such work.

Meta-analysis and other forms of synthetic research have played a critical role in the study of collective action in the management of common-pool natural resources. Scholars have used meta-analysis to identify similar patterns and get a better sense of the multiple empirical manifestations of theoretical concepts. Even though it cannot substitute for primary analysis based on new comparative field research, the practical constraints on collecting new data for broadly comparative research through field research increase the value of meta-analysis. The chapter begins with a short recapitulation of the key features of meta-analysis that were discussed at length in chapter 3.

META-ANALYSIS: A RECAPITULATION

Synthesis of existing research can take varied forms. Meta-analysis, or the "analysis of analyses" (Glass 1976, 3), involves the compilation and analysis of data from existing studies, and contrasts with primary analysis of newly collected data and secondary analysis of existing data. Meta-analysis differs from traditional narrative research synthesis in its use of systematic strategies to integrate data from existing studies. In chapter 3, we defined meta-analysis as a formally structured analysis of analyses that involves systematic coding of data and characteristics derived from existing studies. The meta-analyses discussed in this chapter all involve the coding of qualitative case studies.

The choice between meta-analysis of existing studies and primary analysis involving new field research is not cut-and-dried. The main attraction of meta-analysis is the relatively low cost of accessing existing case studies. By comparison, primary analysis generally requires extended periods of field research and can be quite expensive. Even if qualitative case studies are more accessible than data from the field, converting the information contained in case studies into usable data for meta-analysis is not straightforward. Case studies tend to include different sets of variables and often use diverse measures to capture the same concepts. Meta-analysis thus requires either the adoption of highly abstract coding criteria that offer limited analytical leverage, or the exclusion of data from many studies that provide insufficient information to enable coding of more precisely defined variables.[1] In addition, the findings generated via meta-analysis are weak in regard to external validity because the collection of existing studies constitutes a nonrepresentative sample.

We present two examples of meta-analysis developed by scholars associated with the Workshop in Political Theory and Policy Analysis at Indiana University (the Workshop): the CPR research program and the NIIS research program. We describe the origins of each and the strategies adopted to address known methodological and practical challenges. In particular, we highlight strategies for selecting studies, measuring key concepts, maintaining consistency across observations, controlling data quality, and limiting or compensating for missing data. We discuss the procedures adopted by the CPR research team in somewhat greater detail because they provided the point of departure for the NIIS research program—as well as the International Forestry Resources and Institutions (IFRI) research program discussed in the next chapter. We also offer shorter overviews of several other examples of both meta-analysis and narrative synthesis.

The Common-Pool Resource (CPR) Research Program

The CPR research program was a direct response to the NRC's Panel on Common Property Resource Management (NRC 1986) (see chapter 2). Confronted by the number of cases presented at an NRC conference held in Annapolis during the spring of 1985, Elinor Ostrom started identifying common variables each evening at the conference and sharing these lists widely with other participants. With the case studies presented at the conference and the cases cited within these papers as a point of departure, Fenton Martin (1985) started compiling a bibliography of published and unpublished case studies. To everyone's surprise, it expanded rapidly and soon had more than one thousand entries.[2]

A research team composed of visiting scholars and graduate students at the Workshop decided to develop a meta-database to analyze the very large number of case studies systematically.[3] After an initial planning period, the team began to establish coding forms to record information about key variables that they wanted to use in analysis. Two years of intensive reading and extended discussions went into the design of coding protocols for the CPR research program. Members of the team would formulate and reformulate the structure of the coding forms as they ran into conceptual problems in translating the thick descriptions found in the case studies into reliably coded, structured data. They would develop a section of the coding manual by going back and forth from existing theoretical work to the case description. Once a section was developed based on an initial set of cases, they would see whether it could be used on different cases from entirely different countries and sectors. The team's "field studies" were contained in a large filing cabinet to which all had daily access. Given the low cost of access to their empirical material, the CPR team was able to revise the project coding instruments several times after starting the coding process. This increased the reliability of the final coding, but came at a cost of rereading and revising the coding of those studies that had already been through earlier rounds of coding.

Although the team eventually focused on fisheries and irrigation systems with some forestry cases, the coding protocols were designed so that they could be applied to different resource sectors (E. Ostrom et al. 1989). The coding instruments were built on the Institutional Analysis and Development (IAD) framework. Workshoppers had developed it to understand collective action and self-governance in diverse settings (Kiser and Ostrom 1982). Oakerson (1986) had elaborated it further for the study of the commons (see chapter 2 and Thomson, Feeny, and Oakerson 1992). The guidance of the IAD framework and knowledge of a variety of case studies helped the team develop coding protocols that reflected theoretical concepts and made sense in a wide variety of field settings.

Thus the CPR research program adopted the model-centered approach typical of meta-analysis of case studies (Rudel 2008). In model-centered meta-analysis, theory—in this case, the IAD framework—guides the identification and definition of variables to be coded based on information contained in the case studies. The IAD framework directs attention to the actors, rules or institutions, relationships among actors and among institutions, actions, and outcomes associated with a collective-action situation. The CPR research program opted to screen cases based on research quality and to use relatively precise operational definitions to guide coding. These decisions limited the number of cases that could be coded and increased the quantity of missing data. The next two sections describe strategies adopted to develop and implement operational definitions for theoretical concepts and to minimize problems of missing data that arose from the use of theoretically precise criteria for coding.

Defining Variables

To engage in model-centered meta-analysis, researchers must translate the varied terminology in case studies using a coding scheme that is consistent and rigorous. This task is all the more challenging for variables that are inherently difficult to measure and observe in field settings. These issues affect many variables. We focus on the measurement of the potential unit of collective action, a variable that is critical to the study of collective action, difficult to recognize in the field, and measured in diverse ways in empirical studies.

An appropriation subgroup is defined as those users who have similar rights to and responsibilities for the resource, similar dependency on the resource, and similar exposure to variations in supply, and who also withdraw broadly similar quantities of the resource (E. Ostrom et al. 1989). The coding manual for the CPR database refers to an "appropriation subgroup" as the set of actors that may engage in collective action. The term *sub*group recognizes the possibility of important differences within the total population of individuals using a given resource. The definition of a subgroup does not require formal organization or collective action. Groups that have organized institutions for collective decision making are coded as appropriation organizations.

The distinction between subgroups and organizations greatly facilitates the empirical study of collective action. It provides a standard unit for observing and measuring potential collective action. It also encourages the collection of data about groups that have overcome collective-action problems as well as those that have not. Since groups may act collectively for some but not all aspects of resource management, this modular approach also facilitates analysis that distinguishes among types of collective action. Despite these conceptual and analytical advantages, application of the subgroup concept can be challenging. The multidimensional definition refers to rights and responsibilities as well as to actual patterns of use and dependency on the resource. The definition misses groups for which these dimensions do not coincide.

The CPR database includes data on a large variety of potential dependent variables, including the establishment or survival of institutions for collective management of common-pool resources, effective management of those resources, and the robustness of management arrangements. The presence of rules that limit the number of appropriators, restrict rights of use and appropriation, and define the responsibilities and duties of appropriators indicates collective action for resource management. Data on the dates of operation provide an indicator of the survival of institutions. The CPR database allows assessments of effective management in terms of sustainability, correlation with resource quality, rule adherence, and limitations of violence as a means of conflict resolution. The management arrangements themselves can also be assessed in terms of equity, efficiency, stability, and robustness.

Compensating for Gaps in Case Materials

Meta-analysis is constrained by the quality of the source materials, the set of measures that can be gleaned from them, and the sample presented by source materials. The CPR research team developed four procedures to limit the extent of missing data and/or increase confidence in the quality of included data: the use of multiple sources per case where possible, screening of source materials, inquiries to authors of case studies, and the inclusion of unpublished case studies. These procedures could not eliminate all problems associated with missing data and sampling, but they increased confidence in the quality of the data and improved the team's understanding of the limitations of their data.

First, whenever possible, the research team drew upon multiple studies to inform the coding for a resource and set of subgroups. The use of multiple studies raised confidence in the quality of the data and increased the number of variables that could be coded.[4] Second, for each source, team members completed a screening form on which they evaluated the quality of the original case material and the degree to which it addressed the core variables in the meta-analysis. Data were entered into the meta-database only for those sources written in light of considerable fieldwork and containing information about the crucial variables identified by the team. These included basic information about the participants using a resource, strategies used by these participants, the condition of the resource, and the presence or absence of rules-in-use for regulating harvesting. A six-page screening form was filled out for all sources that were read and considered potentially appropriate for coding.

A frustrating aspect of doing meta-analysis is the large number of studies that have to be read and screened before one can find a sufficient N of cases that cover core variables thought to influence collective action for the management of natural resources. To obtain sufficient information about 47 irrigation systems, the team screened over 450 documents (Tang 1994). They screened several hundred papers to obtain sufficient information about 30 coastal fisheries located around the world (Schlager 1994). Other scholars doing careful meta-analysis have faced similar problems. Pagdee, Kim, and Daugherty (2006), for example, screened 110 articles related to forest management in order to analyze 31 cases involving some aspects of local participation. Rudel (2008) reported that he had screened nearly 1,200 studies for an earlier meta-analysis of 268 cases of tropical forest cover change.

Third, the team appealed directly to authors of source materials to help clarify key variables they had mentioned in their original studies. Inevitably, many studies used definitions for key variables that differed from the definitions used by the CPR research team. Other studies did not define key concepts or did not provide enough information for coding. The team was able to fill some of the resulting gaps by sending the completed coding forms to authors. Authors of source materials were asked to verify the coding and fill in missing data from their field notes if possible. This process did increase the reliability of the coding given an author's concern that the team understood the study correctly. On the other hand, this process did not substantially reduce missing variables as the missing information often concerned variables that were not of major interest to the field researcher and had not been recorded in the field in the first place.

Although there is no way of knowing how representative the sample might be, the fourth strategy of including unpublished, as well as published, studies limited the risk of "publication bias."[5] The team was blessed with the hard and skilled work of Fenton Martin and Charlotte Hess, who searched out unpublished cases from a variety of sources. For example, they checked published papers for additional references—particularly unpublished papers—and then wrote to the authors to obtain these papers for the Digital Library of the Commons, an online depository of papers related to common-pool resources.[6] Thus studies that might otherwise have been overlooked were included and recorded in a manner that made them readily accessible to other scholars.

Contributions

A large number of cases had already demonstrated that collective action on the commons was possible and widespread, and that neither individual private property rights nor centralized state control was required for sustainable management of common-pool resources. Establishing the CPR database made it possible to analyze variation in the success of collective action on the commons. Researchers have used the CPR database to address four broad questions: (1) What difference do different property rights make? (2) Which characteristics of a group affect the ability to organize successfully? (3) How does the type of collective challenge influence a group's capacity to organize an effective response? and (4) What types of regimes—institutions for sustaining collective action—are robust over time?

PROPERTY RIGHTS

It was widely assumed and seemed reasonable that "property rights" were an essential foundation for effective organization of a CPR, yet reading extensive CPR case studies forced the team to develop better conceptual foundations to overcome the ambiguities identified in the theoretical literature. A widespread confusion that dominated the literature in the second half of the twentieth century equated the concept of property rights with the existence of a right by one party (individual, family, organized group, or government) to sell all rights to another party. The right to transfer or sell one's rights is referred to as the right of alienation. Many scholars presumed that unless users had alienation rights, they did not have property rights (Alchian and Demsetz 1973; Anderson and Hill [1977] 1990; Posner 1975; but see Bromley 1989; Buck 1988). Some of the early confusion about the capability of users to develop their own effective governance system related to the presumption that without the right of alienation resource users had no property rights and were indeed trapped in overuse. There are, however, many well-defined and operational common-property systems that have existed for a long time without the right of alienation (McKean 1982, 1986; Netting 1981).

As the team read and coded more and more common-pool resource case studies, they kept finding established resource regimes that had survived for long periods of time where the users did *not* have the right to sell their holdings. This led Edella Schlager and Elinor Ostrom (1992) to draw on the earlier insights of Ciriacy-Wantrup and Bishop (1975) and John R. Commons ([1924] 1968) to think of property-rights systems as containing *bundles* of rights rather than a single right. They defined and coded the presence or absence of a series of five rights that were found in empirical studies of operational resource systems in the field (Schlager and Ostrom 1992, 250–51):

Access: a right to enter a defined physical property.

Withdrawal: a right to harvest the products of a resource such as timber, water, or food for pastoral animals.

Management: a right to regulate the use patterns of other harvesters and to transform a resource system by building improvements.

Exclusion: a right to determine who else will have the right of access to a resource and whether that right can be transferred.

Alienation: a right to sell or lease any of the above four rights.

They then posed the possibility that one can relate the different ways that these bundles are combined to a set of positions that individuals hold in regard to operational settings. They noted that rights of access, withdrawal, management, exclusion, and alienation are cumulative or nested. Rights of withdrawal, for instance, cannot be exercised without rights of access. They proposed a terminology to describe expanding bundles within the hierarchy of possible rights. An authorized user has only rights of access and withdrawal. A claimant has these rights plus management rights, while proprietorship adds rights of exclusion. Ownership encompasses the full set of rights. Examples from the CPR database illustrated each bundle of rights and grounded the typology empirically. Conceiving of property rights in this manner has been widely accepted by scholars who have studied diverse property-rights systems around the world (Brunckhorst 2000; Degnbol and McCay 2007; Paavola and Adger 2005; Trawick 2001b).

The CPR database also enabled systematic evaluation of the importance of particular rights for successful management of specific types of shared resources. In most of the cases where users did not have rights of alienation but did manage their resource effectively, users did have rights of management and/or exclusion and used these to manage a resource. Although case studies had already raised questions about the necessity of rights of alienation, analysis of the CPR database confirmed the widespread occurrence of sustainable management in the absence of rights of alienation.

Schlager (1994) analyzed the patterns of rights and outcomes for a set of inshore fishery cases that were well documented by the original case author. Schlager found that possessing at least the three rights held by a claimant (access, withdrawal, and management) did affect the capabilities of fishers from inshore fisheries to self-organize. Having the authority to exclude others (being a proprietor) gave fishers even more capabilities to ensure that others did not invade their inshore fishery and allowed still further investment in regulating use and investment. She did not find that having the right of alienation was as essential as claimed in the literature. In regard to irrigation systems, Tang (1994) found that having the rights of a proprietor made a substantial difference in regard to the long-term management, but having the full rights of an owner was not crucial. In many common-property systems that have been sustained over long periods of time, none of the resource users has had the right to alienate their other rights. Thus the right of alienation is *not* the key defining right for those who have been responsible for designing and adapting common-property systems in the field. Many users of common-pool resources have effective property rights even though their bundles of rights may not include the right of alienation.

CHARACTERISTICS OF THE GROUP

Case studies suggest that inconsistencies in the relationship between group characteristics and successful collective action reflect multiple forms of group heterogeneity. In a pair of articles, Ruttan (2006, 2008) uses the CPR database to distinguish several forms of heterogeneity and successful collective action, evaluate the relationship between particular forms of heterogeneity and collective action, and consider a variety of hypothesized causal mechanisms. Ruttan's statistical analyses show that the nature of the relationship between heterogeneity and collective action depends on (1) the form of heterogeneity, (2) the measure of successful collective action, and (3), as discussed further below, the type of natural resource.

Ruttan (2006) distinguishes social heterogeneity associated with forms of social difference that impede communication (e.g., caste, ethnicity, language, religion) from heterogeneity in cultural views related to the natural resource and its use. Both forms of sociocultural heterogeneity are distinct from economic heterogeneity, measured in terms of family incomes (Ruttan 2008). Successful collective action might refer to levels of participation, provision of collective goods (e.g., institutional choice, organized enforcement), or outcomes related to the condition of the resource (Ruttan 2008).

While economic heterogeneity seems to facilitate collective action under certain conditions, little evidence exists that sociocultural heterogeneity has any positive influence. Where wealthy groups of users depended heavily on the resource and levels of economic heterogeneity were high, collective benefits were more likely to be provided (Ruttan 2008). On the other hand, economic heterogeneity appears to dampen compliance with rules-in-use. Ruttan (2006) does not find much evidence of a direct negative relationship between sociocultural heterogeneity and collective action, but there appears to be an indirect effect. Sociocultural heterogeneity is associated with lower levels of trust, and lower levels of trust are associated with less success in collective action.

THE NATURE OF THE COLLECTIVE CHALLENGE

Case studies had suggested that the conditions affecting collective action on the commons depend upon the particular types of collective action under consideration and the characteristics of resource systems. The inclusion of cases related to different types of natural resources in the CPR database enables comparisons of the relative difficulty of collective action across types of collective tasks and resources.

Schlager (1994) examined the rules adopted by forty-four subgroups of fishers in thirty fisheries to deal with appropriation externalities, technological externalities, and assignment problems. Appropriation externalities arise when individual fishers fail to coordinate on overall levels of extraction. Technological externalities arise when the use of gear interferes physically with the activities of other fishers. And assignment problems refer to the difficulty of coordinating the distribution of fishing effort across stable clusters of fish with variable productivity. Schlager (1994) found that several subgroups of fishers had developed rules that effectively addressed technological externalities and assignment problems. Although the data did not support statistical analysis of responses to appropriation externalities, none of the groups of fishers had adopted restrictions on the fish harvested. Schlager speculated that differences in responses to collective challenges reflected differences in their severity.

Likewise, Ruttan (2006) found that different forms of sociocultural heterogeneity influenced collective action related to fisheries and irrigation systems in different ways. Although sociocultural heterogeneity presented an obstacle to collective action by lowering trust for both resources, the most influential form of sociocultural heterogeneity depended on the resource. Social heterogeneity that interfered with communication limited trust among users of irrigation systems, but had little influence on collective action related to fisheries. For fisheries, cultural differences in views related to the resource system and its use were associated with lower levels of trust and collective action. Ruttan (2006) speculated that these differences reflect the relative complexity of the resource and social patterns of use. In fisheries, cultural views of the resource may correspond to differences in the species harvested or the type of fishing gear used. Externalities related to particular forms of engagement with the fisheries are a well-documented source of conflicts (e.g., Berkes 1986a, 1986b; Schlager 1994) and can be expected to constrain collective action. Since irrigation systems are single-purpose resources, designed to distribute water, different cultural perspectives seem less likely.

The management challenge associated with a common-pool resource depends upon the structure of the resource itself and whether the rules-in-use are linked effectively to this structure. Tang (1992, 1994) found that the effectiveness and efficiency of irrigation systems depended on the fit between the rules allocating water and responsibilities with the physical domain. When rules create clear and persistent inequalities in the allocation of water or responsibility for maintenance, the disadvantaged irrigators have little incentive to contribute to the maintenance of the irrigation system. More equitable arrangements encourage all irrigators to contribute to maintenance of the system and thus enhance its performance.

In a comparative analysis of different types of common-pool resources, Schlager, Blomquist, and Tang (1994) found that two characteristics of the resource were particularly important: the mobility of resource units (such as water and fish) and the possibilities for storing the resource units. Because these two conditions vary independently of each other, four distinct types of resources can be distinguished: stationary resources with the possibility of storage, stationary resources without any possibility of storage, mobile resources with the possibility of storage, and mobile resources for which storage is impossible. Schlager and colleagues argue that the mobility of a resource raises the costs of collective action and makes it more difficult for resource users to recognize how their resource use influences resource condition. The possibility of storage, on the other hand, facilitates the development of institutions for managing shared resources by decreasing the intertemporal risks associated with lower levels of consumption.

ROBUST REGIMES

Not only did the CPR database further document the possibility that resource users would themselves overcome dilemmas to create their own institutions; it also provided evidence that many of these institutions had survived for long periods of time—even centuries in some instances. After working with colleagues to amass, read, and code a large number of individual cases of long-lasting and of failed systems, Elinor Ostrom, using Kenneth Shepsle's (1989) definition of a robust institution, tried to find specific rules that were associated with the systems that had survived for a long period of time. Shepsle defined an institution as robust if it was long-lasting and the operational rules had been devised and modified over time according to a set of higher-level rules (which institutional analysts would usually call collective-choice rules). These higher-level rules might themselves be modified slowly over time.[7]

After devoting a large segment of a sabbatical spent in Bielefeld, Germany, to reading cases, writing them up, redoing statistical analysis, and struggling to find specific rules that worked in many settings, Ostrom finally dropped the idea of identifying the *specific* rules that tended to generate success. She moved up a level in generality to try to understand broader institutional regularities among the systems that were sustained over a long period of time. The concept of "design principle" seemed an apt characterization of the regularities derived from this perspective. These regularities were not design principles in the sense that the irrigators, fishers, forest dwellers, and others who had invented and sustained successful common-property regimes over several centuries had these principles overtly in their minds. The effort was to identify the core underlying lessons that one could draw out from the cases of long-sustained regimes, and then to compare these successes with the failures to assess whether the failures were characterized by the same features.

Identification of common features or design principles related to long-term robustness of institutions to govern common-pool resources required a return to the source materials and the development of new concepts that were not in the coding forms. Ostrom referred puzzles and draft text to the authors of case studies that were discussed in the manuscript for *Governing the Commons* (Ostrom 1990), where the eight design principles were first articulated. Fortunately, scholars who had undertaken the earlier case studies were very helpful in checking out the overview and correcting any misinterpretations. Since the design principles are described extensively in Ostrom (1990, 2005), we give only a brief overview of them here.

1. *Well-Defined Boundaries*: The boundaries of a resource system, as well as the set of individuals or households with rights to the resource, should be clearly defined. The clarity of the social boundary rules influences incentives for cooperation. Clarity of the boundaries of a resource system limits problems related to externalities. Rule enforcement becomes easier when both types of boundaries are well defined.

2. *Proportional Equivalence between Benefits and Costs*: Rules-in-use should allocate benefits associated with a common-pool resource in proportion to contributions of required inputs. Rules that respect proportionality are more widely accepted as equitable. Perceived inequity may lead some participants to refuse to abide by rules they consider to be unfair.

3. *Collective-Choice Arrangements*: Most individuals affected by a natural resource regime should be authorized to participate in making and modifying its rules. This principle increases the likelihood that rules fit local circumstances, change over time to reflect local environmental and social dynamics, and are considered fair by participants. Common-property institutions that empower local elites—rather than most local resource users—are likely to generate policies that benefit the elites disproportionately; these arrangements are not consistent with the second design principle (for examples, see Ensminger 1990; Platteau 2003).

4. *Monitoring*: The individuals charged with monitoring rule adherence and resource conditions should be accountable to users. Reliable monitoring raises confidence among users that they can cooperate without the fear that others are taking advantage of them. Robust, self-organized resource regimes tend to select their own monitors.

5. *Graduated Sanctions*: Sanctions for violated rules should be graduated. Graduated sanctions signal that infractions are noticed while allowing for misunderstandings, mistakes, and exceptional circumstances that lead to rule breaking. They encourage individuals who

have broken a rule to resume compliance in order to enjoy ongoing trust.

6. *Conflict-Resolution Mechanisms*: There should be rapid, low-cost, local arenas to resolve conflicts among users or between users and officials. Some conflicts arise because participants interpret in different ways a rule that they have jointly made. Simple, local mechanisms that get conflicts aired immediately and produce resolutions that are generally known in the community can limit the number of conflicts that reduce trust.

7. *Minimal Recognition of Rights*: The rights of local users to make their own rules should be recognized by the national or local government. Resource regimes that lack official recognition have operated over long periods but have had to rely almost entirely on unanimity as the rule used to change rules. Otherwise, disgruntled participants who oppose a rule change can go to the external authorities to threaten the regime itself! Changing rules using unanimity imposes high transaction costs and prevents a group from searching for better-matched rules at relatively lower costs.

8. *Nested Enterprises*: When common-pool resources are part of a larger system, governance activities should be organized in multiple nested layers. Small-scale units can match rules to local conditions, but larger-scale institutions are also needed to govern interdependencies among smaller units. The rules allocating water among major branches of an irrigation system, for example, may differ from the rules used to allocate water among farmers along a single distribution channel.

The possibility that the design principles synthesize core factors affecting the likely long-term survival of a CPR institution has captured the interest of a large number of scholars. This list has now been examined in depth by a variety of scholars (see Crook and Jones 1999; Guillet 1992; Marshall 2008; Morrow and Hull 1996; Weinstein 2000). A recent meta-analysis of 112 published articles by a variety of scholars evaluated the validity of the design principles for explaining successes or failures in diverse common-pool resources. Two-thirds of these articles confirm the relevance of the design principles that have now been slightly revised to improve the clarity of Principles 1, 2, and 4 (M. Cox, Arnold, and Villamayor-Tomas 2009).

Overall Assessment

Prior case studies provided the source material for the CPR database as well as informing the choice of variables to be included in it. The

CPR database, however, enabled forms of analysis that were not possible with case study research alone. Its structured coding of large numbers of case studies makes it possible to move beyond the proof of plausibility typical in case study research. Scholars have used the CPR database to identify repeated relationships, analyze sources of variation, and disentangle complex relationships. Scholars used the CPR database to tease apart multifaceted phenomena like property rights, disentangle several empirically distinct forms of heterogeneity, and explore empirical differences associated with different forms of collective action and types of common-pool resources. Although deriving the design principles underlying robust institutions for collective action on the commons went beyond concepts coded in the CPR database, it would not have been feasible to identify these without the struggle involved in developing and using the database.

The CPR database cannot support analysis of average effects, and it cannot be used to establish that repeated patterns are representative. Nonetheless, the CPR database provides the ability to distinguish general patterns from idiosyncratic situations, and this is a precondition for any scientific advancement. Further, the CPR database provided solid experience in developing coding forms based on the IAD framework that provided a strong foundation for the establishment of further large-N empirical studies. The Nepal Irrigation Institutions and Systems (NIIS) database that is discussed in the next section is a direct descendant of the CPR database.

NIIS: A Hybrid Approach

In 1988, members of a Workshop team studying decentralization (E. Ostrom, Schroeder, and Wynne 1993) were invited to Nepal to study the impact of the decentralization policies there. Before going to Nepal, Ostrom contacted Norman Uphoff at Cornell University to ask for the names of Nepali scholars who had studied natural resources, and who could give her a more objective view of how decentralization was working in Nepal than the team members could attain by relying entirely on government officials and the people they recommended to be interviewed. Fortunately, Dr. Prachanda Pradhan, who had undertaken a large number of case studies of irrigation systems and had many more in his file drawers, was very receptive to Ostrom's queries about decentralization and particularly about diverse ways of organizing irrigation systems in Nepal. Ostrom returned from her first visit to Nepal—the first of many—with copies of about fifty case studies in her luggage and knowledge that many others were listed in the references of these documents.

Thus, while most of the time and effort during the rest of 1988 and 1989 was spent coding and analyzing the CPR database, the possibility was evolving of creating a second meta-database focusing on one resource sector in one country. More than one hundred documents about irrigation systems in Nepal were eventually obtained, and, as described below, researchers eventually undertook fieldwork to check out the data as coded, complete missing data, and add additional sites.

The research team[8] spent most of 1990 designing the NIIS database with the expert programming of Sharon Huckfeldt, developing a coding manual, and designing seven coding forms building on the lessons learned from the CPR meta-database. The team benefited from in-depth knowledge of irrigation in Nepal brought to the team by Ganesh Shivakoti and Paul Benjamin. Case material included reports, dissertations and theses, reports from Rapid Rural Appraisals, field notes from expatriate advisers, and published books and articles. Upon completion of the first round of coding, team members realized that the number of missing values—even for very well-crafted studies—would limit statistical data analysis to a small set of cases for which *all* major variables had been described by the original case author. To expand the set of cases that could be included in analysis, team members decided to undertake rapid fieldwork for sites where the case author had already identified most of the relevant variables. Thus the database ended up as a hybrid; it combines coding of case studies with new fieldwork (E. Ostrom, Benjamin, and Shivakoti 1994).

The NIIS research team has continued to collect new data, about additional irrigation systems, with work to fill in missing data from the original case studies continuing whenever the team is in the field. While in the field, team members also verify the data that have already been entered from the case. The NIIS database currently includes data on 236 separate irrigation systems in 29 of Nepal's 75 districts. Data for three time periods for 19 irrigation systems push the total number of observations up to 274.[9]

Adaptation of the CPR Protocols

The NIIS team took the coding protocols from the CPR research program as a point of departure. The team benefited from the CPR team's investment in the development of broadly applicable measures for theoretically rigorous concepts. Nonetheless, the NIIS team modified a few variables and adopted some distinct strategies. The CPR coding protocols, for example, defined the appropriation subgroup as a set of individuals with similar rights to and responsibilities for the resource, similar levels of dependency on the resource, similar vulnerability to fluctuations in the supply of the resource, and similar rates of withdrawal. The NIIS research program refers to the unit of potential collective action as the subgroup, defined as the set of individuals with similar rights to and responsibilities for water in the irrigation system. This new definition retains the distinction between a group with the potential for collective action and evidence of actual collective action. The change made it possible to code as a subgroup any set of individuals that has similar rights and responsibilities even if members of the group differ in dependence on the resource, vulnerability to fluctuations in supply, or patterns of use. It also made possible analysis of the implications of heterogeneity in dependence on the resource or patterns of use for the probability of collective action by individuals with similar rights and responsibilities.

Studies of irrigation systems, including NIIS, tend to focus on the operation of the system, both in terms of infrastructure maintenance and performance in delivering water to crops. The NIIS research program includes indicators that allow connections to be drawn between institutional design and resource management. The length and number of canals, for example, reflect the challenge facing the irrigators in mobilizing resources to invest in the development and maintenance of the irrigation system. Information on the flow of water to the head end and the tail of a system, and the yield of crops produced, makes the connection between the existence of a shared infrastructure and the effective management of the shared water resource.

Measurement and Sampling

The NIIS research program has successfully avoided or limited many of the measurement problems that are typically associated with meta-analysis. Although recognition of rigorously defined concepts in case studies posed a problem for both the CPR and NIIS databases, it was a less severe problem for the NIIS research program. First of all, irrigation groups are objectively easier to identify than a user group related to an inshore fishery or a forest. The structure of irrigation systems makes it relatively straightforward to identify who is linked by their location next to a distribution canal. Second, fieldwork conducted by the NIIS team compensated for shortcomings in source materials. Third, simplification of the definition of a subgroup made it easier to apply.

The use of targeted fieldwork reduced problems of missing data but still did not produce a representative sample of all irrigation systems in Nepal. In fact, it would be impossible to draw a random sample because records of existing irrigation systems are grossly incomplete. It is clear that some districts are overrepresented in the NIIS database but, with no inventory of farmer-managed irrigation systems in Nepal, much less a district-by-district breakdown,[10] there is no way to determine how much the sample differs from the population of irrigation systems. NIIS researchers can be confident about the internal validity of their findings but can assess their external validity only by reference to consistency with other studies.

Priority in conducting supplementary fieldwork went to those systems with data problems that were also relatively *accessible* given the extreme time and cost involved in traveling to remote systems where no roads existed. As discussed below, early analysis found very substantial differences between farmer-managed (FMIS) and agency-managed irrigation systems (AMIS). At that time, the NIIS database contained data for 127 systems, of which 104 were built and managed by farmers and 23 were constructed and managed by the government of Nepal. To be sure that the findings were not due to a small sample of AMIS, researchers undertook a second field trip to Nepal in the summer of 1993; 23 new AMIS were added to the database, and missing data were collected for 4 AMIS already in the system but relatively incomplete. Further, some fieldwork was completed for projects with a specific geographic focus. For example, a collaborative project between the Institute of Agriculture and Animal Sciences in Chitwan and Indiana University has focused on irrigation systems in Chitwan district.[11]

Contributions

Studies conducted with the NIIS database have evaluated three types of factors thought to influence the performance of irrigation systems: ownership and management rights, investments in physical infrastructure, and characteristics of the group of irrigators. These findings raised policy-relevant questions about the value of centralized and capital-intensive strategies for providing irrigation. They also confirmed the importance of two design principles identified by Ostrom (1990): proportionality in benefits and costs, and collective-choice arrangements that involve individuals affected by the resource system.

While most farmers in Nepal own land, most own small parcels of less than one hectare. They are relatively homogeneous with similar preferences in regard to obtaining water for rice production during the monsoon and winter seasons and various crops during the spring. Farmers in Nepal have long exerted local authority to create their own water associations, construct and maintain their own systems, and monitor and enforce conformance to their rules (see Benjamin et al. 1994; Lam, Lee, and Ostrom 1997; Sengupta 1991; Yoder 1994). The irrigation systems constructed and maintained by farmers tend to rely on low-tech construction techniques including building nonpermanent headworks from mud, trees, and stones. International aid agencies have provided considerable funding to government agencies in an effort to upgrade the engineering standards.

Analysis of the NIIS database found substantial difference in performance between those systems owned and governed by the farmers themselves and those owned and operated (but, in some cases, not governed) by a national governmental agency. In a detailed analysis of 150 farmer-governed and agency-governed irrigation systems in Nepal, W. F. Lam (1998) develops three performance measures: (1) the physical condition of irrigation systems, (2) the quantity of water available to farmers at different seasons of the year, and (3) the agricultural productivity of the systems. Using multiple regression analysis techniques so as to control for environmental differences among systems, Lam finds several variables strongly related to these dependent variables. One is the form of governance of the system. With other variables held constant, irrigation systems governed by the farmers themselves perform significantly better on all three performance measures. This variable has the largest explanatory power of any variable in Lam's analysis, including the physical size of the system, terrain characteristics, and the number of farmers.

Thus farmers with long-term property rights, who can communicate, develop their own agreements, establish the positions of monitors, and sanction those who do not conform to their own rules, are likely to grow more rice, distribute water more equitably, and keep their systems in better repair than is the case in government systems. While there is variance in the performance of these Nepali systems, few perform as poorly as government systems—when other relevant variables are held constant. Since many of the government systems rely on high-tech engineering, the capability of farmers to increase agricultural production on their "primitive systems" while they also provide the labor to maintain and operate the system, is particularly noteworthy. These substantial differences in performance between AMIS and FMIS were confirmed again in an analysis of the expanded database containing 229 irrigation systems (Joshi et al. 2000).

Lam's (1994, 1996, 1998) work with the NIIS database also speaks to the debate about the relationship between group characteristics and collective action on the commons. Lam (1994, 182) found no evidence of a significant relationship between the number of users or the amount of land included in the service area and any of the three performance variables he studied. Heterogeneity in terms of access to water interfered with collective action related to the maintenance of shared infrastructure, but not consistently. Those closer to the headworks have an incentive to consider the interests of those near the tail of the irrigation system when they depend on their labor for frequent repairs to the headworks. Lam's analyses of 136 small- to medium-size irrigation systems revealed that investments in technology can reduce incentives to contribute to the maintenance of shared infrastructure when they increase heterogeneity in interests and endowments of group members (Lam 1996, 1998). This is what happens as a result of investments in the headworks of irrigation systems that reduce the need for repairs to the headworks. These investments also reduce the interdependency between irrigators at the top and bottom of the irrigation system, and thus the incentives for cooperation in infrastructure maintenance (E. Ostrom and Gardner 1993).

In a recent paper, Lam and Ostrom (2009) examine the process and impact of an innovative irrigation assistance project that was undertaken in one district of Nepal in the mid-1980s by analyzing NIIS data related to changes in system structure and performance over three time periods. They conducted a statistical analysis of some of the key variables that are likely to affect the diverse patterns of change, as well as an analysis of the influence of configurations of core variables using Qualitative Comparative Analysis (QCA). They found that the original and later investments in system infrastructure are but one factor that may lead to longer-term success—but not by itself, as has been so often recommended in the development literature. They found that unless the farmers organize themselves and create their own rules, and augment their rules through collective action or by imposing fines on those who violate rules, infrastructure investment alone is not sufficient for achieving sustainable higher performance.

Overall Assessment

Supplementation of existing studies with quick field visits greatly increased the completeness and quality of the data in the NIIS database. Nonetheless, the database does not offer a random sample of irrigation systems in the country. The focus on accessibility helped to stretch limited resources to gain more data at the cost of reinforcing a bias in the data. Moreover, the NIIS database contains data for a single type of resource in a single country. Compared with the CPR database, the NIIS database offers limited geographical scope and variety of contexts. On the other hand, investments in the quality of data have enabled more rigorous analyses of farmer-managed irrigation systems in Nepal that have important policy implications.

OTHER SYNTHETIC STUDIES

A number of other scholars have also synthesized lessons from case studies related to natural resources and environmental change. Like the CPR research program, some encompass a wide variety of issues related to diverse natural resources around the world (e.g., Agrawal 2001b; Baland and Platteau [1996] 2000; Burger and Gochfeld 1998). Like the NIIS research program, others focus on specific issues (e.g., Feeny et al. 1998; Nugent and Sanchez 1999; Poteete and Ostrom 2004a; K. Walker 2009), types of natural resources (e.g., Agrawal 2004; Geist and Lambin 2001, 2002; Leal 1998; Nagendra 2008; Pagdee, Kim, and Daugherty 2006; Peluso and Vandergeest 1995; Poteete and Ostrom 2004b; M. Richards 1997; Rudel 2005, 2008), or geographical regions (e.g., Nugent and Sanchez 1999; Peluso and Vandergeest 1995; M. Richards 1997; Rudel 2008). All of these integrative studies sort through a large number of existing studies to identify consistent relationships, areas of disagreement, and, in some cases, topics that have been relatively neglected. These studies use synthetic analysis to define the research frontier and suggest directions for future research.

Additional Examples of Meta-Analysis

While all of these syntheses draw on a large body of existing studies, only nine overtly use meta-analysis (Agrawal 2004; Geist and Lambin 2001, 2002; Nagendra 2008; Nugent and Sanchez 1999; Pagdee, Kim, and Daugherty 2006; Rudel 2005, 2008; K. Walker 2009). An even smaller number are concerned with management or use of natural resources by the people who use the resource (Agrawal 2004; Nugent and Sanchez 1999; Pagdee, Kim, and Daugherty 2006; K. Walker 2009). Agrawal (2004) and Pagdee, Kim, and Daugherty (2006) examine decentralization of natural resource management to local communities, while Nugent and Sanchez (1999) analyze variation in the centralization or degree of hierarchy in Sudanese tribal institutions. K. Walker (2009) examines the incentives influencing illegal harvesting in protected areas.

Pagdee, Kim, and Daugherty (2006) conducted a meta-analysis of 69 cases of community forestry to evaluate the general influence of 43 independent variables identified from the literature. A series of simple, mostly bivariate, statistical tests suggested that community forestry is more often deemed successful in terms of economic efficiency, ecological sustainability, or equity when property rights are clear and secure, institutional arrangements are effective (e.g., in monitoring and sanctioning to enforce rule compliance), and community members have incentives to participate.

Agrawal's (2004) meta-analysis includes data from 55 cases of decentralized management of forests and wildlife in 30 countries in Africa and Latin America. The data confirm evidence from case studies (e.g., Agrawal and Ostrom 2001; Ribot, Agrawal, and Larson 2006) that decentralization programs generally transfer a limited range of rights to local communities. Decentralization, even if limited, is most often initiated by a coalition involving central government and either international donors (especially for wildlife) or local actors (especially for forestry). Decentralization is (somewhat) more extensive when backed by a coalition involving both the central government and local actors.

In a meta-analysis of ethnographic data on 41 Sudanese tribes, Nugent and Sanchez (1999) investigate sources of variation in centralization of *local* tribal institutions. They find that spatial variability in rainfall is associated with common property and less hierarchical tribal institutions. While they suggest that resource conditions influence collective action related to both the development of property rights and community institutions, they are not able to address these dynamics with data gleaned from their ethnographic source materials.

K. Walker (2009) combines meta-analysis with game theory to understand the extent of illegal harvesting in protected areas around the world. She first developed a formal model of the monitoring dilemma based on earlier models of Tsebelis (1989) and Weissing and Ostrom (1993). The game was composed of two players: managers and resource users. For every round, the managers had to decide whether to monitor or not, and the resource users had to decide to abide by the law or illegally harvest from a protected resource. She posited that three factors influence the extent of illegal harvesting: (1) whether the resource itself is under dispute, (2) the relative costs and benefits to the manager of monitoring, and (3) the relative value to the users of resource units. Walker conducted a meta-analysis with data from 116 cases of protected areas in 35 countries to evaluate the empirical applicability of her game-theoretic model. Substantial illegal harvesting was reported in 54 percent of the cases; the outcome predicted by her model matched the reported outcome for 76 percent of the cases. Because the costs of monitoring in many large protected areas are high and frequently outweigh the potential benefits of finding rule-breakers, imposing sanctions, and reducing harvesting, monitoring is sporadic in such settings. Given irregular monitoring, illegal resource harvesting is rather common in protected areas even when managers try to increase carrot-and-stick strategies to induce higher levels of compliance.

Scholars are also turning to meta-analysis to synthesize findings from the growing number of social science experiments related to collective action. Sally (1995), for example, conducted a meta-analysis of all the social dilemma experiments he could locate in the social science literature between 1958 and 1992. From an initial count of more than 100 studies, he developed a database that contained 130 distinct treatments from 37 different studies. Sally had to exclude many of the experimental studies conducted early in this period, as researchers had not yet developed consistent ways of describing their experimental designs or results. Sally found that communication among experimental subjects was consistently related to their achieving a higher level of cooperation—contrary to the presumption of game theory that communication was only a form of "cheap talk" that could not affect outcomes.

Bowles (2008) analyzes the findings from 42 experimental studies of diverse types of social dilemmas. In the supplemental online material for his article, he provides a useful table describing the relevant subject pool, the particular treatments involved, and the results. Bowles finds that participants in many social dilemmas are able to draw on other-regarding preferences and norms to achieve better outcomes than are predicted by conventional theory. Using external economic incentives to try to increase outcomes in social dilemma experiments, however, had counterproductive results. Instead of complementing the internal incentives of participants, economic incentives tended to compromise the participants' sense of "self-determination" and reduced the importance of intrinsic motivations.

These studies demonstrate the value of synthetic analyses, and meta-analysis in particular, for engaging in broadly comparative research and for gaining an overview of a large body of contradictory findings. Where large-N cross-national research is rare in primary analysis based on new fieldwork, it is the norm in meta-analysis based on case studies. Most of these meta-analyses include cases from two or more continents. Meta-analysis makes it possible to compare alternative hypotheses or identify multiple causal patterns to an extent that is simply impossible in comparisons of a smaller number of cases.

Yet meta-analysis does have limits. Even with the use of multiple search engines, the number of cases identified for inclusion in these studies is small relative to the large number of potential explanatory variables (Agrawal 2001b). When relatively small sample sizes do not support multivariate analysis, it is not possible to assess fully the relative importance of independent variables or the possibility of interaction effects. Small sample sizes also limit the reliability of attempts to analyze regional or other subsamples. When authors report the regional breakdown of their sample, regional imbalances become apparent. Two-thirds of the cases analyzed by Pagdee, Kim, and Daugherty (2006) are Asian, for example, while Nagendra (2008) draws over half of the cases in her meta-analysis of studies related to change in land cover in protected areas from Latin America. Since there are reasons to expect causal patterns to vary with ecological patterns (Rudel 2008), conclusions suggested by regionally imbalanced samples could be misleading.

An Example of Narrative Synthesis

Narrative synthesis relies on qualitative integration of findings from existing studies. It does not involve the structured analysis of data or characteristics coded from source materials. Although exhaustive citations can compensate in part for formal meta-analysis, such citations do not consistently report evidence for *and* against conclusions reached. Descriptive statistics from formal meta-analyses not only provide more information; they also facilitate replication. Nonetheless, meta-analysis is not always appropriate. Scholars should engage in narrative synthesis when a body of literature is relatively small, lacks consensus on key concepts and measurements, or utilizes a wide variety of research designs (Bangert-Drowns 1995). A narrative approach is better able to draw connections between distinct but related literatures. Even when meta-analysis is possible and advisable, it should be combined with a qualitative discussion of how the meta-analysis relates to the broader literature (Bangert-Drowns 1995; Light and Pillemer 1984; Rudel 2008; Slavin 1986). Baland and Platteau's ([1996] 2000) synthesis of theoretical and empirical studies of natural resource management by rural communities demonstrates the potential of the narrative approach.[12] The limitations of this influential narrative synthesis are strikingly similar to those associated with meta-analysis.

Baland and Platteau ([1996] 2000) addressed three overarching themes: the likelihood of sustainability of natural resource use under communal management, conditions affecting collective action in natural resource management, and challenges to the sustainability of collective action by rural communities. Their analysis draws upon studies with a wide variety of research designs and theoretical perspectives. As is typical in narrative reviews, they do not explain how they compiled existing studies for their analysis, nor do they mention a formal coding scheme.

Baland and Platteau's ([1996] 2000) favored style of presentation involves comparison and evaluation of alternative interpretations and measurements of key concepts in terms of both logical consistency and empirical value. For example, they identify groups with the potential for collective action in various ways. Their chapter 10 focuses on collective management of natural resources by traditional village societies that "are relatively closed, are not permeated by a market logic (or are only superficially so), and are to a large extent insulated from the rule of a centralized state machinery" (189). Elsewhere, they speak of "the corporate custodian community" (217).[13] Yet even extremely rural populations have long been affected by trading networks and other interactions with external actors (e.g., Wilmsen 1989). Indeed, in chapter 11 Baland and Platteau acknowledge the rarity of traditional villages and examine the influence of the state, demographic changes, and market integration on rural villages.

Subsequent analysis describes the unit for collective action variously as village- or group-based, or as local-level. Flexibility in identification of who is (or could be) acting collectively allows Baland and Platteau to draw upon findings from case studies that define the unit of collective action in a variety of ways. On the other hand, this approach obscures differences between different units of collective action as well as possible divisions within larger units of collective action such as villages. This trade-off is comparable to the one meta-analysts face when choosing between precise definitions that are not widely reflected in the literature and general definitions that offer limited analytical leverage.

Baland and Platteau allow for and discuss alternative interpretations of concepts. Their critiques of alternative interpretations and measurements of key variables often culminate in suggestions for more rigorous conceptualizations. Their preferred interpretations are often innovative, with scant representation in the existing empirical literature. In their discussion of resource conservation, for example, they insist that success should be claimed only if conservation occurred as a result of intentional actions by the group (188). As they note, many authors have paid more attention to the consequences of local institutions than to the underlying collective goals. Likewise, they observe that studies of the influence of group size on collective resource management often do not distinguish carefully between the effects expected as a consequence of changes in interpersonal dynamics that accompany changes in group size and those associated with the heterogeneity of the group (300–301). Use of Baland and Platteau's ([1996] 2000) more rigorous definitions should help future empirical studies address simmering debates. Deviation from past interpretations limits their capacity to evaluate relationships based on existing empirical studies. At best, they are sometimes able to glean relevant data from empirical studies that use somewhat different definitions but provide rich details about their cases.

Baland and Platteau's ([1996] 2000) synthesis of theoretical economics research on collective action and empirical studies of natural resource management by rural communities identified many unanswered questions about the importance of group size and heterogeneity for collective action. They confirmed suspicions that market pressures and government interventions pose threats to common-property institutions, but also raised questions about the prospects for comanagement or other forms of cooperation between local communities and national governments. Like studies that rely explicitly on meta-analysis, the narrative approach adopted by Baland and Platteau distinguishes common patterns from idiosyncratic events, teases apart multifaceted concepts, and helps make sense of seemingly contradictory findings from case studies. While meta-analysis would increase confidence in the generality of patterns and hypothesized sources of variation, the narrative approach allows for the integration of highly diverse material. The narrative approach also gave Baland and Platteau greater flexibility to go beyond the literature in their discussions of concepts and hypotheses.

PROGRESS AND CONTINUING CHALLENGES

As a line of research develops, synthetic analysis becomes increasingly valuable. In this chapter, we have surveyed advantages and limitations associated with meta-analysis as a relatively inexpensive technique for synthetic analysis. We have highlighted two significant challenges. First, the pool of available studies does not constitute a representative sample. The external validity of analyses related to general patterns and average effects depends on a representative sample of field-based observations. It is not possible to build a representative sample from existing studies because scholarly interests and the publication process produce a biased sample. Meta-analyses can partly compensate for publication bias by including unpublished studies, but unpublished studies are by their very nature less accessible than published studies. Large-N studies based on new fieldwork offer greater control over measurement and sampling, but the need for fieldwork and the associated costs limit the possibilities for such research. For many social scientific issues, meta-analysis is much less expensive, and thus much more feasible, than new fieldwork.

Second, it is difficult to glean consistently measured concepts from source materials that reflect diverse local contexts, research questions, and theoretical perspectives. Meta-analyses must develop consistent concepts to bring order to the diversity of approaches found in the case study literature. Although meta-analyses do not produce new primary observations and are limited by inconsistencies in their source material, it is the use of consistent concepts in coding that enables structured comparison of source material. Structured comparisons reveal areas of agreement and disagreement, consistencies and inconsistencies, in that material. The research programs reviewed in this chapter have made important contributions, despite the absence of scholarly consensus about concepts and measures, because they offer very clear definitions and careful evaluations of several alternative interpretations of particularly complex concepts. Transparency about concepts and measures greatly enhances the value of research, regardless of the method used.

The scarcity of comparable data, the costs of large-N studies, and the lack of conceptual consistency about a wide range of social science concepts make the generation of large-N databases based on new data daunting. When used effectively, meta-analysis increases the analytical value of past research. Even if findings derived from meta-analysis are not entirely representative, they distinguish common patterns from correlations found in only a handful of cases and, when combined with QCA, can identify multiple configurations.

Meta-analysis represents a valuable strategy for getting a sense of the bigger picture *before* incurring the costs of new research. Because meta-analysis suggests ways to improve the precision and focus of data collection, it can reduce the costs and improve the analytical value gained from other methods. Meta-analysis can inform the set of variables to be considered in broadly comparative large-N field-based research, and how they are measured. Experiments and agent-based models can evaluate the hypothesized causal mechanisms behind repeated empirical patterns. Meta-analysis also provides valuable guidance for the selection of cases for new case study research (Gerring 2007a, 2007b; Lieberman 2005). The meta-analyses reviewed in this chapter have informed many subsequent studies.[14] In other words, while meta-analysis cannot offer the final word, it does provide an essential bridge between case study research and research based on other methods.

CHAPTER 5

Collaborative Field Studies

IN CHAPTER 3, we introduced two strategies for large-N analysis of field-based observations: meta-analysis of case studies and field-based studies. As discussed in chapter 4, meta-analysis can identify common patterns and suggest explanations for variations in the case study literature, but does not eliminate the need for large-N field studies. Meta-analysis is constrained by features of past research, such as the set of variables considered by the studies included in the analysis, inconsistent conceptualization and measurement of variables across studies, and the unrepresentative nature of the sample presented by existing studies. Large-N analyses based on broadly comparative fieldwork are needed to establish the external validity of relationships suggested by other methods, including case studies, meta-analyses, experiments, and formal models.

In practice, large-N field studies are not necessarily broadly comparative, much less representative of the global population of common-pool resources (see chapter 3). It is not surprising that relatively few scholars have compiled or analyzed large-N data sets on collective action for natural resource management. There is only so much any individual researcher can accomplish when research demands intensive fieldwork and substantial local knowledge.

The near nonexistence of cross-national field-based empirical research should be cause for concern. Apparent patterns at one scale of analysis may not hold at other scales of analysis (Gibson, Ostrom, and Ahn 2000). Worse, analysis based on nonrepresentative samples may be misleading. Moreover, given theoretical arguments and mounting evidence that institutions as well as ecological structure strongly influence outcomes, good science requires comparisons across a variety of institutional and ecological settings.

Can methodological and practical challenges to broadly comparative research be overcome through collaboration? This chapter assesses the extent of collaboration and the implications for methodological practices in peer-reviewed journal articles related to collective action for natural resource management that were published from 1990 through 2004.[1] We find that collaborative research increased markedly over this period but is not associated with an increase in the number of observations or the geographic scope of the study. It seems that collaboration does not offer an easy solution to the practical challenges of broadly comparative field-based research. To better understand why, we examine several examples of collaborative research. We describe the origins and participants, key research questions, geographic scope, and variety of data collection goals for each research program. We also summarize the contributions and limitations of each program. We conclude the chapter with a comparison of the strategies, successes, and challenges encountered by these research programs, as well as some thoughts about how to encourage more collaborative research. We return to this theme in chapter 10.

Collaboration in Field-Based Research, 1990–2004

Field-based data collection is the most reliable way to get comparable data with external validity and the only way to do over-time studies. Ultimately, since there are limits to the time and financing available for data collection, trade-offs exist between the number and type of variables measured, the quality of data for each observation, and the number of cases for which data can be collected. The expense and practical difficulties of collecting multiple forms of high-quality data mean that most studies include cases from only one or two countries or, frequently enough, a single region within one country. Collaborative partnerships should be able to mobilize more resources and cover more cases with fewer compromises in the quality of data on each case.

While only 5.4 percent of the articles on collective action for natural resource management published 1990–99 had more than two authors, the share of such articles accounts for fully 20.7 percent of the articles published from 2000 to 2004.[2] The prevalence of studies with thirty or more observations on the main unit of analysis increases as the number of authors increases from one to four or more. Where only 12.0 percent of single-authored articles could be categorized as large-N studies, 27.8 percent of all articles with two or more authors had thirty or more observations. The participation of more than one author is not, however, associated with broader geographic coverage. In fact, no discernible relationship exists between the number of authors and geographic scope of analysis. It seems that collaboration more often involves scholars who share an interest in a particular country than it does scholars working on similar questions across geographic contexts—at least among scholars working on collective action for natural resource management. Collaboration results in more intensive fieldwork involving survey research or multidisciplinary data collection.

Self-identified products of larger collaborative research projects account for a modest but increasing fraction of these field-based articles: 16.1 percent of articles published 1990–99 and 35.3 percent of articles published 2000–2004. Larger projects include partnerships between organizations (usually two or more universities or research centers—8.1 percent of all articles), larger networks (all articles produced by the International Forestry Resources and Institutions [IFRI] research network—5.2 percent),[3] and projects sponsored by either a national government or an international organization (16.3 percent). This period saw substantial increases in articles associated with the IFRI research network and projects funded by governments and international governmental organizations.

In the 1990s, large-N studies were 67.8 percent more likely in publications that mentioned an institutional partnership (e.g., between universities or research centers) or project funding from a government or nongovernmental organization than in publications that mentioned no larger project. By 2000–2004, however, the proportion of large-N studies had increased considerably among publications that made no mention of a larger project. Publications associated with institutional partnerships were still 60.4 percent more likely to involve large-N analysis than publications that did not involve a larger project, but large-N analyses were only 20.3 percent more common in publications funded by government projects or international-governmental organizations. No relationship exists between participation in a larger collaborative research project and the geographic scope of the study.

The lack of a clear relationship between participation in a larger project and the scope of the data cautions against any expectation that partnerships and networks offer easy solutions to the challenges of broadly comparative research. Nonetheless, partnerships and networks offer an attractive strategy for overcoming the obvious physical limits to what any single researcher can achieve working independently.

To get a better sense of the opportunities and constraints associated with collaborative research, we look more closely at four examples of collaborative research programs involving new field research: two smaller research partnerships, the Consultative Group on International Agricultural Research (CGIAR), and the International Forestry Resources and Institutions (IFRI) research program. The two smaller research partnerships, as described below, were supported by specific grants and research centers and had a relatively limited duration and geographic scope. These partnerships are typical of initiatives by clusters of individual researchers interested in gaining greater depth or scope through collaboration. CGIAR is an alliance or network sponsored by an international organization and government partners in various countries. Collaboration is loosely coordinated; there are no common research protocols nor is there a common database. The IFRI research program involves a more structured network of collaborating research centers, common data collection protocols, and a common database. Developed by scholars associated with the Workshop in Political Theory and Policy Analysis at Indiana University, IFRI builds on experiences with the CPR and NIIS research programs discussed in chapter 4.

Collaboration makes it possible to spread the costs of data collection while retaining comparability. It can thus broaden the comparative scope of research while retaining the intensity of data collection associated with qualitative research.[4] As the number of partners in collaborative research increases, members face increasing challenges in reaching consensus on concepts and methods. There is a trade-off, of course, between maintaining flexibility and ease of comparative analysis.

Our examples range from small-scale partnerships to global networks, and from relatively loose coordination to more structured use of well-defined common methods. They have adopted a variety of strategies for balancing clear and consistent conceptualization against recognition of multiple interpretations of concepts in the literature, the need to adjust measures to local context, and diversity in perspectives among collaborators. We now consider the extent to which several examples of collaborative research have succeeded in balancing these competing goals.

Two Research Partnerships

We consider the contributions and limitations of two research partnerships that are described in some detail in articles published between 1990 and 2005.[5] These projects involved three to four institutional partners. Both collected data on subnational units of observation related to the use and management of common-pool resources. A collaborative project on community-based management in Tanzania encompassed thirty-eight common-pool resources in twelve villages in six districts. The Traditional Management of Artisanal Fisheries (TMAF) research project collected several types of data about fishing households and fishery management systems in three major fisheries in northeastern Nigeria. For each project, we describe origins and participants, discuss research goals and strategies, and assess contributions and limitations.

Community-Based Management of Common-Pool Resources in Tanzania

With support from the British Department for International Development (DFID), this collaborative project addressed several gaps in information about common-pool resources in semiarid regions of Tanzania (Lovett, Stevenson, and Kiwasila 2002; Quinn 2001; Quinn et al. 2007). Scholars at the Centre for Ecology, Law and Policy (CELP) at the University of York, the Institute for Resource Assessment at the University of Dar es Salaam, and Norconsult (Tanzania) Ltd. collected data about the use and management of thirty-eight common-pool resources in twelve villages in six semiarid districts of Tanzania during 2001 and 2002 (Quinn 2001).[6] The project assessed patterns of reliance on common-pool resources, existing management regimes, and individual perceptions likely to affect the use and management of these natural resources.

Consultations with government officials and key informants guided the selection of six districts with semiarid conditions for which background information was available from past research. The team selected two villages within each district to gain variation in the mix of livelihood strategies and ethnic groups. Data collection involved a variety of methods, including reviews of documentary evidence, semistructured interviews with key informants, structured individual interviews for a risk-mapping exercise, Participatory Rural Appraisal (PRA) exercises, and a household survey (Lovett, Stevenson, and Kiwasila 2002). Key informants were identified through the use of a snowball approach, expanding from district and local officials to include villagers actively involved in local management of common-pool resources (Quinn et al. 2007). Inadequate information about a mobile population prevented the use of a probability sample for the risk-mapping exercise; the team instead used an opportunity sample of 105 individuals (Quinn et al. 2003).

The partnership between CELP, the University of Dar es Salaam, and Norconsult (TZ) Ltd. has contributed to understandings of social heterogeneity within rural communities, perceptions of risk associated with rural livelihoods, and institutional arrangements for the management of a variety of common-pool resources. Individual perceptions of risk varied with livelihood strategies and gender (Quinn et al. 2003). While most villagers were concerned about access to water, perceived risks associated with access to land, water, and social amenities like education and health care were more pervasive and more severe among pastoralists than among agriculturalists. Men perceived greater risks related to access to natural resources, while women were more concerned about risks related to education, health, and social position. Differentiation in the incidence and severity of perceived risks associated with particular problems can be expected to influence collective action for the management of common-pool resources.

Rural Tanzanians do manage a variety of local natural resources collectively. Common-property regimes for the management of forests, grasslands, and water were found in all twelve villages. One village had a fourth common-property regime for the management of a lake; another managed a conservation area collectively. Quinn et al. (2007) compare customary arrangements for managing forests, grasslands, and water with the eight design principles that Ostrom (1990) identified as widely associated with the endurance of common-property institutions.

The design principles provided a helpful tool for analyzing management regimes. For example, they drew attention to the serious challenges that arise from ambiguous authority over common-pool resources and to the threats to sustainability from management systems that lack mechanisms for monitoring and adjusting to changing conditions. Of the thirty-eight common-property regimes, only eight adhered closely to *all* eight design principles. Deviations occurred where resource conditions associated with a semiarid climate raised the costs of institutional development, villages chose not to formalize customary norms as village bylaws, tensions existed between the traditional and formal systems of village governance, or location-specific projects or designations superseded local authority. The collaborators concluded that while they found many practices consistent with the design principles, adherence to every design principle is not necessary for successful long-term management (Lovett, Stevenson, and Kiwasila 2002; Quinn et al. 2007).[7] Institutional ambiguity offers some advantages when resource systems feature considerable uncertainty, as is the case for semiarid grasslands. The design principles are silent on questions related to the design of institutions that adequately address severe ecological uncertainty.

The Tanzania partnership conducted several forms of archival and field-based research within a relatively short period. The project has improved knowledge about the diversity of common-pool resources in semiarid Tanzania, village-level management of these resources, and the significance of common-pool natural resources for rural Tanzanians. Although collaboration undoubtedly increased the number of observations and the geographic scope of this research program, participants still felt significant resource constraints. The final technical report acknowledged that the project involved more literature review than new data collection, and noted that time constraints forced the team to rely on PRA techniques rather than on more in-depth qualitative research methods (Lovett, Stevenson, and Kiwasila 2002). Collaboration cannot fully compensate for the relatively short duration of most research grants.

Traditional Management of Artisanal Fisheries in Nigeria

Scholars at the University of Portsmouth (UK), the University of Maiduguri (Nigeria), and the Federal University of Technology, Yola (Nigeria), launched the Traditional Management of Artisanal Fisheries (TMAF) project to address information gaps related to fisheries and fishery management in Nigeria. The project conducted a multifaceted analysis of three fisheries in northeastern Nigeria: the Upper River Benue, Lake Chad, and the Nguru-Gashua Wetlands (Neiland, Madakan, and Béné 2005; Sarch 1996; Sarch et al. 1996). Project goals ranged from documentation of village-level systems for fishery management to analysis of their sustainability and socioeconomic significance. TMAF enjoyed support from 1993 through 1997 from the British Overseas Development Administration (ODA) and the Department for International Development (DFID).

In the absence of up-to-date and centralized demographic information, the first task involved the identification of fishing villages associated with the three fisheries. The team collected lists of villages and households from a variety of local government officials and traditional leaders, local primary health centers, reports developed for specific projects, government publications, and local nongovernmental organizations (Sarch et al. 1996). A total of 194 fishing villages were identified based on village location, size, and the presence of fishers among the residents.

Data collection involved a household survey, plus specialized surveys of management systems, markets, and fishermen. Data collection techniques included standardized interviews of household heads, semistructured interviews with key informants, and participatory forms of research. Distinct samples were drawn for different aspects of the project (Sarch et al. 1996). The survey of management systems involved participatory research activities with village leaders and elder fishermen in 53 randomly selected villages. For the household survey, the team randomly selected 66 fishing villages and 1,316 household heads within those villages. The survey included both fishing and nonfishing households to support assessments of household-level contributions to fishing. For these larger village and household surveys, random sampling increased generalizability and value for policymaking (Neiland, Weeks, et al. 2000). Other forms of data collection involved smaller samples. Participatory appraisals of traditional management systems were conducted in 12 villages. Team members relied on weekly visits to three fish markets for their market analysis and monitored environmental conditions (e.g., temperature, rainfall, water levels) in three locations. All samples included observations from each of the three fisheries.

TMAF documents the diversity of fisheries in the Upper River Benue, Lake Chad, and the Nguru-Gashua Wetlands. Natural features of the aquatic environment, socioeconomic characteristics, the importance of fishing to local livelihoods, and historical and recent developments all vary significantly (Neiland, Jaffry, et al. 2000; Neiland, Madakan, and Béné 2005; Sarch et al. 1996). While fishing on Lake Chad centers on the lake, for example, seasonal pools and floodplains are important fishing sites in the Upper River Benue and the Nguru-Gashua Wetlands (Neiland, Jaffry, et al. 2000). The household survey found considerable heterogeneity among fishing households as well (Neiland, Jaffry, et al. 2000; Neiland, Madakan, and Béné 2005). There is marked regional differentiation in household characteristics and patterns of fishing, but also substantial socioeconomic heterogeneity among fishing households within each region (Neiland, Jaffry, et al. 2000).

While fishing is important in all regions, its contribution varies across regions and across households within each region. In all three fisheries, fishing and farming are complementary activities. Most households engage in both activities. Households that fish and farm are at least as productive as households that only farm; in the Lake Chad region, participation in both activities correlates with higher household productivity (Neiland, Madakan, and Béné 2005). Sarch (1996) offers two alternative explanations for the advantages gained from fishing in Lake Chad and draws out the policy implications of each. Most fishing in Lake Chad occurs during seasonal floods that follow the harvest; households that fish and farm use the earnings from one activity to purchase inputs (e.g., fishing gear, seeds) for the other activity. Limited access to capital may reduce farming productivity by limiting investment in inputs and prevent the purchase of gear required for fishing. If differential access to capital accounts for the differences in productivity, then restrictions on fishing may increase investment in farming. It is also possible, however, that participation in fishing contributes to productivity by reducing vulnerability to high rates of inflation and low-interest earnings from savings. When farming revenues are not cycled into fishing during the seasonal floods, those assets erode between agricultural seasons, decreasing investments in agricultural inputs. In this case, restrictions on fishing will have a negative influence on the broader economy.

By Nigerian law, all natural resources, including fisheries, are owned by the federal government. In practice, lack of capacity and financing limit the effectiveness of state management. Very few villages (10 percent) relied on modern management systems (Neiland, Madakan, and Béné 2005; Neiland, Weeks, et al. 2000). Traditional systems of fishery management remain pervasive, even where modern systems of state administration are operational (Neiland, Madakan, and Béné 2005; Neiland, Weeks, et al. 2000; Sarch et al. 1996). More than half of the villages had predominantly traditional systems of fishery management (58 percent), while modern and traditional management systems coexist in the remaining villages (32 percent).

Modern management systems typically prioritize sector-wide revenues, while traditional systems emphasize the socioeconomic contributions to particular fishing communities (Neiland, Madakan, and Béné 2005; Neiland, Weeks, et al. 2000; Sarch et al. 1996). Although government policy mandates diverse forms of regulation, the local governments charged with implementation generally focus on licensing and the collection of fees (Neiland, Weeks, et al. 2000). Traditional systems emphasize regulation of access (Neiland, Madakan, and Béné 2005; Neiland, Weeks, et al. 2000). While some traditional management systems regulate fishing gear or fishing seasons, these techniques are less widespread. Traditional authorities do not regulate access to protect fishing stocks; permission to fish is denied only during fishing festivals (Neiland, Weeks, et al. 2000). Rather, traditional authorities view control over access to fisheries as a mechanism for generating revenue (Neiland, Madakan, and Béné 2005; Neiland, Weeks, et al. 2000). In some cases, traditional authorities redistribute the revenues from fishing to enhance livelihoods in the broader fishing community; elsewhere, however, these revenues exacerbate socioeconomic and political inequalities (Neiland, Madakan, and Béné 2005).

Neiland, Madakan, and Béné (2005) evaluated the institutional performance of the traditional management systems against five criteria: achievement of self-set goals, efficiency (few disputes, limited effort required for compliance), the ability to adapt to progressive change, resiliency or the ability to survive sudden shocks, and equitability (perceived fairness). On average, the traditional systems surveyed by the TMAF project are doing well in terms of achieving their own goals and dealing with compliance and conflicts. Traditional systems have had variable success in responding to sudden shocks. The systems have adjusted to some progressive technological and hydrological change, but have adjusted less well to demographic and economic changes. Commercialization and increasing socioeconomic differentiation are exacerbating long-standing inequities.

The spread of more efficient gear, declining traditional authority, and demographic changes do increase the risks of overexploitation (Neiland, Jaffry, et al. 2000). During the colonial period, increased mobility, more efficient fishing gear, and increased market value had diverse consequences for fishery management. Some traditional management systems adapted to these changes, but others collapsed or gave way to privatization (Neiland, Madakan, and Béné 2005). The diversity in fishing management systems documented by TMAF suggests that similar diversity is likely in response to current and future changes. Neiland, Weeks, et al. (2000) predict that traditional management systems will persist because they are currently strong and do not face serious challenges from the modern state. Fishing households are able to absorb some change because fishing represents only one element of a mixed livelihood strategy. Because the rate of change has not been too rapid, institutional adaptation is easier.

TMAF generated a tremendous variety of observations over a five-year period. Collaboration increased the variety of research activities undertaken by the project, while division of labor increased its geographic scope. The richness of this project also reflects its somewhat longer duration. The result is a multistranded, high-quality study of three fisheries in northeastern Nigeria. Findings from the large random-sample surveys can be generalized to households and management systems throughout these three fisheries, but not further. Indeed, TMAF documents considerable diversity in traditional systems for fishery management, fishing practices, and the contribution of fishing to the local communities. It is exactly this high degree of institutional diversity and the contextual nature of social-ecological relationships that heighten both the importance of fieldwork and the difficulty of broadly comparative analysis. Perhaps the methods developed by TMAF could be applied in studies of other fisheries. Based on the effort invested in TMAF, a cross-national study of this nature would require a large number of collaborators and substantial financial support.

Thoughts about Research Partnerships

Partnerships create opportunities for enriching research. Collaboration enables the collection of a greater variety of observations and use of a greater diversity of methods by bringing together scholars with different disciplinary backgrounds and skills sets. Coordination of research efforts can increase the scale and scope of research in terms of the number of observations, the types of observations, geographic coverage, and the variety of research questions that can be addressed. Research partnerships have played a crucial role in filling information gaps, documenting important forms of diversity, and analyzing social-ecological relationships. Collaborative analyses have suggested potentially general relationships that merit investigation in other settings. Nonetheless, participation of a handful of institutions in collaborative research over a three-to-five-year period cannot fully overcome the obstacles to broadly comparative field-based research. The scarcity of data on collective action and common-pool natural resources is simply too severe. Can broader forms of collaboration overcome these challenges?

CGIAR: A GLOBAL RESEARCH ALLIANCE

 The Consultative Group on International Agricultural Research (CGIAR) describes itself as an "alliance" of international researchers, research centers, and programs working to support national and international agricultural science (http://www.cgiar.org/index.html). Members include international organizations, governments, and foundations. The alliance supports fifteen international research centers that focus on particular resources or issues, e.g., the Center for International Forestry Research (CIFOR), the International Food Policy Research Institute (IFPRI), the International Livestock Research Institute (ILRI), the International Water Management Institute (IWMI), and the World Fish Center.[8] These research centers engage in collaborative research with other national and international research centers, governments, and civil society organizations, including farmers' associations. CGIAR promotes research around particular issues or thematic concerns through a number of systemwide and eco-regional initiatives (http://www.cgiar.org/impact/initiatives.html).

The systemwide program on Collective Action and Property Rights (CAPRi) supports research on collective action and property rights within the CGIAR alliance and beyond in a variety of ways. The compilation and dissemination of bibliographic materials and the provision of grants encourages CGIAR scholars to pay attention to collective action and property rights in their research. Scholars from across the CGIAR network come together for CAPRi workshops to discuss thematic issues, share common concerns, and exchange ideas. CAPRi also organizes conference panels and disseminates working papers, policy briefs, proceedings, and books.

CGIAR scholars, with the encouragement and support of the CAPRi systemwide program, are making important contributions to the study of collective action and the management of common-pool natural resources. The themes and approaches found in CGIAR-affiliated scholarship mirror the broader body of work related to collective action and common-pool natural resources. CGIAR scholars seek to understand patterns of natural resource use and management and their social, economic, and environmental consequences. Many are concerned about community-based natural resource management, comanagement, and other forms of decentralized natural resource management (e.g., Campbell et al. 2001; Meinzen-Dick, Raju, and Gulati 2002; Oyono 2004a, 2004b; Pacheco 2004; Resosudarmo 2004; Samad and Vermillion 1999; Sundar 2001; Thompson, Sultana, and Islam 2003). Several CGIAR studies underline the social and environmental damage caused by government policies that undermine local autonomy, involve inappropriate forms of decentralization, promote unsustainable economic development strategies, or fail to address economic crises (Brown and Ekoko 2001; Campbell et al. 2001; Levine, Sheng, and Barker 2000; Oyono 2004a; Pender et al. 2004). Others analyze conflicts, coordination, and cooperation among those using common-pool resources (Brown and Ekoko 2001; McCarthy and Vanderlinden 2004; Meinzen-Dick, Raju, and Gulati 2002; Levine, Sheng, and Barker 2000; Pokorny and Schanz 2003).

Substantive concerns vary somewhat depending on the natural resource under consideration. Sources of variation in collective responses to environmental risk receive considerable attention in studies of pastoral management of arid and semiarid lands (McCarthy et al. 2000; McCarthy and Vanderlinden 2004). Studies of irrigation systems focus more on social interactions and distributional issues that influence contributions to infrastructure provision and maintenance (Kurian and Dietz 2004; Makombe et al. 2001; Meinzen-Dick 2007; Meinzen-Dick, Raju, and Gulati 2002).

Thus far, no component of CGIAR has embarked on an effort to use the alliance's networks to build a cross-national database of comparable data. Rather, scholars and centers prefer less-structured initiatives that encourage research on particular themes but do not define the content or methods for data collection. CGIAR's thematic approach encourages the adoption of research designs that are matched to local context but also reflect prior research by other CGIAR scholars. Effective synthesis of the volume and diversity of research produced by the CGIAR alliance presents an ongoing and significant challenge. To meet this challenge, the CAPRi systemwide program invests heavily in the synthesis and the diffusion of research findings so that findings at one center influence research at other centers and beyond.

IFRI: An International Research Network

In 1992, in her capacity as head of the Food and Agriculture Organization's (FAO) Forest, Trees and People Program, Marilyn Hoskins sought to develop a program of research on interactions between people and forest management. She approached researchers at the Workshop at Indiana University about the possibility of adapting the theoretical framework and database structure of the CPR and NIIS research programs for the study of forestry.[9] This inquiry prompted development of the IFRI research program.

IFRI differs from the earlier research programs developed at the Workshop in its primary reliance on new fieldwork rather than existing studies, in its shift in attention to more complex and multiple-product forest resource systems, in its organization as a research network, and in the intention to develop over-time, comparative studies. Collaborating Research Centers (CRCs) are active in Africa, Asia, Latin America, and North America. As of 2009, there are 12 IFRI CRCs in 11 countries (see http://www.sitemaker.umich.edu/ifri/home). Individual scholars are also affiliated with IFRI. Arun Agrawal of the School of Natural Resources and the Environment at the University of Michigan became the lead coordinator for the IFRI research program in 2006; colleagues at Indiana University continue their participation.

Data for 241 unique sites with 350 forests in 17 countries had been entered into IFRI's common database as of July 1, 2009.[10] IFRI researchers conduct repeat studies of forest sites every three to five years. The database includes data for 80 sites that have been studied at least twice and 24 sites for which exactly three visits have been completed.[11] This represents a relatively large number of data points for a fairly broad set of countries and variables.

IFRI has achieved an unusual breadth of sustained collaboration and accumulated a significant amount of cross-national data relevant for the study of collective action related to common-pool forest resources. In light of these unusual features, we discuss IFRI's strategies for data collection and coordination in some detail. We then summarize major contributions by IFRI researchers and discuss the challenges encountered.

Strategies for Data Collection

Data collection encompasses biophysical measures of forest conditions, demographic and economic indicators about forest users, and information about institutions affecting use of forest resources. For each study site, data are collected about a variety of conceptually distinct entities, such as forests, user groups, and forest products. Separate data collection protocols correspond to each conceptual entity or capture relationships between conceptual entities. A research team will use one protocol to collect data about forest products such as firewood, medicinal plants, or building materials, and another to collect data about each group that uses the forest.

The basic social unit of analysis for the IFRI research program is the user group, defined as a set of individuals with the same rights to and responsibilities for forest resources.[12] IFRI methods often identify several user groups that are active in a forest. Groups that have established a more formal organization for collective decision making are coded as forest associations. If a forest association exists, it may represent one or more user groups. Forest associations may encompass a large proportion of forest users, or they may be formed by a subset of forest users. The relational database structure facilitates the collection and storage of data for sites that vary tremendously in the number of forests, settlements, products, and user groups.

The distinction drawn in data collection between user groups and organizations or forest associations is characteristic of the modular approach to data collection adopted by the CPR, NIIS, and IFRI research programs. Data collection protocols capture multiple indicators of potential concepts of interests and do so in a way that allows a number of different combinations in analysis. Since the number of variables for which alternative conceptualizations are measured increased with each generation of research on collective action, the IFRI research program includes multiple empirical indicators for a wider variety of variables than did the CPR research program.

IFRI seeks to balance conceptual and methodological coherence with a capacity for ongoing adaptation. The network meets every two years and can make adjustments in research protocols based on earlier findings and incorporate new research questions. The IFRI protocols represent the core, not the limit, of data collection. Studies frequently combine IFRI research with household surveys or remotely sensed images (Agrawal and Gupta 2005; Jagger et al. 2009; Nagendra, Karmacharya, and Karna 2005; E. Ostrom and Nagendra 2006; Tucker et al. 2005; Vogt et al. 2006). Other forms of supplemental data collection include standardized surveys of village-level organizations or information related to donor projects, government programs, or laws (Agrawal and Chhatre 2007; Agrawal and Goyal 2001; Agrawal and Yadama 1997; Andersson 2004; Andersson, Gibson, and Lehoucq 2006).

Strategies for Coordination

Organization as an international network of researchers and research centers circumvents problems of limited scope associated with most large-N studies (Tucker and Ostrom 2005). It makes possible more rapid accumulation of comparable data on a broader geographic scale than any single researcher could manage. Nonetheless, coordination of a dispersed network of scholars in a multidisciplinary study of complex and diverse field sites presents a variety of challenges. IFRI has developed extensive documentation, organizes regular training sessions and meetings, and uses electronic media to promote methodological consistency and collaboration across the network.

The use of common research instruments and techniques for data collection provides a foundation of conceptual consistency in the IFRI research program (Gibson, McKean, and Ostrom 2000; Wertime et al. 2007).[13] The IFRI Field Manual provides extensive explanation of common research questions, key concepts, recommended field methods, and the database structure (Wertime et al. 2007). Detailed discussion of the relational database structure and each of the data collection protocols examines underlying assumptions and highlights common challenges encountered in the field. Sketches from early field experiences and hypothetical situations illustrate key concepts. Where alternative measurement strategies exist (e.g., for sampling forest plots), the Field Manual explains the alternatives and offers advice on how to choose among them.

An annual training program introduces newcomers, such as graduate students and new members of existing teams, to the IFRI method. Regional training programs provide additional reinforcement for new and existing participants. For field-based research programs such as IFRI, accuracy in identification of user groups depends on the observational skills of field researchers. Differences in rights and responsibilities can be subtle and informal. Probing questions may be needed to distinguish between differences in practice and rights; if only youth collect berries, it may mean that older people lack time for berry collection rather than that they lack the right to engage in this activity. Careful training and supervision of research teams helps ensure attentiveness to these sorts of subtleties in the field.

Biennial networkwide meetings offer regular opportunities for the group as a whole to propose changes and weigh their relative benefits and costs. Most major changes have occurred after having been vetted at one or more biennial meetings. Biennial meetings also offer opportunities to share findings, exchange ideas and techniques, and connect with colleagues at other centers who are working on similar issues. Regional meetings and the organization of panels at international conferences present additional opportunities for face-to-face interaction. A full-time IFRI research coordinator facilitates communication across the network between meetings by moderating a Listserv and editing a newsletter (see IFRI Web site).

Contributions and Challenges

IFRI scholarship addresses a wide range of issues related to collective action and the management of forestry resources. Many IFRI studies evaluate the social and environmental implications of government policies involving decentralization (e.g., Agrawal 2005; Andersson, Gibson, and Lehoucq 2006; Ghate 2008; Varughese and Ostrom 2001; Webb and Shivakoti 2008), protected area management (Hayes 2006; Hayes and Ostrom 2005; Merino Pérez and Hernández Apolinar 2004; Tucker 2004), or state control (Dorji, Webb, and Shivakoti 2006; Sudtongkong and Webb 2008; Webb and Dorji 2008). Others compare social, economic, and environmental outcomes under alternative property regimes (Gibson, Lehoucq, and Williams 2002; Nagendra et al. 2007; E. Ostrom and Nagendra 2007; Thoms, Karna, and Karmacharya 2006; Tucker 1999) or examine the dynamics within communities that manage their forests informally, in the absence of a government-sanctioned decentralization program (Ghate 2004; Gombya-Ssembajjwe 1997). IFRI scholars have developed indexes that distinguish between the creation of collective rules and action to implement and enforce collective rules (Varughese 1999). The presence of informal institutions for forest management has been confirmed with evidence of forest conditions that deviate from patterns predicted by optimal foraging (Banana, Gombya-Ssembajjwe, and Bahati 2001; Becker and León 2000; Gibson 2001; Schweik 2000).[14]

As a group, these studies call into question the advisability of blueprint solutions to the challenges of common-pool natural resource management. These studies also provide repeated evidence of gaps between formal policies and institutions and conditions on the ground. These points are further reinforced in a series of IFRI studies on the importance of effective monitoring and enforcement for the success of community-based forest management (Agrawal and Goyal 2001; Banana and Gombya-Ssembajjwe 2000; Ghate and Nagendra 2005; Gibson, Williams, and Ostrom 2005; E. Ostrom and Nagendra 2007).

IFRI includes multiple measurements of several concepts related to the development of institutions for the management of common-pool resources. Several studies have compared alternative measurements to demonstrate contingent relationships. These sorts of analyses have demonstrated that the relationship between collective action and group characteristics such as group size and heterogeneity, for example, depends on the form of collective action and heterogeneity (see review in Poteete and Ostrom 2004a). Similarly, Poteete and Welch (2004), by comparing rules that five communities in southern Indiana had developed for firewood, ginseng, and morel mushrooms, showed that resource complexity has an independent influence on institutional development.

IFRI researchers have faced a challenging scientific problem when trying to undertake cross-national research related to the outcomes of collective action on forest conditions. The extensive forest mensuration undertaken in a random sample of plots generates valid measures for comparison within the same ecological zone. Gautam (2002, 98), for example, examined whether the size of a user group was related to several measures of forest conditions: the number of trees, the average diameter at breast height (DBH) of sampled trees, their average height, and the number of species for a set of Nepal sites within a similar ecological zone. He found that group size was not correlated with forest conditions in a straightforwardly negative manner, but that the forests governed by the very largest groups were in worse condition than those governed by smaller- to medium-size groups.

Comparisons of these direct measures of forest conditions for sites that cross ecological zones can, however, be misleading. Fortunately, the team was advised at the time of the design of the research instruments to ask the forester or biologist who supervised the forest mensuration to provide an evaluation of forest condition for the forest just measured compared to others known to the researcher in the same zone. Forest users were also asked whether forest conditions were improving, remaining about the same, or becoming worse over time. These measures have been useful in analysis for studies within a single zone as well as essential for comparing across ecological zones. Varughese (1999, chap. 3), for example, used these assessments to evaluate the relative influence of population pressure and village-level collective action on forest conditions in eighteen villages in Nepal's middle hills. He found no relationship between the current quality of forest conditions or changes over time and either size of group or the rate of population growth; the level of collective action in the village provided a better predictor of forest conditions.

Several studies have used these evaluations by forestry specialists or by forest users to conduct large cross-national studies. Gibson, Williams, and Ostrom (2005) found strong evidence of the importance of regular monitoring and enforcement. Hayes and Ostrom (2005) and Hayes (2006) use the same measure to demonstrate the lack of any difference in forest conditions within officially designated protected areas as contrasted to other institutional arrangements. Chhatre and Agrawal (2008) explore how enforcement interacts with a variety of other independent variables for 152 forests around the world. Other IFRI scholars have linked IFRI forests to reference forests that have had very little use but are otherwise similar to facilitate comparison across ecological regions (Becker and León 2000; Schweik 2000; Tucker et al. 2008).

As the number of repeat visits increases, it becomes possible to analyze *changes* in the basal area, diameter at breast height (DBH), or stem count as dependent variables since the forest mensuration data are obtained within the same forest over time. E. Ostrom and Nagendra (2006) and Coleman (2009a) show that collective action by local forest users to monitor forest conditions is one of the most important factors associated with improvements in forest conditions. In light of the repeated findings of the importance of monitoring, Coleman and Steed (2009) examined factors that might be associated with the likelihood that local users would themselves monitor each other in one hundred IFRI forests located in fourteen countries. They found that the variable with the strongest impact on local monitoring was whether local users had rights to harvest some forest products from a forest—or, in essence, they had something to lose if the forest condition deteriorated.

IFRI has made it possible to answer the call for broadly comparative cross-national research on collective action for the management of common-pool natural resources. Nonetheless, until recently, most of IFRI's publications relied on data from a single country, and many analyze data for a subset of sites within a country. The relative scarcity of cross-national data analysis even within a research program designed to conduct such research reflects the conceptual challenges of comparing forest conditions across ecological zones. In addition, IFRI scholars have a greater sense of ownership and understanding of data that they were involved in collecting. They often focus on data from their own countries in order to address national-level policy debates. These issues present general constraints on collaboration for broadly comparative field-based studies of collective action and common-pool resources. Over time, however, IFRI's production of cross-national studies has increased.

COMPARING THE STRATEGIES AND DRAWING IMPLICATIONS

As we have shown, scholars have pursued a variety of strategies for accumulating data for a larger set of observations about collective action in natural resource management. To varying degrees, these efforts have attempted to balance the pursuit of more observations with the preservation of detailed information about particular cases of (potential or actual) collective action. Here and in the previous chapter, we have described examples of meta-analysis, a hybrid of meta-analysis and field data, a narrative synthesis of the literature, and collaborative research. These research programs vary in the diversity of natural resources considered, geographic scope, duration, and costs. Tables 5.1 and 5.2 summarize the basic characteristics of each research program and the strategies adopted to maintain conceptual consistency and comparable data.

The comparability and reliability of empirical findings depend on conceptual consistency. Yet an extreme insistence on conceptual and methodological consistency runs counter to the evolutionary nature of learning. Knowledge advances through the refinement of concepts and methods in response to findings from past studies. These research programs have not limited their attention to any single form of collective action. Openness makes the research programs attractive to a variety of scholars with overlapping but not identical research questions. Diversity of approaches has merit; comparisons of alternative conceptualizations of hypothesized relationships can help advance knowledge more rapidly. The lack of consistency in measurement of collective action does raise the risk of miscommunication between scholars who use the same terms to describe somewhat different phenomena. Clear explanations of variables and how they have been measured offer the best defense against miscommunication.

Each strategy has strengths and weaknesses. None stands out as obviously superior to the others. Given the success of each strategy, social scientists would be well advised to conduct meta-analyses and form collaborative networks for a broader array of topics. Meta-analysis has been applied mostly to quantitative analyses of clinical and experimental research. Yet it seems particularly attractive when case studies are beginning to accumulate about an issue at a scale of analysis that makes large-N field studies especially costly and difficult to organize. Meta-analysis is well suited to address the scarcity of comparable data about social phenomena at the subnational level.

The inherent limitations of working with case studies as source materials mean that meta-analysis will never eliminate the desirability of large cross-national databases founded on original fieldwork. By spreading the costs of such endeavors, research networks make the creation of such databases possible. Several well-established collaborative programs exist for survey research (e.g., the World Values Survey), but fewer in other areas.[15] It can be difficult to coordinate on other types of fieldwork, given the importance of contextual elements. IFRI's strategy of using common concepts and measures for a core set of variables, while allowing the addition of variables for particular centers, regions, or sites, represents a compromise that can also help researchers in other fields achieve collaboration across diverse contexts.

Even in collaborative research, it has proven difficult and costly to accumulate enough comparable data over time to support substantial numbers of large-N analyses with policy units, common-pool natural resource systems, or actual or potential units of collective action as the unit of analysis, whether at the national or the cross-national level. Resource constraints, career incentives, and collective-action problems among researchers all help explain why the promise of collaborative research has not yet been more fully realized. More financial and institutional support from universities and granting agencies for collaboration, and especially for long-term collaborative research, could help overcome these obstacles. The comparison of the smaller research partnerships with IFRI highlights the importance of long-term financial support. Both TMAF and the Tanzania partnership faced trade-offs between data quantity and quality. TMAF opted for a more intensive study of a single region instead of a more superficial treatment of additional fisheries. The Tanzania project chose to rely on PRAs rather than more intensive field methods in order to cover 12 villages in 6 districts. Support from a changing set of international donors (FAO, Ford Foundation, MacArthur Foundation, and NSF) has made it possible for IFRI to accumulate data for 241 study sites and conduct more than 80 repeat studies over the course of more than ten years. The current network of 12 research centers in 11 countries represents a threefold expansion from the initial 4 centers in Bolivia, Nepal, Uganda, and the United States. IFRI's international scope would have been comparable to that of other research partnerships had its funding run out after five years. Even with the important findings that IFRI researchers have made, it has been very hard to obtain long-term funding, as this is still unusual for social science research.

TABLE 5.1
Examples of large-N studies of collective action in natural resource management: basic characteristics

A. Meta-analyses, hybrids, and narrative reviews

Research program	Strategy	Resources	Geographic scope of data	Sampling strategy
CPR database	Meta-analysis	Fisheries, irrigation systems, and (a few) forests	Cross-national: 86 case studies	Availability, quality, and resource type. Screened 1,600 case studies for quality information about a specific case; considerable time spent in field by author; and inclusion of key information on resource characteristics, management rules, user strategies, and outcomes.
Baland and Platteau ([1996] 2000)	Narrative review	Fisheries, forestry, game, grazing, groundwater, irrigation, and land	Cross-national: 113 or more[a]	Availability and fit (thematic and methodological). Survey of available socio-anthropological material based on field studies.
NIIS	Hybrid	Irrigation systems	National: 236 unique cases[b]	Availability and convenience. Survey of available studies; accessibility of systems; proximity of systems; structured sampling of additional systems mentioned in official records.

[a]Baland and Platteau do not report the number of cases. This is an estimate based on a count of empirical studies cited in the text of part II.
[b]Revisits have been conducted at some sites in the NIIS database; these are not counted here.

B. Field-based collaborative approaches

Research program	Strategy	Resources	Geographic scope of data	Sampling strategy
TMAF	Partnership of three universities	Fisheries	Subnational: three fisheries in northern Nigeria	Random or purposive, depending on the research component.
CELP—University of Dar es Salaam—Norconsult (TZ) Ltd.	Partnership of two universities and a research firm	Pastures and water	Subnational: 12 villages in 6 districts in Tanzania	Purposive semiarid districts. Villages that reflect ethnic and ecological variation.
CGIAR	"Alliance" of research centers, civil society organizations, and governments	Agriculture, fisheries, food, forests, genetic resources, livestock, particular crops, water	Cross-national—but not collated	No coordinated sampling strategy.
IFRI	Network of research centers	Forestry	Cross-national: 241 unique cases[a]	Networkwide: uncoordinated. Availability of interested partners in a given country; availability of funding. Within country: purposive for country, region, or grant/project.

[a]Revisits have been conducted at some sites in the IFRI database; these are not counted here.

TABLE 5.2
Examples of large-N studies of collective action in natural resource management: strategies for conceptual consistency and comparable data

A. Narrative reviews, meta-analyses, and hybrids

Research program	Defining the unit of collective action	Evidence of collective action	Measuring independent variables
CPR database	Subgroup: those who have similar rights to and responsibilities for the resource, similar dependency on the resource, and similar exposure to variations in supply, and who withdraw similar quantities of the resources.	Establishment and survival of common-property resource system; effective management in terms of sustainability, resource quality, rule adherence, limitation of violence; equity, efficiency, stability, robustness of arrangements. Limits on the number of appropriators, restrictions on rights of use and appropriation, and definition of the responsibilities/duties of appropriators.	Some allowance for measuring multiple forms of some variables, such as social differentiation and heterogeneity across and within subgroups.
Baland and Platteau ([1996] 2000)	Chap. 10: members of traditional village societies, defined as "relatively closed, . . . not permeated by a market logic . . . , and . . . to a large extent insulated from the rule of a centralized state machinery" (189). Chaps. 11–12: village or group-based or local-level common-pool resource management.	The existence of conservation rules consciously designed for conservation that actually achieve conservation (188); long-term survival of local institutions (183).	Not clear whether any coding system was used. Allows for and discusses alternative interpretations of concepts. Discusses and critiques alternative conceptualizations and suggests own preference, although preferred conceptualization may not have much representation in literature surveyed.

Research program	Defining the unit of collective action	Evidence of collective action	Measuring independent variables
NIIS	Subgroup: those who have same rights to water in an irrigation system. Not necessarily all farmers using the irrigation system since different farmers may have different rights.	The length and number of canals, information on flow, and the relationship of system performance to seasons and crops.	Modular approach with multiple empirical indicators of many variables.

B. Field-based collaborative approaches

Research program	Defining the unit of collective action	Evidence of collective action	Measuring independent variables
TMAF	Fishery—encompasses all fishing villages	Sustainability of fishing levels; avoidance of overcapitalization.	Semistructured interviews and structured household survey.
CELP—University of Dar es Salaam—Norconsult (TZ) Ltd.	Common-pool resource management regimes	Evaluation in terms of Ostrom's design principles for long-enduring CPRs. Adequacy of management for sustainability, effective prevention of open access.	Semistructured interviews and PRAs guided by checklists of questions plus a structured household survey.
CGIAR	No standardized definition	No standardized definition.	No standardized list, definitions, or methods for measurement.
IFRI	User group: those with the same rights to and responsibilities for a forest	Biological data and comparisons with patterns expected with optimal foraging; resource mobilization; collective activities in the forest; and the development of rules for access to and use of forest resources.	Modular approach with multiple empirical indicators of many variables.

Larger research networks such as CGIAR and IFRI have achieved significant cross-national membership but, until recently, produced relatively more single-nation studies than cross-national analysis. The CGIAR alliance, with its large number of institutional members, broad geographic reach, and access to official sources of funding, has the potential to undertake truly international and long-term research. To date, CGIAR has provided general support for research on collective action through the CAPRi program but has not developed a common research strategy. Considering the diversity of researchers involved with CGIAR, it would probably be difficult to agree on even a minimal set of research protocols. Because research activities are not tightly coordinated, the collation of comparative results and the identification of cross-national patterns present ongoing challenges. Indeed, it is CAPRi's mission to meet these challenges.

IFRI is the only field-based research network of which we are aware that has accumulated a large enough quantity of sufficiently comparable data to support large-N cross-national analysis with a policy unit, ecological system, or actual or potential unit of collective action as the unit of analysis. And even then, IFRI researchers have frequently analyzed a subsample of data from a single country. The use of common data collection protocols addresses problems of comparability in a technical sense, but does not eliminate the substantial challenges of drawing sound comparisons across cultural, ecological, and political contexts. It took time for sufficient data to accumulate and for IFRI scholars to develop analytical techniques that enabled rigorous comparisons across ecological zones. Now, however, IFRI is producing a steady flow of large-N research that involves comparisons across countries and ecological zones (Chhatre and Agrawal 2008; Coleman 2009a; Coleman and Steed 2009; Gibson, Williams, and Ostrom 2005; Hayes 2006; Hayes and Ostrom 2005; E. Ostrom and Nagendra 2006; Poteete 2001, 2002; van Laerhoven 2008).

Collaborative research makes it possible to accumulate the number of observations from a variety of countries required for broadly comparative analysis while retaining a foundation of qualitative data collected through rigorous fieldwork. Collaboration does not overcome all challenges associated with the study of collective action in natural resource management—or any other topic with a subnational unit of analysis. All of the examples that we surveyed made trade-offs between the intensity and the breadth of their research. Scholars involved in collaborative research must also balance local idiosyncrasies and individual research interests with the need for common methods. Nonetheless, collaborative research offers the greatest promise for identifying general patterns—and anomalies—based on quality field-based data about units of analysis relevant for the study of collective action, as well as other topics for which data are scarce and costly to collect.[16]

PART THREE

Models and Experiments in the Laboratory and the Field

CHAPTER SIX

Experiments in the Laboratory and the Field

NOW THAT WE HAVE discussed various methods of field research in part II, we will discuss the use of controlled experiments in this chapter. Controlled experiments are generally used to test hypotheses. Experiments in the laboratory and the field on common-pool resources have confirmed a number of observed phenomena in case studies and shown that in controlled replicable situations, self-governance can happen more often than was earlier predicted. Although experiments have debunked claims that collective action was impossible, this method has not yet led to the development of a fully specified and unified alternative theory of collective action in commons dilemmas. Chapter 9 will present a beginning effort in this direction. Experimental studies have shown the importance of the role of communication, especially "cheap talk," where participants communicate without the ability to enforce promises. Furthermore, they have demonstrated the willingness of participants to forgo income by sanctioning those who did not cooperate.

Experimental studies regularly contradict expectations from formal models based on behavioral assumptions of individual utility maximization of material returns. The inconsistency between formal theory and experimental evidence accelerated the search for alternative behavioral models that can explain observed experimental results. This has led especially to the positing of a diversity of alternative utility functions that include positive preferences for returns to others in the group as well as changes due to norms, and alternative models of learning (Camerer 2003; Henrich et al. 2004). These developments are part of a larger movement in the social sciences with the maturation of behavioral game theory (Camerer 2003) and neuroeconomics in recent years (Glimcher 2003).

This chapter provides an overview of experimental methods and discusses their strengths and weaknesses with reference to research on collective action on common-pool resources. In a chapter focused on a synthesis of findings, we cannot also cover all of the methodological questions. For an introduction to the methodology of experiments itself, we refer the reader to Friedman and Sunder (1994), Kagel and Roth (1995), and Camerer (2003). We will especially focus on the role of communication and costly sanctioning. At the end of the chapter, we highlight some new developments that include experiments with more sophisticated ecological dynamics and more diversity in the types of decisions participants can make.

The Experimental Method

In a typical experiment, the experimenter creates an environment where a number of human subjects make decisions in a controlled setting. Human subjects voluntarily consent to participate in an experiment prior to participating. They receive instructions on the actions about which they can make decisions and outcomes that depend on the decisions of all in the experiment. Participants make each decision in private by writing it on a paper form or entering it on a computer. Salient incentives are provided in terms of monetary returns depending on the decisions made, or other relevant rewards.[1]

Experiments related to collective action and the commons represent a form of social dilemma where human subjects face a situation in which private interests are in conflict with interests for the group. For many decades psychologists, economists, political scientists, and scholars from other disciplines have used experiments to study social dilemmas (Dawes 1973; Dawes et al. 1986; Frohlich and Oppenheimer 1992; Kagel and Roth 1995; Wilke, Messick, and Rutte 1986). In this chapter, we focus mainly on a subset of these experiments that are most related to the study of governance of natural resources—those focusing on public goods and common-pool resources.

The main goal of experiments is to test well-defined hypotheses under controlled conditions or to study the effects of variables for which theory may be less explicit. In organizing an experimental research program, one starts with the design of a baseline experiment to represent a simplified decision setting. Then, one carefully changes one attribute of the situation at a time and conducts multiple experimental sessions for each change in design. Researchers have a level of control over an experimental setting that is impossible to achieve in natural field settings. A well-designed experiment has internal validity in that one knows with high levels of certainty what conditions are present in an experiment and how these relate to conditions specified in a theory (Camerer 2003). Replications of an experiment by researchers in another setting with different participants also help to confirm or challenge the results. Replications provide insights as to whether the results are due to the design of the experiment and not due to unaccounted factors in the way an experiment was conducted in one setting.

Laboratory experiments lack the external validity of well-designed field studies as described in part II, but field studies lack the internal validity of laboratory experiments. In a multimethod approach to the study of collective action, both experiments and field studies are important foundations for testing and developing theory. Experimental results may challenge and falsify an existing theory, but neither experimental nor field research can definitely establish a proof for a theory. Outcomes of experiments are not definitive. As with the findings from all research methods, we need to be open to reevaluating everything, including our own presumptions in designing and analyzing the experiments (V. Smith 2009).

Owing to concerns about external validity of laboratory experiments with student subjects, there is an increasing use of field experiments within experimental economics, where subjects are recruited in the field (Harrison and List 2004). Such experiments are also performed for the study of collective action for common-pool resources (e.g., Cardenas 2000; Lopez et al. forthcoming). In field experiments, the participants have had more salient experience with commons dilemmas and are more demographically diverse. Harrison and List (2004) distinguish three types of field experiments: artifactual field experiment (an abstract game with nonstandard subject pool), framed field experiment (same as artifactual field experiment but with field context in the community, task, or information set that the participants can use), and a natural field experiment (where the subjects are not aware that they are in an experiment). The field experiments discussed in this chapter fall into the category of artifactual field experiments.

While it is never possible to establish a perfect experiment, extensive methodological work has been undertaken since the pathbreaking work of Vernon Smith. Smith (1982) challenged social scientists to exhibit great care in the design of experiments and to ensure that the assumed structure was clear to the participants. Researchers can do so by pretesting instructions extensively, paying participants well, and making payments consistent with the outcomes obtained in the experiment. Further, experimental researchers have developed a commitment to share experimental instructions and their data with one another and to encourage replication in order to ensure that there was nothing "unique" about the implementation of an experiment. Still further, experimental studies are used to "test bed" competing strategies for implementing new public policies (see Plott and Porter 1996).

Many social dilemma experiments have been performed at universities in developed countries with participants from university settings, such as undergraduate students. The initial reasons for this selected sample of participants are accessibility, control for the experimenters, and lower overall costs. While laboratory experiments conducted in a university setting usually pay participants more than they would earn in an hourly position in the same location, the costs of setting up the experiment, recruiting participants, conducting the experiment, and recording data generated in the experiment are substantially lower than for experiments conducted in field settings. It is important to recognize that observed behavior can vary between different pools of participants—for example, between undergraduate students in the United States and villagers in rural areas in developing countries (Henrich et al. 2004). It is reassuring to know, however, that a recent study of postgraduates from forty-one countries around the globe replicated findings from a similar experiment conducted with undergraduate students—enhancing confidence in the findings from earlier studies (see discussion below and Ahn, Ostrom, and Walker 2009). In recent years, scholars have increasingly used field experiments, however, where resource experiments are performed with participants who have a more salient dependence on common resources. While the costs of organizing these experiments are substantial, they help establish where the behavior of actual resource users is similar to or differs from that of participants recruited on a university campus.

Besides the external validity question, another challenge of laboratory experiments is the potential sensitivity of the results to small changes in the design (Cookson 2000; Tversky and Kahneman 1981). Such changes can be the result of the wording of the instructions (Cookson 2000), whether payoffs are framed as gifts or subtractions from an initial endowment (J. Cox et al. 2009; Sefton, Shupp, and Walker 2007), or even the name of the experiment (Ensminger 2004). While this is also a positive attribute of experiments—since one likes to understand the effect of different variables—it calls for substantial pretesting before the experiments are performed; moreover, researchers must replicate the experiments to test the robustness of the findings.

Laboratory Experiments of Relevance to the Study of the Commons

With regard to the governance of social-ecological systems, studies of public goods and of common-pool resources are both important. As discussed in chapter 2, the conventional theory sees the provision of public goods and management of shared natural resources as social dilemmas. Formal models of these situations most frequently assume self-interested rationality. In other words, each individual is expected to choose the action associated with the individually best payoff based on expectations of what the other actors will do. The Nash equilibrium is a stable outcome from which no player has an incentive to deviate given the expected behavior of the other player(s).[2] Game-theoretic models of public goods provision and appropriation from common-pool resources predict a Nash equilibrium of noncooperation. Further assumptions made in almost all formal models of social dilemmas include the following:

1. decisions about strategies are made independently and simultaneously;
2. participants cannot communicate with one another in any way;
3. all participants have complete and common knowledge of the exogenously fixed structure of the situation and of the payoffs to be received by all individuals under all combinations of strategies; and
4. no external actor (or central authority) is present to enforce agreements among participants about their choices.

When these assumptions are made for a game that is not repeated, the theoretical prediction derived from noncooperative game theory is unambiguous—zero cooperation. If such a game is finitely repeated and everyone shares complete information about the structure of the situation, the predicted outcome for every iteration of the game is again the Nash equilibrium of the constituent game. The presumption is that if individuals would not cooperate in the last game of a series, they would not cooperate in the second-to-last game, the third-to-last game . . . all the way back to the initial game (Luce and Raiffa 1957). This is called backward induction (but see Axelrod and Hamilton 1981; Boyd and Richerson 1988).

Numerous experiments have been designed to evaluate the behavioral assumptions and hypothesized causal mechanisms underlying these predictions. To measure levels of cooperation in experiments on commons dilemmas, the Nash and cooperative equilibria need to be sufficiently different. If the assumptions behind formal models are accurate, observed levels of cooperation in experiments should be very low. A series of laboratory experiments during the last three decades have shown that participants do invest in the provision of public goods substantially more than is predicted by noncooperative theory (Isaac, McCue, and Plott 1985; Isaac and Walker 1988a; Isaac, Walker, and Thomas 1984; Isaac, Walker, and Williams 1994; Marwell and Ames 1979, 1980, 1981).[3]

On the other hand, participants overharvest common-pool resources even more than is predicted by theory (E. Ostrom, Gardner, and Walker 1994; E. Ostrom, Walker, and Gardner 1992) unless given an opportunity for face-to-face communication, in which case they do better than predicted. Depending on the return rate from investments in a public good, the higher-than-predicted initial contribution rate remains the same or decreases with the number of rounds. Without communication or costly sanctioning, the majority of the common-pool and public goods experiments show that the average investments move toward the Nash equilibrium. However, at the start of the experiment, participants in common-pool experiments overharvest more than the Nash equilibrium, while they contribute more than the Nash equilibrium in the public goods experiments. Laboratory experiments have consistently shown that communication is a crucial factor for achieving cooperative behavior (Brosig 2002; E. Ostrom, Gardner, and Walker 1994; Sally 1995).

Public Goods Experiments

The standard linear public goods provision experiment is frequently referred to as a Voluntary Contribution Mechanism (VCM) (Isaac and Walker 1988a). A public goods experiment can be characterized by the number of individuals (N), the marginal per capita return (*mpcr*), the number of repetitions (T), and the initial endowment of token resources for each participant (ω). The marginal per capita return (*mpcr*) is the marginal addition to total outcomes that results from one more unit invested in joint returns as compared to individual returns. A linear public goods provision game involves a free-rider problem if *mpcr* < 1 and N × *mpcr* > 1. Suppose, in a given round, individual *i* contributes x_i of ω for the provision of the public good. The participant's payoff (π_i) is

$$\pi_i = \omega - x_i + mpcr \sum_{j=1}^{N} x_j \qquad (6.1)$$

The equilibrium prediction, assuming individuals maximize their own monetary payoffs, is that the public good will not be provided at all.

We present two generally observed patterns from the linear public goods provision experiments that scholars should address in their efforts to provide coherent theoretical explanations. The general observed patterns are illustrated with data on six experimental treatments of Isaac and Walker (1988a) and Isaac, Walker, and Williams (1994), which differ in regard to *mpcr* and group size. The observed trend has been replicated in many follow-up studies (e.g., Ledyard 1995). The first general observed pattern is that the average contribution to the public good varies with group size and *mpcr* (figure 6.1). The second general observed pattern is the large variation of individual decisions (figure 6.2).

The average level of contribution for the provision of public goods and its change over time differs across experimental settings. Some extreme experimental conditions with low *mpcr* (e.g., 0.3) show a rapid convergence to almost complete free-riding. Other treatments with relatively high *mpcr* show a pattern of stabilization of the contribution level around 50 percent of the total endowment. Yet other experimental conditions exhibit trends in between the two extremes. All typically show overall decreases in contribution level over rounds of decisions. The gradually declining trends of contributions also hold for experiments of longer durations, such as 40 or 60 rounds, but the rate of decrease in contributions is lower (Isaac, Walker, and Williams 1994). Controlling for *mpcr*, it appears that the larger the group size, the higher is the contribution level. This can be seen most clearly in figure 6.1 when one compares three treatment conditions: for *mpcr* 0.3, the groups of size 4 (filled diamond) show the lowest contribution; groups of size 10 (filled triangle) show a noticeable increase in the contribution level compared to that of the group of size 4. And the groups of size 40 show contribution levels around 50 percent without a clear declining trend. But this apparently benign effect of group size is not present for the *mpcr* value of 0.75. Both groups of size 4 and those of size 10 show very similar trends of contribution when the *mpcr* is 0.75.

Variance in contribution levels across participants in a given round is another important characterizing factor of public goods experimental results. In some rounds, all participants contribute a similar proportion of their endowment. Obviously, this is more likely when the average contribution is near zero. In other rounds, one observes a diversity of contribution levels, ranging from 100 percent to 0 percent. An interesting observation comes from a session in Isaac, Walker, and Williams (1994), with *mpcr* = 0.3 and group size 40. The participants in the session all had experience with previous social dilemma experiments. As figure 6.2 shows, contribution levels tend to move toward extremes of zero or 100 percent over time. In the experimental session, about 20 percent of participants contribute all of their endowments to the public goods account. The proportion of complete contributors increases to 40 percent by the final round of the experiment. At the same time, the proportion of complete free-riders also increases from 10 percent in round 1 to over 30 percent in round 10. Thus, by the final round, the full contributors and the complete free-riders together constitute more than 70 percent of the group. This micromechanism generates the stable group-level contribution shown in series (40, 0.3), marked by hollow circles, in figure 6.1.

The results summarized above offer several puzzles from the perspective of noncooperative game theory. In the public goods provision environment, especially for some parameterizations that are inconsequential from the perspective of the noncooperative theory, there is just "too much" cooperative play. What aspects of the public goods game are fostering the degree of cooperation exhibited, and what explains the interaction between the level of cooperation, *mpcr*, and group size?

In their efforts to explain discrepancies between the theory and the data, Isaac, Walker, and Williams (1994) consider several possible explanations, including learning and/or the failure of backward induction.

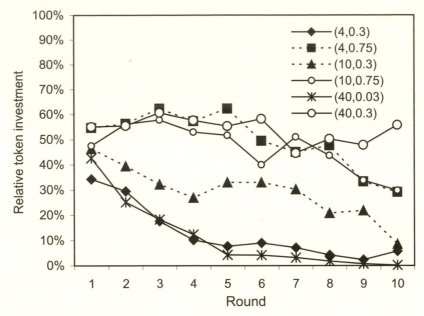

Fig. 6.1. Average contribution over the round for the six different treatments. The number of participants and the *mpcr* are given in brackets. *Source*: Adapted from Janssen and Ahn 2006.

Their experiments with richer information sets and longer game horizons, however, suggest that there is more going on than just learning the consequences of alternative strategies. Complementing this research, Laury, Walker, and Williams (1995) investigate the public goods provision setting in an operationalization in which (1) group members' identity is anonymous and (2) participants' decisions and earnings are anonymous to both other group members and the experimenters. Their results parallel those reported by Isaac, Walker, and Williams. Anonymity (or the lack thereof) does not appear to be a significant variable that can be used to explain behavior in the public goods provision setting.[4]

It is interesting to consider the "knife-edged" prediction of the theory for the public goods game (Isaac, Walker, and Williams 1994). If the *mpcr* > 1, a 100 percent allocation of all tokens to the group good is the single period dominant strategy. If the *mpcr* < 1, zero allocations of tokens to the group good is the single period dominant strategy. On the other hand, in experimental payoff space, if the *mpcr* is near 1, the payoff consequences of different strategies are minimal from an individual's perspective but can be great from the group's perspective. The greater the *mpcr*, the greater the gains from some form of group (subgroup) co-

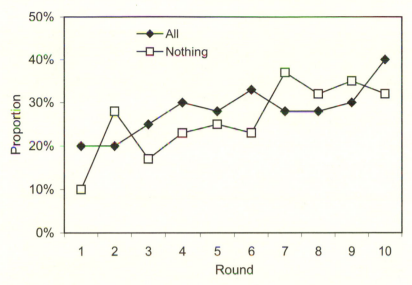

Fig. 6.2. Increasing variance across participants over time in a public goods experiment with *mpcr* equal to 0.3 and group size equal to 40. *Source:* Adapted from Janssen and Ahn 2006.

operation. Further, holding *mpcr* constant, in any public goods setting, increasing group size increases the gains from a group achieving some form of implicit cooperation. In efforts to overtly model *mpcr* and group size as an artifact of the game that may affect behavior, several modeling approaches have been suggested.

Ledyard (1995) proposed an equilibrium model in which individuals get some satisfaction (a warm glow) from participating in a group that implicitly and successfully cooperates. In modeling a "warm glow," Ledyard's assumption is related to the work of Andreoni (1989, 1995). Individuals are distinguished by types, based upon the strength of their "warm glow" preferences.[5] Under certain assumptions about the population distribution of preferences, Ledyard finds that (1) there can be deviations from complete free-riding even in a single-shot game, and (2) individuals will be more likely to deviate from complete free-riding in large groups. In recent years, a diversity of representations has been proposed to include other-regarding preferences (Bolton and Ockenfels 2000; Charness and Rabin 2002; J. Cox, Friedman, and Gjerstad 2007; Fehr and Schmidt 1999, for example). All these preference formulations make a trade-off between individuals' own earnings and the earnings of others, and vary in whether they penalize inequality or just weigh the average of individuals' own earnings versus the earnings of others.

Isaac, Walker, and Williams (1994) propose a nonstandard "for-ward"-looking model of behavior. Their model is nonstandard since it moves away from the logic of backward induction for finite repetitions of a game. Participants are considered to be forward-looking in the sense of gains from cooperative play. Participants allocate tokens toward the group good in an effort to solicit cooperation. Their approach is composed of three principle components: (1) the assumption that individual i believes his/her decisions will have a signaling content to others, (2) a benchmark earnings level for measuring the success of signaling, and (3) the formulation of a subjective probability function for evaluating the likelihood of success. In this model, ceteris paribus, the likelihood that a signal (allocations to the group account) will succeed increases with both group size and *mpcr*.

Janssen and Ahn (2006) tested a diverse set of other-regarding prefer-ence formulations, signaling behavior, and learning models on experimen-tal data from Isaac and Walker (1988a) and Isaac, Walker, and Williams (1994). Janssen and Ahn concluded that if the experimental data are to be explained, heterogeneity of preferences, signaling, and learning need to be included in a hybrid model using maximum likelihood estimations with penalties for increased complexity of the model.

On another theme, some scholars explain contributions by the structure of the situation rather than by diverse preference functions. They posit that individuals are willing to contribute if others do since they would be better off, but are unwilling to be a "sucker" by contributing when oth-ers do not contribute, as only the defectors get good returns. Bagnoli and Lipman (1989) develop a theoretical model, for example, where simul-taneous, voluntary contributions to the production of a discrete public good are guaranteed to be returned if insufficient contributions are made to provide the good. Theoretically, this payback mechanism creates a sense of security for each individual that their contributions will be ac-cepted only if others contribute sufficiently that the public good can be obtained. Otherwise, all will receive the same payoff and no public good will be produced. Bagnoli and McKee (1991) tested the prediction and found strong empirical support for it. Participants were more willing to contribute to public goods when they were assured that they were pro-tected against free-riding by those who did not contribute.[6]

Common-Pool Resource Experiments

A common-pool resource (CPR)—such as a lake, an irrigation system, a fishing ground, a forest, the Internet, or the stratosphere—is a natural or man-made resource from which one person's use subtracts units not available to others, and it is difficult to exclude or limit users once the resource is provided by nature or produced by humans (E. Ostrom, Gardner, and Walker 1994). Consequently, one of the important problems facing the joint users of a common-pool resource is known as the "appropriation problem." This means that given the incentives, individuals may appropriate more resource units when acting independently than they do when they find some way of coordinating their appropriation activities. Joint users of a common-pool resource often face many other problems including assignment problems, technological externality problems, provision problems, and maintenance problems. And the specific character of each of these problems differs substantially from one resource to the next. The initial CPR experiments of E. Ostrom, Gardner, and Walker (1994) focused on appropriation problems, since those are what most policy analysts associate with "the tragedy of the commons." In more recent experiments, discussed on pages 164–67, more focus is given to ecological dynamics.

The initial CPR experiments of E. Ostrom, Gardner, and Walker (1994) started with a static, baseline situation that was as simple as the researchers could specify without losing crucial aspects of the problems that real harvesters face. A quadratic production function was used for the resource itself—the payoff that one participant could obtain was similar to the theoretical function specified by Gordon (1954). The experiments were formulated in the following way. The initial resource endowment of each participant consisted of a given set of tokens that the participant allocates between two markets: Market 1, which had a fixed return; and Market 2, which functioned as a collective resource and had a return determined in part by the actions of the other participants in the experiment. Each participant i chose to invest a portion x_i of his/her endowment of ω in the common resource Market 2, and the remaining portion $\omega - x_i$ is then invested in Market 1. The payoff function as used in E. Ostrom, Gardner, and Walker (1994) was

$$u_i(\mathbf{x}) = \begin{array}{ll} 0.05 \cdot \omega & \text{if } x_i = 0 \\ 0.05 \cdot (\omega - x_i) + (x_i / \sum x_i) \cdot F(\sum x_i) & \text{if } x_i > 0 \end{array} \tag{6.2}$$

where

$$F(\sum x_i) = (23 \cdot \sum_{i=1}^{8} x_i - 0.25 \cdot (\sum_{i=1}^{8} x_i)^2)/100 \tag{6.3}$$

According to this formula, the payoff of someone investing all ω tokens in Market 1 ($x_i = 0$) is $0.05 \cdot \omega$. The return for Market 1 is like a fixed wage paid according to the hours invested in working. Investing a part or all of the tokens in Market 2 ($x_i > 0$) yields an outcome that depends on the investments of the other participants. If the participants behave according to the noncooperative game theory, they will invest according to the Nash equilibrium, where each participant maximizes payoff given the strategies chosen by the other participants.

Basically, if appropriators put all of their assets into their outside option, they receive a certain return equal to the amount of their endowment times an unchanging rate. If appropriators put some of their endowed assets into the outside option and some into the common-pool resource, they get part of their return from the outside option and the rest from their proportional investment in the common-pool resource.

The participants received aggregated information, so they did not know each individual's actions. Each participant was assigned tokens as their endowment in each round of play. In the first set of experiments, each participant received 10 tokens in each round. In later experiments, this was increased to 25 tokens. Their outside opportunity was valued at $.05 per token. They earned $.01 on each outcome unit they received from investing tokens in the common-pool resource. Participants were informed that they would participate in an experiment that would last no more than two hours. The number of rounds in each experiment varied between 20 and 30. In addition to being told the payoff function specifically, participants were provided with look-up tables that eased their task of determining outcomes depending on their own and others' decisions.

With these specifications, the predicted outcome for a finitely repeated game, where participants are not discounting the future and each participant is assumed to be maximizing monetary returns, is for each participant to invest 8 tokens in the common-pool resource for a total of 64 tokens. By design, the prediction is similar for both endowment levels (10 and 25). At this level of investment, they would each earn $.66 per round in the 10-token experiments and $.70 per round in the 25-token experiments.[7] The participants could, however, earn considerably more if the total number of tokens invested in the common-pool resource was 36 (rather than 64). This optimal level of investment would earn each participant $.91 per round in the 10-token experiment and $.83 per round in the 25-token experiment. The baseline experiment is an example of a commons dilemma in which the game-theoretic, predicted outcome involves substantial overuse of a common-pool resource (Nash equilibrium), while a much better outcome could be reached if participants were to lower their joint use relative to the Nash equilibrium.

Participants interacting in baseline experiments substantially overinvested as predicted. Participants in the 10-token experiments achieved, on average, 37 percent of the maximum earning from the common-pool experiment available to them, while participants in the 25-token experiments received –3 percent (E. Ostrom, Gardner, and Walker 1994, 116). At the individual level, participants rarely invested 8 tokens—the predicted level of investment at the Nash equilibrium. Instead, all experiments provided evidence of an unpredicted and strong pulsing pattern in which individuals appear to increase their investments in the common-pool resource until there is a strong reduction in yield, at which time they tend to reduce their investments leading to an increase in yields. The pattern is repeated over time. At an aggregate level, behavior approximates the predicted Nash equilibrium in the 10-token experiments, but is far worse than predicted in the early rounds of the 25-token experiment and only begins to approach the predicted level in later rounds.

INSIGHTS FROM PUBLIC GOODS AND COMMON-POOL RESOURCE EXPERIMENTS IN THE LABORATORY

One way of viewing the discrepancy between theoretical predictions and experimental results of both public goods provision and CPR game situations is that the standard noncooperative theory may offer a useful method for organizing the behavior of some individuals, but not *all*. As we suggested above, the narrow rational-choice model of maximizing individual returns can be used to explain behavior in some situations and about some individuals, but not all. In repeated experiments without communication, the group average moved toward the Nash equilibria in the last rounds of the experiment. Even in experiments with many repetitions, however, equilibria strategies are seldom observed for all individuals in a group. Participants pursue a diversity of strategies that can be roughly categorized into selfish rational behavior, altruistic behavior, and conditionally cooperative behavior. The last of these strategies covers the largest segment of the observed behavior and refers to participants who have a tendency to cooperate if others cooperate. In this section, we will discuss a number of additional treatments that are performed with both public goods and CPR games: face-to-face communication, heterogeneity, and costly sanctioning. In contrast to the prediction of conventional theories, "cheap talk" has a positive effect on cooperation and participants invest in sanctioning others.

Face-to-Face Communication in the Laboratory

In face-to-face communication experiments, participants were authorized to communicate with one another in a group setting before returning to their terminals to make their own private decisions. This provided an opportunity for "cheap talk," where agreements are not enforced by an external authority. In the context of noncooperative game theory, "cheap talk" is viewed as irrelevant. The same outcome is predicted as in the baseline experiment, since a participant can promise to cooperate but no external "third party" ensures that the promise is fulfilled (Harsanyi and Selten 1988, 3).

In typical repeated communication experiments, participants first made ten rounds of decisions in the context of the baseline appropriation game. After the tenth round, participants listened to an announcement that they would have an open group discussion before each of the next rounds of the experiment. The participants left their terminals and sat in a circle facing one another. After each discussion, they returned to their terminals to enter their anonymous decisions. Participants used face-to-face communication to discuss together what strategy would gain them the best outcomes and to agree—if possible—on what everyone should invest in the subsequent rounds. After each decision round, they learned what their aggregate investments had been. Thus they learned whether total investments were greater than those they had agreed to. While in many rounds, participants did exactly as they had promised one another they would do, some defections did occur. If promises were not kept, participants used this information about the aggregate investment levels to castigate the unknown participant(s) who had not kept to their agreement.

This opportunity for repeated face-to-face communication was extremely successful in increasing joint returns in the CPR experiments where participants in the 10-token setting obtained close to 100 percent of the maximum available returns (E. Ostrom, Gardner, and Walker 1994, 154). In the 25-token experiments, participants also improved their overall performance to 75 percent of the maximum available returns. The temptation to defect, however, was greater in the 25-token experiments. It is important to note that participants were not able to identify the individual decisions of the other participants.

That participants had internalized norms regarding the importance of keeping promises is evidenced by several of their behaviors. Simply promising to cut back on their investments in the common-pool resource led most participants to change their investment pattern. Second, participants were indignant about evidence of investment levels higher than promised and expressed their anger openly. Third, those who broke their promise tended to revert to the promised level after hearing the verbal tongue-lashing of their colleagues. Communication experiments with public goods provision dilemmas show an increase in contributions (Isaac and Walker 1988b; Orbell, van de Kragt, and Dawes 1988). Bochet, Page, and Putterman (2006) found that chat-room communication is almost as effective as face-to-face communication.

The combined impact of group size and face-to-face communication was studied in a series of experiments carried out with 189 scholars or PhD students from 41 countries around the world who attended summer seminars at Indiana University between 1998 and 2003 or one held at the Slovak Academy of Sciences in June 2007 (Ahn, Ostrom, and Walker 2009). The experiment was always held on the first morning, when the participants did not yet know each other. Twenty-one participants were brought together in one room and told that they had been assigned to one of three groups jointly harvesting from a common-pool resource and using the core CPR experiment described above (and in E. Ostrom, Gardner, and Walker 1994). In the first two rounds, participants remained in a large room and no communication was allowed. For the third and fourth rounds, participants were allowed to engage in face-to-face communication in this large group but still did not know who the others were in their own group. In the fifth and sixth rounds, the participants were divided into their groups and went to three smaller rooms to continue face-to-face communication. The communication permitted in the third and fourth rounds in a large group did lead to a substantial increase in cooperation, and payoffs were much closer to optimal than to the predicted Nash equilibrium. The capacity to know who was in their group and to discuss options with known colleagues during the fifth and sixth rounds enabled participants to gain sufficient trust to move very close to optimal. After the experiment, participants stressed the importance of knowing who was in their smaller group for increasing trust and willingness to cooperate.

Findings from these communication experiments are consistent with a large number of studies of the impact of face-to-face communication on the capacity of participants to solve a variety of social dilemma problems (see E. Ostrom and Walker 1991; Sally 1995). While the findings confirm that communication makes a major difference in outcomes, some debate exists as to *why* communication alone leads to better results (Buchan, Johnson, and Croson 2006). In some experiments, research showed that increased performance with communication is not due to better understanding of the experiment (Edney and Harper 1978; Kerr and Kaufman-Gilliland 1994). In the CPR experiments where the quadratic equation was used for the payoff function, participants did initially spend time trying to be sure they understood what the group optimum was and how to allocate that to individuals. A review by Shankar and Pavitt (2002) suggests that voicing of commitments and development of group identity and norms seem to be the best explanation for why communication makes a difference.

Another reason may be the revelation of a participant's type since the uncertainty of participants' types is a source of incomplete information in experimental games. For example, face-to-face communication (and resulting verbal commitments) may change participants' expectations of other participants' responses. In particular, if a participant believes that other participants are reciprocators (i.e., will cooperate in response to cooperative play), that participant may play cooperatively to induce cooperation from others. In this case, cooperating can be sustained as rational play in the framework of incomplete information regarding participant types.

In another set of experiments where five out of eight subjects had to contribute a small sum in order to enable a communication round, E. Ostrom and Walker (1991) found that the cost of getting to a communication period was a barrier. Some groups were not able to organize communication rounds effectively. Others had difficulty using communication regularly enough to deal with players who had not kept their prior agreements. In the main, however, these groups were able to increase the efficiency of their investments from 42 percent to 80 percent (E. Ostrom and Walker 1991, 317).

Heterogeneity

Steven Hackett, Edella Schlager, and James Walker (1994) conducted a set of CPR experiments where they explored whether communication could ameliorate the problems identified in field settings related to heterogeneity among appropriators. As we discussed in earlier chapters, the literature from field settings has repeatedly listed heterogeneity as a serious deterrent to cooperation (Hackett 1992; R. Hardin 1982; Libecap and Wiggins 1984; Wiggins and Libecap 1987). For example, Kanbur argues,

> theory and evidence would seem to suggest that cooperative agreements are more likely to come about in groups that are homogeneous in the relevant economic dimension, and they are more likely to break down as heterogeneity along this dimension increases. (1992, 21–22)

The task of agreeing to and sustaining agreements for efficient CPR appropriation is more difficult for heterogeneous appropriators because of the distributional conflict associated with alternative sharing rules. In heterogeneous settings, different sharing rules may produce different distributions of earnings across appropriators. While all appropriators may be made better off by cooperating, some will benefit more than others, depending upon the sharing rule chosen. Consequently, appropriators may fail to cooperate on the adoption of a sharing rule because they cannot agree upon what would constitute a fair distribution of benefits produced by cooperating.

In order to address appropriator heterogeneity, the Hackett, Schlager, and Walker experimental design allows for two levels of input endowments. One subset of appropriators have large endowments; the remaining appropriators have small endowments. Parameters were chosen so that the Nash equilibrium is symmetric within appropriator type, but asymmetric across type; large appropriators allocate more inputs to the CPR than do small appropriators.[8] This is accomplished by having the small participants' endowment be a binding constraint in equilibrium. While the asymmetric Nash equilibrium depends critically on the endowment parameter ω, the group payoff maximizing level of allocation does not. Many different rules can distribute individual allocations to the CPR such that total rents from the CPR are maximized. Since endowments are heterogeneous, different rules (e.g., equal allocation to the CPR versus CPR allocations proportionate with endowment) imply different wealth distributions. Such inequities may lead to disagreement over the type of sharing rule, and ultimately to a reduction in CPR rents.

In order for communication to enhance joint CPR payoffs, the appropriators must agree on (1) the target level of group allocations to the CPR and (2) a strategy for allocating the target input allocation across appropriators. They must also create the trust in one another's reciprocity to attenuate cheating, since agreements are nonbinding. The existence of heterogeneity in endowments and in historic allocation levels has no effect on (1) but presumably elicits disagreement over (2), which in turn may impair the development of trust. Participants knew with certainty the total number of decision makers in the group, their own token endowment, the total number of tokens in the group, the productivity characteristics of the CPR, and the number of decision rounds in the current treatment condition. Individual token endowments were publicly known. After each round, participants were shown a display that recorded their profits in each market for that round, total group token allocations to Market 2, and a total of their cumulative profits for the experiment. During the experiment, participants could request, through the computer, this information for all previous rounds for the current treatment condition. Participants received no information regarding other participants' individual allocation decisions. The specific parameters used for these experiments were that each small participant was endowed with 8 tokens per round, each large participant with 24.

Participants engaged in two (consecutive) ten-round sequences of the asymmetric game. In the first ten rounds, participants were not allowed to communicate. In the final ten rounds, the participants were informed that prior to each decision round they would have the opportunity to discuss the allocation problem. In the first ten rounds, the groups' actions converged toward a Nash equilibrium. After face-to-face communication between rounds was permitted, the observed behavior at the group level moved toward a cooperative equilibrium. Thus, even in situations of heterogeneity of endowments, "cheap talk" leads to an increase in cooperative behavior.

Sanctioning Experiments

Participants in most field settings related to natural resources are able to communicate with one another on a face-to-face basis, at least from time to time, either in formally constituted meetings or at social gatherings. Further, in many field settings, participants have also devised a variety of formal or informal ways of sanctioning one another if rules are broken. In fact, the amazing speed with which irrigators responded to a perceived infraction while Ostrom was studying a system in Nepal led her to urge Roy Gardner and James Walker to help design an experiment where they could study monitoring and sanctioning in the lab (see chapter 10). Engaging in costly monitoring and sanctioning behavior was not consistent with the theory of norm-free, complete rationality (Elster 1989, 40–41). Thus it was important to ascertain whether participants in a controlled setting would actually pay in order to assess a financial punishment on the behavior of other participants. The short answer to this question is yes.

Participants played ten rounds of the baseline CPR game modified so that the individual investments in each round were reported as well as the total outcomes (E. Ostrom, Walker, and Gardner 1992). Participants were then told that in the subsequent rounds they would have an opportunity to pay a fee in order to impose a fine on the payoffs received by another participant. The fees ranged in experiments from $.05 to $.20 and the fines from $.10 to $.80. In brief, the finding from this series of experiments is that much more sanctioning occurs than the zero level predicted. Most of the sanctions were directed at subjects who had ordered high levels of tokens. Participants react both to the cost of sanctioning and to the fee/fine relationships. They sanction more when the cost of sanctioning is less and when the ratio of the fine to the fee is higher (E. Ostrom, Walker, and Gardner 1992). Participants did increase gross benefits through their sanctioning but *reduced* their net returns substantially owing to the high use of costly sanctions.

Similar findings exist for public goods provision experiments where punishers typically punish low contributors (Fehr and Gächter 2002; Yamagishi 1986). The higher the level of sanctioning, the higher the level of contributions observed in public goods experiments (Nikiforakis and Normann 2008). With the cost of sanctioning taken into account, a low penalty level will not increase the contributions to the public goods to outweigh the extra costs. Sanctioning is primarily directed at those who defected, but a few sanctions appear to be directed by those who had been fined in a form of "blind revenge" against those who were cooperators and whom they thus suspected of having sanctioned them (Saijo and Nakamura 1995). Furthermore, the spiteful behavior disappears when the cost of sanctioning is the same as the penalty (Falk, Fehr, and Fischbacher 2005). When participants are allowed to punish back, the benefit of punishment is reduced (Cinyabuguma, Page, and Putterman 2006; Denant-Boemont, Masclet, and Noussair 2007; Nikiforakis 2008). In those experiments, participants could make an additional punishment decision after they had a first decision round on punishment. Without communication and agreement about a punishment rule, subjects do use punishment in both public goods and common-pool resource games more than is predicted by theory. As a result, gross payoffs are increased but net payoffs are reduced by the cost of punishment.

Casari and Luini (2009) explored the robustness of these findings as well as whether a "consensual" punishment rule would improve net pay-offs. In a public goods setting, with five participants from a group of twenty participants randomly assigned to each round, Casari and Luini compared a "consensual" treatment to simply allowing subjects to sanction one another simultaneously or sequentially. In the consensual design, a subject is actually punished only if two or more other subjects indicate a willingness to pay for a sanction. When only one subject indicates a willingness to sanction, no change is made in any of the earnings of participants. The researchers found that under the consensual design, contribution levels increased and that net payoffs were higher. By contrast, allowing any subject to sanction any other subject frequently led to the punishment of high contributors, as had occurred in public goods experiments with costly punishment discussed above.

When participants are allowed to move between groups, they tend to choose the group in which sanctioning is possible (Gürek, Irlenbusch, and Rockenbach 2006). In this public goods experiment, individuals could choose each round to join the group with or without costly sanctioning. Initially, fewer than half of the participants joined the group with costly sanctioning. The level of contributions in this group, however, was twice as high as that of the group without costly sanctioning. By the end of thirty rounds, almost all the participants joined the group with the costly sanctioning option where the contributions reached almost 100 percent and few sanctions were needed.

FIELD EXPERIMENTS

A drawback of laboratory experiments is the rather homogeneous subject pool in terms of age, education, and experience with governing natural resources that are salient to them. Performing experiments outside a university setting leads generally to greater diversity in the participant pool. Performing experiments outside an educational setting requires special attention to avoid any negative impacts on the local host communities. It is also important to have good connections with the local leaders and to have pretested the experiments with participants similar to the antici- pated subject pool.

A very interesting series of replications and extensions of CPR ex- periments has been conducted by Juan-Camilo Cardenas (2000) and colleagues using field laboratories set up in school buildings in rural Co- lombia rather than a computer-based laboratory on a university campus. Cardenas initially invited more than two hundred villagers to participate in a series of experiments. Several closely paralleled the ones conducted at Indiana University, while others addressed an extended set of ques- tions. The villagers whom Cardenas invited were actual users both of lo- cal forests, for the extraction of firewood, natural fibers, and log timber, and of local water resources. One of the basic questions he wanted to pursue was whether experienced villagers, who were heavily dependent on local forests for wood products, would behave in a manner broadly consistent with that of undergraduate students at an American Big Ten university.

The answer to this first question turned out to be positive. He wrote his instructions in Spanish and in a manner that would be easily under- stood by villagers. Instead of tokens—which are an easy medium for un- dergraduates to understand—he asked villagers to decide on how many months a year they would spend in the forest gathering wood products as contrasted to using their time otherwise. Each villager had a copy of a payoff table, which was the same as that of the other seven participants. The table showed that as the number of months that each individual spent in the forest increased, the individual would gain more returns but that the return to all of them depended on everyone's keeping the har- vesting time to a very low level.

In the baseline, no-communication experiments, Cardenas found a pat- tern similar to earlier findings with participants from Indiana University. Villagers substantially overinvested in appropriation from the resource. While there was considerable variation among groups, villagers on aver- age achieved 57.7 percent of their optimal return in the last three rounds of the baseline experiments (Cardenas 2000, 316).

Face-to-face communication enabled the villagers to increase efficiency on average to 76.1 percent of optimal. Surveys filled in after the experi- ments were completed were used by Cardenas to explain the considerable variation among groups. He found, for example, that when most mem- bers of the group were already familiar with common-pool resources such as the collective use of a mangrove, they used the communication rounds more effectively than when most members of the group were dependent primarily on their own assets. Cardenas also found that "social distance and group inequality based on the economic wealth of the people in the group seemed to constrain the effectiveness of communication for this same sample of groups" (Cardenas 2000, 317; see also Cardenas 2003).

Cardenas, Ahn, and Ostrom (2004) discuss communication experiments in Colombia in which no communication was allowed in the first ten rounds, and three treatments were distinguished for the last ten rounds of the experiment. Besides the default case of no communication, Cardenas and colleagues distinguished a one-shot communication of five minutes before round 11, and repeated communication after each round from round 11 onward. When there was repeated communication, the level of extraction was lower than the default level and remained at that level. A one-shot communication round led initially to the same reduction of extraction, but this extraction level increased over the rounds to a level between the default and the repeated communication treatments in round 20. The ability of participants to convince each other repeatedly of their willingness to cooperate is the proposed explanation for the greater effectiveness of repeated communication.

Cardenas, Stranlund, and Willis (2000) report on another fascinating extension. In five experiments, the villagers were given a chance to communicate after the initial ten rounds of the baseline condition. In five other experiments, they were told that a new regulation would go into force that mandated that they should spend no more than the optimal level of time in the forest each round (which, in this case, was one month per villager). They were told that there would be a 50 percent chance that conformance to the rule would be monitored each round. The experimenter rolled a dice in front of the participants each round to determine whether an inspection would take place. If an even number showed up, there would be an inspection. The experimenter then drew a number from chits numbered between 1 and 8 placed in a hat to determine who would be inspected. Thus the probability that anyone would be inspected was 1/16 per round—a low but realistic probability for monitoring forest harvesting in rural areas in developing countries. The monitor checked the investment of the person whose number was drawn without revealing the result to others. If the person was over the limit imposed, the penalty was subtracted from the payoff to that person. No statement was made to others as to whether the appropriator was complying with regulations or not.

The participants in this experimental condition actually increased their withdrawal levels in contrast to behavior when no rule was imposed and face-to-face communication was allowed. What was remarkable about this experiment was that participants who were simply allowed to communicate with one another on a face-to-face basis were able to achieve a higher joint return than the participants who had an optimal but imperfectly enforced external rule imposed on them. Other scholars have also found that externally imposed regulations that lead to higher joint returns "crowded out" voluntary cooperative behavior arrived at independently or through communication (see Frey and Oberholzer-Gee 1997; Reeson and Tisdell 2008). Vollan (2008) conducted a framed field experiment in Namibia and South Africa and found that the crowding-out effect depended on three factors: how controlling versus supportive is the external intervention, the level of trust within a society, and the level of self-determination within the group.

In recent field experiments conducted in coastal fishing villages of Colombia, Lopez et al. (forthcoming) conducted a series of experiments to dig even deeper into the conditions whereby external policies complement or retard local efforts to cooperate. In the first set of ten rounds of a public goods experiment, individual contributions (but not the real names of the subjects) were posted on a board that all participants could see. Then participants chose to sanction or not to sanction another participant at a cost to themselves. The introduction of public knowledge and costly sanctioning in these experiments produced very high contributions. In a second stage, Lopez and colleagues introduced an external requirement that each participant contribute all of his or her tokens to the public good; randomly selected subjects were to impose a fine if a violation of this rule was found. In this second condition, participants contributed fully, and sanctions imposed by the participants or the external authorities were rarely incurred. Thus, in an experiment where participants perceived complementarity between their own actions and those of an external enforcer, as well as having public information to assure them that others were following the rules, contributions to the public good were close to optimal.

Ernst Fehr and Andreas Leibbrandt (2008) have conducted an interesting set of public goods experiments with fishers who harvest from an "open-access" inland lake in northeastern Brazil. They found that a high percentage (87 percent) of fishers contributed in the first period of the field experiment, and that contributions leveled off in the remaining periods as in laboratory experiments. Data obtained about expectations of the contributions of others was found to be positively related to a fisher's own contribution levels in the first period—thus most of the fishers were "conditional cooperators." Fehr and Leibbrandt also examined the mesh size of the nets used by individual fishermen and found that those who contributed more in the public goods experiment used nets with bigger mesh sizes. Larger mesh sizes allow young fish to escape, grow larger, and reproduce at a higher level than they do if they are caught when they are still small. In other words, cooperation in the field lab was consistent with observed cooperation related to a real CPR dilemma: do you individually capture more fish today or let some escape so they can replenish the stock that you and others can draw on in the future? The researchers conclude that the "fact that our laboratory measure for other-regarding preferences predicts field behavior increases our confidence about the behavioral relevance of other-regarding preferences gained from laboratory experiments" (Fehr and Leibbrandt 2008, 17).

Velez, Stranlund, and Murphy (2009) report on common-pool experiments in fishery villages in Colombia. During their field experiment, they also asked about the expectations the participants had about the actions of others. With this information they could test different motivational drivers for their decisions such as self-interest, altruism, reciprocity, inequity aversion, and conformity. Their analysis indicates that their data are consistent with conformity, not with reciprocity, altruism, and inequity aversion. Given the contrast to Fehr and Leibbrandt (2008), it is evident that more research on this topic needs to be performed.

Toward a New Generation of Experiments of Commons Dilemmas

Experiments on CPRs and public goods have shown that many predictions of the conventional theory of collective action do not hold; more cooperation occurs than predicted, "cheap talk" increases cooperation, and participants invest in sanctioning free-riders. Experiments have also established that there is motivational heterogeneity in investment or contribution decisions as well as in decisions on sanctioning.

Several recent developments in experimental design indicate directions for the next generation of experiments to make them more relevant with regard to findings from case studies. The first development is the inclusion of specific ecological dynamics. A substantial literature focuses on the fit between institutions and ecological dynamics (e.g., Young 2002). An institutional arrangement that works effectively for one resource problem might be a dismal failure if applied to another resource problem (Acheson 2006). This would not be so problematic if clear classifications of case studies existed. For example, whether the resource units are mobile (fishery, pastoralism) or whether infrastructure is developed to guide the resource flow (irrigation systems) have been identified as important attributes of resources affecting behavior (Janssen, Anderies, and Ostrom 2007; Schlager, Blomquist, and Tang 1994). Some initial experiments have been performed with more dynamic common-pool resources. When the common-pool resource could probabilistically be destroyed (Walker and Gardner 1992), or when cost of extraction was dependent on decisions in previous rounds (Herr, Gardner, and Walker 1997), the level of overharvesting was increased compared to the levels observed in the traditional static setting discussed earlier in this chapter.

The second development is to enhance the focus on the innovation of formal rules for more complex dilemma situations. This is possible if we allow more types of decisions to be made during the experiments. Current experiments that include sanctioning and communication take into account only the level of investment. They do not include discussions about who is allowed to appropriate when and where, with what technology, and how monitoring is arranged. More complex rule structures become relevant when one includes more complex ecological dynamics.

The third desirable development is the creation of large-scale experiments. An increasing number of social activities leave digital trails that can be collected by sophisticated data-mining techniques. This leads to the possibility of collecting large over-time data sets of social dynamics. In recent years, social scientists have started to realize the research potential of the digital worlds as natural experiments—for example, by studying the societies of online games (Bainbridge 2007; Castranova 2005) or the institutions of open source software projects (Schweik and English 2007). Moreover, the Internet provides a unique opportunity to perform large social science experiments in a controlled setting (Dodds, Muhamad, and Watts 2003; Resnick et al. 2006). The increasing use of virtual worlds by the younger generation also provides new research opportunities (Bainbridge 2007). We will discuss some initial results from these new developments.

New Developments in Laboratory Experiments

In typical commons dilemma experiments, participants make decisions and type in numbers on a computer screen with the payoff table as their information source. In a recent set of dynamic resource games, participants are able to make decisions in real time and to chat via text messages.

Janssen et al. (2008) introduce an experimental environment that is designed to have a much richer set of possible decisions by participants.[9] A group of participants interact in real time to harvest tokens from a spatially explicit renewable resource. Participants move their avatars[10] on the screen and make decisions on where to go on a grid and harvest tokens, and how fast to move on the screen. Therefore, they make dozens of decisions during the few minutes of each round in an experiment. Instead of one decision per round (and perhaps twenty-five to thirty decisions in the full experiment), participants can make many hundreds of decisions during an experiment—if they agree on ways to allocate either space or time to one another so that they do not overharvest the resource and face an empty screen with no more decisions to be made.

Owing to the richness of the experimental environment, it is suitable for the study of how participants innovate rules in a complex environment. They cannot make an estimate of the total quantity of resource units available, but they can see resource renewal patterns and craft innovative rules for allocating space and time to one another as a way of improving their returns from the use of the common resource. Another benefit of this experimental environment is the link with agent-based modeling. With this experimental environment, actual people make decisions within a dynamic artificial environment for which we can record all the decisions. This enables us to test alternative models of decision making with the recorded data.

By using chat via text messages between the rounds, we can record all relevant information about the communication and analyze the content of the communication. Earlier experiments have shown that text chat and face-to-face communication do not lead to significant differences in results (Bochet, Page, and Putterman 2006). As is expected, communication increases performance. In contrast with traditional experiments, the availability of the whole communication stream makes it possible to analyze the content and identify what aspects of communication lead to higher performance. Initial analysis reported in Janssen (forthcoming) shows that more text messages and more equal contribution of text messages explain differences in performance between groups, rather than the content of the messages (in line with Buchan, Johnson, and Croson 2006).

An example of a recent experimental design brings a number of participants together in a spatially explicit environment of hundreds of cells. Participants harvest a token by moving their avatar's location on top of the token. They move their avatar by pressing the arrow keys (left, right, up, and down). Participants can collect tokens during a number of rounds, each of which is approximately four minutes. Each token harvested is worth a few cents. The resource renewal rate is density dependent. That is, as the number of tokens around an empty cell increases, the probability increases that in the next time step a token will appear on the empty cell (see figures 6.3 and 6.4). The probability p_t is linearly related to the number of neighbors: $p_t = p^* n_t / N$ where n_t is the number of neighboring cells containing a token, and N (= 8) the number of neighboring cells. The parameter p is defined in such a way that the renewal of the resource is quick enough to be observed by the participants, but sufficiently slow that the participants experience a dilemma between immediate, individual benefits and longer-term, group benefits. If participants rapidly collect as many tokens as they can, they will quickly exhaust the resource and no tokens will remain on the screen. Once every token has been harvested, no chance exists for any new tokens to be created during an experimental round.

In these experiments, participants begin with an individual practice round to get familiar with the environment. Then an individual round is performed with monetary incentives. Subsequently, the participants are randomly matched into groups for a number of group rounds with a size of the resource that is four times that of the individual round. When participants have not been able to communicate, a tragedy of the commons is observed (figure 6.5). After communication, the resource size is maintained, leading to a 70 percent higher earning. The participants mainly agree to split the resource into four equal parts, and to wait and harvest slowly for a few minutes. The time left is known to the participants, and they typically formulate a rule that "with x seconds left take what you can."[11]

This dynamic environment can be adjusted to diverse sets of stylized ecologies mimicking resource dynamics of fishery, pastoralism, and forestry by changing mobility of resources, spatial heterogeneity of regrowth, and visibility of the resource. The software of this new-generation experiment can be found at http://commons.asu.edu/.

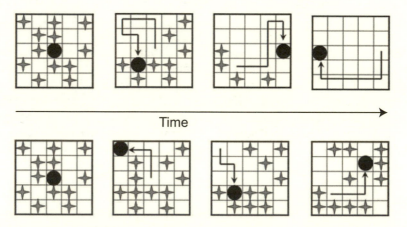

Time

Fig. 6.3. Four snapshots of two harvesting strategies by two different types of subjects in a hypothetical situation of a 5 × 5 resource, where resource units are depicted by star-shaped objects. On the top row in the figure above, the subject moves his/her avatar (circle) eight steps per time period. On the bottom row, the subject moves his/her avatar only four steps per time period. *Source*: Adapted from Janssen and Ostrom 2008, 377.

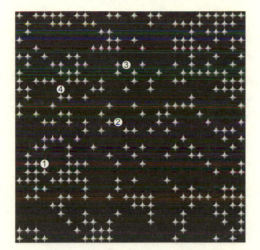

Fig. 6.4. Screen view of the renewable resource, where the diamond-shaped tokens are the potentially regenerating resource units, black cells are empty cells, and the four dots are the avatars of the participants.

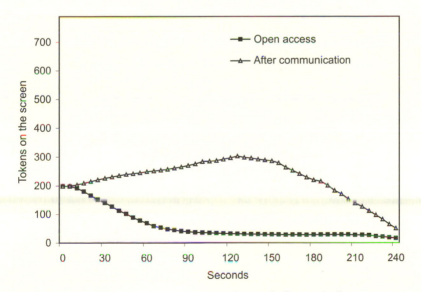

Fig. 6.5. Average resource size over six experiments before and after communication.

Toward a New Generation of Field Experiments

Like the laboratory experiments, a new development in field experiments is the inclusion of more relevant ecological dynamics and the change of formal rules in studying the ability to overcome common-pool resource dilemmas. Cardenas, Janssen, and Bousquet (forthcoming) discuss three kinds of experiments representing dilemmas in forestry, fishery, and irrigation. In contrast to the laboratory experiments where subjects do not share experiences in harvesting resources on which they directly depend, are assigned "tokens," and use simple pencil-and-paper or computerized designs, experiments in the field are with stakeholders who face the dilemmas of harvesting natural resources without destroying them in their daily lives. The ecological dynamics are stylized but well understood by the participants.

The experiments were held in three villages in Thailand and three villages in Colombia. Villages were selected that relied extensively on use of one of three resource appropriation activities: fishery, forestry, and irrigation. For each location, permission to perform experiments was given, when needed, by the heads of villages. After two years of experimental design and pretests, the experiments were conducted during the first six months of 2007. Typically, four days of experiments were followed by in-depth interviews with a sample of relevant stakeholders of the village and extensive discussion with villagers about the formal and informal rules of resource use in their own community.

In each village, all three resource games were conducted with 4 groups of 5 people. As a result, 360 individuals participated in the first set of experiments. The general outline of the experiments is as follows. After instructions and practice rounds, the participants play ten rounds. They are not told the number of rounds in advance. After the tenth round, three different rules are presented to the participants. They then vote on which rule they wish to have implemented in a subsequent series of rounds. The three rules represent a property type of rule, a lottery type of rule, and a rotation type of rule, and are all aimed at solving the resource dilemma.[12] In the property type of rule, only a certain quantity of harvest is allowed. In the lottery type of rule, the order in which participants have legal access to the resource is randomly drawn. In the rotation type of rule, the order in which people have legal access to the resource is predetermined. The participants turn in their vote, and are asked to fill out a brief survey on their opinions about characteristics of the rules, before the result is announced. If two rules get two votes, an additional round of votes between those two candidates is used to define the final chosen rule. Ten rounds are played with the new rule implemented. The first round after the vote has the same starting situation as round 1 of the experiment.

In the forestry game, the basic decision was how much to take from a renewable resource. In the fishery game, there were two decisions to be made each round: where to fish and how much effort to put in. When more than a certain level of effort was put into fishing in one location, the payoff table for that location flipped to a low payoff table. This could be reversed only if the site experienced a low harvest level for two rounds. In the irrigation game, the participants first needed to decide how much to invest in the public good, the infrastructure that generates an amount of water available for farming. Then, in an order of upstream to downstream, participants could take from the water available.

Initial insights are that participants do not harvest all of the resources, and that the social and ecological dynamics are path-dependent. Once a fishery group ends up with low payoff tables, it is difficult for them to get out of the trap. An irrigation group where upstream participants take unequal shares experiences a lower investment in subsequent rounds in the public good by downstream participants. Another initial finding is that participants' trust in others in the community has a significant correlation with cooperative behavior in contrast to experience with typical rules related to a particular type of resource. Most groups favored the rotation rule when voting on the rule for the last ten rounds. A property type of rule was the least favorite among the resource users. Cardenas, Janssen, and Bousquet (forthcoming) are currently investigating in more detail how the prior experience of the participants affected their choices and behavior in the experiments.

Conclusion

Experiments have strong internal validity. This makes it possible for scholars to replicate important findings of others. Although small changes in the design of the experiments can lead to different results, the ability to replicate results leads to the slow accumulation of an ever more robust understanding. Another strength of experiments is their ability to test hypotheses from theory or observations of fieldwork. With regard to collective action of the commons, it is remarkable that field observations that were inconsistent with predictions from formal theory have been replicated repeatedly in controlled settings in the laboratory and in field experiments. It is now well established that "cheap talk" leads to increased cooperation in social dilemmas. Furthermore, costly sanctioning can have a positive effect on cooperation, especially if this is combined with communication or when costly sanctioning is self-imposed.

A disadvantage of laboratory experiments on common-pool resources and public goods is the lack of external validity given the simplicity of the designs, the frequent use of undergraduate students, the knowledge of the human subjects that they are in an experiment, the short time period in which decisions are made, the use of monetary incentives, and the abstract dilemmas given to the human subjects. Field experiments bring more context into the experiments and use subjects who have relevant knowledge of collective action on the commons. Nevertheless, results from field experiments cannot themselves be generalized.

The pros and cons of experiments also show the importance of combining them with other methods such as those described in part II. Case studies provide important observations of how particular groups are or are not able to overcome collective-action dilemmas. The importance of such mechanisms can then be tested in a controlled experiment. Large-N studies provide an estimation of the effect of variables such as group size and heterogeneity, attributes of a resource, and broader governmental policies. Experiments can then provide quantitative data to test alternative formal models of human decision making in collective action.

CHAPTER SEVEN

Agent-Based Models of Collective Action

IN CHAPTER 6, we discussed how predictions of the impossibility of collective action are generated by formal models of social dilemmas that rely on assumptions regarding individual maximization of short-term benefits to self. In this chapter, we discuss agent-based modeling as one type of formal modeling that begins to identify the conditions under which cooperation can evolve.

Agent-based models explicitly define boundedly rational agents who are interacting with subsets of a whole population. The main aim of such models is to identify the set of microlevel mechanisms within which broader-level patterns evolve, such as cooperation in commons dilemmas. The models can be used to compare alternative explanations that are derived from the field and experimental studies described in chapters 2–6.

The modeling work described in this chapter is a brief and necessarily incomplete overview of the large body of work in the area of agent-based models of collective action. This chapter should not be read as a tutorial on agent-based modeling. For those who would like to learn more details about the methodology, we refer to Tesfatsion and Judd (2006), Miller and Page (2007), Gilbert (2007), and http://www.openabm.org/. We focus on the central topics that also are addressed in other chapters in this book, namely, under what conditions is a group of resource users more likely to engage in self-governance, engage in monitoring, and follow their own rules or those that external authorities impose on them.

A BRIEF INTRODUCTION TO AGENT-BASED MODELING

Essentially, agent-based models are computational representations of autonomous agents who interact with each other at a micro level leading to broader-level patterns. Agent-based models are information-processing algorithms based on various assumptions about the cognitive ability of the individual agents and the topology of their interactions (networks). Since there is a lot of freedom to specify the type of agents and their interactions, it is important to be explicit in the assumptions one is using in the models.

We will first discuss cellular automata, the simplest class of agent-based models. Cellular automata consist of agents without cognitive complexity and who interact only with their neighboring agents on a regular grid. All agents (cells) have the same transition strategies that define how states of cells change. Next, we briefly discuss networks that are important in defining the topology of interactions between agents. Finally, we introduce more advanced agent-based models that include cognitive processes. These tools can be used to develop simulation models in which one can do controlled experiments with a large number of computerized agents interacting with each other, and one can test the consequences of specific assumptions. As such, these simulation models can be used to explore the conditions under which cooperation emerges.

Cellular Automata

Originally, the cellular automata (CA) approach was introduced by John von Neumann and Stanislaw Ulam during the 1940s and 1950s at the Los Alamos National Laboratory. Most influential was the work of von Neumann on a reductionist model of life and self-reproduction, which was published after his untimely death (von Neumann and Burks 1966). A CA is a system with an environment of cells that can have a limited number of states. Time goes by in discrete steps. According to some (deterministic) strategies set by the researcher,[1] which are the same for each cell, the state of a cell in the next time step depends on its own present state and the states of all its surrounding cells in the present period. The resulting surprisingly complex dynamics that evolved from this simple set of strategies has led scholars in many disciplines, since the early 1970s, to study complex dynamic behavior of systems using the CA approach. The essential properties of a CA are:

- a regular n-dimensional lattice (in most cases, n is one or two dimensions), where each *cell* of this lattice has a discrete state; and
- a dynamical behavior, described by so-called *strategies*. These strategies describe the state of a cell for the next time step, depending on the states of the cells in the *neighborhood* of the cell.

The basic element of a CA is the *cell* that is represented by *states*. In the simplest case, each cell has the binary state 1 or 0, which may represent cooperate/defect in a social dilemma, adopt/not adopt a product, or built environment/nature in terms of land use. In more complex simulations, the cells can have multiple states. These cells are arranged in a lattice. The most common CAs are built in one or two dimensions. The cells can change state by transition strategies, which determine the state of the cells for the next time step. For example, if the cell with the highest payoff in the neighborhood in the last time step was a cooperator, cooperate in the next time step. Another example is for a cell to adopt a new innovation if x percent of the neighboring cells have also adopted it. In cellular automata, a strategy defines the state of a cell as a function of the *neighborhood* of the cell. The neighborhood defines the sphere of influence of the cells, and the type of neighborhood can affect the results of the simulations. The most common neighborhoods for two-dimensional CA are given in figure 7.1.

CAs have been very successful as theoretical models of complexity and have been applied to diverse natural sciences. A drawback of using CA for representing social agents is its extreme simplicity. For example, social networks are more complex than the local neighbors on a lattice. The number of possible states in which a social agent can be may be too large to be efficiently represented as a CA. Owing to these limitations, automata portraying social processes are represented by agents rather than cells, and the topology of interactions of agents is represented by networks.

Networks

Networks represent a given system in terms of its localized components, referred to as nodes, and the relations between these components, known as links. The social networks relevant for the study of collective action typically consider agents as nodes and social relations as links. Although quantitative studies of social networks have a history that stretches over a century (Freeman 2004), a tremendous growth has occurred during the

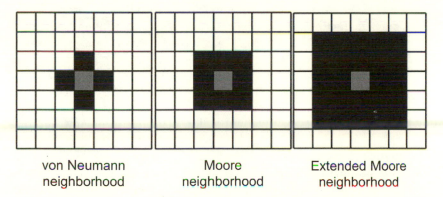

| von Neumann neighborhood | Moore neighborhood | Extended Moore neighborhood |

Fig. 7.1. Examples of cellular automata. The gray cell is the center cell; the black cells are the neighborhood cells. The states of these cells are used to calculate the next state of the (gray) center cell according to the defined strategy.

last few years of the study of the structure and dynamics of diverse types of social and biological networks. Social network analysis is a method of research for understanding the structure of a system and is based on graph theory and statistics. In recent years, caricature network types have been formulated that capture key network metrics found in empirical studies of various disciplines, such as small-world networks (Watts and Strogatz 1998) and scale-free networks (Barábasi and Albert 1999).

Small-world networks are characterized by high clustering and short-cuts within the network. This means that for many nodes in a social network, friends of friends are friends, but occasionally an agent has contacts with an agent in a very different part of the network. The combination of local clusters and occasional shortcuts generates the result that agents within such a network are connected with just a few steps. Scale-free networks represent the observation that there are many nodes with only a few connections, and only a few nodes with many connections. Network structure can have an impact on the level of cooperation in collective-action situations (Gould 1993), and we will discuss some of these findings from agent-based modeling later in this chapter.

Agents

Within agent-based models, agents are defined as autonomous decision-making algorithms. Agents can be goal-directed (satisfying or maximizing their posited utility), reactive (automatic responses to changes in the environment), and capable of interacting with other agents. One of the difficulties of this method is in balancing reactive and goal-directed behavior. Developing models with agents who have only reactive behavior is relatively simple. Much of humanlike behavior, however, can be represented as a combination of reactive and goal-directed behavior. An example of an agent with goal-directed behavior is a selfish rational agent who uses all information available to make decisions that maximize expected benefits to self. Although this agent model provides a good description of human behavior in highly competitive markets, as is confirmed in experimental studies, it is not satisfactory for the description of behavior in various decision situations of collective action (see chapter 9).

For decision situations involving collective-action problems, motivation, fairness, and preferences play an important role, and these characteristics may vary within the population of human agents. Furthermore, decision problems related to environmental management are often so complex that it is not likely that any one actor has full information and understanding of the problem and is able to evaluate all possible options. Models of bounded rationality have been used as an alternative (Simon 1955). Models of bounded rationality assume that people act intentionally but do not engage in utility maximization. In response to the costs of searching for information and cognitive limitations on processing information, people regularly make decisions based on partial information and heuristics or shortcuts. Furthermore, using concepts from psychology, we are able to include dimensions of economic agents such as emotions, motivations, and perceptions. Once the tight framework of the selfish rational actor is loosened, however, many frameworks are possible, and choosing the "right" one for analysis of a process is difficult. Within behavioral economics, attention has been paid mainly to models of learning that explain observed behavior in experiments (Camerer 2003). Others focus on fast and frugal heuristics of how individuals make choices about simple problems under time pressure (Gigerenzer et al. 1999).

A scheme of a simple model of two agents interacting with each other and their common resource is given in figure 7.2, which provides the simplest description of agent-based models applied to common-pool resources. Agents derive information from the environment that informs the perception they have about the state of their shared resources. Based on their goals and attributes, agents make decisions about what actions to perform, and these actions affect the environment. The agents can interact indirectly—for example, by affecting the common resource—or directly by communication. Communication might be used to exchange information about possible strategies, knowledge about the resource, and agreements about how to solve collective-action problems. The main dilemma concerning the architecture of agents with regard to the study of ecosystem management is the degree of complexity embodied in the agent. The models discussed in this chapter mainly focus on very simple decision strategies. In chapter 8, we will discuss the development of agent-based models based on diverse types of empirical data.

Strengths and Weaknesses of Agent-Based Models

Case study analysis, meta-analysis, and human-subject experiments have generated a series of observed behavioral regularities that are not explained by rational-choice theory or other theories typically used in studying collective action. Heterogeneity of preferences, other-regarding preferences, and bounded rationality are thought to be important components in understanding the observed regularities. A strength of agent-based modeling is the focus on interactions between agents. These agents are typically boundedly rational and vary in their attributes within the agent population. In chapter 8, we will discuss in more detail how to connect the empirical findings with agent-based modeling.

With agent-based models, it is possible to explore the consequences of alternative assumptions in order to compare models with empirical

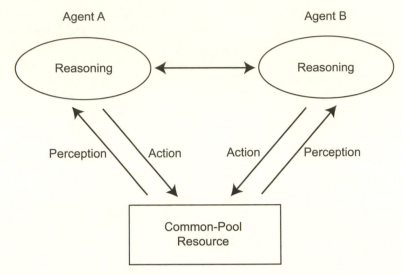

Fig. 7.2. A scheme of cognitive interactions between two agents and their shared common-pool resource. *Source*: Adapted from Janssen 2005a, 162.

findings. Since agents consist of a set of procedures for what to do in which context, models can be developed that are based on observations instead of the logical elegance of analytical models. For example, we can be specific in the type and quality of information the agent derives and how this information is processed. The capacity to process information, cognitive capacity, can also be manipulated in a systematic way. Agents can vary in their attributes, motivations, and social network connections. This increase of complexity can be relevant if we want to develop formal models of the newly emerging diagnostic theory of collective action of the commons that emphasizes the role of context. Still, agent-based models are logically consistent, and the results can be replicated. One can use agent-based modeling as a form of deductive reasoning to generate outcomes that can then be tested in new human-subject experiments or in the field.

A weakness of agent-based modeling is the current infancy of testing agent-based models in a rigorous way. The next chapter focuses in more detail on the challenges of developing empirically grounded agent-based models.

Some practical concerns also exist. Agent-based modeling is not yet taught widely in undergraduate and graduate programs within the social sciences. As a consequence, getting acquainted with the method, and learning programming skills and the art of modeling, involve a steep learning curve. A further challenge arises from the lack of widely practiced protocols for documenting work in agent-based modeling carefully so that scholars can check and build upon each other's work. These challenges are acknowledged by the agent-based community who are organizing themselves within the OpenABM consortium (http://www.openabm .org) to address a number of these issues.

We now highlight several important contributions of agent-based modeling to the theory of collective action and the study of common-pool resource management. The most relevant contributions have addressed five distinct sets of questions: (1) How do cooperative strategies evolve in repeated Prisoner's Dilemma games? (2) How do spatial patterns of relationships influence collective action? (3) How does indirect reciprocity affect the evolution of cooperative strategies? (4) Under which conditions can costly punishment evolve? and (5) How do social or meta norms evolve?

Repeated Prisoner's Dilemma

Cooperation among Egoists

One of the classic studies that started the wide use of agent-based models is the study of how cooperation in social dilemma situations can emerge. Scholars have used the Prisoner's Dilemma (PD) game to model a wide variety of social situations, including harvesting from a common-pool resource (Dasgupta and Heal 1979; D. Richards 2001; Ridley 1998). In the classic example of a PD game, two individuals are held as prisoners in separate cells and accused of being partners in crime (Rapoport and Chammah 1965). These two agents are not able to communicate. Both have to make a decision independently of each other whether to cooperate or to defect. When both cooperate, they both receive three tokens. If both defect, they both receive one token. If one cooperates and one defects, the cooperator receives nothing, while the defector receives five tokens. What will the agents do? In table 7.1, the payoff table of a Prisoner's Dilemma is presented. A selfish rational agent will reason that if the opponent will cooperate, it is best to defect, while if the opponent defects, the best strategy is to defect too. If the agent assumes that the opponent has the same reasoning as herself, the agent will defect. The result is that selfish rational agents are expected to defect, and the Nash equilibrium is mutual defection.

In his classic work on predicting equilibria in game-theoretical models, Nash assumed selfish rational players. Do real people adopt this strategy in a Prisoner's Dilemma game? As discussed in the previous chapter, experimental work has shown that people do not always behave like selfish

TABLE 7.1
Payoff table of a Prisoner's Dilemma

	Agent B cooperates	Agent B defects
Agent A cooperates	(3,3)	(0,5)
Agent A defects	(5,0)	(1,1)

rational actors. Agent-based models can be used to develop models based on agents making decisions with simple strategies that can explain the observed behavior in experiments.

In the late 1970s, political scientist Robert Axelrod invited colleagues to submit an entry to a tournament he was organizing (Axelrod 1984). The tournament consisted of agents, represented as algorithms, playing a finitely repeated Prisoner's Dilemma game. The instructions were that each submitted algorithm would play 200 rounds against each submitted algorithm, including itself, and an algorithm that randomly plays cooperate and defect. A winning strategy needed to anticipate what other submitted entries might look like. According to the Nash equilibrium, always defecting would be the rational submission, but a wide variety of strategies were submitted. Some of the 14 entries were complex strategies with many lines of code. The simplest entry was also the winning entry and was submitted by psychologist Anatol Rapoport. The strategy, Tit-for-Tat, starts with cooperation and then repeats the decision made by the opponent in the previous round. This means that the strategy reciprocates cooperation and punishes defection. As long as the opponent cooperates, the agent continues cooperating. When the opponent defects, the agent will also defect the next round and continue to defect as long as the opponent defects.

Axelrod organized a second tournament and more people submitted entries. One change to the original tournament was that the length of the number of rounds was not fixed. The game might end in any round with a small probability. The expected length of the number of rounds was still 200. Those who entered knew the results of the first tournament, and several variations on Tit-for-Tat were submitted. The best-performing of the 62 entries was again Tit-for-Tat.

Evolving Strategies in Prisoner's Dilemma Tournaments

Does this mean that Tit-for-Tat is the best possible strategy in finitely repeated Prisoner's Dilemma games? No, since the performance in the game depends on the population of strategies submitted to the tournament. If all of the other strategies are "defect always," the best entry is also "defect always," owing to the difference made in the first round. Axelrod (1987) decided to simulate an evolution of tournaments. Random strategies are deployed at the outset, and strategies that do well are copied and imitated. Over repeated rounds, strategies that perform well evolve over a number of tournaments. The good strategies that evolved were not Tit-for-Tat strategies per se, but variations.

In order to simulate tournaments, Axelrod needed to formalize the space of possible strategies that could be submitted. He assumed that agents have a memory of three rounds. Based on the actions of the opponent in the previous three rounds as well as their own actions, 64 ($4 \times 4 \times 4$) possible combinations can be defined (4 refers to the number of possible results of a two-person game: CC, CD, DC, and DD). For each possible history, the agent may decide to cooperate or to defect. This leads to 2^{64} possible strategies that agents may propose using this rather rigid way of developing strategies.

Since we also need to define whether agents cooperate or not in the first three rounds, we add $3 + 3$ rounds, leading to a total of 70 possible combinations, and 2^{70} possible strategies. It is impossible to evaluate each possible strategy for each possible set of opponents in a tournament. So it is not possible to definitely prove which strategy works the best. We can, however, simulate possible evolutions of tournaments. Axelrod uses concepts from genetic algorithms to simulate such an evolution (Mitchell 1998).

A genetic algorithm consists of a population of solutions to a problem that evolves over time. For each generation, each solution is evaluated and a fitness score is defined. In Axelrod's case, it was the score of a strategy in the tournament against all other agents. The higher the score, the better the solution, and the higher the chance that this solution will be used in the next generation of an evolving tournament. A solution is coded as a bit-string, which is a string of 0's and 1's. For example, 1 represents cooperation and 0 represents defection. The length of the string is 70. Each location refers to a specific action, cooperate or defect, given a specific history.

The next generation is created based on the performance of the solutions in the existing generation. There are different ways to select the "parents." Axelrod randomly draws two solutions and selects the one with the higher score for the next generation. Once a new set of parents is selected, crossover and mutation operators are applied to the parents in order to generate novel strategies. With crossover, two parents are randomly drawn, and they swap a piece of bit-string. The location where the bit-strings are broken is randomly defined. Mutation entails the swapping of a 0 to a 1 or a 1 to a 0 with a small probability for each location on the bit-string.

As a result, the strategies of playing repeated Prisoner's Dilemma games evolve over time. Over the generations, the average score of the strategies increases (figure 7.3). The resulting strategies mimic some important characteristics of the Tit-for-Tat strategy: never defect first, reciprocate cooperation, punish defection, and be forgiving. Such variation may allow two defections of the opponent before defecting, or initially start with defection instead of cooperation.

SPATIAL GAMES

Spatial Social Dilemma Games

People do not interact randomly with each other as if we were particles in a well-mixed gas. A number of studies in recent years have analyzed the spatial structure of interactions and its effect on collective action. A simple model that shows the importance of space is that of Martin Nowak and Robert May (1992). They developed a spatial model where the environment is a 99 × 99 square lattice with fixed boundaries. Each cell represents an agent who plays a Prisoner's Dilemma game each round with its neighbors in a Moore neighborhood (see figure 7.1). In each round, an agent has to decide to play C (cooperate) or D (defect) against all neighbors. The payoff of the Prisoner's Dilemma is 1 when an agent and her neighbor cooperate, and greater than 1 when the agent defects while the neighbor cooperates. A zero payoff is the result in the other two cases: mutual defection, and cooperation by the agent and defection by the neighbor, both lead to a zero payoff. The sum of all games played with neighbors is the total payoff of the agent. At the beginning of each step, the agent will copy the best strategy of the agents in the Moore neighborhood. When you start with all cooperators, except the agent in the center, you will derive interesting patterns of cooperators and defectors. Cooperation and defection can coexist in a spatial setting.

Nowak and May therefore show that spatial structure of interactions may affect the level of cooperation. Huberman and Glance (1993) criticized the findings of Nowak and May (1992) by showing that the results are sensitive to the way information is updated. When agents do not update their strategies all at the same time, but asynchronously, the defector strategy will spread rapidly. Nowak, Bonhoeffer, and May (1994) confirmed this finding, but the coexistence of cooperation and defection is still possible for a variety of parameter values. Helbing and Yu (2009) show that cooperation can also evolve if not all cells contain agents and agents can move to other empty cells that they expect to lead them to higher rewards.

A recent contribution analyzes the consequences of different network structures. The Nowak and May model assumes a regular lattice, while

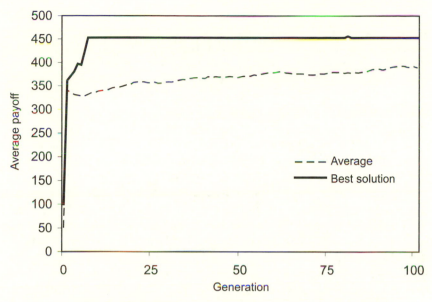

Fig. 7.3. Average and best score of 100 runs of a population of solutions for 100 generations of repeated Prisoner's Dilemma games.

empirical social networks differ in the degree distribution of links and clustering of agents (see the section on networks above). Santos and Pacheco (2005) show that in Prisoner's Dilemma games, cooperation emerges for a wider set of assumptions if the network is scale-free instead of a regular lattice. A more general finding about the spatial structure on the possibility of cooperation in repeated social dilemmas is presented by Ohtsuki et al. (2006). They provide a simple heuristic that is a good approximation for all graphs that they have analyzed, such as cycles, spatial lattices, regular graphs, random graphs, and scale-free networks. The heuristic says that natural selection favors cooperation, if the benefit of the altruistic act, b, divided by the cost, c, exceeds the average number of neighbors, k, which means $b/c > k$.[2]

Spatial Public Goods Games

We will not review the comprehensive literature on spatial games here; rather, we will focus on public goods games because of their relevance for natural resource management. Hauert and colleagues study the evolution of cooperation in spatial public goods games (Brandt, Hauert, and Sigmund 2003; Hauert et al. 2002; Hauert and Szabo 2003). They show that when agents are able to leave a game, defectors, cooperators, and nonplayers coexist in a dynamic environment (Hauert et al. 2002).

Hauert and Szabo (2003) tested the consequence of different geometries of interactions and found that cooperation is higher on honeycomb versus square geometries. This means that the findings of theoretical models on cooperation are not necessarily robust to assumptions about the structure of local neighborhoods. On the other hand, larger neighborhoods, and thus larger groups that share the public good, reduce the level of cooperation.

Another line of explanation focuses on the possibility of evolutionary group selection (M. Wade 1977, 1978; D. Wilson 1983; Wright 1945). A group that includes more altruistic agents derives higher average fitness for its members. The higher average fitness is likely to lead to more offspring of agents in the successful group, even though within each group the altruistic agents are less fit than their selfish neighbors. It is known that low demographic mobility is also a crucial factor for the evolution of altruistic traits (Killingback, Bieri, and Flatt 2006; Wright 1945). A number of recent models use group selection as a way to mimic cultural evolution in human history, such as the model of Boyd et al. (2003), which is discussed below in the section on costly punishment.

Many models that examine group selection build on the "Haystack model" of John Maynard Smith (1964). In Haystack models, agents are divided into a number of groups in which games are played, and asexual reproduction takes place within each group. At the end of the reproductive phase there is a dispersal phase, where the entire population is pooled and new groups are randomly formed from the pooled population. For Haystack models where the games are Prisoner's Dilemmas, the only stable equilibrium is one of mutual defection (see Bergstrom 2002; Cohen and Eshel 1976).

Janssen and Goldstone (2006) combine the reproduction and dispersal phases. In fact, their model resembles trait-group selection where a trait can be negatively selected in each and every local group of a global population and yet can be positively selected in the population overall (D. Wilson 1975). In agreement with studies like Wright (1945) and Killingback, Bieri, and Flatt (2006), low demographic mobility proves to be the most crucial factor for the evolution of altruistic traits.

Indirect Reciprocity

If agents interact with others who are non-kin and with whom they have no history of interaction, why is mutual defection not a necessary outcome? Tipping models, derived from the pathbreaking work of Schelling (1960, 1978), predict levels of cooperative behavior. Instead of presuming that all other players initially have full information in the sense that they know for sure what strategies others will take, in a tipping model players prefer to cooperate with others when a significant proportion of the others do cooperate but are initially uncertain about the proportion of others who intend to cooperate. In other words, their beliefs about the distribution of types of players are not initially in equilibrium. Thus tipping models do have multiple equilibria that depend largely on the initial actions of some of the players. As shown in figure 7.4, if only a few players are expected to cooperate by keeping their harvesting levels at a low level (expected cooperation at L), then most of the players will not cooperate, as they would perceive themselves to be "suckers" benefiting others more than they benefited themselves. But if the expected level of cooperation is relatively high (above the tipping point, T), then more and more players will cooperate. Over time, in a tipping model, players may come close to approximating an optimal level of harvesting (O).

In line with the tipping point model, the work on indirect reciprocity explains why actors may cooperate with non-kin strangers. The main mechanism to explain cooperation assumes that agents have ways to signal their intentions. The theories of indirect reciprocity and costly signaling show how cooperation in larger groups can emerge when the cooperators can build a reputation.[3]

Nowak and Sigmund (1998) proposed a simple model where agents play social dilemmas, and a symbol that represents some aspect of past

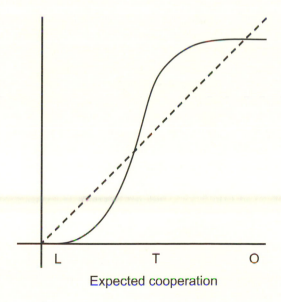

Expected cooperation

Fig. 7.4. Tipping model of levels of cooperation.

behavior is attached to the agents, resulting in high levels of cooperation. Frank (1987) earlier developed an analytical model of one-shot
games where he analyzed equilibria for different assumptions about the
information from signals and costs of adapting the signals. Other studies
equip agents with tags and symbols, and show that cooperation levels
are enhanced when agents cooperate only with other agents carrying the
same symbols (Hales 2001; Lindgren and Nordahl 1994; Riolo, Cohen,
and Axelrod 2001), or that agents learn to detect trustworthy symbols
(Janssen 2008). Macy and Skvoretz (1998) use symbols related to the
types of players' behavior. Note that there is an important difference
between cooperating with similar agents and detecting whom to trust. If
tags lead similar agents to interact more frequently, this will enhance the
likelihood that cooperators with similar tags will team up. In fact, tags as
used in the above studies lead similar agents to end up in repeated interaction. Janssen (2008) let agents, who are equipped with tags, play one-
shot Prisoner's Dilemma games and found that the use of tags does not
lead to repeated interaction. Owing to learning and inheritance of knowledge from parents, agents learn to make decisions in social dilemmas. In
Janssen (2008), agents can evolve to have other-regarding preferences,
and in the evolutionary process agents will learn to recognize egoists who
subsequently are outperformed by conditional cooperators.

The combination of learning and evolution that drives the evolution
of conditional cooperators in Janssen (2008) resembles the analytical
work of Güth and Kliemt (1995, 1998). They show that retributive emotions can survive in evolutionarily stable ways if it is possible for players
to know in advance whether the person with whom they are playing is
characterized by a "strong conscience" or a willingness to impose punishments if cooperation is not selected. Bester and Güth (1998) examine
the possibilities for other-regarding preferences to evolve over time in a
population facing social dilemmas. Using an indirect evolutionary approach in which preferences become endogenous, they show that including another in one's utility function depends on the favorable response of
the other to cooperative moves. Family members, in particular, are more
likely to have other family members in their utility functions, but the argument of these authors differs from the kin-selection argument.

The evolution of other-regarding preferences within a family is linked
not to genetic transmission but rather to the fact that family members are
better informed about each other. Signaling concern for others by giving
to charity may also increase the likelihood that such preferences can survive and multiply in a population of nonrelated individuals. Further, the
evolution of preferences that include benefits to others is more likely to
emerge in populations where individuals are not anonymous and can use
symbols to identify their type (Ahn, Janssen, and Ostrom 2004). Agent-
based models can more explicitly include the topology of interactions

between agents, the heterogeneity of preferences, and decisions made. Addressing the same problem by both analytical models and agent-based models strengthens the robustness of findings, since both types of models have their strengths and weaknesses.

Agents can use reputation to decide with whom to cooperate or even with whom to play in a social dilemma. In the models of Schluessler (1989) and Vanberg and Congelton (1992), the agents with successful strategies are those who exit when the opponent defected in the previous game. In fact, these strategies do not tolerate errors. Stanley, Ashlock, and Tesfatsion (1994) and Ashlock et al. (1996) allowed agents to choose partners, and their chosen partners to refuse offers, based on the known history of interactions with other players.

EVOLUTION OF COSTLY PUNISHMENT

It has been suggested that costly punishment is an important factor in the evolution of cooperation in large human societies. As discussed in chapter 6, laboratory experiments on public goods and common-pool resources have shown that participants are willing to give up monetary returns to punish noncooperators (Fehr and Gächter 2002; E. Ostrom, Walker, and Gardner 1992). From an evolutionary perspective, it is puzzling why individuals would accept a reduction of their own payoff so as to decrease the payoff of other individuals. The possibility of the evolution of costly punishment in human societies has been demonstrated by various modeling studies.

We first discuss various game-theoretical models of punishment before we turn to the contributions of agent-based modeling. Contingent strategies can encourage cooperation by threatening punishment for defection. Fudenberg and Maskin (1986) posited that it was possible for subjects to eliminate free-riding if some players made a firm commitment to follow a "grim trigger" strategy. A grim trigger strategy involves a permanent switch from cooperation to defection once anyone fails to cooperate. This self-enforcing, positive equilibrium is possible only if all players commit themselves to punish others and deter defection by their known strong commitment. In addition to the grim trigger strategy, theoretical work led to an explosion of possible equilibria predicted by noncooperative game theory. Among the predicted equilibria are strategies yielding the suboptimal Nash equilibrium, the optimal outcome, and everything in between.

The grim trigger strategy uses defection as a way to punish defection that may lock participants into the deficient equilibrium. Punishment in field settings usually involves some action other than defecting oneself on an agreement. Since punishing someone else usually involves a cost for oneself and produces a benefit for everyone, it is a second-order social dilemma (Oliver 1980; Yamagishi 1986).

Hirshleifer and Rasmusen (1989) partially tackled this problem by modeling the problem as a two-stage game with a cooperation stage followed by a punishment stage where both are repeated many times. With a costless punishment strategy, they demonstrate that a strategy of cooperating, punishing nondefectors, and then punishing those who did not punish defectors is an equilibrium. Hirshleifer and Rasmusen find that in large populations, the strategy of cooperate and then punish any defectors will increase cooperation if (1) defectors respond to punishment by a single player by cooperating thereafter, and (2) the long-run benefits to the punisher exceed the costs they pay for punishing someone else. This strategy survives both with strategies that initially defect but cooperate if punished, and with strategies that cooperate but do not punish under some conditions. Increasing group size reduces the probability that this strategy will induce cooperative behavior owing to increases in the cost of punishing a larger set.

Boyd and Richerson (1992) built a two-stage evolutionary model based on Hirshleifer and Rasmusen's model of a large population from which groups of size n > 2 are selected. In their model, any individual can punish any other individual second stage, but there is a cost to the punisher and to the punished. The same group continues for the next round dependent on a probability function. Strategies are modeled as if they were inherited. They allow errors to occur in the execution of a cooperative strategy, but all other strategies are executed as intended. After the rounds of interaction are completed, the more successful strategies are reproduced at a higher rate than are the less successful strategies. In this model, an increase in group size requires an offsetting linear increase in the number of interactions to achieve similar levels of collective action. They also find that moralistic strategies "which punish defectors, individuals who do not punish noncooperators, and individuals who do not punish nonpunishers can also overcome the problem of second-order cooperation" (Boyd and Richerson 1992, 184). When moralistic strategies are common, defectors and cooperators who do not punish are selected against owing to the punishment directed at them. "In this way, selection may favor punishment, even though the cooperation that results is not sufficient to compensate individual punishers for its costs" (Boyd and Richerson 1992, 184). These moralistic strategies can stabilize any behavior—a result that is similar to the famous "folk theorem" that any equilibrium can be stabilized by such punishing strategies as the grim trigger.

Boyd et al. (2003) extend this work using an agent-based model, which makes it possible to define more specific cultural group selection processes. They show that costly sanctioning can evolve when initially the agents are nonpunishing defectors. They consider a population that is divided into N groups of size n. An agent can contribute or not to a public good in each period. If an agent contributes, he or she will incur a cost c to produce a total benefit b that is shared equally among group members. If an agent does not contribute, but defects, the agent will incur no costs and produce no benefits. If the fraction of contributors in the group is x, the expected payoff for contributors is $1 + bx - c$ and the expected payoff for defectors is $1 + bx$, so the payoff disadvantage of the contributors is a constant c independent of the distribution of types in the population.

After a decision is made to contribute or not, a cooperating agent makes a decision to punish or not each defector in his or her group. This will reduce each defector's payoff by p/n at a cost k/n to the punisher. If the frequency of punishers y is sufficiently high, the cost of being punished exceeds the cost of cooperating ($py > c$). Hence contribution is more beneficial, especially when a contributor does not invest in punishment. In fact, punishers suffer a fitness disadvantage compared with nonpunishing contributors. This is the reason punishment is considered to be altruistic and mere contributors are "second-order free-riders." When there is almost no defection, the payoff disadvantage of punishers relative to contributors approaches zero.

Boyd et al. (2003) assume that there are N groups of population size n. All participants individually decide first whether they will contribute or not and then whether they will penalize defectors. In the next step, individuals encounter other group members with probability $1 - m$ and an individual from another group with probability m. An individual i who encounters an individual j imitates j with probability $W_j/(W_j + W_i)$, where W_x is the payoff of individual x in the game, including the costs of any punishment received or delivered. This leads to selection of higher payoff-deriving strategies and migration of strategies between groups. Boyd et al. (2003) show that high levels of cooperation emerge for group sizes of up to sixty-four persons, a reasonable proxy for group sizes of our hunter-gather ancestors as well as for many small-scale contemporary communities, if costly punishment is allowed. Hauert et al. (2007) show that costly punishment can also evolve in spatial public goods games, using group sizes of five agents, if an agent can decide not to participate in the public goods game. Only with the option of not participating, however, do punishers evolve.

EVOLUTION OF SOCIAL (META) NORMS

Axelrod (1986) was among the first to tackle how norms supporting cooperative strategies, which were not the strategies leading to a Nash equilibrium, could be sustained over time. He posited that individuals could adopt norms—meaning that they usually acted in a particular way and were often punished if they were not seen to be acting in this manner. He posited that some individuals develop a norm to punish those who defected in social dilemmas, as well as the concept of a meta norm—a norm that "one must punish those who did not punish a defection" (Axelrod 1986, 1109). With punishment norms backing cooperative norms, and the meta norm of punishing those who did not punish defectors, Axelrod was able to develop an evolutionary theory of cooperation consistent with evidence from the field.

Recent evolutionary models by Kameda, Takezawa, and Hastle (2003) have developed these ideas even further. In a formal analysis of a set of simplified strategies, these authors explore the viability of a "communal-sharing strategy" that cooperates when in the role of resource acquisition and imposes sanctions on others if they engage in nonsharing behavior. They establish that the communal-sharing strategy is a unique evolutionarily stable strategy that blocks any other strategy from successfully invading for a wide range of parameters. Kameda and colleagues also undertook a simulation of the performance of multiple strategies when ten players are involved and their strategies could evolve over time. Here, they observed that free-riding could become the dominant strategy over multiple generations owing to the problem of second-order free-riding in regard to norm enforcement. When they added an "intolerant" norm enforcer who is willing to bear extra costs for excluding others who are second-order free-riders on the enforcement of cooperative norms, the simulated ten-person games tended to sustain cooperative sharing over a very large number of generations. In field settings of robust social-ecological systems, one does tend to find some members of self-organized groups who are "fired up" about the need for everyone to follow the rules and norms they have evolved over time. Some groups rotate the role of being the local enforcer among their membership (as we discuss in part II), so no one has to bear the cost of monitoring and enforcing at all times, while each of them is "super-charged" with the responsibility for local monitoring for a specific time on a rotating basis.

FUTURE CHALLENGES

Many scholars have addressed collective-action problems and the governance of common resources using formal methods, especially game theory and agent-based modeling. Most of the work focuses on the evolution of cooperation and informal rules (social norms) (Axelrod 1984, 1986; R. Hoffmann 2000; Nowak 2006). We are also interested in the evolution of formal rules that include explicit descriptions of possible sanctions when an agent is caught breaking a rule (Crawford and Ostrom 2005). Therefore, monitoring and sanctioning are also important actions that we need to explain. In recent years, a number of studies have considered the emergence of costly punishment (Boyd et al. 2003). Those studies focus on the emergence of cultural norms to give up resources to punish defectors in well-defined social dilemmas.

We expect that a future development will be adding an additional level of complexity and studying the evolved composition of rule sets for complex social dilemmas. Initial attempts have been reported in Janssen and Ostrom (2006a), where the artificial agents could agree to accept a rule that would reduce their individual short-term returns to enable them to derive higher long-term returns. For simplicity's sake, only one candidate rule set was provided in the model to the agents. The next step is the study of the evolution of the institutional rules themselves.

Janssen (2005b) proposed a framework to model the evolution of institutional rules. The basic idea is that there is a population of rules, encoded as a bit-string, and these rules can tackle certain challenges of solving collective-action problems. We are interested in how a *community* is able to deal with a variety of challenges, and how the community is able to adapt its rules to deal with the challenges. Furthermore, it would be interesting to understand how communities may learn from one another, even if the regimes of challenges are not equal.

Rules can be encoded as a string that consists of rule components. These components might be created in different libraries consistent with the different components of the grammar of institutions, such as Attributes, Deontic, Aim, Conditions, Or else (aka ADICO) (Crawford and Ostrom 2005).[4] The syntax of the grammar of institutions contains five components, as follows:

- Attributes, which describe which members of the group the statement applies to;
- Deontic, which holds a verb from deontic logic: *must/obliged*, *must not/forbidden*, or *may/permitted*;
- Aim, which describes the action to which the deontic applies;
- Conditions, which describe when, where, how, and to what extent the statement applies; and
- Or else, which defines the sanction to be applied for noncompliance with a rule.

Different compositions of these components lead to strategies, norms, or rules. Shared strategies are written with attributes, aim, and conditions components; norms add the deontic to this; and rules add the or else component.

If we follow this framework, a rule consists of these five parts. Each part is built up from a library of potential rule structures, like the ADICO framework of Crawford and Ostrom (2005). Different components of the library are combined into one rule (figure 7.5).

Empirical studies show that the number of rules fluctuates over time (March, Schulz, and Zhou 2000). New challenges arise, and new rules are created, while other rules may die out. The main difficulty in formalizing the process of rule development will lie in the process by which agents decide on a new rule. Initial results of lab experiments (Janssen and Ostrom 2008) indicate the importance of participant experience, which is difficult to quantify. Is there a pattern in which groups change the rules of the game? Such a pattern might be a consequence of acquired heuristics that people use for specific information structures of the decision problem (Gigerenzer and Selten 2001; Goldstein and Gigerenzer 2002), or culturally transmitted practices (Richerson and Boyd 2005).

Building on earlier work where groups of agents share common resources (Boyd et al. 2003; Burtsev and Turchin 2006; Janssen and de Vries 1998), agents can be assumed to have a mental map of how different rule components lead to better governance of the common resources, represented as a single-layered neural network,

$$S = w_0 + \sum_{i=1}^{N} w_i x_i \tag{7.1}$$

where S is the score for a rule component, w_i the weights, and x_i the input information. The weights can be updated in the following way,

$$\Delta w_i = \lambda \, (O - E[O]) \cdot x_i, \tag{7.2}$$

where Δw_i is the adjustment to the ith weight, λ is the learning rate, E are the outcomes of the social-ecological system, and $O - E[O]$ is the difference between the expected and observed outcomes of the system.

The inputs into the mental model of the agents are based on the general diagnostic framework proposed by E. Ostrom (2007) and discussed in chapter 9. The basic idea is to organize an analysis of how attributes of (1) a resource system (e.g., fishery, lake, grazing area), (2) the resource units produced by that system (e.g., fish, water, fodder), (3) the users of that system, and (4) the governance system jointly affect (and are indirectly affected through feedback from) the patterns of interactions and resulting outcomes achieved at a particular time and place.

The output score is an estimate of the importance of different model components. The agents use this mental model to define which components of the rule library to combine. Agents may have different preferences for appropriate rules. The collective-choice rules define how individual "votes" at an operational level are aggregated toward a decision to add

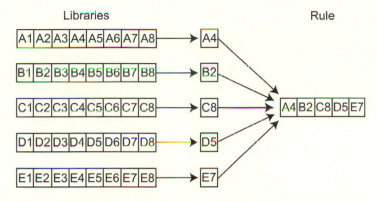

Fig. 7.5. Process of constructing a rule from the libraries.

a new rule to the social-ecological system (figure 7.6). Agents may exchange experiences with other agents related to their mental model of the rule set as they interact within a social network within their community. There might also be an exchange of experiences between groups, for example, due to kinship or exchange relationships (initially assumed to be exogenous relations).

With the model, we can perform controlled experiments to investigate the conditions under which effective rules are developed to manage the shared resources. We will investigate the impact of different collective-choice rules and compare it with our experimental findings and the literature of field studies (Janssen, Anderies, and Ostrom 2007). Furthermore, we will also test the implications of uncertainty on the types of rule systems that evolve.

Using stylized models, we have the opportunity for exploring new situations, such as the impact of resources with multiple stable states (Scheffer et al. 2001) on the ability of groups to define effective rule systems. Furthermore, such a research agenda can facilitate the exploration of the path-dependencies of rule systems, and how certain collective-choice rules may facilitate or hinder effective adaptation for particular types of resource dynamics.

Conclusion

Since the 1980s, agent-based modeling has been increasingly used as a formal method to study the conditions under which boundedly rational agents can evolve cooperation at various scales. The stylized models show that agents with limited cognitive capacities can form groups of

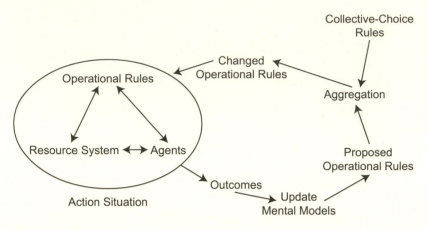

Fig. 7.6. Schematic model of rule evolution.

cooperators when they are able to signal their past behavior by using tags; they can interact repeatedly; they can decide not to participate in a social dilemma; they can use costly punishment; and various groups are interacting with each other.

Agents who evolve in most computational experiments are not blindly self-seeking but conditionally cooperative. If there are only one-shot interactions without signaling, cooperative strategies are not likely to evolve. This resembles the experimental evidence that without communication, behavior in public goods and common-pool resource experiments approaches Nash equilibria.

The theoretical insights of the stylized models show the importance of communication. Communication can help to signal willingness to cooperate, exchange information on the reputation of others, and (un)knowingly signal one's trustworthiness. Note that communication within agent-based models does not go beyond signaling of traits of agents, and does not involve persuasion and/or negotiation. What we do not yet know very well is how informal rules, or norms, get institutionalized in formal arrangements such that cooperation can evolve at higher scales. With large populations, it will be challenging to evolve common norms, and therefore formal rules become essential to enforce cooperative agreements. But how do agents know what kinds of rules are effective, and how do they aggregate their individual preferences into formal agreements?

This chapter provided numerous illustrations of how surprising findings from case studies and experiments have stimulated model development that could explain the observed patterns. Agent-based models are appropriate for this task since they can include heterogeneity of agent characteristics, agent-agent interactions, evolution of agents' characteristics, and learning. Agent-based models can also be used to explore possible behavior of not-yet-observed combinations of assumptions. A limitation of the current state of agent-based models is the rather abstract and artificial nature of the models. Therefore, we focus in the next chapter on how social scientists can begin to combine agent-based models with case study research and experiments.

CHAPTER EIGHT

Building Empirically Grounded Agent-Based Models

IN THIS CHAPTER, we discuss recent efforts to develop empirically grounded agent-based models. Field studies and experiments have shown that individuals overcome the challenges of collective action associated with management of common-pool resources far more frequently than is predicted by conventional theories of collective action (see part II and chapters 6 and 7). These empirical findings call into question the model of rational utility-maximization upon which the conventional theory is based. The findings suggest the importance of communication, trust and reciprocity, normative considerations, interactions among multiple types of actors, and the cognitive challenges presented by complex ecological systems. In principle, agent-based models make it possible to evaluate how well alternative models of human behavior and social interactions account for empirical observations. In practice, linking the observations from field studies, experiments, and agent-based models presents a major challenge. It is not yet clear how to combine the different methods. This chapter discusses recent developments in combining empirical studies with agent-based models, and the new findings derived from this activity. These new developments combine field studies, meta-analysis of case studies, laboratory and field experiments, and role games with agent-based modeling.

Reflecting the diversity of methods used to derive empirical information on social and social-ecological systems, different approaches have been developed to ground agent-based models empirically (Janssen and Ostrom 2006c). Some efforts use empirical observations to develop agent-based models in an attempt to achieve a better understanding of the dynamics behind particular observations. Others compare data generated by theoretically informed agent-based models with empirical observations from experiments or field studies as a form of theory testing. We also discuss the use of agent-based models and experiments as a way to inform subsequent decision making by participants, as a form of action research.

The various studies presented in this chapter all discuss the importance of heterogeneity of attributes and preferences of the actors in order to explain observed patterns. This justifies the use of agent-based modeling to study collective action and the commons. On the other hand, various studies discussed in part II have shown that we have limited insight as to how heterogeneity affects the success of collective action. Better understanding of when and how diverse forms of heterogeneity affect collective action is thus an important topic on a longer-term agenda.

COMPARING SIMULATIONS WITH DATA

Since this chapter focuses on empirically grounded agent-based models, it is important to provide some context to the challenge to compare models with data. If we have high-quality data and a well-defined formal model, we can use conventional statistical methods to calibrate the model. As chapters 2–6 have shown, the qualitative and quantitative data we use to study the commons come from different sources. It is important to know the context in which the data are collected in order to use the data appropriately to evaluate a model. Owing to the challenges of data collection, we will use different methods to evaluate models. When data are derived in a situation that is less dependent on the local context, we may rely on statistical methods. But when data are derived within a specific local context, we may need alternative methods to evaluate models, including feedback from stakeholders.

Given the difficulty of obtaining high-quality data about decision making in collective-action situations, and given the explicit inclusion of cognitive, institutional, and social processes in agent-based models, achieving good statistical performance or matching patterns is not sufficient. In some cases, no quantitative data exist on which a statistical analysis can be performed. Other criteria one can use are these:

- Is the model plausible given the current scholarly understanding of the processes?
- Can we understand why the model is doing well?
- Did we derive a better understanding of our empirical observations?
- Does the behavior of the models coincide with the understanding of relevant stakeholders about the system?

We will now turn to a discussion of the different ways agent-based models are combined with empirical data. We will distinguish different research goals in empirically grounding the formal models, which will also require different criteria to evaluate the success of the empirically grounded agent-based models.

Different Approaches to Combine Empirical Data and Agent-Based Models

Dependent on the type of information that is available and the questions of interest to the researchers, we can distinguish several approaches. The choice of approach involves a trade-off between generalizability and context. This is somewhat similar to the problem of model selection (Pitt, Myung, and Zhang 2002). Some studies focus on generalization of the results; others try to apply a model to a specific case—this is true both of empirical studies such as those discussed in part II and of models and experiments discussed in part III. On the other hand, we also face the trade-off between a few subjects and a large number of subjects. With a few subjects, we can focus more often on the cognitive processes and derive high-quality data about individual decisions and circumstances. When there are many subjects, we can distinguish among types of subjects who differ in their level of other-regarding preferences, discount rates, and types of learning (see Janssen and Ahn 2006). With thousands of subjects, empirical information on the decision-making process of subjects is rarely available.

Including an awareness of these trade-offs—generalizable versus context-specific, and small versus large population size—we distinguish four approaches for utilizing empirical information to help confirm patterns observed in agent-based modeling: (1) models based on *stylized facts*, (2) models of behavior in laboratory and field *experiments*, (3) *role games* and companion modeling, and (4) models based on specific *case studies*.

When a large number of high-quality observations exist, one can derive statistical distributions and other *stylized facts* from the empirical data. These stylized facts are often the starting point for models such as those using meta-analysis of case studies. What are the simple rules that generate these stylized facts? A popular example of such a stylized fact is the power law distribution,[1] as observed in many systems, such as city size, firm size, and the number of links in networks like Web sites and sexual contacts (Axtell 2001; Barabási and Albert 1999; Liljeros et al. 2001). In the collective-action situations discussed in this book, the moderate level of cooperation, the existence of sanctioning, the crucial role of monitoring in the effectiveness of resource institutions, and the increase of cooperation after communication are (qualitative) stylized facts.

Using relatively uncomplicated models of the decisions of simple reactive agents,[2] scholars can investigate the modeled conditions under which they can derive statistics similar to the observed stylized facts. When one has a large amount of high-quality data, one may have more success in detecting stylized facts quantitatively. Therefore, we see applications of this approach for data-rich areas of investigation. For example, a successful application area is finance (e.g., Bouchaud 2001; LeBaron 2001), where large amounts of high-quality data are available. In relation to governing commons dilemmas, digital commons can provide examples of such an approach—for example, congestion on the Internet (Huberman and Lukose 1997), or free-riding in file-sharing networks (Adar and Huberman 2000). One typically detects distributions of frequency of congestion levels, or distributions of the share of users who are contributing files to peer-to-peer systems. If models are developed to describe these patterns, they are rooted in the mathematics of physics and use common sense to develop the relationships. But such empirical distributions would also be interesting to develop and test in models grounded in collective-action theory.

A second approach—*controlled experiments*—uses laboratory and field experiments to test computational models. Laboratory and field experiments provide a highly abstract, controlled environment in which social scientists can test very precise hypotheses. Agent-based models are used to formulate alternative models of human decision making. In this way, agent-based models can be used to test which alternative behavioral models best explain the experimental data. Social scientists use such experimental data on markets or social dilemmas together with agent-based modeling (Camerer 2003; Duffy 2006).

Controlled laboratory experiments are of limited use when one is interested in the broader context in which particular subjects make their decisions. A third approach that enables the researcher to include better ways of representing context is the use of *role games* and companion modeling. One develops a role game based on the situation in a particular community, and the subjects then play the roles they normally play. Observations from the role game are used to develop agent-based models (Barreteau, Le Page, and D'Aquino 2003; Bousquet et al. 2002; Etienne 2003), and the results are evaluated by the stakeholders—the players themselves. With evaluation by stakeholders, we mean that results of simulations are shown and stakeholders can give feedback on whether the results are plausible given the situations the researchers intend to simulate. Since the stakeholders have played the role games and as a consequence have a good understanding of what the models attempt to capture, they can evaluate whether the simulations of the game would be in line with their own experiences. The stakeholders can also debate whether the game is different from their perceived reality.

The fourth approach is agent-based models based on *case studies* and field studies. Based on different types of information about a specific system, one develops agent-based models that represent the system as precisely as feasible. This hybrid method is a common approach in land-use change modeling, agricultural economics, fisheries, and electricity markets.[3] In such studies, one has multiple sources of field data but incomplete information to observe quantitatively the microlevel dynamics of the system such as decision-making processes in the past and present. Data from remote sensing, surveys, census data, field observations, and the like, are used to develop the different components of the system such as agents representing farmers and other landowners, land use patterns, and ecological dynamics. One is often interested in understanding the interactions between the different components of the system, and in using the model to explore different policy scenarios. Because of the different sources of information, there are methodological challenges in how to include various types of observations such as ethnography (Huigen, Overmars, and de Groot 2006), surveys (Berger and Schreinemachers 2006; Brown and Robinson 2006), and agricultural census data (Happe, Kellermann, and Balmann 2006). Basically, these methodological challenges come down to how to collect relevant information by sampling to generate agent populations that represent the relevant distributions of agent attributes and decision rules at different levels of scale.

We picture the four approaches in figure 8.1. The first two approaches focus on generalizability; the latter two focus more on the "fitting" of a particular case. Each approach has unique characteristics and usefulness. Chapter 7 discussed agent-based models that seek to understand (qualitative) stylized facts in large populations of agents. We will now discuss the other three approaches in more detail.

Agent-Based Models of Laboratory and Field Experiments

Since the behavior of participants in many collective-action experiments is not consistent with predictions using a rational-choice model of individuals maximizing individual payoffs, an important question is this: What types of models of human behavior explain the observations? A recent development is the use of agent-based models to test alternative models that replicate the patterns of the participants in the laboratory experiments (Duffy 2006). We will now discuss a number of examples of agent-based models that seek to replicate patterns observed in the common-pool resource (CPR) and public goods provision experiments discussed in chapter 6. We highlight models of psychological motivations, trust and reciprocity, reputations, learning, social preferences, and signaling in situations involving the appropriation of CPRs and the provision of public goods. Since there is no standardized method for evaluating simulations with empirical data, we will see different methods resulting in different insights. We conclude the section by synthesizing the findings of the various studies.

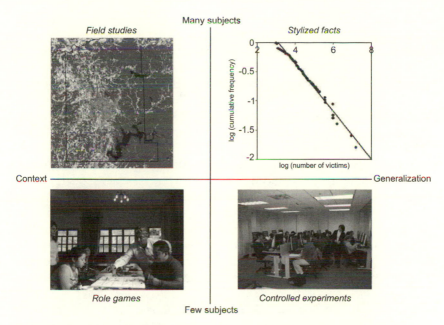

Fig. 8.1. The different types of approaches to combine empirical information and agent-based modeling. *Sources*: Top-left figure is an adapted version of a remote-sensing figure of land uses in Monroe County (Indiana, U.S.A.) by Cynthia Croissant, Laura Carlson, Glen Green, Tom Evans, Shanon Donnelly, and Charles Winkle. Top-right figure is based on Cederman (2002, fig. 1). Bottom-left photo was taken by Marco Janssen. Bottom-right photo was provided by James Russell. Adapted from Janssen and Ostrom 2006c.

Peter Deadman pioneered the use of agent-based models to explore the experimental data. In the first such study, Deadman (1999) defined agents who had a portfolio of possible strategies. The portfolio was based on information from exit interviews conducted after the sessions of CPR experiments (E. Ostrom, Gardner, and Walker 1994). In each round, Deadman programmed the agents to choose one of the strategies of the portfolio to be activated based on expected performance. After each round, the strategies were evaluated by the agent based on the expected and experienced performance of the strategies in previous rounds.

One of the strategies investigated by Deadman attempts to maximize the individual return received in each round by comparing investments in resource appropriation in previous rounds with the resulting returns. If returns on tokens invested are increasing, then more tokens are placed in resource appropriation. If returns on tokens invested in resource appropriation are decreasing, then fewer tokens are placed in harvesting from the CPR. Another strategy mentioned by participants was to compare average returns between investing in the CPR and investing in the fixed return, and then to increase the tokens allocated to the market that performs better. The last type of strategy directly compares an individual agent's investment with the investments of the group as a whole. Deadman's agent-based model showed similar fluctuations in aggregated token investment levels in resource appropriation, as had been observed in the laboratory experiments reported in E. Ostrom, Gardner, and Walker (1994).

Following up on the previous study, Deadman, Schlager, and Gimblett (2000) introduced communication between agents in their model. During communication, agents are assumed to pool their experience in regard to the various strategies they have used. In this way, all agents derive a similar map of which strategies work well. As in the laboratory experiments where communication was allowed, investment levels moved closer to the optimal level of full cooperation. This suggests that communication may contribute to higher levels of cooperation because it enables social learning.

Deadman's combination of agent-based models with experimental data was pathbreaking, but the design of the agents in his models was not grounded in a theoretical framework of decision making, and the models were evaluated in an ad hoc fashion. Subsequent studies have used this approach to evaluate theoretically informed models of human behavior. Jager and Janssen (2002), for example, based their agent-based model on a metatheoretical framework of psychological theories and tested their model on data from common-pool resource experiments. In their theoretical framework, an agent is assumed to have different types of needs, including subsistence, identity, and exploration. Depending on whether the needs of the agent are satisfied or not, and whether the agent is uncertain or not about the expected payoffs, an agent uses one of four decision rules: deliberation, social comparison, repetition, or imitation. An unsatisfied agent spends more cognitive energy (e.g., deliberation or social comparison) than does a satisfied agent (who relies more on repetition and imitation). An uncertain agent uses information from other agents (social comparison or imitation) instead of relying on individual information (deliberation or repetition). The difference between social comparison and imitation is that during social comparison an agent checks whether copying the strategy of another agent leads to an expected improvement of the utility. Jager and Janssen found that agent-based models in common-pool resource settings needed to include other-regarding preferences, satisficing instead of maximizing behavior, a small probability to explore new options (curiosity), and heterogeneity of preferences.

The model of Jager and Janssen (2002) was based on theories from social psychology. Castillo and Saysel (2005) tested a formal representation of the behavioral theory of collective action (E. Ostrom 1998) on field experimental data. This behavioral theory focuses on the links between the trust that individuals have in others, the investments others make in trustworthy reputations, and the probability that participants will use reciprocity norms. They develop a model of this theory using data from field experiments performed with inhabitants of Providence Island in the Colombian Caribbean Sea, where fish and crab resources are essential to livelihoods. Black crab production has increased in the past fifteen years to satisfy both trade and tourist demands. Depletion of the fishery has caused observable increases in labor inputs and more extensive harvesting by the fishers.

Castillo and Saysel (2005) developed a systems dynamics model based on the behavioral theory of collective action. They formulated causal relationships among the components of the theory through feedback loops, representing the interactions between trust, reputation, and reciprocity among the residents. The model operates at the individual level, whereby a five-player real-life setting is represented as five artificial decision-making agents.

The model was calibrated through the use of data from field experiments in the Caribbean coastal area of Colombia. The experiments used traditional common-pool resource settings where a group of five villagers play ten rounds without communication or external regulation and then ten rounds with either communication or external regulation. The participants in the experiment were recruited from fisher and crab-hunter communities in Colombia (Cardenas, Ahn, and Ostrom 2004).

The participants in these field experiments had the opportunity to harvest from a virtual common-pool resource where there was a discrepancy between individual and collective interests measured in monetary incentives. As described in chapter 6, in half of the experiments the participants were allowed to communicate between each round during the last ten rounds of the experiment. In the external regulation treatment, during the last ten rounds the experimenter indicated that a new harvest rule was to be used, and that one player would be chosen randomly in each round to be monitored and would receive a penalty if (s)he had harvested more than was allowed. If followed, the external rule would enable participants to make the cooperative solution and earn the most money. The experiments with communication converged to the cooperative solution. The experiments using the external regulation and punishment design performed well initially, but produced more and more defections from cooperative behavior over time.

Simulations using the agent-based model were able to replicate the experimental data for both the communication and regulation-punishment treatments. Further, a rigorous analysis was performed to test whether the developed model was robust for more extreme conditions and assumptions. The formalized model of E. Ostrom (1998) was found to be structurally robust, as implemented by Castillo and Saysel, and could explain the observed behavior in the experiments by the fishermen and crab hunters at Providence Island in Colombia.

The studies by Deadman, Castillo and Saysel, and others evaluated model performance based on whether the qualitative patterns produced by the agent-based model were similar to the patterns generated in a set of experiments. Janssen and Ahn (2006) performed a more rigorous, quantitative analysis that compared the empirical performance of alternative decision-making models to explain the outcomes in a large set of public goods experiments without communication (Isaac and Walker 1988a; Isaac, Walker, and Williams 1994). They developed a hybrid model based on the experience-weighted attraction-learning model of Camerer and Ho (1999), the general model of social preferences developed by Charness and Rabin (2002), and the best-response model with signaling based on Isaac, Walker, and Williams (1994).

In contrast with the previous studies, Janssen and Ahn focus on the problem of parameter calibration and the evaluation of the model performance in terms of individual- and group-level statistics. All models outperform the selfish rational actor model as an explanation of observed behavior. The essential elements of the model that enhance its performance are the inclusion of other-regarding preferences and satisficing behavior. This is similar to Jager and Janssen's (2002) finding for common-pool resources and the conclusions in Ebenhöh and Pahl-Wostl's (2008) literature review.

Instead of having researchers craft models of decision making for the participants, we can ask participants to develop models of how they would like to make decisions in the experiments. Using the *strategy method*, participants who have been in earlier experiments can program strategies that will interact with each other in an agent-based model (Selten, Mitzkewitz, and Uhlich 1997). Keser and Gardner (1999) apply the strategy method to common-pool resources. Their common-pool resource game consisted of a constituent game played for twenty periods. Sixteen students, all experienced in game theory, were recruited to play the game over the course of six weeks. In the first phase of the experiment, they played the common-pool resource game online three times. In the second phase of the experiment, the tournament phase, they designed strategies that, after implementation as agents, were then used to develop an agent-based model where the agents play their strategies against each other. The harvesting rate of the average participant was in line with the Nash equilibrium. At the individual level, however, fewer than 5 percent of participants played in accordance with the game equilibrium prediction. Although the strategy method makes it possible to derive the direct intentions of the participants, it is not useful for comparing and contrasting different theories because the strategies are not theoretically grounded.

Combining agent-based modeling and laboratory experiments of complex dynamic social dilemmas is a relatively recent development. The research described above demonstrates considerable potential for testing alternative theories of human behavior. Huge methodological challenges still exist, however, in regard to parameter estimation and model comparison. For example, Salmon (2001) showed that identification of the correct learning models using econometrics techniques leads to potential problems. Salmon generated experimental data by simulating normal-form games using a number of learning models so that he could test four different econometric approaches for the accuracy with which they distinguished the individual models by which the data were generated. The econometric techniques were not successful in classifying the data correctly according to which learning model was used. Wilcox (2006) did a similar experiment to test the implication of the assumption of homogeneity of the participants. If the agent population is heterogeneous in parameter values, serious problems in accuracy of parameter estimation are created.

What do we mean by a better model? There is a difficult trade-off in fitting the data and in keeping the model simple. The more complicated the model, the more parameters, equations, and so forth, to describe the model, the better the model fits the data compared to a simpler model. The final model might, however, lack external validity as it is too specific for explaining a particular data set. The best model balances goodness of fit with the ability to generalize. In an effort to balance these, Pitt, Myung, and Zhang (2002) propose to use maximum likelihood estimation but include a penalty for the complexity of the model beyond the number of parameters included.

Because agent-based models have a more complicated structure than do typical linear models of decision making, we do not meet the implicit assumptions of using maximum likelihood estimation. Agent-based models explicitly assume that decisions are not made independently, and noise terms are not necessarily distributed according to a Gaussian distribution. Furthermore, estimation of the behavior of a representative agent on an individual level may not provide a good calibration of an individual-level model that generates emerging patterns at aggregated levels, as the analysis of Janssen and Ahn (2006) illustrates. Since patterns at different levels and scales are of interest to those who are studying collective action within social-ecological systems, an alternative approach to compare models is pattern-oriented modeling (Grimm et al. 2005).

Pattern-oriented modeling originates from ecology and defines a number of quantitative patterns including uncertainty ranges at different levels of temporal and spatial scale. An example is the average level of contribution to public goods in figure 6.1. A model version, a certain parameterization, is considered to be sufficient if all observed empirical patterns are reproduced by the model. Janssen, Radtke, and Lee (2009) applied this pattern-oriented modeling approach to data from the dynamic and spatial laboratory experiments discussed in chapter 6 and identified less than 0.1 percent of the parameter combinations that generate all patterns within the uncertainty ranges. This means that only a small subset of the parameter combinations lead to model outcomes that are within the uncertainty ranges of the empirical data. This also means that there is more than one parameter combination that cannot be distinguished given the uncertainty of the empirical data. Instead of trying to find one best model version, pattern-oriented modeling tries to identify a set of acceptable model versions given the empirical uncertainty.

In all the efforts to test agent-based models on experimental data, we find some commonalities. All studies show that it is necessary to include other-regarding preferences, heterogeneity of preferences, and satisficing behavior in order to explain the observed behavior.

ROLE GAMES AND COMPANION MODELING

Companion modeling is a participatory approach to develop agent-based models with stakeholders living in villages in developing countries (Barreteau 2003). By including the various viewpoints of stakeholders and using those viewpoints in exploring future scenarios of local and regional cases, it stimulates a process of collective learning (Röling 1996). It is important to recognize that the main goal of companion modeling is to contribute to actual problem solving within local communities, not to test theories of collective action.

The companion approach consists of three stages in a cyclical process. First, field observation and a literature review provide information to generate explicit hypotheses. In the next stage, a simple model is developed based on the existing knowledge. Third, role-playing games are used to derive concrete information about the decision-making processes in the villages of interest. The original model will then be enhanced by the observations and discussed with the stakeholders who were involved with the role game. Since the role game and the simulation model include similar processes and interfaces, the stakeholders can judge the social validity of the model.

The companion modeling approach was developed in 2000 as a way to incorporate local knowledge into agent-based models. Since agent-based models were typically based on theory or general logic, scholars who apply agent-based models to specific case studies lacked methods to extract relevant information to make the models fit with the local context. When Barreteau and Bousquet (2000) were studying the underutilization of irrigated systems in the Senegal River Valley in north Senegal, an agent-based model was developed to simulate an archetypal irrigation system. The agents represent farmers, a bank, and water allocation groups. The processes deal with the circulation of water and credit and with interactions about their allocation and access to them. The model was used in role-playing experiments to test its potential as a negotiation support tool and to test the model with the agents they try to simulate (Barreteau, Bousquet, and Attonaty 2001). The deployment of a role-playing game was found to be useful for testing the model and interacting with local stakeholders. This led Bousquet et al. (2002) to the idea of companion modeling, which interactively combines agent-based modeling and role-playing games, and employs the latter to acquire knowledge, build and validate the agent-based model, and use the model in the decision-making process. They hoped that participation in companion modeling would help local stakeholders understand complex decision-making situations and would contribute to improved social outcomes. The approach has been applied to a number of case studies, as reviewed in Bousquet et al. (2002).

An interesting example is given in Gurung, Bousquet, and Trébuil (2006), who performed companion modeling with two villages in Lingmuteychu watershed, Punakha District, west-central Bhutan. One village was located upstream in the watershed, and the other was downstream. The role games made the residents of the upstream village aware that they constrain the water use of the downstream villages through their own water use and cropping patterns. A subsequent round of role games and models was developed, and more villages were included to develop possible solutions for sharing the water. At the end of the process, a multivillage agreement was signed to manage the watershed collectively. Gurung, Bousquet, and Trébuil (2006) cannot prove that companion modeling enhanced the process of solving the collective-action problem, but the anecdotal evidence strongly suggests that it did.

We will now discuss some examples of companion modeling that were used to derive better insights related to natural resource problems. In Etienne (2003), an agent-based model was developed to simulate strategies for natural resource management in the Causse Méjan, a limestone plateau in southern France characterized by a rare grassland-dominated ecosystem endangered by pine invasion. In an effort to facilitate discussion of alternative long-term management strategies for the sheep farms and the woodlands, contrasting perspectives on land resources from foresters, farmers, and rangers of the National Park of Cévennes were represented at different spatial scales. A series of exercises with different stakeholder groups was performed to confront them with the consequences of their viewpoints and those of the other stakeholders. As a result of this iterative process, it was possible to select a set of feasible scenarios stemming from the current actors' perceptions and practices, and to suggest alternative sylvopastoral management strategies based on innovative practices.

D'Aquino et al. (2003) describe their project on irrigation systems in Senegal. Since 1997, they have experimented in the Senegal River Valley with agent-based modeling intertwined with role-playing games. Their approach is aimed to include as much knowledge about the local participants as possible. This development of methodology may contribute to additional tools for resource users and public infrastructure providers to self-govern their common resources since companion modeling tools can help develop a common understanding of the resource dynamics and potential conflicts. In some cases, as in Bhutan (Gurung, Bousquet, and Trébuil 2006), the companion modeling process led to agreements between communities.

Pahl-Wostl (2002) discusses a similar development that she calls participatory agent-based social simulation. This modeling technique focuses on the development and use of integrated models with stakeholders in a particular problem setting. In various participatory sessions, information is derived from stakeholders on how they view the problem, what the main variables in their mental models are, and how they interact with viewpoints of other stakeholders. For example, Hare and Pahl-Wostl (2002) illustrate in a Swiss case study how they use knowledge elicitation techniques to retrieve relevant information from stakeholders that can be used to categorize the stakeholders to inform the design of agent-based models. The resulting models are used with stakeholders to facilitate learning and discovery of potential solutions in the collective-action problem of the study.

Guyot and Honiden (2006) perform another step and introduce "agent-based participatory simulations." In these agent-based simulations, human participants control some of the agents in an attempt to merge agent-based models and role-playing games. The typical role-playing game depends on face-to-face interaction among participants using physical objects like cards and game boards. Through the computerization of all the interactions, all information can be recorded, processed, and used to improve the understanding of participants and organizers. An example would be to introduce "assistant agents" who provide suggestions for actions to the human participants. This type of role game bears a similarity to the recent developments in laboratory experiments as discussed in chapter 6.

Barreteau, Le Page, and D'Aquino (2003) argue that such role-playing games are good tools for communication among stakeholders, but that it is difficult to reproduce the results. Systematic comparison of the results is difficult since many factors are uncontrolled. When players play again, they may change the context of the game owing to their learning experience in the previous experiment. Therefore, companion modeling may be used not only for scientific investigation, but also as part of action research[4] to enhance the ability of communities to solve collective-action problems.

MODELS OF CASE STUDIES

When developing models of collective-action situations in local and regional case studies, one typically has a diversity of qualitative and quantitative data. Most of the agent-based modeling research that has drawn on specific case studies as an empirical foundation has focused on modeling a whole social-ecological system and not a specific research question related to collective action. Many of these models seek to identify processes that can account for observed patterns of change in land use and land cover. More generally, they attempt to untangle social-ecological interactions by modeling how actors respond to and influence ecological change, both as individuals and in the aggregate. What crops do farmers choose to put on their land, and how does this affect erosion patterns? How do we describe how agents decide when to deforest particular areas of land? Models of agents' decision making can be based on particular theories, such as rational-choice theory, or on decision strategies derived from ethnographic studies. The empirical data for these models are sometimes based on official statistics, such as remote sensing, census data, and economic statistics, supplemented with survey data (e.g., Manson and Evans 2007). We will discuss some examples later in this section.

Some models are based on ethnographic data obtained through participant observation. By using participant observation, one derives both qualitative and quantitative data about the behavior of resource users (e.g., Bharwani et al. 2005; Huigen, Overmars, and de Groot 2006). Only a few studies have used this approach as their main source of information to build agent-based models. In the few cases that do, the ethnographic data are used to define the behavioral models of the agents, but additional information—such as remotely sensed spatial data about resource conditions like forest cover for different points in time—is used to develop the model.

Bharwani et al. (2005) developed an agent-based model of a case study of smallholder farmers in a village in Vhembe district, Limpopo Province, South Africa. The focus of their study was on how information on seasonal climate outlooks may affect agricultural strategies. Ethnographic knowledge elicitation tools were used to derive decision trees of farming decisions for different climate and market conditions (Bharwani 2006; Bharwani et al. 2005). Poor farmers were found to respond more to climate signals than did better-off farmers, who focused more on market conditions. If the resilience of the poor farmers is to be increased, the information they receive about expected long-term weather conditions (climate signals) needs to be highly accurate. The model analysis shows that poor farmers benefit only if expected long-term weather patterns are correct at least 85 percent of the time.

Huigen, Overmars, and de Groot (2006) developed a land-use model based on ethnographic histories of farm households in San Mariano, the Philippines. These histories provided information on when to buy seed, when to plant seed, when to bring crops to the market, when to extend farming, and when to resettle. Combining this information with remote-sensing data on land cover, Huigen and colleagues were able to calibrate the model on historical land-cover data and explore diverse scenarios of land-use change. Smajgl, Leitch, and Lynam (2009) developed an agent-based model based on the IAD framework discussed in part II, in light of conducting in-depth case studies of four social-ecological systems in the outback of Australia. While each of the cases had quite different attributes, using a common framework that was discussed with local residents and officials proved to be of considerable value in producing the report and useful policy recommendations.

Wilson, Yan, and Wilson (2007) developed an agent-based model of lobster fishermen in Maine that addresses collective action related to natural resources. The state of Maine had initiated a voluntary participant observation program that resulted in precise recordings of the location of lobster catches using a logbook program where locations of counts of legal, sublegal, egg-bearing, and V-notched lobsters were recorded for each trap haul. Upon each entry of catch statistics, a date, time, and location identifier was retrieved from an onboard global positioning system (GPS). The agent-based model was based on a learning classifier system where agents learned behavioral strategies. The set of possible behavioral strategies was based on strategies observed being used by real fishermen. The model could replicate the main spatial and temporal stylized facts of the data. Furthermore, it shows under which conditions groups of fishermen defend their territories against encroachment by other fishermen—similar to findings of long-term case studies of these fisheries (Acheson 2003).

Spatial data can be used to derive maps of physical infrastructure, biophysical characteristics (e.g., soil), political and institutional boundaries, land use, and land cover. These data can then be used as input into agent-based models, as maps of the environment within which the agents interact, through derived measures such as travel costs, proximity between agents, and the like. Many agent-based models on land-use change have their primary data set based on geographic information systems and remotely sensed spatial data (see Parker et al. 2003). An interesting example of combining companion modeling with remotely sensed data is Castella, Trung, and Boissau's (2005) model of deforestation in Vietnam. Using companion modeling in various villages, they developed—in an iterative way—a model of a "typical" community. They used this information to build models at a regional scale and used remote-sensing data on land cover to test the regional model.

Manson and Evans (2007) discuss two models that aim to explain historical change in forest cover of regions of the Americas. One model focuses on deforestation in southern Yucatán in Mexico, and the other model focuses on reforestation in Monroe County, Indiana (U.S.A.). Both models use households as the relevant units for constructing agents. They needed to assume heterogeneity of household characteristics and decision making in order to explain the observations. This result leads to the conclusion that effective policies that may stimulate collective action on land cover cannot rely on one, and only one, policy to encourage conservation since households will vary in their type of response to each policy.

Remotely sensed data can also be used to analyze fishery resources where movement of boats and locations of catching fish are recorded. Dreyfus-Leon (1999) presents a basic model to mimic the search behavior of fishers. The search has two steps: first, which area to fish and, second, how to move around in a fishing ground. In Dreyfus-Leon and Kleiber (2001), the model of fishers' behavior was applied to yellow-fin tuna fishing in the eastern Pacific Ocean. The tuna vessels searched for the tuna schools during a fishing trip. An interesting Turing test[5] was performed to assess the performance of the model by asking experts, fishers, and tuna researchers to identify which tracks were simulated and which were real. The experts were not able to provide the correct answer more frequently than random choice. This gave the modelers some confidence in their results.

Two scenarios were considered in the Dreyfus-Leon analysis: one with no fishing regulation and another with an area closure during the last quarter of the year. In the scenario without regulation, fishing effort was allocated primarily near to the coast and where high concentrations of tuna were detected. In the scenario with regulation, redistribution of effort was uneven but increased in neighboring areas or in areas relatively near the closure zone. Decrease in effort was evident only in the closed area. Effort redistribution when regulations are implemented is not well understood, but this modeling approach can help fishery managers to envisage some regulation effects in the fishery.

Household surveys can be instrumental to define types of agents and how they are distributed on the landscape, as found in several of the above studies. Classes of agents may differ in their preferences, income, knowledge, and other factors, and may affect the aggregated patterns of the simulations. Brown and Robinson (2006) based their model of urban sprawl on a survey of residential preferences within southeastern Michigan, and identified seven groups of residents with similar preferences and similar characteristics of location. Then they developed a highly stylized model of residential development and explored the consequences of agent heterogeneity on the simulated patterns. Preferences were related to nearness to urban services, including jobs, aesthetic quality of the landscape, and similarity of agents to their neighbors. Brown and Robinson found that the way they represented the heterogeneity in the landscape had a significant effect on model outcomes, aggregate patterns of development sprawl, and clustering.

Berger and Schreinemachers (2006) also discuss methodological challenges in the use of survey data. Since agent-based models are often stochastic, and agent characteristics are generated by probability distributions, it is not clear how one parameterizes agent-based models for a specific empirical case with a modest number of observations for each category of agent. Since one defines a limited number of agent types, it is not evident that generating a large population of agents based on survey data results in simulations that are consistent with the data. Berger and Schreinemachers use regional data from Uganda to run their initialization of the agent-based model of land-use change only when the generated data about household characteristics are statistically similar to the observed data. In this way, multiple runs can be generated that are consistent with empirical observations.

METHODOLOGICAL CHALLENGES

This chapter has discussed a diverse set of studies that uses agent-based models together with empirical approaches such as laboratory and field experiments, companion modeling, case studies, and surveys. The combination of these approaches increases the balance between internal and external validity. The use of agent-based models makes them internally consistent and ensures consistency with theoretical considerations. Testing the models on empirical data, sometimes together with stakeholders, makes these models fit the specific context of the application.

Field studies and experiments present a convincing challenge to the rational-choice model of utility maximization and suggest elements for an alternative model. Even in tightly controlled laboratory experiments, however, it is not possible to observe actual decision-making processes. Experiments repeatedly find that communication bolsters cooperation, but do not explain why. Likewise, field studies highlight the importance of a common understanding of how a resource responds to use, and hint at the variety of ways by which groups reach a common understanding. Empirically grounded agent-based models make it possible to evaluate whether hypothesized processes are consistent with empirically observed patterns of behavior. The studies reviewed in this chapter suggest that observed levels of cooperation are consistent with heterogeneity among actors, with at least some agents holding other-regarding preferences, and suggest that communication may bolster cooperation because it facilitates social learning. These studies also provide support for the role of experience, including experiences gained through role-playing and participation in companion games, in improving social outcomes.

In this chapter, four types of empirical approaches are distinguished as a foundation for agent-based modeling—*stylized facts*, *controlled experiments*, *role games*, and *case studies*—reflecting variation in the number of human subjects involved and whether the model is focused on a specific context or on an effort to provide generalizable results. In larger research programs, we see scholars using different approaches within one project (Manson and Evans 2007), for example, by testing decision-making models on experimental data, which are then used within a case-specific model. Or they develop role games in various villages that are then generalized to a module in a regional-scale agent-based model (Castella, Trung, and Boissau 2005).

Although the approaches discussed in this chapter apply to other quantitative methods as well, it is important to keep in mind the unique characteristics of agent-based modeling. With agent-based modeling, one explicitly describes the decision processes of simulated actors at the micro level. Owing to the actions of the agents and their interactions with other agents, patterns of agent behavior emerge at a higher level. The development of such models based on empirical data requires information about how agents make their decisions, how they forecast future developments, and how they remember the past. What do they believe or ignore? How do agents exchange information? And does the structure of agent interactions (trade, kin, organization) affect the higher-level scale phenomena?

The ability to look at nonlinear models at different scales—individual and social—is promising but makes it challenging to develop empirical tests. The models often involve strong simplifications of known processes in order to quantify and abstract the observed behavior. They focus on quantitative information and make assumptions about mechanisms (such as preferences or decision-making strategies) that are not, or are only indirectly, observable. The fact that the models generate quantitative *results* does not necessarily mean that these are quantitative *predictions* that can be used in various contexts. Therefore, researchers need to be cautious about accepting results as universally applicable.

Obviously, combining various methods of modeling, data collection, and analysis leads to the necessity for larger groups of collaborators, who are equipped with knowledge of and experience with different methods, to work together. To successfully engage collaboration, projects need to be relatively long-term. New methodological skills may need to be acquired along the way as new empirical challenges emerge. Such projects typically consist of junior and senior scholars in a network of different organizations that also creates challenges for project communication.

Conclusion

Empirically grounded agent-based modeling builds on the various methods discussed in this book and enables the comparison of different assumptions on the ability to explain observed patterns of collective action. Such an approach is typically a team effort of scholars from various disciplines over a long period of time. Empirically grounded agent-based models can also be part of a practical problem-solving endeavor in which stakeholders are involved in the modeling process. Such models do not have the goal of testing theories, but they may germinate new directions for theory development.

The recent increase of empirical applications of agent-based models also raises new methodological challenges. How can we evaluate simulations with data if the model represents evolving processes with limited predictability? A likely avenue is to compare observed patterns from the data at different spatial and temporal scales with distributions of agent-based models. Given the variability in the simulations and the uncertainty in the data, multiple versions of a model might meet all the relevant patterns. Hence, instead of fitting the model to the data, families of model versions are identified that reproduce the most important empirical patterns. Besides the scientific and quantitative testing of models, qualitative validation using stakeholder insights or using Turing tests may offer important alternative methods of model testing for more context-dependent applications.

In sum, the recent developments in empirically grounded agent-based models bridge the different methods discussed in this book and are likely to become interesting integrative approaches for future research on collective action and the commons.

PART FOUR

Synthesis

CHAPTER NINE

Pushing the Frontiers of the Theory of Collective Action and the Commons

IN THIS CHAPTER, we synthesize how the theory of collective action and the commons has evolved through the use of multiple research methods. Research based on field studies, laboratory and field experiments, game theory, and agent-based models has conclusively demonstrated that it is *possible* for individuals to act collectively to manage shared natural resources on a sustainable basis. Numerous field studies have illustrated the existence of robust collective action that endures over generations. In response to these findings, theory related to collective action and the commons has evolved considerably. For example, field research informed conceptual clarifications related to types of goods and property rights and the rich set of rules used to manage resources. Experiments established the importance of communication and trust in initiating and sustaining collective action. Agent-based models enable scholars to test how diverse combinations of strategies, resource characteristics, and spatial factors combine over time to create situations where cooperation is sustained or disappears. The earlier conventional theory is no longer viewed as the only relevant theory for understanding the commons (Copeland and Taylor 2009; Vatn 2009).

If earlier puzzles have been addressed, new puzzles have emerged and pose significant analytical challenges. Research based on multiple methods suggests that collective action related to common-pool resources (CPRs) is far more complicated than the conventional theory had assumed. The evidence does not support the assumption that individuals always maximize expected, short-term, material returns to self in isolation from other actors. A large number of conditions influence the prospects for collective action (Agrawal 2007; E. Ostrom 2007). Further, findings from research involving a variety of methods suggest that many of these relationships are context-specific (de Oliveira, Croson, and Eckel 2009).

To move beyond the conventional theory of collective action and the commons without getting mired in complexity, we need to build on theoretical developments related to three levels of analysis: (1) individual human behavior, (2) the microsituation including the immediate variables impinging on individuals in a collective-action dilemma, and (3) the broader social-ecological context. The need for three interrelated theoretical efforts is a tad overwhelming, but we need to recognize the importance of all three levels.

Reliance on the theory of human behavior derived from market theory is a core reason for earlier failures to explain why some resource users self-organize and others do not, as well as why some government policies to solve overharvesting work and others do not. The theory of human behavior used to explain and predict likely outcomes in social dilemmas must reflect the strong, accumulated evidence about human behavior in the field, in experimental settings, and in more recent models (E. Ostrom 1998). Focusing on a richer theory of human behavior, however, is not sufficient by itself. A better theory of human behavior alone cannot explain why individuals tend to behave more cooperatively in some contexts and not in others.

We know from extensive empirical research that the specific variables structuring the immediate microenvironment facing individuals have a strong impact on levels of cooperation. Whether the individuals who are interacting know one another, communicate, trust one another to cooperate, and have accurate information about the situation they are in, all affect the likelihood that individuals will cooperate in a dilemma situation, as we elucidate below. We need to integrate these findings into our theoretical understanding of the commons. Further, we also need to understand how the broader context, including the immense complexity of natural resource and political economic settings in which commons dilemmas occur, affect specific human interactions and outcomes.

The big challenge in updating the conventional theory is how to avoid the extremes of overly simple or overly complex theories. Ontological frameworks offer an analytical strategy for recognizing complexity without being overwhelmed by it. Ontology refers to the essence of reality. Our earlier references to ontology in chapter 1 concerned assumptions about the essential nature of reality in terms of causality, such as the relative influence of structure and agency, and the degree to which universal patterns exist. An ontological framework identifies the most essential features of complex systems. A linguistic construction, such as a concept, is seen as composed of subconcepts, which are in turn composed of subconcepts, and further subconcepts. The multitier, ontological framework described later in the chapter (and in E. Ostrom 2007) begins to identify the many variables that *may* be involved in some types of collective-action dilemmas at one level, but are not involved in all collective-action dilemmas at all relevant levels.

We need to build a diagnostic theory of social-ecological systems, grounded in an ontological framework, to learn which attributes of a system—and potentially subtypes and even subtypes of subtypes of these attributes—are important in the analysis of one type of problem in a particular context. These attributes are likely to change as the problem changes and/or the context changes. We cannot present a finished product for these efforts in this chapter. These theoretical tasks will require further work by many scholars over many years. We can, however, build on the extensive research reported in parts II and III of this book to provide a better theoretical understanding and a more coherent framework for future work than was available several decades ago.

The rest of this chapter first provides a synopsis of the developments reviewed in parts II and III of the book. Then, we summarize current thinking about a behavioral theory of individual action. Next, we discuss the need to unpack the concept of context into a microsituational level and a broader scale. Then, we focus on the most relevant aspects of a microsituation that affect the likelihood of cooperation in social dilemmas. In the fifth section, we examine the broader scale affecting collective action. There we discuss an ontological framework for examining relevant contextual variables at a broader level that affect outcomes in diverse microsituations. We then propose a diagnostic approach that identifies the large *sets* and *subsets* of variables that potentially affect patterns of interactions and outcomes. This strikes a good balance between theoretical oversimplification and the complexity represented in context-specific explanations. We conclude with a brief overview of the challenges for future research.

SYNOPSIS OF RESEARCH DEVELOPMENTS REVIEWED IN PARTS II AND III

Garrett Hardin's (1968) dramatic pronouncement that local users were inexorably trapped in overusing a commons appeared more than four decades ago. Given the consistency of Hardin's prediction with the work of H. Scott Gordon (1954) and Anthony Scott (1955) before him, with predictions from the theory of collective action (Olson 1965), and with non-cooperative game theory of that era, few saw reasons to challenge it. A sufficient number of well-known examples existed where common-pool resources were severely overharvested that the theory was considered credible by many scholars and policymakers, and became the conventional theory of the commons.

The conventional theory was pristine in the simplicity of its model of human behavior but made strong assumptions about information conditions. Individuals are assumed to have complete information about the structure of the situation they are in, including the preferences of other actors, the full range of possible actions, and the probability associated with each outcome resulting from a combination of actions. Each individual is assumed to select the strategy leading to the best expected outcome for self. Thus individuals faced with a one-shot or finitely repeated social dilemma situation, with a payoff structure that brought more immediate returns if they did not cooperate while others did, would not cooperate.[1] Regardless of the microsituational structure or broader context, all individuals in a dilemma situation would maximize short-term returns to self (see figure 9.1). No one would cooperate.

The theory presumed that external analysts could develop models showing how a preferred rule would change incentives leading to changes in actions so as to produce optimal outcomes. These optimal rules could hypothetically be imposed on participants who would change their behavior, but not their inner decision-making processes (see figure 9.2). Based on the conventional theory, many analysts thought that the *only* way to solve the commons problem was to impose a "solution" from the outside.

Fortunately, scholars who conducted case studies of diverse resource systems all over the world were not blinded by the conventional theory. They simply wrote about what they found in their field sites. In many instances, their findings contradicted the presumption that it was impossible for local users to self-organize. As discussed in chapter 2, the early case study findings were so widely scattered among different disciplines and types of resource systems that the challenge they represented to the validity of the conventional theory was not well recognized until the mid-1980s. The scholarly and policy world owes a considerable debt of gratitude to the National Research Council for organizing a Panel on Common Property Resource Management. The panel brought attention to the existence of not just one but hundreds of counterexamples to the predictions derived from the conventional theory of the commons. The possibility of collective action has now been confirmed in many field-based studies, experiments, and agent-based models. Because of the strong findings generated through a diversity of approaches, scholars, policy analysts, citizens, and officials now understand that collective action is *possible* and can address problems related to overuse of natural resources.

Successful collective action is not, however, the *only* possibility. Case studies have documented numerous examples of once-successful collective arrangements that failed to survive market pressures, government interventions, technological changes, demographic changes, or ecological changes. In other cases, collective action never emerged. What accounts for varied success in collective action to manage common-pool natural resources? The studies reviewed in parts II and III of this book provide numerous suggestions. These studies have highlighted the importance of (1) cognitive limitations and risk aversion, (2) social interactions and norms, and (3) interactions among contextual conditions.

Field studies and meta-analysis have shown that, in fact, shared resource systems (including irrigation works, fisheries, forests, rangelands, water systems, etc.) present management challenges that vary considerably. The conventional theory assumed that management of any shared

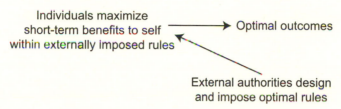

Fig. 9.1. Conventional theory of collective action.

Fig. 9.2. Conventional solution to collective-action dilemmas.

natural resource could be modeled as a single-shot Prisoner's Dilemma. If resource users value risk spreading over single-shot yields, however, as has been shown to be the case in some field studies, rewards for cooperative behavior may be considerable. Further, because of the variability and complexity of biological and physical dynamics affecting natural resources, the cognitive challenges presented by natural resource management also vary across settings. How can theory address the influence of *cognitive limitations and risk* on individual decision making and collective action?

In the lab, once subjects are enabled to talk about their puzzle in a face-to-face group,[2] most develop joint strategies as well as the trust and reciprocity needed to carry out these strategies, contrary to the conventional theory. Within a few rounds, they reduce overharvesting substantially and improve their individual and joint outcomes. These findings echo behavior in the field where, as discussed in part II, many groups that use inshore fisheries, forests, irrigation systems, and pastures have used communication to develop a diversity of norms and rules to enable them to reduce overharvesting (Sandberg 2008). As we discuss in the next section, although social interaction certainly conveys information about the planned behavior of other actors, its role in establishing and enforcing norms seems to be at least as important for encouraging collective action. An improved theory must be able to account for *normative influences on human behavior.*

Field-based studies, experiments, and agent-based models have identified a large number of contextual variables that influence collective action, including microsituational conditions, such as group size and heterogeneity, and macroconditions, such as market pressures, property rights, and government policies. It seems that few if any of these variables influence collective action in a uniform manner. Evidence has mounted that the simple policy prescriptions that are so often recommended as panaceas—privatize, turn over to the government, or create communal rights—can also fail (see Berkes 2007; Brock and Carpenter 2007; Meinzen-Dick 2007; Wilson, Yan, and Wilson 2007). Simple solutions for complex problems are not likely to work. Considerable evidence has been gathered, from both the field and the laboratory, that outcomes are influenced by *combinations* of factors.

The importance of cognitive limitations and risk, social interactions and norms, and interactions among contextual variables has been confirmed in numerous studies based on case studies, cross-national comparisons, experiments, and agent-based models. Current theories of collective action do not fully address interactions among these conditions. The theoretical challenge has several aspects. An improved theory should offer the tools for simplification that are inherent in theoretical analysis while allowing for complexity. It should allow for complexity and contingency without losing sight of patterns that apply to multiple cases. And it should account for cases that were well explained by the conventional theory as well as the many cases that deviate from the older theory. The research reviewed in parts II and III of this book presents a challenge to theory but also provides building blocks for an improved theory. The next sections draw out those building blocks, beginning with movements toward a more general behavioral theory of human action.

Toward a More General Behavioral Theory of Human Action

The clear and unambiguous predictions derived from the conventional theory of collective action have been replaced with a range of possible outcomes, including some that are far more optimistic. The theoretical and empirical enterprise has, however, become more uncertain and complex. Explanations can no longer rest entirely on the model of the individual facing a particular type of payoff function. Instead, as shown in figure 9.3, an explanation of cooperation must be based on individual learning and norm-adoption, as well as the influence of microsituational and broader contextual variables, in generating variable levels of cooperation. We believe that behavior is more directly influenced by the microsituational variables, which in turn are influenced by the broader contextual variables. However, some methodological approaches do not explicitly include the microsituational context and assume a direct link between broader context and observed behavior, indicated by the thin line in figure 9.3.

Scholars who yearn to have one simple theory to explain human behavior in all settings find this frustrating. It is particularly upsetting to

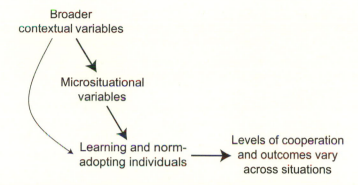

Fig. 9.3. Cooperation in collective-action dilemmas in behavioral theory.

have one theory—rational-choice theory—that explains how individuals achieve close-to-optimal outcomes in competitive market settings, but fails to explain how individuals will or will not cope with social dilemmas.[3] Simply assuming that individuals are socialized into seeking better group outcomes does not explain the obvious fact that groups struggle with this problem and often fail to obtain jointly beneficial outcomes (Dietz, Ostrom, and Stern 2003). It is not an acceptable scientific strategy to hold onto a theory because it has done so well in one type of situation when it does not predict behavior well in many other types of situations.

We need to recognize that what has come to be called rational-choice *theory* is instead one *model* in a family of models that is useful for conducting formal analyses of human decisions in highly structured, competitive settings, as we discuss in chapter 6. It should be thought of as a model of human behavior when individuals face highly competitive settings and do not remain in the game unless they focus narrowly on benefits to self. As Alchian (1950) demonstrated long ago, competitive markets eliminate players who do not maximize profits. Further, markets generate limited, but sufficient, statistics needed to maximize profits. The institutional structure of a market rewards individuals who make economically rational decisions and who can then be modeled as if they were determinate, calculating machines. Predictions of the conventional model are well-supported empirically for behavior in competitive markets and other highly structured and competitive environments (C. Holt 2007; Lian and Plott 1998; V. Smith 1962; V. Smith and Walker 1993). When it is used successfully, the rational-choice model is largely dependent for its predictive power on the structure of the situation involved (Satz and Ferejohn 1994). In other words, the specific attributes of the situation within which individuals interact are more important in predicting outcomes than is the model of rational behavior and the assumption that the payoffs create a dilemma situation (Orbell et al. 2004).

In their effort to understand the extensive research that has challenged the validity of the model of rational behavior used so successfully in predicting behavior in highly competitive situations, scholars have attempted to modify this model at the margins to retain simplicity while accounting for deviations from the assumption that individuals maximize their own utility. These modifications posit other goals that humans appear to seek beyond immediate material benefits, or acknowledge cognitive limitations and varied attitudes toward risk. The fact that many participants cooperate even in one-shot social dilemma situations indicates that their preferences are not entirely dictated by the monetary payoffs they receive in the experiments. Thus allowing for norms and social preferences is *necessary* in explaining the dynamics of these action situations, but not *sufficient* for predicting cooperation.[4]

All of the detailed models of human behavior that have been developed to explain deviations from the conventional model predict behavior well in some nonmarket situations but do not make accurate predictions across a full diversity of social dilemmas (see Janssen and Ahn 2006). Thus it is unwise to settle on a single new *model* of individual behavior to replace the model of fully self-interested behavior. It is more productive to posit broad theoretical attributes of human behavior that can help explain why individuals act in particular ways in one situation versus another. The weight of an explanation for cooperation in social dilemmas must lie both in the general theory of human behavior *and* in specific characteristics of the microsituations they are in as they are embedded in a broader context.

Assumptions of a Behavioral Theory

A broader theory of human behavior views humans as adaptive creatures who attempt to do well given the constraints and opportunities of the situations in which they find themselves (or the ones that they seek out) (Jones 2001; Simon 1955, 1957, 1999). Humans learn norms, heuristics, and full analytical strategies from one another, from feedback from the world, and from their own capacity to engage in self-reflection and imagine a differently structured world. They are capable of designing new tools—including institutions—that can, for good or evil purposes, change the structure of the worlds they face. Multiple models are consistent with a behavioral theory of human actions, including a model of complete rationality when paired with specific models of repetitive, highly competitive situations.

Basically, a behavioral theory of human decision making in dilemma settings is based on three core assumptions:

1. Actors possess incomplete information about the structure of the situation in which they are interacting with others, but they may acquire more complete and reliable information over time, especially in situations that are frequently repeated and generate reliable feedback to those involved.
2. Actors have preferences related to achieving net benefits for self, but these are combined in many situations with other-regarding preferences and norms about appropriate actions and outcomes that affect their decisions.
3. Actors use a variety of heuristics in making daily decisions that may approximate maximization of net benefits (for self and others) in some competitive situations but are highly cooperative in other situations.

If, as we assume, decision making relies on learning and adaptation, other-regarding preferences and norms, and heuristics, then trust can play a central role in influencing the prospects for collective action. We discuss each of these basic assumptions and then draw out the implications for the centrality of trust.

INCOMPLETE INFORMATION WITH LEARNING

In most common-pool resource settings, it would be unrealistic to assume that all individuals make decisions in light of having complete information about all of the structural aspects of the situation they face. Instead of assuming that complete and perfect information is a universal property of the individual decision maker, in a behavioral theory one assumes that structural elements of a relevant situation affect the accuracy and completeness of the information that an individual possesses.

It is reasonable, for example, to assume full information when predicting behavior in laboratory experiments given the substantial effort that most researchers expend to provide all participants with the same and accurate information about the structure of the situation. Participants are informed of the number of other participants, the actions they can and cannot take, the payoffs for different combinations of actions, and whether the experiment will be repeated with (or without) the same linkage among participants. Individuals rarely have full and complete information in nonexperimental settings, but they do learn. Learning is more likely in a relatively simple situation that is repeated without major structural changes. One can assume that individuals learn more accurate information over time about other participants, the individual actions that are allowed or forbidden and how these are linked to outcomes, and their individual and joint payoffs. Learning is more difficult in structurally complex situations and when the structure of the choice situation changes unpredictably. Under these circumstances, actors may not learn, or they may draw inaccurate "lessons" from their experiences.

Learning takes many forms. In addition to gaining a better understanding of the structure of the choice situation, individuals learn norms and social rules, how particular individuals typically behave (reputations), and individual heuristics or rules of thumb to guide behavior in specific types of situations.[5] We turn to these other forms of learning in the next two subsections.

NORMS AND OTHER-REGARDING PREFERENCES

In addition to learning more reliable information, individuals also learn norms. By norms, we mean that the individual attaches an internal valuation—positive or negative—to taking particular types of action in specific situations. Crawford and Ostrom (2005) refer to this internal valuation as a delta parameter that is added to or subtracted from the objective costs of an action or an outcome. Knack (1992) refers to negative internal valuations as "duty." The strength of the commitment (Sen 1977) made by an individual to take particular types of future actions (telling the truth, keeping promises) is reflected in the size of the internal positive or negative weight (delta parameter) that they add to their preference function.

Analytically, individuals can be thought of as learning norms of behavior that are relatively general and fit a wide diversity of particular situations. Cox and colleagues posit that individual behavior in a particular setting is affected by an individual's initial emotional or normative state and then by direct experience with others in a specific setting (J. Cox 2004; J. Cox, Friedman, and Gjerstad 2007; J. Cox, Sadiraj, and Sadiraj 2008). The underlying norms and direct experience in a particular setting combine to affect orientations toward reciprocity. There are multiple ways of representing these social preferences.[6]

Fairness and justice are among the norms used by many individuals in dealing with collective-action settings (Frohlich and Oppenheimer 1992). The maximal net return to a group may be obtained in a manner that is perceived to be fair or unfair by those involved—using the general concept that "equals should be treated equally and unequals unequally" (see Isaac, Mathieu, and Zajac 1991). Fehr and Schmidt (1999) propose another explanation for experimental observations, namely, *inequity aversion*, which is a dislike of unequal outcomes per se, independent of whether they have been the result of kind or of hostile intentions. When participants are symmetric in regard to all strategically relevant variables, the only real fairness issue relates to the potential capability of some to free-ride on others (Dawes et al. 1986). When participants differ, however, finding an allocation formula perceived by most participants as fair is far more challenging (Eckel and Grossman 1996; Rawls 1971). In most cases, however, theorists have argued that when participants think that a proposal for sharing costs and benefits is fair, they are more willing to contribute (Biel and Thøgersen 2007; Blount 1995).

Simply assuming that individuals adopt norms is not sufficient to generate a prediction of when individuals will or will not cooperate in a dilemma situation. As de Oliveira, Croson, and Eckel (2009, 19) point out, "individuals may have a stable preference to 'do the right thing,'" but even with this stable preference, "observed behavior may vary by context because the perception of the 'right thing' would change." Multiple aspects of particular situations combine to enhance the importance of following norms and valuing returns to others or of ignoring these. Factors such as not knowing who else is involved, or learning that others are not cooperating, may deter an individual—one who has strong norms or other-regarding preferences—from giving any weight to these in this situation. Who wants to be a sucker or to help those who are free-riders?

HEURISTICS

When theorists use a model of complete rationality, they assume that individuals have access to complete information—information about all potential actions that one could take, all outcomes that could be obtained, and all strategies that others could take. The conventional model also assumes that individuals will consider all available information when making decisions. In fact, many situations in life do not generate complete and accurate information about all potential actions, all outcomes, and all strategies. Even when individuals can acquire information, it may be costly for them to do so. In other situations, the volume and complexity of information is overwhelming. In most everyday situations, individuals use heuristics—rules of thumb—that they have learned over time regarding responses that tend to give them good (but not necessarily optimal) outcomes in particular kinds of situations. In frequently encountered, repetitive situations, such as those faced by pastoralists roving with their animals, individuals learn better and better heuristics that are tailored to particular situations. In other words, over time, individuals develop rough approximations of the benefits and costs of actions they can take in a particular setting. Individuals may also follow normative commitments without calculating the exact level of shame or pride they would experience for making a particular decision in a situation (Vatn 2009). With repetition and sufficiently large stakes, individuals may learn heuristics that approach best-response strategies and thus approach local optima (Gigerenzer and Selten 2001; Ortmann et al. 2008). Heuristics perform less well in responding to rapid changes, especially sudden shocks, and highly unpredictable conditions.

Theorists interested in collective action have examined the potentially positive effects of participants' adopting simple heuristics when they are in a social dilemma situation. Morikawa, Orbell, and Runde (1995), for example, examine the efficacy of using the simple heuristic of "expect others to have the same dispositions as yourself." They conduct a simulation where each agent in a population of ten thousand agents is matched to another agent. Two different versions of matching are considered: matching with one random individual from the whole population, or matching with an agent in close spatial proximity. Those simulated agents whose payoff is above the mean are multiplied by two, while those whose payoff is below the mean are eliminated from the simulation. Their simulations generate the prediction that the heuristic will be most valuable when social dilemmas occur among those in close proximity. Other heuristics, such as "always take your share," may lead to negative outcomes in some situations.

Using a behavioral theory of individuals who learn from past history and current interactions in a situation, who are other-regarding (to some extent), and who hold internal norms related to their behavior, is still consistent with assuming that individuals do a *rough* benefit-cost calculation to evaluate which actions they should take or which heuristics to use in a particular situation. When the situation of concern is primarily commercial and framed by a competitive market, a researcher can gain a relatively reliable estimate of the expected financial benefits and costs of an action. If it is an over-time situation characterized by risk, the researcher has to make a rough estimate of the discount rate and how other participants would estimate the risks involved.

The Centrality of Trust

In situations where individuals can acquire a reputation for being trustworthy and for using positive and negative reciprocity, others can learn to trust those with such a reputation and begin to cooperate so as to sustain higher returns for all (Fukuyama 1995; E. Ostrom 1998; Rothstein 2005). Levels of trust can act as a heuristic guiding the choice among alternative norms. Thus at the core of an evolving theoretical explanation of successful or unsuccessful collective action is the internal link between the trust among participants in a common-pool setting—or a more general collective-action situation—and the increased probability that all participants will use reciprocity norms (see figure 9.4).

The conventional theory of collective action does not include *any* reference to the concepts of trust and reciprocity, even though the distin-

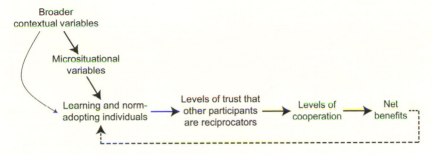

Fig. 9.4. Effect on cooperation of microsituational and broader contexts.

guished economist Kenneth Arrow (1974) had long ago pointed to the essential role of trust between partners as the most efficient mechanism for governing transactions. The prediction of an outcome was based entirely on the payoff function, so little theoretical attention was given to how contextual variables at multiple levels affect cooperation.[7]

When some individuals initiate cooperation in a repeated situation, others may learn to trust them and be more willing to adopt reciprocity themselves, leading to higher levels of cooperation, even though cooperation may not reach 100 percent (Milinski, Semmann, and Krambeck 2002). And, when more individuals use reciprocity, gaining a reputation for being trustworthy is a good investment as well as having an intrinsic value. Thus levels of trust and reciprocity are mutually reinforcing. This also means that a decrease in either can generate a downward cascade leading to little or no cooperation—unless there are appropriate ways of sanctioning noncontributors that reverse a trend downward.

Unpacking the Concept of Context

Extensive research on collective action has shown that more people cooperate than is predicted by the conventional theory, but substantial variation in behavior exists across and within situations.[8] We are less able to predict precise outcomes in collective-action situations than in highly structured competitive situations. With the extensive research reported in parts II and III of this book, however, we have gained further insights into how combinations of microsituational and broader contextual variables affect decisions made by individuals who learn the benefits and costs of cooperation, who value norms and returns to others to some extent, and who use heuristics rather than a full plan of action. Thus our next theoretical task is to begin to develop tools to help unpack the concept of context.

As mentioned in the introduction to this chapter, in addition to a better understanding of human behavior, movement beyond the conventional theory of collective action requires theoretical developments at two levels: the microsituation in which individuals directly act, and the broader context related to the social-ecological system in which individuals make decisions in the field. Analysis of the broader context requires a multi-tier ontological framework for unpacking the huge number of potential variables relevant to the diverse resource dilemmas that occur in field settings. We will defer that discussion until the next section of this chapter and focus now on context at the micro level.

The Microsituational Context

In evaluating whether to trust that it is safe to cooperate (and that the chances of being a sucker are relatively low), individuals have to use information about the structure of the situation they are in—and the behavior of others that they may be able to observe over time. A social dilemma situation in which an individual has *no* information about who else is involved and makes an *anonymous* decision relieves many individual participants of the need to follow norms or value outcomes for others. It also enables a researcher to make a relatively clear prediction that a substantial proportion of individuals in such situations will *not* cooperate. Overharvesting tends to occur when resource users do *not* know who all is involved, do not have a foundation of trust and reciprocity, cannot communicate, have no established rules, and lack effective monitoring and sanctioning mechanisms.[9]

As discussed in chapter 6, subjects in an experiment presented with a common-pool resource problem substantially overharvest when they do not know who is in their group, receive no feedback on individual actions, and cannot communicate. One-shot experiments using double-blind designs, where the participants know that their decisions are kept anonymous and that even the experimenter will not know what they do, tend to generate the most self-regarding behavior. In a recent synthesis of dilemma experiments, Ebenhöh and Pahl-Wostl (2008) found that the level of cooperation was lowest in those experiments in which the identity of others was not known, anonymity was fully protected, and there was no chance to build a reputation.

The Impact of Microsituational Variables on Cooperation

Given the extensive results of experiments that use microsituational variables in their design and a behavioral theory of human action, we are slowly gaining confidence that we can explain and predict when participants in many social dilemmas related to the use of natural resources will achieve higher joint and individual payoffs. We are now able to move beyond resting all explanatory weight on models of human behavior or simply asserting that "context" makes a difference.[10] The core problem that needs to be solved in order to increase cooperation is creating trust among participants that others are reciprocators, and that cooperating will not make an individual a sucker.

Thus we start with the prediction that participants in a repeated social dilemma are more likely to cooperate when they trust that other participants will cooperate, expect higher benefits than costs, and do not think that noncontributors will take advantage of contributors (Frohlich and Oppenheimer 2001). It is easier to evaluate these hypotheses in laboratory experiments than in field settings.[11] With repetition of the experimental conditions and replication of them by other scholars, one can assess whether (1) a particular situational variable has a consistent, predicted impact on behavior in a diversity of settings; (2) its impact depends on the combination of structural variables present; or (3) it had an impact in one setting only and should not play a role in future theoretical development. The following six microsituational variables have been found to increase trust and positive outcomes in multiple experimental social dilemmas.

S1 *High marginal per capita return of cooperation.* If *mpcr* is high, each individual can recognize that his/her own contributions make more of a difference than they would with low marginal per capita returns, and that others are more likely to recognize this and contribute.

S2 *Security* that contributions will be returned if not sufficient. If an individual's contribution will be returned if not enough others contribute, each individual is safeguarded against being a sucker and is more willing to contribute.

S3 *The reputations of participants are known.* Even when individuals may not know specifically with whom they are clustered, knowing enough about fellow participants' past history of being a contributor is likely to increase cooperation levels when the reputation is positive.

S4 *Longer time horizon.* Participants can reason with themselves that showing a willingness to contribute early may lead others to contribute, and the longer the time horizon involved, the better the return on individual investment. In one-shot settings, cooperation is higher than conventional theory predicts, but some participants will not cooperate at all.

S5   Capability to choose to *enter or exit* from a group. This enables participants to enter microsettings where others are cooperating at a higher level and to leave when they are dissatisfied with outcomes.[12]

S6   *Communication* is feasible with the full set of participants. Even sending structured messages to each other can increase trust. When discussion is organized in a face-to-face manner, the way words are spoken, facial expressions, and physical actions help individuals assess the trustworthiness of others and the willingness to contribute. Participants frequently use this opportunity to convince each other of the appropriateness of a norm that they should follow. Even when participants have unequal assets for investing in a public good or common-pool resource, being able to communicate about alternative formulas that could be used to achieve a fair distribution of costs and benefits can help increase trust and joint payoffs.[13]

The above six structural variables have been shown in multiple microsituations to have a positive impact on levels of cooperation. Three structural variables are associated with a diversity of outcomes.

S7   *Size of group.* When individuals face a public goods problem, they are more likely to contribute in larger groups than in smaller groups. In a public goods situation, cooperation by any individual increases the *non*subtractive benefits to all without affecting individual costs. Contrariwise, in a common-pool resource, each unit harvested by one individual is subtracted from those available to others. As the group gets larger, the fear of being a sucker (by not harvesting while others harvest) may increase.

S8   *Information about the average contributions is made available.* In public goods settings, cooperation levels tend to shift downward over time, and where individuals see that downward trend, they also tend to stop contributing. In a common-pool resource, information about past overuse may lead some individuals to pull back and harvest less out of fear of losing all future opportunities, while others might increase harvesting.

S9   *Sanctioning capabilities.* Depending on how a sanctioning capability is established, the ratio of the cost of sanctioning, and the cost of being sanctioned, whether rewards can also be issued, and whether there is communication, some situations with sanctioning capabilities allocated to individuals increase joint returns, and joint returns are decreased in others. One has to examine the effect of sanctioning capabilities on the levels of trust or distrust they engender.

There is a tenth structural variable that differs across microsituational variables and usually is associated with low levels of cooperation:

S10 *Heterogeneity in benefits and costs.* When it appears to some participants that others will receive more benefits without paying more costs, those with fewer assets may be unwilling to contribute—especially if there is no way to communicate about how to share costs and benefits.[14] Heterogeneity in positions and in access reflects differences in power. Small subgroups can create effective arrangements to appropriate more resources for themselves and suppress access to others. Olson (2000) developed the notion of "stationary bandits" to explain such rent-seeking behavior.

The substantial number of carefully designed experiments that have been conducted by researchers in many laboratories (as well as in related field experiments) provides a solid empirical foundation for developing this initial list of microsituational variables that affect levels of cooperation, as illustrated in figure 9.5. The list of variables, as well as the identification of subcategories of variables, is likely to grow over time as more experimental research is undertaken related to collective action. Currently, these variables have been used primarily to structure microsituations in order to test theory. They can also be used diagnostically in efforts to understand, and potentially modify, microsituations, such as small work-teams, where cooperation is low.

The Challenge of Linking Contextual Scales

Several recent efforts to conduct the same experiments in a variety of field settings illustrate that behavior is affected both by the microsituational variables used in conducting an experiment and by the broader contextual variables that affect the field settings where experiments were run. Henrich et al. (2004, 2005), for example, decided to ascertain whether the findings from lab experiments with undergraduate students enrolled in universities located in developed countries would stand up at all when conducted in multiple developing countries. They conducted a series of ultimatum and public goods games in fifteen small communities located in Africa, Asia, and Latin America. Two major findings from this study help to explain why microsituational and broader contextual variables are both important in the understanding of cooperation.

First, Henrich and colleagues found that behavior and outcomes were broadly similar in most of the same experimental games conducted across the societies included in their study. Second, they found that the culture and environment in which an experiment was conducted also affected the behavior of participants and the outcomes. In societies where individuals engaged in little trade or other forms of cooperative behavior,

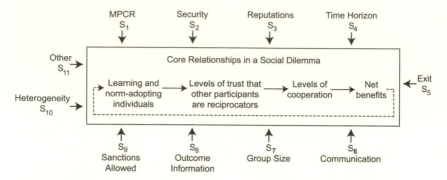

Fig. 9.5. Microsituational variables affecting trust and cooperation in collective-action dilemmas.

participants were the least cooperative in the experiments. In societies organized around trade and team efforts, participants were most cooperative. As discussed in chapter 6, colleagues in Colombia have also found not only similarities in experimental results across diverse field settings in the same country, but also some variations due to different ecological and historical factors of a field site (Cardenas 2000, 2003; Cardenas, Janssen, and Bousquet forthcoming; Lopez et al. forthcoming).

The link between situational variables and the capacity of participants to gain trust and cooperate in microsituations, such as those found in laboratory experiments or small groups who harvest together from a resource, is easier to explain than is the link from broader contextual variables to level of cooperation in field settings. The vastly more numerous contextual variables observed in the field, and the challenge of measuring them precisely, make theoretical predictions related to field studies far more difficult. And yet research conducted in the field, in field laboratories, and through the use of agent-based models repeatedly confirms that the broader context influences the likelihood of cooperation. In the next section, we argue that a diagnostic theory grounded in an ontological framework begins to offer the tools needed to tackle the challenge of studying the influence of broader contextual variables as well as their interactions with specific microsituations and general processes of human behavior.

THE BROADER SCALE AFFECTING COLLECTIVE ACTION

A crucial challenge at the current stage of development is the need to move toward theories of collective action and common-pool resources that acknowledge complexity and multiple levels of analysis, yet offer meaningful analytical leverage, can be tested, and can be improved over time. To accomplish this difficult task, we need to recognize the importance of developing ontological frameworks and diagnostic theories, and learn how to use both. The Institutional Analysis and Development (IAD) framework first developed in the early 1980s (see chapter 2) is an ontological framework that has been useful in organizing empirical research, but has not included as many ecological variables as are needed in future research.

Diagnostic theories have been developed over time in medicine, biology, and information sciences to enable scholars to understand causal processes within complex, nested systems. Answers to initial research questions identify further questions that need to be addressed in a repeated process until one has found answers to illuminate the causal processes that are leading to a set of outcomes of interest. Since there are many potential dependent variables to explain, one needs to develop a set of related theories rather than just a single theory. Ontological frameworks complement the development of powerful diagnostic theories.

Ontological Frameworks

Ontological frameworks are widely used in biology, medicine, and informatics to lay out the nested nature of the elements of a complex system (Madin et al. 2007; Salafsky et al. 2008). When we have a medical problem, for example, a doctor will ask us a number of initial questions and take regular measurements. In light of that information, the doctor proceeds down a medical ontology to ask further and more specific questions (or prescribes tests) until a reasonable hypothesis regarding the source of the problem can be found and supported. Ecologists study problems occurring within ecological systems, and their ontology of questions depends on the specific processes and problems they are studying in a particular area. A biologist may be interested in the growth patterns of one particular mammal living in that ecology. The research questions asked about the life patterns of a particular animal (including humans) differ substantially from those asked about other animals, or about an ecology composed of the interaction of many animals and plants. Further, a biologist would expect that the processes related to a specific animal will differ somewhat when that animal is studied in different ecological zones.

Doctors, biologists, and ecologists are more comfortable than are social scientists with the notion of analytic systems within systems within systems, where the researcher has to determine the appropriate system—and variables within it—to address a particular set of questions. Within the social sciences, Herbert Simon (1985, 196) introduced a concept that he called a hierarchic system,[15] by which he meant

> a system that is composed of interrelated subsystems, each of the latter being in turn hierarchic in structure until we reach some lowest level of elementary subsystem. In most systems in nature it is somewhat arbitrary as to where we leave off the partitioning and what subsystems we take as elementary.

When we think about a particular collective-action problem, we need to think about which of the attributes of a system are likely to have a major impact on the patterns of interactions and outcomes to be explained. The researcher picks the focal system to address a particular set of questions and the relevant variables operating at that level for addressing this question. To address an interesting question, one usually also examines processes occurring at one or two levels above and below that focal system. No focal system is correct for all questions. Nor is there a set of variables at any particular level that is always involved for any of the important questions a researcher may want to address.

An Ontological Framework of Social-Ecological Systems

As a point of departure, we draw on a multitier framework first presented in an article titled "A Diagnostic Approach for Going beyond Panaceas" (E. Ostrom 2007). The broad first tier of this framework relates resource systems and their units with governance systems and users that together generate interactions and outcomes (see figure 9.6). An initial unpacking of the first tier leads to a very large set of variables that may characterize any of the basic systems identified at the first tier (see discussion of table 9.1 below). The second-tier variables may be further unpacked into third-, fourth-, or fifth-tier variables—depending on the question being asked and whether different subtypes of a variable tend to generate different outcomes in particular types of processes.

The framework can be used to study a wide variety of questions related to any particular resource system, ranging in scale from a small inshore fishery to the global commons. A scholar interested in explaining a particular puzzle would first identify the type and size of a resource system, its resource units, the governance system related to it, and the users that are relevant for answering that question. The question might be why fishers in Kafue Flats fisheries of Zambia do not engage in collective action (Haller and Merten 2008), or why two fishery communities on the coast of Mexico were able to self-organize while a neighboring community was not (Basurto and Ostrom 2009).

Scientists trying to understand multiple cases that vary in regard to the first tier identified in figure 9.6 need to design research so that cases

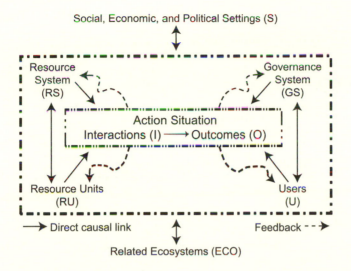

Fig. 9.6. The first tier of a framework for analyzing a social-ecological system. *Source*: Adapted from E. Ostrom 2007, 15182.

are broadly similar in regard to either the left or the right side of the figure. Thus a social scientist may want to hold the resource system and its units constant for a particular study, so these are not different while the scholar is trying to understand the impact of diverse rules on user behavior leading to outcomes. An ecologist, on the other hand, might want to hold the governance systems and attributes of users relatively constant in choosing cases to study so that differences in the resource system can be examined without substantial simultaneous interaction with social structure.

The broad social-ecological system (SES) framework presented in figure 9.6 provides a "frame" for our earlier focus on how microsituational variables impact on the core relationships in a social dilemma. In figure 9.7, we illustrate the nesting of microsituations examined in figure 9.5 within the broader context of figure 9.6. By doing this, we illustrate the complexity of relationships between the broader context of a situation as it impacts the structure of the situation of the actors at the micro level. While some explanations of outcomes may focus more at a microsituational level and others at a broader level, both are needed at times to explain delicate relationships between the broader context and the microsetting.[16]

To begin to diagnose causal patterns that affect interactions and outcomes, one needs to incorporate a subset of "second-tier" contextual variables that are contained within the first tier identified in figure 9.6 that have an impact on outcomes. The list of second-tier variables (and two

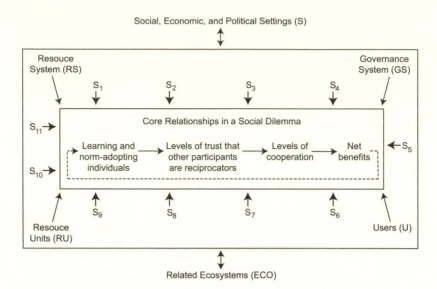

Fig. 9.7. SES broader context as affecting microsituations.

third-tier variables) in table 9.1 constitutes an initial effort to help group and classify important variables in an ontology of potential importance for the analysis of multiple theoretical puzzles related to SES outcomes. Table 9.1 does not contain the "final" list of potentially relevant second-tier SES variables. As more research is undertaken, the framework will be improved over time.

Listing a variable in a framework is not equivalent to developing a well-defined theoretical question. No theory would include *all* of the second-tier variables (or the many third- and fourth-tier variables) that affect some of the important processes occurring within SESs. A list of variables is not a theory. The intention of developing the SES framework is to help scholars, officials, and citizens to understand the *potential* set of variables and their subvariables that can be important in analyzing diverse theoretical questions related to the governance of resources.

Predicting Self-Organization Drawing on the SES Framework

When will users invest in making rules related to their use of a common-pool resource? This is an important question to which a very general theoretical answer can be given. Users of a resource system will continue to harvest resource units, without trying to self-organize, unless they perceive that the benefits they would receive from a change in their rules will

TABLE 9.1
Second-tier variables in framework for analyzing a social-ecological system

Social, Economic, and Political Settings (S)	
S1- Economic development. S2- Demographic trends. S3- Political stability. S4- Technology. S5- Government resource policies. S6- Market incentives. S7- Media organization.	

Resource System (RS)	Governance System (GS)
RS1- Sector (e.g., water, forests, pasture, fish)	GS1- Government organizations
RS2- Clarity of system boundaries	GS2- Nongovernment organizations
RS3- Size of resource system*	GS3- Network structure
RS4- Human-constructed facilities	GS4- Property-rights systems
RS5- Productivity of system*	GS5- Operational rules
RS5a- Indicators of the productivity of system*	GS6- Collective-choice rules
	GS6a- Local collective-choice autonomy*
RS6- Equilibrium properties	GS7- Constitutional rules
RS7- Predictability of system dynamics*	GS8- Monitoring & sanctioning processes
RS8- Storage characteristics	
RS9- Location	

Resource Units (RU)	Users (U)
RU1- Resource unit mobility*	U1- Number of users*
RU2- Growth or replacement rate	U2- Socioeconomic attributes of users*
RU3- Interaction among resource units	U3- History of use
RU4- Economic value	U4- Location
RU5- Size	U5- Leadership/entrepreneurship*
RU6- Distinctive markings	U6- Norms/social capital*
RU7- Spatial & temporal distribution	U7- Knowledge of SES/mental models*
	U8- Importance of resource*
	U9- Technology used

Action Situation [Interactions (I) → Outcomes (O)]	
I1- Harvesting levels of diverse users	O1- Social performance measures (e.g., effective rules, efficient, equitable, accountable, sustainable)
I2- Information sharing among users	
I3- Deliberation processes	
I4- Conflicts among users	O2- Ecological performance measures (e.g., overharvested, resilient, diverse, sustainable)
I5- Investment activities	
I6- Lobbying activities	
I7- Self-organizing activities	O3- Externalities to other SESs
I8- Networking activities	

Related Ecosystems (ECO)	
ECO1- Climate patterns. ECO2- Pollution patterns. ECO3- Flows into and out of focal SES.	

Source: Adapted from E. Ostrom 2007, 15183.

be greater than the costs involved (Axtell 2009; E. Ostrom 2001, 2009b). Appendix 9.1 contains a short formal theoretical analysis of the benefit-cost analysis involved in changing rules. The conclusion of this theory is that when the expected benefits of changing of rules exceed the perceived costs of this effort for a winning coalition of users, the users will choose a new set of rules. Otherwise, they will continue with the old.

The prediction of the formal theory is clear. The challenge in doing empirical fieldwork, however, is that accurately measuring the perceived benefits and costs for the users of an SES is almost impossible. The broader contextual variables that affect perceived benefits and costs differ substantially across settings but can be measured more reliably than individual perceptions. To diagnose when users are likely to invest in self-organization in field settings, one needs to relate broad contextual variables to the likely benefits and costs perceived by individuals in specific contexts.

Given the extensive fieldwork of scholars focused on explaining collective-action outcomes related to natural resources, as summarized in part II, considerable consensus exists about the set of variables that affects the probability of users' developing or changing rules.[17] We identify below a subset of twelve second- and third-tier variables that are among the most frequently identified variables in empirical studies as affecting whether users will self-organize. We also have placed a star next to these twelve variables on table 9.1. While prior research has found that these variables tend to affect the likelihood of self-organization, this finding should not be equated with an assertion that any of the variables listed below is *always* associated with success or failure in avoiding the tragedy of the commons. Rather, it is the overall combination of these variables in particular settings that affects how participants judge the benefits and costs of new operational rules, and how trust and reciprocity have developed in a setting.[18]

The identified set of variables related to resource systems includes

Size of resource system (RS3)
Productivity of system (RS5)
Indicators of the productivity of system (RS5a)
Predictability of system dynamics (RS7)

Multiple attributes of resource units are potentially relevant. One that has been frequently identified is

Resource unit mobility (RU1)

The variables related to users that are potentially important include

Number of users (U1)
Socioeconomic attributes of users (U2)

Leadership (U5)
Norms/social capital (U6)
Knowledge of social-ecological system (U7)
Importance of resource (U8)

Many of the variables related to the governance system will also be important. Empirical studies (see, for example, Haller and Merten 2008) have repeatedly shown that having collective-choice autonomy to make one's own rules (a third-tier variable) is important:

Autonomy to make own operational rules (GS6a)

Diagnosing Institutional Change

In analyzing empirical cases, the researcher or policy analyst must try to diagnose how the above factors affect the expected potential benefits and costs that users in a particular setting face if they continue old rules or attempt to change them. One would start with the listed variables and ask how they are likely to affect the benefits and costs of users. In particular cases, other variables may enter the diagnostic analysis.

The starred attributes of a resource system are likely to affect the perceived benefits and costs of institutional change in the following ways. The size (spatial extent) of a resource system (RS3) is most likely to be related in a curvilinear way to the likelihood of users' organizing. Very large resources are less likely to be self-organized owing to the high costs of defining and monitoring boundaries as well as the challenge of gaining solid ecological knowledge. Very small resources may not generate a sufficiently valuable flow of products to make it worth the time and effort of users to engage in self-organization.

If a resource system is highly productive (RS5), users may see few reasons to invest costly time and effort in organizing, as there is no apparent need. On the other hand, if the resource is already substantially degraded, the high costs of organizing may not generate sufficient expected benefits. Thus self-organization is more likely to occur after users observe some scarcity, but not too much (Wade 1994). The danger users face, however, if they do not organize a relatively productive resource is that rapid, exogenous shocks, such as landslides or fires, might occur that lead to a change in relative abundance of the resource units, and users may not adapt quickly enough to new circumstances (Libecap and Wiggins 1985). That is why having frequently available, reliable indicators about the conditions of a resource (RS5a) is also important. It affects the capacity of users to adapt relatively quickly to changes that could adversely impact their long-term benefit stream (Moxnes 1998).

A resource flow that is highly predictable (RS7) is much easier to understand and manage than one that is erratic.[19] This is true both for the users themselves and for public officials who may have acquired management responsibilities for a resource of a particular type in a region (Brock and Carpenter 2007). With erratic patterns, it is difficult for users (or for scientists and government officials) to judge whether changes in the resource stock or flow are due to overharvesting or to random exogenous variables. Unpredictability of a resource system may lead users to create a larger common-property unit to increase the predictability of resource availability somewhere in the larger unit (Netting 1972; Wilson and Thompson 1993).

The attributes of the users themselves also affect their expected benefits and costs. The number of users (U1) who rely on a particular resource system may affect the likelihood of self-organization, as discussed in multiple field studies reviewed in part II. The size of a group affects the transaction costs of coming to an agreement as well as the ongoing costs of monitoring the activities of other users. If a group is not large enough to take on the multiple responsibilities of self-organization, however, small size may not be an asset (Agrawal 2001a). As discussed in part II, field studies have also identified multiple socioeconomic attributes of users (U2), including wealth and heterogeneity, that affect whether self-organization occurs. As Libecap and Wiggins (1985) argue, asymmetric private information about heterogeneous assets may adversely affect the willingness of participants to agree to a reduction in their use patterns before considerable damage is done to a resource.

Prior experience with other forms of local organization and development of local leadership (U5) greatly enhances the repertoire of rules and strategies known by local participants as potentially useful to achieve various forms of regulation (Coward 1977; Gooch and Warburton 2009; Wade 1994). Further, users are more likely to agree upon rules whose operation they understand from prior experience, than upon rules that are introduced by external actors and are unfamiliar. Given the complexity of many field settings, users face a difficult task in evaluating how diverse variables affect expected benefits and costs over a long time horizon. In many cases, it is just as difficult, if not more so, for scientists to make a valid and reliable estimate of total benefits and costs and their distribution (Wilson, Yan, and Wilson 2007).

Users who share norms, and trust one another (U6) to keep agreements and use reciprocity in their relationships with one another, face lower expected costs in efforts to achieve better outcomes, as well as lower costs of monitoring and sanctioning one another over time. Users who lack trust at the beginning of a process of organizing may be able to gain trust over time if they initially adopt small changes that most users follow before trying to make major institutional changes. If users do not share a common understanding of how complex resource systems operate (U7), they will find it extremely difficult to agree on future joint strategies. Given the complexity of many common-pool resources—especially multispecies or multiproduct resources—understanding how these systems work (U7) may be challenging even for users who make daily contacts with the resource. In resources that are highly variable (RS7), it may be particularly difficult to understand and to sort out those outcomes stemming from exogenous factors and those resulting from the actions of users. And as Brander and Taylor (1998) have argued, when the resource base itself grows very slowly, population growth may exceed the carrying capacity before participants have achieved a common understanding of the problem they face. Of course, this is a problem facing officials as well as users. Users with many other viable and attractive options, who thus discount the importance of future income from a particular resource, may prefer to "mine" one resource without spending resources to regulate it (Berkes et al. 2006). They simply move on to other resources and become "roving bandits," since they assume that other resources will be available to them. If users do not obtain a major part of their income from a resource (U8), the high costs of organizing and maintaining a self-governing system may not be worth their effort.

Autonomy at the collective-choice level (GS6a) tends to lower the costs of organizing. A group that has little autonomy may find that those who disagree with locally developed rules seek contacts with higher-level officials to undo the efforts of users to achieve their own new rules. With the legal autonomy to make their own rules, users face substantially lower costs in defending their own rules against other authorities.

Linking these broader contextual variables to a theory of institutional change does *not* lead to a conclusion that most users using common-pool resources will undertake self-governed regulation.[20] Many settings exist where the expectation should be the opposite: users will overuse the resource unless efforts are made to change one or more of the variables affecting perceived costs or benefits (Berkes 2007; Meinzen-Dick 2007). Given the number of variables that affect these costs and benefits, many points of external intervention can enhance or reduce the probability of users' agreeing upon and following rules that generate higher social returns (Nagendra 2007). Governments, for example, decide whether to extend autonomy to local groups (GS6a), while NGOs interested in enhancing conservation may invest in training leaders (U5) and building social capital (U6).

Diverse microsituations coexist within broader contexts. Both social scientists and policymakers have a lot to learn about how these micro and broader variables operate at multiple levels and interactively in field settings. There are at least two major challenges. First, microsituations may not be visible to field researchers who have to rely on broader contextual variables when doing research. One of the advantages of case studies, as discussed in chapter 2, is that a researcher who spends extended time in a study site may learn about the presence of smaller, informal groups that either enhance or detract from cooperation at the level of the resource system itself. Second, interactions between diverse microsituations and broader contextual settings present a tremendous analytical challenge. One of the advantages of the Nepal Irrigation Institutions and Systems (NIIS) and International Forestry Resources and Institutions (IFRI) research programs described in chapters 4 and 5 is that they collect data about the broader context as well as microsituational variables, such as extensive information about user groups. The repeated finding that user monitoring is strongly associated with better forest conditions is an example of the importance of microsituational variables as well as the broader contextual variables related to the size of the forest, who owns it, the total number of users, and the like.

Aspects of the larger, macroinstitutional structure surrounding a particular setting may also affect the perceived costs and benefits. Thus external authorities can do a lot to enhance or impede the likelihood and performance of self-governing institutions. Further, when the activities of one set of users have "spillover effects" on others, external authorities can either facilitate processes that allow multiple groups to solve conflicts arising from negative spillovers or take a more active role in governing particular resources themselves.

Researchers and public officials need to recognize the multiple manifestations of these theoretical variables in the field. Users may be highly dependent on a resource (U8), for example, because they are in a remote location and few roads exist to enable them to leave. Or they may be located in a central location, but other opportunities are not open to them owing to lack of training or a discriminatory labor market. Users' discount rates in relation to a particular resource may be low because they have lived for a long time in a particular location and expect that they and their grandchildren will remain in that location, or because they possess a secure and well-defined bundle of property rights to this resource. Reliable indicators of the condition of a resource (RS5a) may result from activities that the users themselves perform—such as regularly shearing the wool from sheep (see Gilles and Jamtgaard 1981)—or because of efforts to gather reliable information by researchers or by external authorities (Basurto 2008; Blomquist 1992; Blomquist and Ostrom 2008). Predictability of resource units (RS7) may result from a clear regularity in the natural environment of the resource or because storage has been constructed in order to even out the flow of resource units over both good and bad years (Schlager, Blomquist, and Tang 1994). Users may have autonomy to make their own rules (GS6a) because national law formally legitimates local self-governance or because national government is weak and unable to exert authority over resources that it formally owns.

When the benefits of organizing are commonly understood by participants to be relatively high, users lacking many of the attributes identified above as conducive to the development of self-governing institutions may still overcome their liabilities and establish effective agreements. The crucial factor is *not* whether all contextual attributes are favorable. Most important is the relative size of the expected benefits and costs they generate as perceived by the participants who constitute a winning coalition given the collective-choice rules in use. All of these variables potentially affect the expected benefits and costs of users, but there may be other contextual variables that are highly relevant in a particular case. It is difficult, however, particularly for outsiders, to estimate their impact on expected benefits and costs given the difficulty of making precise measures of these variables and weighing them on a cumulative scale.[21]

Even in a group that differs on many variables, if at least a minimally winning subset of users harvesting from an overused but valuable resource are dependent on it (U8), share a common understanding of their situation (U7), trust one another (U6), and have autonomy to make their own rules (GS6a), it is more likely that they will estimate that the expected benefits of governing their resource are greater than the expected costs. Whether the rules agreed upon distribute benefits and costs fairly depends on the collective-choice rule used, the history of this group, and the type and degree of heterogeneity in the community.

CHALLENGES FOR FUTURE RESEARCH

In addition to the growing consensus concerning the contextual variables most likely to enhance self-organization, many unresolved issues still exist about collective action and the commons. The research findings in parts II and III of this book have led to cumulative understanding in many regards, but have also generated debate about the effect of scale, heterogeneity, and dynamics on collective action. Understanding the multiple effects of scale, heterogeneity, and dynamics is among the major challenges of future research on the commons.[22]

In regard to the effect of the scale and heterogeneity of a user group and/or of the resource units produced by a resource system, research findings from field studies are diverse. One of the problems with a focus on size of group as a key determining factor is that many other variables change as group size increases. If the costs of providing a public good related to the use of a common-pool resource, say a monitoring system, remain relatively constant as group size increases, then increasing the number of participants brings additional resources that could be drawn upon to provide the benefit enjoyed by all. On the other hand, if one is analyzing the transaction costs of arriving at acceptable allocation formulas, group size may exacerbate the problems of self-governing systems. Future work will need to focus on the combinations of variables that impact on incentives and outcomes rather than presuming that one variable—such as size of group—determines results.

Scale is also important regarding a full SES. A social-ecological system can be considered to function as a nested, hierarchical structure, with processes clustered within subsystems at several scales (e.g., the farm, region, and state) (E. Ostrom and Janssen 2004). The subsystems are semiautonomous, but cross-scale interactions do occur. For effective governance, the different spatial and temporal scales of social and ecological processes need to be taken into account, leading to a "multilevel" governance approach (Delmas and Young, 2009; Duit and Galaz 2008; Vatn 2009; O. Young 2006; O. Young et al. 2006).[23] A multilevel approach will experience challenges due to asymmetries in leadership, relevant knowledge of social and ecological processes at different levels of scale, and differences in dependence on resources. The scale of ecological processes affects the cost of monitoring. To measure effectiveness of climate-change policies, for example, researchers must monitor many different processes at the global and regional scale over long periods of time.

Studying the dynamics of SESs is a major priority for future work (Levin 1999). The characteristics of the resource users and the government system evolve over time owing to technological development, deriving new knowledge, and changing norms and knowledge. Ecological systems evolve and adapt continuously at different temporal and spatial scales. Change might be triggered by predictable cycles, such as seasonal variability, or unpredictable events, such as fires and disease outbreaks. Changes in regime type, government, and policy influence natural resources and the local-level institutions for their management by shaping incentives related to resource use and the scope for local autonomy by resource users. The dynamics of political competition and coalition formation can alter political priorities and influence policy implementation and enforcement, even in the absence of changes in government or policy. If effective and durable institutional arrangements are to be crafted, these temporal and spatial dynamics need to be taken into account (Janssen, Anderies, and Ostrom 2007). It is important to find ways to undertake combined studies of social-ecological systems over time (similar to the IFRI research program discussed in chapter 5) so that future understanding and policies are based on a knowledge of dynamics as well as on static relationships for both the social and the ecological subsystems.

The effects of scale, heterogeneity, and over-time dynamics represent analytical challenges because they involve large numbers of variables in complex, multilevel relationships. An ontological framework along the lines sketched in this chapter provides a tool for disentangling specific relationships while keeping the larger, multilevel picture in sight.

CONCLUSION

The conventional theory of common-pool resources, which presumed that external authorities were needed to impose new rules on those users trapped into producing excessive negative externalities on themselves and others, should be considered a special case of a more general theoretical structure. On the basis of a behavioral theory of human action, microinstitutional analysis, and the analysis of broader social-ecological systems, we now know that the users of some resource systems are trapped into massive overuse, but that this is not the only outcome. When a winning coalition of users concludes that the expected benefits from creating and following their own rules (as well as modifying them over time) exceed the immediate and long-term expected costs, they are likely to reformulate these rules. When users cannot communicate and have no way of gaining trust through their own efforts or with the help of the macroinstitutional system within which they are embedded, the prediction of the earlier theory is supported. Ocean fisheries, the stratosphere, and other global commons come closest to the appropriate empirical referents.

If users can engage in face-to-face bargaining and have autonomy to change their rules, they may well attempt to organize themselves. Whether they organize depends on attributes of the resource system and the users themselves that affect their trust in one another and the benefits to be achieved and the costs of achieving them. Whether their self-governed enterprise succeeds over the long term depends on whether the institutions they design sustain high levels of trust, as well as on the conditions of the resource itself. Users or policymakers who design systems with well-defined boundaries, provide arenas for conflict resolutions and internal policymaking over time, and arrange methods for monitoring and sanctioning nonconformance, are more likely to be successful over time. The design principles of robust social-ecological systems discussed in chapter 4 do themselves appear to be robust given that a substantial number of scholars have examined their relevance for the sustainability of SESs and found them to characterize a substantial number of cases for which over-time data are available (M. Cox, Arnold, and Villamayor-Tomas 2009).

The theory of common-pool resources has progressed substantially during the past half century. There are, however, many challenging puzzles to be examined in future work.

A Theoretical Puzzle: Why Do Some Resource Users Self-Organize and Others Do Not?

LET US POSIT that each user $(i \subset U)$ of a resource system compares the expected net benefits of harvesting, using the old operational rules (GS5O) in use—which may be open access—with the benefits they expect to achieve using a new set of operational rules (GS5N). Each user i must ask whether his/her incentive to change (D_i) is positive or negative.

$$D_i = B_i GS5N - B_i GS5O. \tag{1}$$

If D_i is negative for all users, no one has an incentive to change and no new rules will be established. If D_i is positive for some users, they then need to estimate three types of costs:

C1: up-front costs of time and effort spent devising and agreeing upon new rules;
C2: the short-term costs of implementing new rules; and
C3: the long-term costs of monitoring and maintaining a self-governed system over time.

If the sum of these expected costs for each user exceeds the incentive to change, no user will invest the time and resources needed to create new institutions. Thus, if

$$D_i < (C1_i + C2_i + C3_i) \tag{2}$$

for all $(i \subset U)$, no change occurs. But if, for at least one coalition $K \subset U$, there is a "winning coalition" given the rules-in-use such that

$$D_k > (C1_k + C2_k + C3_k), \tag{3}$$

it is likely that new rules will be chosen.

Some may perceive positive benefits after all costs have been taken into account, while others perceive net losses. Consequently, the local collective-choice rules (GS6a) used to change the day-to-day operational rules related to the resource affect whether an institutional change favored by some and opposed by others will occur. No guarantee exists

---

This appendix draws on an earlier theoretical analysis presented in E. Ostrom (2001).

that any such decisions taken in the field will be optimal. In field settings, everyone is not likely to expect the same costs and benefits from a proposed change.

If there are substantial differences in the perceived benefits and costs of users, it is possible that a minority of users will impose a new set of rules that strongly favors those in the winning coalition and imposes losses or lower benefits on those in the losing coalition (Thompson, Mannix, and Bazerman 1988). If a local chief or other notable has dictatorial powers at the collective-choice level, then only this single person has to estimate that the costs of changing a rule are less than the benefits of a new rule. In this case, of course, there may not be widespread benefits for other members of the group. If expected benefits from a change in institutional arrangements are not greater than expected costs for many of the relevant participants, however, the costs of enforcing a change in institutions will be much higher than they will be when most participants expect to benefit from a change in rules over time. If the group relies on majority rule or a larger collective-choice rule, and if there are several such coalitions, the question of which coalition will form, and thus which rules will result, is a further theoretical issue (see Bianco et al. 2006; Shepsle 1989; and others on coalition building in collective-choice settings). Groups living at the frontier of settlements may need to achieve close to unanimity on a change in their norms rather than being able to choose a new operational rule through some accepted collective-choice process.

Obviously, if one could obtain valid and reliable measures of the perceived benefits and costs of collective action for those involved, those data would be the core information needed to predict when collective action to change rules would occur. Gaining information about specific benefits and costs perceived by users at the time of collective-action decisions is, however, next to impossible. Thus gaining information about the attributes of resource systems and their users (as well as their autonomy to make rules) is an essential step to increase capabilities of diagnosing why some groups do overcome the challenge of collective action and others do not.

CHAPTER TEN

Learning from Multiple Methods

IN CHAPTER 1, we introduced four themes: (1) the interlinking of methodological debates with theory development, (2) the advantages and limitations of multiple methods and collaborative research, (3) practical constraints on methodological choices, and (4) the often problematic influence of career incentives on methodological practice. These themes recur throughout this book. We have shown how theoretical puzzles encourage methodological innovation. For example, scholars turned to meta-analysis to make sense of findings from large numbers of case studies (see chapters 3 and 4). More scholars are now developing agent-based models to account for observed behavior in the field and the lab that is inconsistent with conventional models of decision making (see chapters 7 and 8). Evidence generated by each method has also prompted fundamental rethinking of theory. To revisit just two examples, case studies supported conceptual refinements related to property rights (see chapter 2), and the importance of communication in repeated experiments necessitated a rethinking of assumptions about human behavior (see chapter 6).

Thus each method discussed in this book contributes to ongoing theoretical development.[1] Yet, if each method offers distinctive strengths, each also has important limitations, as we have acknowledged. The internal validity of well-designed lab experiments is usually strong, but external validity is subject to challenge. On the other hand, the external validity of well-designed, large-N field studies is usually strong, but may lack internal validity when researchers are trying to sort out specific causal processes. This book has also drawn attention to many practical challenges—including the influence of career incentives and limited budgets—that constrain methodological choices. We have provided examples of diverse strategies for addressing these challenges. Many of the most exciting responses to theoretical and methodological challenges have involved interdisciplinary research teams and the use of multiple methods.

In this chapter, we look more closely at the opportunities and challenges associated with research that combines multiple methods and disciplines. In doing so, we address each theme for this volume. First, noting that methodological breakthroughs have often played a catalytic role in theoretical breakthroughs, we argue for innovative research that draws upon multiple methods and disciplines to solve the theoretical puzzles presented by complex and contingent interactions between social and ecological systems and at multiple scales (see chapter 9). Second, we illustrate the advantages of research involving multiple methods and disciplines with several examples. In a return to our third theme, however, we also acknowledge that practical constraints present a significant challenge. Collaboration seems to offer at least a partial solution. Yet chapter 5 documented relatively modest increases in collaborative field-based research between 1990 and 2004. The next section of this chapter argues that the scholarly community itself faces collective-action problems in the provision of multimethod research. We consider the influence of career incentives and academic fragmentation on the extent of collaboration, and how universities and funding agencies might encourage more collaborative and interdisciplinary research. We conclude with suggestions for overcoming obstacles to the proliferation of interdisciplinary and multimethod research.

INTERLOCKING DEVELOPMENTS IN METHODS AND THEORY

Theoretical puzzles often encourage methodological innovation, which can in turn lead to new theoretical insights. We have described several examples of complementary interactions between theory and method. Methodological innovations have addressed problems related to both data collection and analysis, and have enabled theoretical advancement. New questions that emerge with theoretical developments encourage alternation among methodological approaches and stimulate methodological innovation and refinement.

In part II, we noted that the large number of case studies found by the National Research Council's Panel on Common Property Resource Management in the mid-1980s presented both theoretical and methodological challenges. Since the conventional theory predicted *no* collective action, it could neither account for the many successful cases nor explain differences between successful and unsuccessful cases. The early use of the IAD framework helped scholars involved in the NRC efforts to describe core aspects of studies conducted in diverse environments by scholars from multiple disciplines with a common metatheoretical language. When the Common-Pool Resource (CPR) research program decided to use meta-analysis to synthesize findings from qualitative studies, this technique was only beginning to gain currency in biomedical research (see chapter 3). Meta-analysis was practically unheard-of in nonclinical research and almost never used to synthesize qualitative research. Adapting meta-analysis to analyze qualitative studies of human uses of fisheries, irrigation systems, pastoral systems, and forests helped break a theoretical impasse. Meta-analysis based on a unifying framework also contributed to theoretical understanding of property rights, the influence of group characteristics and resource type, and the identification of design principles associated with the endurance of institutions for successful common-pool resource management (see chapter 4).

Meta-analysis offers a method for transforming findings reported in existing studies into comparable data; it is compatible with diverse methods of analysis. Standard analytical techniques—regardless of the method for data collection—assess correlations among variables and do not address the possibility of context-specific relationships involving conjunctures of variables. Yet there are theoretical reasons to expect environmental outcomes to vary across ecological zones, and social dynamics to vary across cultural and political contexts. Sociologist Charles Ragin (1987) developed Qualitative Comparative Analysis (QCA) to evaluate hypothesized context-specific conjunctures related to such macro social and political developments as peasant revolts, regime failure, and ethnic political mobilization (see chapter 3). More widespread adoption of this analytical method will make it possible to evaluate empirically the extent to which the set of conditions associated with environmental outcomes differs by region, ecological conditions, political regime type, or other social-ecological conditions. QCA promises to be particularly fertile in combination with meta-analysis (Rudel 2008). Scholars who adopt these techniques must be attentive, however, to the possibility of uneven representation of regions, resource sectors, ecological systems, or regime types in the qualitative literature that may generate misleading results.

Findings from field research and experiments have challenged the conventional theory that predicted noncooperation. With the development of agent-based models, with which one can explicitly define information flows and behavioral heuristics, alternative formal models of microsituational contexts and behavior can be developed. Increasingly, agent-based models are developed to analyze data and findings from experimental data (see chapter 8). These studies confirm the importance of other-regarding preferences and heterogeneity of preferences. Other agent-based models have been developed to illuminate the conditions under which agents evolve who have other-regarding preferences (e.g., Janssen 2008; Sánchez and Cuesta 2005), are willing to sanction others at a cost to themselves (e.g., Boyd et al. 2003; Boyd and Richerson 1992; Hauert et al. 2007), and develop norms of reciprocity and fairness (e.g., Axelrod 1986; Kameda, Takezawa, and Hastle 2003). The assumption of cultural group selection found in various models has led to new empirical research based on ethnographic records and experiments to evaluate the likelihood of cultural group-selection mechanisms (Bowles 2006;

Gächter, Renner, and Sefton 2008). These examples show that the interaction between experiments and agent-based models starts to provide a formal foundation for the theoretical framework laid out in chapter 9.

Each methodological and theoretical breakthrough, however, presents new puzzles (Clarke and Primo 2007). As discussed in chapter 9, social and ecological systems interact in complex and contingent ways, and involve dynamics at multiple scales. The analytical challenges of complexity, contingency, and multiscalar dynamics are *not* limited to environmental issues; they affect a wide variety of topics. Innovative, interdisciplinary research that draws on multiple methods is needed to address multiple contemporary challenges, ranging from the vastly increased levels of carbon dioxide in the atmosphere and the destruction of the oceanic ecosystems, to global economic turmoil and stability and change in political regimes. The next section highlights the importance of combining multiple methods and disciplines in research related to collective action in the management of common-pool natural resources.

METHODOLOGICAL AND DISCIPLINARY CROSS-FERTILIZATION AND THEORETICAL INNOVATION

Most periods of rapid theoretical development have occurred as a result of methodological and disciplinary cross-fertilization. The over-time development of a research program related to collective action and the commons has certainly been enhanced by the use of different methods and insights from multiple disciplines—particularly in linking findings from one method or discipline to others. Anthropologists, ecologists, economists, geographers, historians, legal scholars, political scientists, and sociologists have all added to the growing understanding of the complex, nested social-ecological systems that were initially treated as simple, static, and tragic dilemmas. Psychologists are now joining the interdisciplinary effort (Beckenkamp 2009; Frey and Stutzer 2007; Saunders 2003; Tyler 2008). Recent writings that promote the use of multiple methods suggest, either explicitly or by implication, that any research project will be strengthened by the use of multiple methods. This is not, however, the only way to benefit from methodological complementarities, and, as discussed below, it is not always the best strategy. Methodological and disciplinary cross-fertilization often occurs sequentially, as findings from one method or discipline are probed from different methodological or disciplinary perspectives. Alternatively, a research program may bring together scholars trained in a variety of disciplines and methods (Braude and Low 2010). As the examples below illustrate, both forms of cross-fertilization have yielded theoretical insights. Regular interaction among scholars with varied disciplinary perspectives and methodological approaches increases the likelihood of such cross-fertilization.

Sequential Movement between Methods and Disciplines

In some cases, findings from one method that cannot be explained easily or are not convincing given the theory of the times may be taken more seriously when confirmed through the use of another method. An illustration comes from Ostrom and colleagues' work on irrigation institutions in Nepal. Initial analysis of the Nepal Irrigation Institutions and Systems (NIIS) database found a very strong statistical relationship between the productivity of irrigation systems and farmer management, as contrasted to government management, holding ecological conditions constant (see chapter 4). Farmers had mentioned in interviews that they monitored each other's water withdrawals and contributions to maintenance.[2] Ostrom witnessed a dramatic event in the hills of Nepal that supported their claims.

The farmers were showing the research team a section of an irrigation system where they had made recent investments in upgrading a canal. As they walked along the canal with the team, the farmers discovered that someone downhill had dug into their system, and water was pouring out to irrigate a farm that was not a part of their system. The farmers took immediate action, and completely ignored those of us who were viewing the system with them. Several farmers ran screaming down the hill to find out who had done it. Several others got down on their hands and knees to start repairing the damage that had been done. The reaction was so immediate and so dramatic that it was obvious that the farmers were not engaged in this kind of sanctioning because our research team was present. These were quite automatic responses.

Upon returning from Nepal, Ostrom discussed the incident with two colleagues, Roy Gardner and James Walker, with whom she was exploring the logic and behavior of cooperation by testing game-theoretic models in laboratory experiments. Observation of this powerful response to an infraction reinforced the farmers' own claims about sanctioning infractions. From a methodological perspective, however, there were at least three problems. First, the observation demonstrated that farmers *did* invest in sanctioning, but could not explain *why* they did so. Second, the incident offered little evidence to link monitoring and sanctioning to improved performance in farmer-managed systems. Third, there was no way to evaluate whether the behavior of these farmers was unusual or typical except through reference to previous case studies that had reflected on users' monitoring of each other. Indeed, it would have been easy to dismiss the event as an anomaly. After all, the game-theoretic prediction for such situations was clear: nobody would invest in sanctioning others at a cost to themselves without a clear personal benefit.

Gardner developed a rigorous game-theoretic model of a CPR in which one choice available to resource users was to pay a fee in order to fine someone else. The next question was whether subjects in an experimental CPR setting would monitor and actively sanction one another. Walker then developed and pretested a design that implemented the game theory closely, and the three colleagues began to run this experiment in the lab. Much to their amazement, subjects in the lab did sanction one another (E. Ostrom, Walker, and Gardner 1992). In fact, as discussed in chapter 6, they sanctioned one another at such a high level that the cost to them came close to swamping the benefits they achieved by reducing some of the overharvesting.

Then an inspiration struck. In the field, the farmers were sanctioning one another in systems where they had designed their own rules. The research team decided to explore whether that would make any difference in the lab. They recruited subjects who had been in the first set of experiments so those in the new experiment would have experienced the opportunity and costs as well as benefits of sanctioning. The subjects were given an opportunity to play the same base CPR game again without communication or sanctions. Then they were given an opportunity to discuss and then vote on whether they would like to develop their own sanctioning system. Four out of six groups did establish their own sanctioning system, and the designs differed from one another. The amazing thing was that the groups that designed their own rules achieved 90 percent of the social optimum even after deduction of the costs of the few fines and fees that they had to use.

That finding was rather surprising for game theorists and experimentalists. Monitoring each other's conformance to rules is a third-order social dilemma. Many scholars presumed that users would not solve the first-order dilemma of cooperating with one another, or the second-order dilemma of establishing their own rules; they certainly did not expect them to solve a third-order dilemma of enforcing their own rules. The result was picked up by a substantial number of scholars who explored the role of sanctioning. The basic finding has been repeated in many instances (Cardenas 2009; Carpenter 2007; Falk, Fehr, and Fischbacher 2005; Fehr and Gächter 2000a, 2000b, 2002; Henrich et al. 2006). Experimental studies building on the initial design have made further advances showing that the source of the rules to be followed or of the right to sanction makes a difference in the behavior and results of experiments (Cardenas, Stranlund, and Willis 2000; Lopez et al. forthcoming). While skeptics could dismiss the observation of sanctioning by Nepali farmers as an isolated anomaly, replication of the experimental results by numerous scholars established their internal validity. At least under the conditions modeled in these experiments, individuals consistently demonstrate a willingness to invest in monitoring and sanctioning.

The findings from the experiment led to self-conscious attention to the role of monitoring in the design of the International Forestry Resources and Institutions (IFRI) research program. The IFRI research protocols explicitly direct field researchers to seek and record information about how regularly users monitor harvesting activities by other users. Several articles drawing on the IFRI database have found a strong statistical relationship between user monitoring and better forest conditions (see chapter 5). A recent multivariate analysis by Coleman and Steed (2009) of more than 130 forests in a dozen countries found that, when local forest users are recognized as having a right to harvest (having at least the position of an authorized user), they are more likely to monitor patterns of harvesting by other appropriators. Moreover, their monitoring activity makes a difference in forest conditions. These studies confirm that monitoring occurs in the field as well as in laboratory settings, and that actual resource users are more likely to monitor harvesting activities when they have legally recognized rights to the resource.

These findings from the field and the lab are contrary to earlier theories of crime and punishment (e.g., G. Becker 1993) that predicted the necessity of steep fines imposed by external authorities to deter stealing. This earlier prediction followed from the assumption that the expected value of the punishment had to exceed the value of the illegally taken property. The punishments involved in the lab and reported from the field are not high, nor are the sanctions described in case studies initially high. The benefits of relatively low-level sanctions are related to the central role of trust and norms in enhancing cooperation (discussed in chapter 9) more than to the deterrent role of high sanctions. When the resource users monitor one another and let each other know they have observed behavior that does not conform to their norms and rules, they can have higher trust that others are conforming to their agreements.

There are intriguing parallels between theories of group cooperation related to the use of natural resources and theories of group cooperation in urban areas that have developed independently drawing on survey data (see Sampson, Raudenbush, and Earls 1997) and now field experiments. A recent set of innovative field experiments on the conditions associated with rule breaking in urban areas provides strong evidence that residents are much more likely to break rules against littering or stealing money when the area under observation is filled with "disorderly and illegal" graffiti than when no graffiti is present (Keizer, Lindenberg, and Steg 2008). The graffiti seems to signal a lack of mutual monitoring within the community. Other studies that highlight the limited benefits gained from external monitoring and sanctioning further support the interpretation that self-monitoring and graduated sanctions influence outcomes by building trust. In both the context of natural resource management and that of urban neighborhoods, occasional incursions by external police trying to find out whether anyone has broken rules do not increase trust (Cardenas, Stranlund, and Willis 2000). As discussed in chapter 8, Castillo and Saysel (2005) were able to replicate in an agent-based model the field experimental findings related to the effectiveness of face-to-face communication as contrasted to the imposition of a fine by external authority.

Confirmation of findings in studies that use different methods greatly increases confidence in their internal and external validity. The notion that the users of a common-pool resource would monitor each other's behavior was inconceivable for many scholars in the 1970s and 1980s. Reports of monitoring by farmers in one irrigation system in Nepal would not be considered strong enough evidence to convince scholars and policymakers that the conventional theory was wrong. Repeatedly replicated findings from the experimental lab, however, demonstrated unambiguously that the game-theoretical prediction of no monitoring or sanctioning was incorrect. Adding this variable to large-N field studies brought considerable external validity to the earlier case study and experimental findings. Similar findings for urban settings provide further evidence of the general importance of community monitoring for building trust and encouraging rule adherence. The overall finding of the importance of users' monitoring for building trust among participants in collective-action situations is robust across methods and contexts as well as an important link in the evolving theory of collective action.

Combining Multiple Methods and Disciplines in a Program of Research

To develop formal models for the study of the evolution of institutional arrangements, Janssen—trained as an applied mathematician—used computational methods that had proved to be successful in studying complex adaptive systems (Janssen 2005b; Janssen and Ostrom 2006a). Although some interesting analytical results were derived, Janssen felt that there was not sufficient empirical understanding of how groups create and adapt institutional arrangements in order to develop formal models of, for example, how the actors in the action situation create new rules, what they expect about the cost and effects of these rules (see appendix 9.1), what they expect others will do, and so forth. Existing experimental work was mainly focused on comparing the effects of one institutional arrangement with another, not on how they crafted rules. Janssen concluded that new experiments needed to be done in which the rule crafting could be observed more closely, and that would generate new data that could be used to develop formal models.

In 2004, Janssen received a grant from the then-new Human and Social Dynamics program of the National Science Foundation to pursue a series of experiments to derive empirical observations to develop formal models of governing the commons. From the start, the project aimed to include laboratory experiments with undergraduate students, field experiments, and role games with villagers in Colombia and Thailand. These countries were chosen because of existing contacts with an experimental economist, Juan-Camilo Cardenas, and an ecologist, François Bousquet, who had combined role games and agent-based modeling in Southeast Asia. Other investigators in the project were faculty from diverse disciplines at Indiana University, namely, cognitive scientist Robert Goldstone, computer scientist Filippo Menczer, and political scientist Elinor Ostrom. All investigators were familiar with the details of some of the methods, but not with all. During the beginning of the project, the investigators needed to get familiar enough with each other's method to start designing experiments.

Building upon an existing experimental environment developed by Goldstone (Goldstone and Ashpole 2004), the researchers designed new laboratory experiments in which participants experienced spatial and temporal dynamics. Inclusion of those dimensions was important since meta-analysis of field studies has shown that these are critical to distinguish different types of institutional arrangements (Schlager, Blomquist, and Tang 1994). With these laboratory experiments, microsituational variables could be manipulated, and rule crafting could be observed, especially when communications could be recorded because participants were using text-based chat rooms (Janssen et al. 2008; Janssen and Ostrom 2008). Using high-resolution experimental data, researchers could rigorously test agent-based models (Janssen, Radtke, and Lee 2009).

The field experiments and role games went through two years of preparation before the first experiments could be performed. Owing to differences in methodologies used by the various investigators, new problems needed to be solved if both experiments and role games were to be performed in all six villages in two different countries. This led to innovations that the field experimenter Cardenas developed (Cardenas, Janssen, and Bousquet forthcoming). For the first time, this project combined role games and field experiments. Having the villagers first participate in field experiments, and then, later, adjusting the field experiments into role games in line with their local context, represented innovations in the methodology of role games.

Some laboratory experiments performed later in the project were based on experiences derived from the field experiments. For example, an irrigation game characterized by asymmetry of access to the resource led participants in field experiments to balance efficiency (investment in infrastructure) and equity (allocation of water). This was translated into a downloading game in a laboratory experiment with a similar payoff structure, and similar findings (Janssen, Anderies, and Joshi 2009). In the laboratory experiments, communication was allowed, which resulted in higher levels of cooperation and coordination over the rounds. There was more variability in the outcomes for the field experiments.

The experimental designs that came out of this project would not have been possible if it had focused on one methodology. The interaction of scholars familiar with different methods, who were challenging each other, led to innovative designs that other scholars are now beginning to adopt.[3]

Spaces for Cross-Fertilization

Scholars are more likely to incorporate multiple disciplinary perspectives and methodological approaches in their research if they are familiar with the work of colleagues who use different approaches. Research centers can promote multidisciplinary and multimethod research by creating spaces for regular interaction across disciplinary and methodological boundaries. Cross-boundary exchange encourages cross-fertilization of research traditions and fosters the development of trusting relationships conducive to collaboration.

The Workshop in Political Theory and Policy Analysis provides such a space for cross-fertilization through a combination of structured and self-organized opportunities for interactions among graduate students, faculty, and visiting scholars.[4] Associated graduate students and faculty come from several departments and schools across Indiana University. The Workshop welcomes visiting scholars from around the world, including postdoctoral fellows as well as senior scholars on sabbatical. Through a variety of structured activities, people become acquainted with each other and aware of shared interests. These include a colloquium series and a graduate-level seminar, in which visiting scholars also participate. At the end of each term, the Workshop invites other faculty, postdoctoral fellows, and graduate students to comment, in a miniconference, on research prepared by seminar participants.

By providing meeting space for self-organized working groups involving individuals affiliated with the Workshop and for other meetings of various scales, the Workshop encourages individuals to explore and build upon their common interests. Some groups meet to discuss common readings. Others exchange and comment on one another's papers. Yet others become the springboard for joint research. A number of research projects and programs discussed in this book were formed at or have a connection with the Workshop, including the CPR, NIIS, and IFRI research programs, as well as a number of projects involving experiments and agent-based models. These research programs involved multiple methods and disciplinary perspectives from the outset in part because interaction across these boundaries is so commonplace at the Workshop.

The Workshop is just one example of a research center that fosters disciplinary and methodological cross-fertilization by involving a diverse set of participants in regular activities and creating opportunities for less formal, self-organized exchanges and collaboration. Others include the Agrarian Studies Program at Yale University, the Center for the Study of Institutional Diversity at Arizona State University, the Land Tenure Center at the University of Wisconsin, and the centers for area studies at many universities.

PRACTICAL CHALLENGES

Findings from research involving different methods and disciplines will have a cumulative effect on future research and theoretical developments only if, at a minimum, each scholar has a solid command of at least one method, is conversant with a range of other methods and disciplines, and engages in scholarship produced from a variety of methodological and disciplinary perspectives. Scholars face strong incentives to develop specialized methodological skills. Unfortunately, specialization is not always combined with familiarity—much less serious engagement—with a variety of other methods and disciplines. In this section, we discuss practical challenges related to (1) trade-offs in training and research and (2) professional incentives that constrain cross-fertilization across methods and disciplines.

Trade-Offs in Training and Research

Each individual scholar faces trade-offs between methodological and disciplinary breadth and depth in both training and research activities. Although these trade-offs are especially stark early in a career, when one is making decisions about graduate training, they also exert an ongoing influence on decisions affecting skills development, research, and publishing. Any serious effort to promote more interdisciplinary and multiple-methods research must acknowledge and address these trade-offs.

Realization of the potential contributions from any given method depends on its rigorous application. To use a method well, a researcher must understand the assumptions upon which it is based, follow rigorous procedures in applying it, and understand how to interpret the results accurately and completely. With only superficial familiarity with a method, scholars may not recognize situations when key assumptions have been violated. They may overlook procedures that limit the risk of bias or fail to use diagnostics that can reveal and compensate for problems. They might interpret the results in a misleading manner. Worse, if the method has been applied inappropriately, it will generate misleading results. The need for rigorous methodological training and application to avoid such problems is uncontroversial.

Methodological training generally combines formal coursework with hands-on learning. Most graduate programs provide a foundation in one or two methods through required courses and offer opportunities for applied learning through research assistantships. Opportunities to develop more specialized skills include the Summer School in Methods and Techniques offered by the European Consortium for Political Research and, in the United States, the Inter-University Consortium for Political and Social Research (ICPSR) annual summer institute in research methods, the Summer Institute on Research Design in Cultural Anthropology, Short Courses on Research Methods in Cultural Anthropology, and Field Training in Methods of Data Collection in Cultural Anthropology. Opportunities for training in multiple methods have expanded. The Consortium on Qualitative Research Methods' annual Institute in Qualitative and Multi-Method Research offers training in combining data collection methods. The Empirical Implications of Theoretical Models (EITM) program offers training in how to combine multiple quantitative methods within a single research project (Granato, Lo, and Wong 2010a, 2010b).

Similar issues affect interdisciplinary training and research. Disciplinary training provides a historical foundation in the theoretical approaches and questions and highlights key findings.[5] Grounding in a disciplinary tradition increases the likelihood that new scholarship builds on past scholarship; it promotes scientific progress, at least within each discipline. The degree to which methods, theories, questions, and findings overlap across disciplines, and the regularity with which disciplinary cross-fertilization occurs, depend on the extent to which disciplines share substantive concerns (e.g., biological, ecological, social, physical) and historical roots. Cross-fertilization across the social sciences is commonplace, for example. Interdisciplinary programs that involve scholars across the social and ecological sciences are slowly evolving at some universities (e.g., Arizona State University, the University of California at Santa Barbara, and Harvard University among them).

The trade-offs for graduate students and the programs that train them are immediate. There is incredible pressure to reduce the time required to complete a doctoral degree. University administrators seek to shorten the time to degree to keep costs down. Graduate studies represent a period of deferred earnings for students. In response to these pressures, graduate programs limit course requirements. Students and advisers know that each additional methods course comes at the expense of a substantive course, and that each interdisciplinary course implies the omission of a disciplinary course. These considerations influence choices between disciplinary and interdisciplinary graduate programs and decisions about coursework during graduate studies. Is it better to focus on a single method or discipline or to develop familiarity with several?

Ideally, scholars should have a solid command of their own method and discipline but have sufficient familiarity with other methods and disciplines to engage with them. While it is difficult to meet both goals well within the limited period of graduate training, doctoral programs should provide a strong point of departure for both the development of specialized skills and methodological and disciplinary boundary crossing. One strategy for dealing with this trade-off, which has long been used in the biological and physical sciences, is postdoctoral appointments that enable scholars with a PhD to practice the research skills they have acquired and learn new skills while participating in an interdisciplinary project. Many fewer postdoctoral positions exist in the social sciences than in biophysical sciences, but if funding for interdisciplinary research centers continues to grow, we should see an expansion of postdoctoral opportunities across the ecological and social sciences. This postdoctoral period is also a good time to get the dissertation work published and to start defining one's research agenda for the future. This will reduce the pressure when one starts a tenure-track position and gets recommendations to follow traditional research paths.

Professional Incentives

Trade-offs between methodological and disciplinary depth and breadth do not end with receipt of the doctorate. They affect opportunities for employment and advancement, decisions about research and publication, and competition for grants and other forms of professional recognition. Even when individual scholars feel drawn to interdisciplinary topics and recognize complementarities among methodological approaches, they confront powerful professional incentives to specialize. We highlight two factors that encourage specialization: (1) reliance on methodological and disciplinary assessments of research quality and (2) the priority given to the volume and pace of publication in assessments of productivity.

Young scholars trained in interdisciplinary programs do find it more challenging to secure a good position and move ahead for tenure than do scholars trained in a single discipline. One of the coauthors recently placed a PhD candidate at a distinguished university with a strong interdisciplinary program. The student asked for counseling, as faculty members of this university indicated that multiple publications in the major journals of a faculty member's home department were necessary to achieve tenure at that university. While the candidate already had several articles accepted for publication, they would not contribute to a strong case for tenure down the pike from the perspective of the home department, as they were published by very distinguished, but interdisciplinary, journals. In another instance, a colleague who was up for tenure was recommended unanimously by the faculty member's home department, but one academic at another university recommended against tenure since the faculty member did not have any articles in what the external reviewer considered major disciplinary journals. Fortunately, the rest of the case was so strong that the college committee recommended tenure. Recent reports from the job market suggest that a similar preference for methodological specialization over multimethod research remains widespread, at least in political science (Siegel et al. 2007).

These anecdotes reflect systemic pressures. As discussed in chapter 1, the peer-review process that influences hiring, advancement, publications, and grant applications generally means review by specialists. Consistent reviews are more likely for scholarship within a single area of specialization than for scholarship that draws on multiple methods and disciplines (Lohmann 2007). While the greater difficulty of mastering more than one method or discipline may contribute to this discrepancy, reviewers also approach research outside their own area of specialization with greater skepticism, especially if it combines multiple methods or disciplines and they do not understand or they do not accept the rationale for combining various approaches (Lohmann 2007). The examples presented above suggest that the influence of specialists remains strong even in purportedly interdisciplinary programs, and despite the recent promotion of research combining multiple methods.

Time pressures also influence methodological practices. Academia rewards productivity. The pressure to produce may be especially stark in the run-up to tenure but does not evaporate thereafter. Departments and universities continue to assess productivity when making decisions about teaching assignments, promotion, and internal grants and recognition, among other things. Assessments typically count the number of publications within a given period and consider the quality of publication outlets (Rothgeb and Burger 2009). These criteria for assessment are well known and influence decisions about research and publication strategies. For each new research project, scholars must decide whether to build upon existing strengths or branch out to incorporate new methods, topics, and disciplinary perspectives into their research. Research that requires the exploration of new bodies of literature, the collection of new types of data, and the development of new methodological skills will generally be more time-consuming, as will research involving several forms of data collection and analysis. Time pressures discourage both the combination of multiple methods and disciplines within a single project and investment in a range of methods over the course of a series of projects. Time pressures can also constrain the *scope* of research, by encouraging geographical specialization (see chapter 3). Assessments of productivity are certainly important. Our concern is that, because currently widespread forms of assessment do not fully acknowledge the longer lead time required for research that involves multiple methods or disciplines, fewer scholars undertake such research. The practice of discounting the value of interdisciplinary publications provides further disincentives.

Specialization in methodological training and application *is* a reasonable response to career incentives and other practical considerations. At the same time, the scholarly community benefits tremendously from both methodological cross-fertilization and interdisciplinary research. We have argued throughout this book that collaboration offers a potential solution for these problems. Collaboration makes it possible to incorporate multiple methods and disciplines into a research program by bringing together a team of scholars, each of whom contributes specialized skills. Division of labor can also enhance research productivity. Of course, the potential advantages of collaboration are not always achieved (Sigelman 2009). Team members must be sufficiently familiar with one another's methods and disciplines to communicate effectively, and they must have a sincere commitment to integrating different perspectives. In the next section, we focus on the challenges of collaborative research.

COLLABORATIVE RESEARCH AS A COLLECTIVE-ACTION PROBLEM

In chapter 5, we saw that collaboration increased somewhat in field-based research published as peer-reviewed journal articles between 1990 and 2004. References to larger research projects expanded fairly dramatically over this period, from 16.0 percent to 35.4 percent. Collaborative research projects frequently involved more intensive fieldwork, characterized by multiple forms of data collection by multidisciplinary teams. These patterns show that collaboration can facilitate research involving multiple methods and disciplines. The share of coauthored articles grew more modestly, however, from 51.8 percent in the 1990s to 59.5 percent for 2000–2004.[6] Neither coauthorship nor reference to a larger research project was associated with an increase in cross-national analysis. The more modest growth in coauthorship and collaboration in cross-national analysis reflects the severity of the challenges in overcoming incentives for specialization.

Collaborative research that integrates multiple methods and disciplines into analysis as well as data collection has some characteristics of a public good. Research, once published, enters the public domain, where nearly everyone can benefit from it.[7] Although there are certainly private benefits to producing groundbreaking interdisciplinary research, no guarantee exists that any particular research effort will break ground. And groundbreaking research builds on past research. Most scholars are individually better-off if they invest in specialized skills and publish primarily single-method research in disciplinary journals; they are more likely to get a good job, get their research published quickly, receive tenure, and win grants and awards. The scholarly and policy communities, however, would be collectively better-off if more research made use of multiple methods and integrated insights from a variety of disciplines. In field-based research, a similar argument can be made for broadly comparative research. Collaboration may make integrative research possible, but it is unlikely to yield such research consistently unless the underlying collective-action problem is understood and addressed effectively. We highlight four challenges: individual rewards to individual research, organizational fragmentation, misunderstanding and suspicion of other disciplines and approaches, and long-term funding.

Rewards to Individual and Collaborative Research

If collaboration in multidisciplinary data collection culminated in interdisciplinary analysis, one would expect to see more articles published with a large number of coauthors as references to larger, collaborative research projects increase. Articles that incorporate several methods and disciplines do tend to be coauthored (e.g., Becu et al. 2003; Bray et al. 2003; Neiland, Jaffrey, et al. 2000; Tucker et al. 2008). Yet the vast majority of articles published prior to 2000 had no more than two authors. Even for the more recent period, 2000–2004, only 9.5 percent of the articles had more than three authors.[8] More collaborative data collection had not fully translated into more collaborative data analysis.

As noted above, scholars are rewarded for productivity, evaluated in terms of the volume of publication and the perceived prestige of the publication outlets. Coauthored publications present a puzzle from the perspective of hiring committees, tenure and promotion committees, and others seeking to evaluate scholarly performance.[9] How much credit should a scholar receive for coauthored versus single-authored publications? Scholars who publish frequently with coauthors might be expected to have more publications than others on the grounds that, despite the costs of coordinating efforts, division of labor among coauthors should facilitate research and writing, and thus allow for more rapid publication. Furthermore, evaluators frequently wonder how much an individual contributed to a coauthored publication. Skeptical evaluators often raise the possibility that a scholar might be free-riding on the efforts of coauthors. Such questions increase sharply for publications with more than two or three coauthors. Thus professional incentives not only encourage disciplinary and methodological specialization by individuals; they also discourage forms of collaboration through which individuals could combine their specialized skills.

Much higher levels of coauthorship occur in natural scientific research that relies on the coordinated activities of laboratory-based research teams. The high degree of interdependency among researchers involved in data collection and analysis could present problems if some team members felt that others were benefiting disproportionately from the team's combined efforts. Shared credit for publications provides an incentive for individuals to invest in collective research activities. Just as farmers near the head of an irrigation system are more likely to cooperate for more equitable water distribution when they depend on farmers near the end of an irrigation system for labor on maintenance activities (see chapter 4), interdependence among researchers seems to encourage credit sharing in research publications.

The level of interdependency that characterizes laboratory-based research is rare in the social sciences. Many social scientists engage in research activities that might be supported by paid research assistants but do not involve a research team. They may seek coauthors who have complementary data or methodological skills, but they are also able to publish independently. Even participants in research teams often can produce publications independently or with the participation of a subset of team members. Thus, in the social sciences, coauthorship occurs among scholars who contribute distinct methodological skills or knowledge related to particular topics or locations, but the number of scholars involved is typically limited. Research programs that not only include multiple methods and disciplines but also rely on interdependencies among the various elements should generate more collaborative analysis and more coauthored publications that incorporate multiple methods and disciplines.

Going beyond research programs, there is a need to develop cyberinfrastructure to share data, protocols, and software. Within the natural sciences, it is common practice to share data, as illustrated by the success of data sharing in climate and geological research,[10] and biotechnical information such as the genome project.[11] Within the social sciences, there are modest attempts to share data and models,[12] but in practice it is difficult to get scholars to contribute to this public good. Some scholars have opposed blanket data-sharing policies out of a concern that such policies would either disadvantage research that relies on less standardized forms of qualitative data, or compromise the anonymity of respondents who provide sensitive information. These concerns must be taken seriously, but they should not prevent the development of cyberinfrastructure to facilitate the sharing of more standardized and less ethically sensitive data. Uniform data-sharing policies are unlikely to work well given the degree of diversity of methodological practices. The challenge is to develop policies that effectively encourage data sharing while acknowledging differences in the form and sensitivity of data.

Fragmentation of Academia

The deeply institutionalized and sometimes antagonistic fragmentation of academia hinders the emergence of more integrative research programs. The organization of universities and professional associations reflects and entrenches divisions between the natural and social sciences, the disciplines, and even among methodological and substantive specializations. Competition for resources within universities, departments, and professional organizations can discourage cooperation across organizational subunits. Scholars also divide, often bitterly, over ontological assumptions and normative priorities. Collective action is more likely among actors who interact within existing networks and enjoy high levels of trust. Organizational competition restricts patterns of interaction and, in combination with disciplinary and theoretical differences in worldviews, generates suspicion instead of trust. As such, academic fragmentation represents an important obstacle to research that truly integrates multiple methods and different disciplinary perspectives.

Within universities, organizational structures often group the natural sciences in one school, the social sciences in another. Each school is further divided into departments. Larger departments often rely on internal divisions, frequently based on areas of specialization, to manage departmental business. These organizational divisions facilitate management of the university and specialized training of students. They also enable specialized research that might not generate immediate or tangible rewards. Indeed, Lohmann (2004) attributes the organizational form of the modern university to historical efforts to protect and encourage specialized scholarship in Europe. But organizational forms also influence patterns of interaction. Organizational division not only presents a hurdle to intellectual exchange and other forms of cooperative behavior; it also defines the lines of competition over resources.

Universities do attempt to counterbalance discipline-based departments with interdisciplinary programs and research centers, as discussed above. From the perspective of existing departments, creation of a new interdisciplinary program or center introduces a rival claimant on university resources. Departments may also see threats to their autonomy in requests that they hire faculty to serve interdisciplinary programs, grant tenure and promotion based on criteria set in part by these units, teach students in these programs, or otherwise alter internal procedures and practices to address priorities set elsewhere. These dynamics can be seen in the anecdotes reported above of criteria for hiring, tenure, and promotion that give greater weight to disciplinary over interdisciplinary publications, even for faculty within interdisciplinary programs. Institutionalized divisions represent a serious constraint, but they can be overcome. Vibrant centers of interdisciplinary research do flourish on many university campuses. Such programs are more likely to succeed if they are designed to address likely sources of opposition.

Misunderstandings and Mistrust

Institutional divisions might exacerbate academic fragmentation, but they are not the only—and possibly not even the most important—source of fragmentation. Unfortunately, there are still considerable "battles" among scholars who rely on different methods or assumptions. *Some* scholars engaged in in-depth descriptions of cases challenge the usefulness of efforts to seek general patterns, while *some* who do large-N observational research do not recognize the value of case studies or experiments in untangling causal processes. Likewise, scholars from different disciplines or theoretical perspectives often hold different assumptions about how the world works, or disagree about priorities, both in research and in policy. In the introduction to a special issue of the journal *Public Choice*, titled "Homo Economics and Homo Politicus," that he coedited with Michael Gillespie, Geoffrey Brennan (2008, 431) reflects that

> the ambition to find common ground on which public choice scholars and "political theorists" of a more traditional kind might have profitable exchange is not a trivial one: we start from very different conceptions of what counts as theory—even of what counts as worthwhile scholarship—and from different disciplinary presuppositions as to how differences in approach can most profitably be engaged and resolved.

These sorts of barriers to communication across disciplinary, methodological, and theoretical traditions are not uncommon.

In research related to shared natural resources, for example, tensions between proponents of protected areas and advocates of decentralized management by natural resource users can get highly emotional (Baird and Dearden 2003; Borgerhoff Mulder and Coppolillo 2005; F. Holt

2005). Gravely worried about biodiversity losses and threats to ecosystem processes, some conservation biologists see strict protection as the only solution (e.g., Terborgh 1999). From their perspective, arguments for human use, even if restricted, are naive and shortsighted, and will result in irrecoverable losses. For scholars who believe that complete exclusion from common-pool natural resources is undesirable, it is the advocates of strict protection who are naive. Some do attempt to develop strategies that protect ecological integrity and address the limitations of centralized management.

In analyzing a case from Cambodia, Baird and Dearden (2003, 541) stress that "wholesale replacement of long-practiced resource management strategies by state-dictated national park regulations is seldom an optimal path for forging effective long-term conservation strategies." They argue for flexibility in designing effective schemes that draw on the capabilities of local people but also on larger governmental programs that may help counteract some contemporary pressures to clear land that did not exist at an earlier time. We welcome this sort of pragmatic effort to incorporate responses to the very real challenges of managing common-pool resources into conservation strategies.

Methodological differences sometimes give rise to levels of suspicion and hostility that rival tensions over policy goals. A recent special issue titled "Customs, Commons, Property, and Ecology: Case Studies from Oceania," of the respected journal *Human Organization*, illustrates continuing tensions. The editors brought together a number of interesting case studies that highlighted many of the diverse processes occurring in Oceania in response to diverse forms of globalization. The goal was in part to critique "the over-application of common property theory to customary settings" (Wagner and Talakai 2007, 1). The editors depict "common property theory" as an effort to "develop universal theory for all types of common property systems—grazing lands, forests, fisheries, irrigation systems, village commons, and so on" (2). The poor fit between the case studies in the volume and "the overly neat, essentialized categories of private, common, and public property" is taken as grounds for rejecting common-property theory (5). In the conclusion to the volume, Lieber and Rynkiewich (2007, 90) claim that "common property theory not only does not account for the ethnographic findings in Oceanic societies, but instead distorts data when applied to ethnographic cases. . . . The authors assembled here are at pains to explain why common property theory is inapplicable to their cases, offering alternative generalizations to explain their findings." In fact, important contributions to what Wagner and Talakai call "common property theory" *agree* that the three categories of "private, common, and public property" cannot fully capture the richness of most existing property regimes (see part II).

Unfortunately, the critiques seem to reflect a deep suspicion of different methods and disciplines that contributed to a misunderstanding, and thus misrepresentation, of research on common property and common-pool resources.

We are struck by both the emphasis on the *ethnographic* approach favored by contributors to the special issue and the frequent equation of *comparative* research on common property and common-pool resources with *universalizing* goals. The editors seemingly assume a simple correspondence between methods and theoretical assumptions. While some scholars engaged in comparative, large-N, and experimental research do assume the existence of universal patterns, many others do not. This book has shown how widespread evidence of nonuniversal, context-specific patterns accumulated, not just through ethnographic case studies of the sort included in the *Human Organization* volume, but also through meta-analysis, large-N field-based research, experiments, and agent-based models. The social-ecological system (SES) framework described in chapter 9 is an effort to provide a coherent language for unpacking the rich diversity of factors identified by scholars in the tradition that the editors of *Human Organization* criticize. We have read the individual cases in this special issue with considerable interest. We only wish that suspicion of nonethnographic research had not resulted in a misplaced attack on something called "common property theory."

Fortunately, there are efforts underway to reduce suspicion and misunderstanding across disciplinary and methodological boundaries. Pranab Bardhan and Isha Ray (2008, 655) have brought together a set of anthropologists and economists to highlight some of the divisions between the two disciplines but primarily to "explore the possibilities of bridging some of these divisions." Because they focus on the analysis of local commons, their work is particularly relevant for readers of this book. We strongly recommend their book, *The Contested Commons: Conversations between Economists and Anthropologists* (2008). They honestly discuss the differences in the approaches of the two disciplines but also see that scholars can learn from a serious discussion of these differences rather than engaging in name-calling and useless fights. They delve deeply into the benefits of serious discussions among scholars trained differently, but they also try to understand some of the same problems.

In another good effort to build on the differences among disciplines, De Moor (2008) demonstrates how extensive archival research can address many of the important theoretical questions related to the robustness of common-property institutions. In addition to reporting her findings, she overtly tries to "unite theoretical insights from different disciplines that have been dealing with the 'tragedy of the commons'" (2). These efforts are to be commended. After all, collaboration or even cross-fertilization across disciplines and methodological approaches is unlikely in the absence of trust, and trust is more likely to develop with familiarity.

Long-Term Funding

Several funding agencies have invested heavily in interdisciplinary and collaborative training and research. Examples related to social-ecological systems include the U.S. National Science Foundation (NSF)'s Integrative Graduate Education and Research Traineeship (IGERT) program and the Human and Social Dynamics (HSD) program, and the European Union Seventh Framework Programme on the Environment. IGERT supports innovative efforts to incorporate multiple disciplines and more collaborative research activities into graduate training, while the HSD encourages interdisciplinary research on human behavior. The 2008 HSD competition supported interdisciplinary research on the intersection of human decision making, behavior, and environmental change.[13] The European Union's Framework Programme on the Environment supports multidisciplinary, collaborative research in four areas: (1) climate change, pollution, and risks; (2) sustainable management of resources; (3) environmental technologies; and (4) earth observation and assessment tools. Other components of the EU Framework Programme encourage collaboration by facilitating the formation of research teams and the incorporation of new researchers into such teams. Many other funding agencies also encourage collaborative research that incorporates multiple methods and disciplines. The availability of major grants should help scholars overcome practical challenges and professional incentives that otherwise discourage collaborative and interdisciplinary research.

The IFRI research program illustrates both the value of collaborative, multidisciplinary research and the challenges of securing the funding required to sustain such research over the long term. Consider the case of Evelyn Lwanga Namubiru and the Uganda Collaborative Research Center (CRC) at Makerere University in Kampala. For her doctoral degree at Indiana University, Namubiru (2008) designed a dissertation project to analyze how four different institutional arrangements—private property, national government–owned, joint community-government management, and sacred forests—were affected by multiple changes in national policy over time. Colleagues at the Uganda CRC already had conducted two rounds of field research and had data for two sites for each of these four institutional arrangements. The Uganda team made those data available to Namubiru. With support from a small research grant, Namubiru conducted a third data collection visit to these eight sites. With comparable data for two previous time periods from the Uganda CRC, Namubiru was able to analyze changes spanning roughly fifteen years. The new data that she collected are now on file with the Uganda CRC and available to support future research. A dissertation project that covers three time periods and four types of institutional arrangements would not have been possible in the absence of an ongoing collaboration in which the work of each scholar contributes to a common pool of data available for future researchers.

Funding such an effort for a sustained period of time is, however, quite a challenge. In chapter 5, we noted the effect of resource constraints on the Traditional Management of Artisanal Fisheries (TMAF) research program and a partnership to study institutions for the management of common-pool resources in Tanzania. Support for these projects from the British Department for Overseas Development enabled research that involved multiple methods and disciplines, but resource constraints limited the intensity of research efforts in Tanzania and the geographic scope of both projects. Neither project acquired the long-term funding needed to generate the sort of over-time data that IFRI has accumulated.

IFRI has been fortunate to receive key support for two- or three-year periods at a time from the Food and Agriculture Organization of the United Nations, the National Science Foundation, the Ford Foundation, and the MacArthur Foundation. And yet, even though IFRI has generated a large number of peer-reviewed articles and several books, no funding agencies have been willing to provide an endowment—or even a five- or ten-year grant—to assure the long-term continuity of this long-term effort. Given the repeated findings that as economic and ecological conditions change, institutional arrangements need to be adaptive (Folke et al. 2005), it is crucial that long-term support be secured for a long-term, multicountry, multidisciplinary study that can carefully assess the impact of institutions on ecological conditions in a changing environment. Unfortunately, it is also close to impossible with the current policies of most research funding agencies.

Responding to the Challenges

It seems worthwhile for the scholarly and policy communities to recognize hurdles to collaborative research and strive to lower them. Universities, governments, and nongovernmental granting agencies could encourage more collaborative, broadly comparative, and long-term research by providing greater institutional and financial support. Institutional and financial support would address resource constraints but not collective action and other incentive problems that discourage collective action. Career incentives that reward individual research more than collaborative research clearly discourage collaboration. Reversal of these incentives is not impossible; acceptance of collaborative work does vary over time and across disciplines. An explicit recognition of the value of collaborative research and its policy implications might encourage coordinated efforts to alter career incentives more systematically and rapidly.

Looking Forward

In this book, we document significant progress related to both method and theory. Through our focus on a single, well-defined body of research, we have seen how method and theory can develop together. Findings from a variety of methods provide the building blocks for the development of more realistic theories and related frameworks to replace the highly simplified model once accepted as the conventional theory (see chapter 9). Theoretical refinements of concepts helped account for seemingly contradictory findings related to the influence of group characteristics like group size and heterogeneity, as well as macrocontextual factors such as property rights. We have described a number of methodological innovations that contributed to these important theoretical developments, and that have been spurred by theoretical puzzles. The positive feedback between theory and methods has policy benefits as well. The combination of better methodological tools and greater appreciation of the complex and contingent nature of social and ecological relationships has decreased support for blueprint policy solutions.

This book provides strong evidence of the contributions of a wide variety of methods and disciplines. Arguably, each method and discipline has had the greatest influence when its findings have been taken up, replicated, and probed by scholars using other methods or working in other disciplines. Given the demonstrated gains from methodological and disciplinary cross-fertilization, we enthusiastically encourage scholars to participate in more synthetic and integrative research.

We believe that the scientific community and policymakers would benefit from greater collaboration, more interdisciplinary research, and more multimethod research. In light of the lingering mutual suspicions between different methodological and disciplinary traditions, let us be clear that we are *not* arguing for uniformity in research practices. In particular, we are *not* arguing that *all* research should be collaborative or interdisciplinary, or should use multiple methods. As with other blanket responses to complex problems, any effort to impose a uniform approach to the study of social and ecological phenomena would certainly backfire. As we have noted repeatedly, the gains from disciplinary and methodological cross-fertilization are greatest when scholars with a solid command of their own disciplines and methods interact with each other. The coexistence of a wide variety of specialized research practices with integrative research efforts greatly increases the likelihood that theoretical and methodological innovations will occur and spread. Cross-fertilization may occur *either* through a series of studies that respond to each other using different methods and drawing on diverse disciplinary perspectives, *or* through integration of multiple disciplines and methods within a research program.

We are fully cognizant of the challenges. Our review of research on collective action for the management of common-pool natural resources revealed several important obstacles to disciplinary and methodological cross-fertilization and integration. Scholars typically do not immediately acknowledge evidence that contradicts established theory. Even after contradictory evidence has been acknowledged, improved theories do not emerge immediately or easily. Likewise, methodological practices do not always or immediately change in response to either theoretical developments or methodological innovations. Instead, as we have seen, methodological practices are influenced by practical as well as theoretical considerations. Further serious obstacles arise from professional incentives, organizational divisions, and suspicions of the assumptions and priorities of unfamiliar research traditions.

Although this book focuses on research related to collective action for the management of common-pool natural resources, we believe that our findings related to methodological practices and the interactions between theory and methods apply to a fairly wide range of social scientific and interdisciplinary research. This single research tradition offers examples of a wide variety of methods, including several research programs in which we have participated. While other research traditions might not use the exact same set of methods, the use of diverse methods is pervasive. Because anthropologists, ecologists, economists, geographers, sociologists, political scientists, and others have worked on the challenges of managing shared natural resources, we were able to demonstrate the benefits possible from methodological and disciplinary cross-fertilization and to examine the challenges of interdisciplinary research. The practical problems encountered in research on collective action affect many other research areas, especially topics for which existing data are scarce and field research requires sensitivity to local context. Certainly, the challenges associated with professional incentives are general.

While there are no simple solutions to these challenges, human beings repeatedly demonstrate the capacity to overcome collective challenges. People can change the structure of the situation in which they find themselves. We have reported that trust in other members of a group is especially important for the emergence of cooperative norms. Lack of familiarity with other research traditions limits trust of other disciplines and methods. Universities, funding agencies, and professional associations that promote exposure to multiple methods and disciplines in training, workshops and roundtables, and interdisciplinary centers are creating mechanisms to increase familiarity across different research traditions. The institutional and structural arrangements that undermine trust by pitting different disciplines and methods against each other in competition for resources and status are more difficult to address. The creation of interdisciplinary research centers on university campuses and the provision of grants for collaborative interdisciplinary research will have limited effect unless they involve active efforts to lower these institutional and structural divides. This is where we recommend that future efforts to promote synthetic and integrative research focus their energies.

Notes

1. See Campbell and Stanley (1966) for an earlier recognition of methodological trade-offs.

2. See overviews of methodological developments in Almond and Genco (1977), Gerring (2001, preface), Lasswell (1951), Moses and Knutsen (2007), and Torgerson (1986).

3. See Platt (1986) for an analysis of the changing framing of methodological debates in sociology in the United States between 1920 and 1960.

4. For an insightful analysis of the use of paired comparisons by scholars as diverse in some of their methods as Alexis de Tocqueville, Robert Putnam, Valerie Bunce, and Richard Samuels, see Tarrow (2008).

5. Formerly, the *Post-Autistic Economics Review* (see http://www.paecon .net).

6. Ontology refers to theoretical assumptions about the essence of reality. Ontology may refer to the elements of reality or to how the world works. In this chapter, we are concerned with the nature of causality. In chapter 9, we develop an ontological framework that identifies essential elements of social-ecological systems.

7. Some participants in debates associated with the perestroika movement in political science alluded to a similar dynamic in the immediate postwar period. See, for example, Rudolph (1996, 28).

8. Despite parsimonious statements of hypotheses predicted by formal models, these models often predict highly contingent outcomes. The emphasis on strategic interdependence constrained by structure implies a high level of causal complexity.

9. See Rudel (2005) for an excellent effort to analyze a large meta-database with QCA.

10. King, Keohane, and Verba (1994) targeted qualitative researchers especially in promoting more explicit research design. See Campbell (1975) and Lijphart (1971) for earlier defenses and critiques of small-N research.

11. The process of finding and maintaining a balance between critical distance and social embeddedness can be extremely demanding psychologically (e.g., Fenno 1978).

12. http://www.maxwell.syr.edu/moynihan/programs/cqrm/index.html.

13. For more information about training programs for cultural anthropologists, see the Cultural Anthropology Methods Mall (http://qualquant.net/training/ index.htm).

14. In a review of multidisciplinary research on collective action for natural resource management, we found that nearly half (43.6 percent) of the articles published between 1990 and 2005 had a single author, and that 82.0 percent had no more than two authors (see chapter 4). In a review of articles submitted to the *American Political Science Review*, Sigelman (2009) finds that less than 15

percent of all papers submitted over the six-year period during which he served as editor (2001–7) included more than two authors. The acceptance rate of multiauthored papers did not differ from that of single-authored papers.

15. Examples of program support for collaborative social science research include two- to four-year infrastructure grants for research teams from the Fond québécois de la recherche sur la société et la culture (FQRSC); and up to seven years' support for large-scale collaborative research from the (Canadian) Social Sciences and Humanities Research Council. During the 1990s, the Social Science Research Council and the American Council of Learned Societies (funded by the Ford Foundation) financed a year of *pre*dissertation fieldwork for doctoral students who already had strong training in other methodologies through its International Pre-dissertation Fellowship Program. The (U.S.) National Science Foundation's EITM program supports multimethod research but not fieldwork.

16. Compare Platt (1986) for a related discussion of methods in sociology during an earlier period (1920–60).

17. An interdisciplinary, international group of ecologists and social scientists recently published a "call to action" for fishery-management scholars to work across academic boundaries (Degnbol et al. 2006). Their assessment of the problem, and their way of addressing the problem through interdisciplinary collaboration, are consistent with our own conclusions.

CHAPTER TWO SMALL-N CASE STUDIES: PUTTING THE COMMONS UNDER A MAGNIFYING GLASS

1. Hardin's recognition of a positive role for state property also echoed standard thinking. State property was often presented as a second-best option for situations in which private rights were not possible or desirable for normative reasons. Alchian and Demsetz (1973), however, note that state regulation often creates problems of shirking, and warn that communal property often occurs because the state fails to exercise its rights of exclusion.

2. Kuhn's (1970, 16–19) discussion of the "black swan" illustrates the interpretive challenge.

3. This is similar to George and Bennett's (2005, 18) definition of cases as "instances" of a "class of events."

4. The clarity of natural resource boundaries has been identified as an important condition for successful collective action (E. Ostrom 1990); unclear boundaries also present a challenge for data collection, as we discuss further below.

5. For an introduction to these and related techniques, see Abbott (1997); Bennett and Elman (2006); Brass (2000); Collier, Brady, and Seawright (2004); Dion (1998); George and Bennett (2005); George and McKeown (1985); Gerring (2007b); Ingram, Schneider, and deLeon (2007); Pierson (2003); Skocpol and Somers (1980); R. Smith (2004); and Tarrow (2008).

6. Several innovations in quantitative techniques enable analysis of a greater variety of causal relationships (e.g., Braumoeller 2003; Buckley 2004; Clark, Gilligan, and Golder 2006; Ragin 1987, 2000; Signorino 1999). With the exception of QCA and fs/QCA (Ragin 1987, 2000), these techniques are better suited to

testing assumed causal patterns than to discerning multiple patterns. We look more closely at QCA in chapter 3.

7. Some analytical techniques associated with case study research rely on stringent and often dubious assumptions. But heroic assumptions are not inherent in the method.

8. When case study research loses sight of the broader population, however, parochialism and other forms of conceptual inconsistency emerge (Sartori 1991).

9. Although strategies for increasing observations through within-case comparisons are widely promoted, Munck and Snyder (2007) found that relatively few case studies in leading journals for comparative politics take advantage of such internal observations.

10. Gerring (2007a, 57–61; 2007b) also discusses the challenge of data availability but gives less attention to variation in data availability by topic.

11. While the Internet creates new opportunities for subnational and nonelite populations to circumvent formal publication channels, access remains highly unequal.

12. Later chapters discuss methodological strategies for synthetic learning, including meta-analysis of case studies (chapter 4), collaborative research (chapter 5), field experiments (chapter 6), and empirically grounded agent-based models (chapter 8).

13. As the framework has developed in recent years, the structure of the resource system has been divided into two broad parts: the "resource system" and the "resource units" that are consumed by humans. The concept of rules has been broadened to include a full array of "governance systems," and the structure of the community is now called "users." All of these working parts of a social-ecological system are themselves embedded in a "social, economic, and political setting" and in "related ecosystems" (see E. Ostrom 2007 and discussion in chapter 9).

14. Debates exist about the ability to disprove even invariant hypotheses, especially in light of the fallibility of observation. For examples, see Goldthorpe (1997) and Lieberson (1991). See also the discussion of falsification in Kuhn (1970, 13–19) and Lakatos (1970, 95–102).

15. These citations reflect a very small sample of relevant case studies. Many studies include instances of failures as well as successes or analyze arrangements for communal management that were successful for some time before faltering.

16. A fourth potential reason may be strong economic incentives to convert resource use (particularly land) to gain higher profits.

17. Clear and secure property rights do not prevent depletion of renewable resources under all circumstances (e.g., Baland and Platteau [1996] 2000, 18–23, 294–96).

18. For a more general treatment, see Sjaastad and Bromley (1997). On the distinctions among property, access, and control, see Rangan (1997), Ribot and Peluso (2003), and Sikor and Lund (2009).

19. Shipton (1988) argues that scattered arable plots are another form of risk management, although Fenoaltea (1988) disagrees. Adoption or maintenance of production strategies associated with risk management is also influenced by distributional politics (Agrawal 1999; Mwangi 2007a).

20. Baland and Platteau ([1996] 2000, 365–66) argue that claims for the desirability of small groups rest more heavily on the expectation of homogeneity than on that of benefits from frequent interactions.

21. To be fair, the equation of villages or settlements with community often represents a shorthand used even by commentators who are quite aware of its inadequacy.

22. Balasubramanian and Selvaraj (2003) find that increasing numbers of tube wells in a watershed threaten irrigation tanks both by increasing the need for investment in maintenance in response to higher rates of groundwater withdrawal and by decreasing the likelihood of collective action to provide such maintenance.

23. This community subsequently adopted much more restrictive conditions for new members (Poteete and Welch 2004).

24. Olson (1965) treated all nonexcluded goods as public goods, obscuring differences related to the divisibility of goods and the possibility of depletion. As discussed above, nondivisible and inexhaustible public goods should be distinguished from divisible and exhaustible common-pool resources.

25. The probability of success in this case is lowered further by the general absence of conditions that favor collective action (Altricher 2008). The point here is that collective action will yield little in the absence of an understanding of how to achieve collective goals.

26. Some of the material in NRC (1986) was later published as Bromley et al. (1992).

27. We surveyed the research questions and hypotheses suggested by these edited volumes as part of our discussion of synthetic studies in chapter 3.

28. The concern here is with cross-fertilization and synthesis, not collaboration. As discussed in chapter 5, some research networks do persist for extended periods.

29. Until 2006, the name of the organization was the International Association for the Study of Common Property. The name was changed to encompass research on a greater diversity of "commons," such as digital commons.

CHAPTER THREE BROADLY COMPARATIVE FIELD-BASED RESEARCH

1. Breadth of comparison refers to the geographic scope, historical scope, and, for our focal area of research, the diversity of types of natural resources included in an analysis. In this chapter, we are particularly concerned with geographic scope.

2. We gratefully acknowledge the competent research assistance of Agnes Koós, who conducted the bibliographic search and compiled the meta-database discussed in this chapter.

3. Academic Search Premier (EBSCO) is the largest multidisciplinary database of scholarly articles (EBSCOhost Research Databases 2005). Nonetheless, no database indexes all scholarly outlets. We evaluated potential biases by comparing unscreened results generated by EBSCO and Web of Science for articles published in a single year (2004), using a subset of search terms: common-pool resource,

commons, community management, community-based management, collective action, and common resource management. Together, the two databases identified 480 unique articles. Of these, Academic Search Premier identified 68 percent compared with 58 percent for Web of Science. Only 27 percent of all articles appeared in both databases. The most obvious differences concerned clearly off-topic research that would be dropped during the screening process. For example, Web of Science identified more ecological studies with a biophysical focus and more theoretical (nonempirical) analyses of collective action, while Academic Search Premier listed book reviews as scholarly articles and identified more biomedical studies. Both databases index the most important outlets for empirical, social science, and interdisciplinary research related to natural resources. We believe that there would be much more overlap after screening. Although no bibliographic database would include all relevant articles, the breadth of coverage offered by Academic Search Premier generates relatively comprehensive results and reduces the likelihood of bias.

4. The strategy of searching on one term at a time decreased the likelihood of missing relevant articles but retrieved many off-topic citations. Off-topic articles included those about collective action in other domains, concerned with the House of Commons rather than natural resource commons, or related to particular natural resources but not to collective action. The winnowing process relied primarily on abstracts, supplemented by reviews of full articles when abstracts did not clearly address our selection criteria.

5. Poteete and Ostrom (2008) analyzed a more encompassing set of articles and used slightly different coding rules. Here, we analyze only articles that rely on field-based studies of collective action by natural resource users. The analysis does not include articles that were not empirical or not field-based, nor does it include those concerned with collective action among politicians or policymakers rather than natural resource users. For differences in coding, see the discussion below of the main unit of analysis. Some coding errors were discovered and corrected during recoding.

6. In some of these articles, more attention is devoted to other units of analysis. In Poteete and Ostrom (2008), the "main" unit of analysis refers to the unit of analysis to which the article devotes the most attention. The alternative interpretation of the "main" unit of analysis results in only marginal differences in the patterns reported but more accurately reflects our theoretical concerns.

7. The central limit theorem assumes that the underlying population is normally distributed. Although it is not obvious that the normality assumption makes sense for the distribution of outcomes of interest related to collective action, the thirty-observation rule of thumb offers an attractive—and relatively obtainable—point of reference.

8. We did identify several additional publications with cross-national scope that were not empirical or based on field research. These include literature reviews, analyses of published data, and synthetic analyses.

9. Additional large-N analyses have been published since 2004 (e.g., Chhatre and Agrawal 2008; Gibson, Williams, and Ostrom 2005). The policymaking unit of analysis refers to collective action by resource users analyzed according to jurisdiction and does not include analyses of collective action by policymakers (e.g.,

Andersson 2004; Andersson, Gibson, and Lehoucq 2006) or governments (e.g., in international agreements).

10. At the extreme, Wilson et al.'s (1999) analysis of the Lake Victoria's Nile perch fishery involves an internationally shared resource yet is presented as a case study of a single resource system.

11. A number of large-N studies based on fieldwork have been reported in papers and books (e.g., Bardhan 2000; Jodha 1990; Lam 1998; Shivakoti and Ostrom 2002; Somanathan, Prabhakar, and Mehta 2002). All of these large-N studies analyze data from a single country.

12. These debates reflect differences in the relative importance given to the evaluation of correlations and the tracing of processes (Bennett and Elman 2006; Brady and Collier 2004) and different expectations about the generality of social patterns (Ragin 1987).

13. Note that an additional four large-N studies collected data for the full population within their study area. Other strategies for sampling included structured sampling, convenience samples, voluntary responses to mail questionnaires, and snowball samples.

14. Spatial sampling guided by Global Positioning System (GPS) technology offers an ingenious strategy for avoiding biases associated with incomplete official lists (Landry and Shen 2005).

15. Secondary analysis refers to the reanalysis of a database constructed from primary data (Glass 1976).

16. Meta-analysis does not eliminate reviewer bias, but greater transparency about procedures makes it easier for other scholars to identify bias (Bangert-Drowns 1995; Slavin 1986).

17. We do agree, however, with those who caution against pooling data from studies with different research designs (e.g., Slavin 1986).

18. Only some of these studies concern collective action or common-pool natural resources.

19. A related technique, fs/QCA, moves away from dichotomous coding by using fuzzy sets (Ragin 2000). Graduated coding of qualitative data allows for intermediate outcomes but, in the absence of accepted protocols, gives rise to new puzzles.

20. Shelby and Vaske (2008) encounter a similar terminological problem. In the study of the human dimensions of leisure science, several analyses of other analyses have been published but are generally considered "comparative analyses." Shelby and Vaske accept the terminological distinction because the "comparative analyses" that they reviewed analyzed data that were from other studies, but not derived from the research reports from the other studies. Meta-analyses related to common-pool resources, however, have relied largely on data included in publications and other research reports. As discussed in chapter 4, meta-analysts have contacted case study authors to track down missing data, but this is also a recommended practice among meta-analysts of experimental and quasi-experimental research.

21. Decisions about methodological practices also reflect the relative rewards to different analytical strategies in terms of grants and professional recognition. We take up this point in chapter 10.

22. Although the specific statistical techniques that have been developed are suitable for meta-analysis of quantitative research and cannot be used in the meta-analysis of case studies, the logic of testing for bias associated with research design applies with equal force to all forms of meta-analysis. It is only a matter of using techniques that are appropriate for different types of data.

Chapter Four Meta-Analysis: Getting the Big Picture through Synthesis

1. A third option begins with highly inclusive criteria, but then involves repeated rounds of recoding to evaluate more precise variable definitions. See chapter 3 and Rudel (2008).

2. Charlotte Hess and Emily Castle have continued the massive effort to keep up with the literature in this area. "The Comprehensive Bibliography of the Commons," with over 57,000 citations, can be accessed through "The Digital Library of the Commons (DLC)" Web site (see http://dlc.dlib.indiana.edu/). The DLC itself is a depository of papers on these issues; it contained more than 4,500 papers as of August 1, 2009.

3. During the 1985–86 academic year, William Blomquist and James Wunsch met regularly with Elinor Ostrom to build on the effort to identify variables that were described in a large number of cases identified by the NRC. In 1986, Ostrom was able to hire Edella Schlager and Shui Yan Tang as research assistants, Sharon Huckfeldt as a programmer, and Julie England as a database manager on a National Science Foundation grant to embark on a project titled "The Role of Institutions in the Survival and Efficiency of Common-Pool Resources." This grant also supported a diversity of formal theoretical work and our first empirical studies in the experimental laboratory. Arun Agrawal worked on forestry cases while a visiting scholar at the Workshop before conducting his own PhD fieldwork in India.

4. Ruttan (2006, 845–46) provides a list of the irrigation and fishery cases and source materials.

5. See discussion of this problem in chapter 3.

6. See note 2 for more details.

7. In the more recent literature on complex systems, the concept of "robustness" focuses on adaptability to disturbances: "the maintenance of some desired system characteristics despite fluctuations in the behavior of its component parts or its environment" (Carlson and Doyle 2002, 2538; see also Anderies, Janssen, and Ostrom 2004).

8. Ganesh Shivakoti and Paul Benjamin worked closely with Ostrom to revise the CPR coding forms for this purpose. During the period of developing the NIIS database, the research team brought several experts, including Robert Yoder, Anthony Bottrall, Robert Hunt, and Mark Svendsen, to the Workshop to review the draft manuals and forms and suggest revisions based on their own in-depth knowledge of biophysical, social, and institutional factors likely to affect performance of irrigation systems.

9. Julie England, pers. comm., December 31, 2008.

10. Ashok Regmi, pers. comm., July 30, 2004.

11. Consequently, sixty-seven systems (28.4 percent) in the database are located in Chitwan alone (Julie England, pers. comm., December 31, 2008).

12. Baland and Platteau consider experimental studies in their section on theoretical developments. We discuss the experimental method in chapter 6.

13. Notions of relatively isolated corporate communities were common among anthropologists and others at midcentury (e.g., Wolf 1957).

14. According to the Web of Science database, at least 2,416 articles have cited E. Ostrom (1990), and at least 332 have cited Baland and Platteau ([1996] 2000) as of June 29, 2009.

CHAPTER FIVE   COLLABORATIVE FIELD STUDIES

1. See chapter 3 for a description of the database used in this analysis.

2. By comparison, Sigelman (2009, 509) reports that 16.0 percent of the articles accepted for publication by the disciplinary journal the *American Political Science Review* from fall 2001 through summer 2007 had more than two authors. Likewise, 14.6 percent of all papers submitted during this period had more than two authors.

3. We discuss the IFRI research program below.

4. Similarly, George and Bennett (2005) argue for more collaboration as a way to increase the use of multiple *methods* in research projects.

5. Other examples of larger projects include the Central and Eastern European Sustainable Agriculture framework project (Theesfeld 2004), the Community Perspectives of Land and Agricultural Reform project undertaken by the University of Witwatersrand and West Virginia University (Woodhouse 1995), and the Making Agriculture Sustainable project encompassing five European countries (Oerlemans and Assouline 2004).

6. The CELP Web site describes a cross-national project on Common Pool Resources (http://www.york.ac.uk/res/celp/webpages/projects/cpr/cprmenu.htm) that includes Botswana, Mexico, Nepal, Spain, and Zimbabwe as well as Tanzania. The article by Adhikari, Di Falco, and Lovett (2004) appears to be a product of this broader initiative. The Web site suggests no more than loose coordination of research across components, and it seems that CELP did not have partner institutions in all of these countries.

7. Ostrom (1990) did not argue that congruence with *all* eight principles was either necessary or sufficient. As discussed in chapter 4, the design principles are currently being revised in light of the large number of studies in which other scholars have assessed their relevance.

8. The other centers are the Africa Rice Center (WARDA), Biodiversity International, Centro Internacional de Agricultura Tropicale (CIAT), Centro Internacional de Mejoramiento de Maiz y Trigo (CIMMYT), Centro Internacional de la Papa (CIP), the International Center for Agricultural Research in the Dry Areas (ICARDA), the International Crops Research Institute for the Semi-Arid Tropics (ICRISAT), the International Institute of Tropical Agriculture (IITA), the International Rice Research Institute (IRRI), and the World Agroforestry Centre (ICRAF).

9. See chapter 4 for a discussion of the CPR and NIIS research programs.

10. As of July 1, 2009, the IFRI database contained data from sites in Bhutan, Bolivia, Brazil, Colombia, Ecuador, Guatemala, Honduras, India, Japan, Kenya, Madagascar, Mexico, Nepal, Tanzania, Thailand, Uganda, and the United States (Julie England, pers. comm.).

11. Updates of the common database occur periodically as new data come in from CRCs.

12. Despite the name change, an IFRI user group is conceptually equivalent to an NIIS subgroup, but in relation to a resource system that generates a greater variety of natural products (see chapter 4).

13. Each research team maintains a local database and periodically sends data for inclusion in the networkwide database.

14. A number of dissertations have been completed using IFRI data, including Andersson (2002), Benjamin (2004), Coleman (2009b), Futemma (2000), Hayes (2007), Jagger (2009), Namubiru (2008), Pacheco (2007), Regmi (2007), Schweik (1998), Silva-Forsberg (1999), Thoms (2004), van Laerhoven (2008), and Varughese (1999).

15. The Research Network on Gender Politics and the State (RNGS), established in 1995 and involving nearly forty scholars in sixteen industrialized countries, is a noteworthy exception. See the RNGS Web site (http://libarts.wsu. edu/polisci/rngs/).

16. Meta-analysis *can* build on rigorously collected qualitative field research; realization of this potential depends on the care taken in screening source material (see chapter 4).

CHAPTER SIX   EXPERIMENTS IN THE LABORATORY AND THE FIELD

1. The experiments discussed in the chapter typically involve a sample of participants (students in laboratory experiments who are not regularly related as students or assistants to the researchers running the experiment), use no deception, and provide monetary incentives.

2. The Nash equilibrium is named in honor of John Nash, the Nobel Prize–winning theorist who first proposed this concept.

3. Subjects in many dilemma experiments such as Prisoner's Dilemma and Investment games do "cooperate" at a higher level than predicted by the conventional theory (see E. Ostrom 2009a for an overview). In one of the more fascinating earlier experiments, conducted by Liberman, Samuels, and Ross (2007), the same Prisoner's Dilemma game was played with two framings. In the experiment that was labeled as "the Community Game," 71 percent of the participants chose to cooperate. When the same experiment was labeled "The Wall Street Game," the rate of cooperation fell to 33 percent—still a significant proportion given the theoretical prediction of no cooperation.

4. In common-pool resource experiments, as discussed in the next section, anonymity negatively affects cooperation levels.

5. Also see Palfrey and Rosenthal (1988, 310), where they model "uncontrolled preferences," which derive from "acts of social cooperation or contribution, the utility of altruism or social duty."

6. In another series of experiments, Bagnoli, Ben-David, and McKee (1992) did not find support for a second theoretical model developed in Bagnoli and Lipman (1989) involving a somewhat complicated agreement by participants on the level of contributions—an agreement that, if followed, would lead to optimal equilibria. This again illustrates one of the strengths of testing theory through experiments in the laboratory where very precise operationalizations can be made, and theorists are enabled to see which of their predictions hold in practice and which do not.

7. To provide similar monetary income among the two treatments, participants were paid one-half of their computer returns in the 25-token experiments.

8. The Nash equilibrium can be made symmetric even with large- and small-endowment appropriators. In particular, a symmetric Nash equilibrium results as long as the small-endowment level is greater than or equal to that required for equilibrium play. In such a case, small-endowment appropriators simply have a lower input allocation level in the outside market relative to large-endowment appropriators.

9. The software was based on Goldstone and Ashpole (2004), who performed experiments on foraging behavior.

10. A graphical image of a participant on the computer screen.

11. This is the expected end-of-round effect. In Janssen et al. (2008), the time left for the round was not known, and participants were eager to get tokens as soon as possible since they were uncertain about the amount of time left.

12. In our meta-analyses and large-N studies, we had found that these three rules were frequently used in the management of fisheries, forests, and irrigation systems. See Lobe and Berkes (2004) for an example of a lottery rule used in the coastal fisheries of southern India.

Chapter Seven Agent-Based Models of Collective Action

1. In the cellular automata literature, one typically uses the term *rules* instead of *strategies*, but we use *strategies* to be consistent with our use of the words *strategies*, *norms*, and *rules* in this book.

2. Which is the same as when *mpcr*, as defined in chapter 6, is greater than 1.

3. See, for example, Alexander (1987); Gintis, Smith, and Bowles (2001); Leimar and Hammerstein (2001); Lotem, Fishman, and Stone (1999); Nowak and Sigmund (1998); Wedekind and Milinski (2000); and Zahavi (1977).

4. Smajgl, Izquierdo, and Huigen (2008) provide another agent-based modeling approach to endogenous rule change based on the ADICO framework.

Chapter Eight Building Empirically Grounded Agent-Based Models

1. A power law distribution refers to distributions where a small number of the population receives a large share. In contrast to a normal distribution, the power law distribution has a fat tail, a significant probability of an extreme outcome (Clauset, Shalizi, and Newman 2009).

2. Simple reactive agents have automatic responses to decision problems and do not spend effort to evaluate the consequences of their decisions. An example is an agent who copies the decision of his/her most successful neighbor if the neighbor is more successful than the agent him/herself. See chapter 7.

3. See, for example, Balmann et al. (2002); Berger (2001); Bower and Bunn (2000); D. Brown et al. (2005); Dreyfus-Leon and Kleiber (2001); Evans and Kelley (2004); and Wilson, Yan, and Wilson (2007).

4. Action research refers to problem-solving activity led by individuals (such as professional scholars) who work with others (such as stakeholders) to improve the way they address issues and solve problems. The concept was introduced by Kurt Lewin (1946).

5. A Turing test is an experiment where one tries to distinguish a human from a machine (Turing 1950). In the original Turing test, a human judge engages in a natural language conversation via text messages with one human and one machine, each of which tries to appear human. If the judge cannot reliably tell the machine from the human, the machine is said to have passed the test.

CHAPTER NINE   PUSHING THE FRONTIERS OF THE THEORY OF COLLECTIVE ACTION AND THE COMMONS

1. The theoretical predictions for an indefinitely repeated social dilemma included all possible actions from full cooperation to no cooperation at all—regardless of the structure of the immediate microsituation.

2. Recent experiments where participants can exchange text messages only with unknown other participants also lead to significant improvements (Janssen forthcoming).

3. James Buchanan (1984, 5) articulated the earlier view of most economists when he wrote that "The burden of proof rests with those who suggest wholly different models of man apply in the political and economic realms of behavior."

4. Psychologists have debated whether predictions could be based on attributes of individual personalities or the specific situation that individuals face. Given this puzzle, Waichmann and Requate (2008) recently undertook a careful test of the personality traits of subjects in Cournot duopoly experiments where participants have to decide without communication how much to produce. They assessed whether personality traits affect subjects' behavior. They found that personality traits did help predict individual behavior in the first few rounds of an experiment. On the other hand, they found that "after subjects have gained experience, their behavior is largely independent of their personality traits" (Waichmann and Requate 2008, 11). In concluding their analysis, they state, "Our findings support the hypothesis that it is the situation rather than the personality characteristics of the subjects that mainly determines their behavior" (ibid.).

5. Evolutionary psychologists have produced substantial evidence that humans have an inherited capacity to learn rules and norms—similar to the capacity to learn a language (see Cosmides and Tooby 1992, 1994). These include the norms of reciprocity and trust. Such learning requires exposure to repeated situations where other individuals who are respected (such as parents) reiterate the importance of following these norms. Further, humans have also learned how to detect

cheaters when they can see each other's faces (Farrelly and Turnbull 2008; Verplaetse, Vanneste, and Braeckman 2007).

6. See, for example, Andreoni (1989); Bolton and Ockenfels (2000); Charness and Rabin (2002); J. Cox, Friedman, and Gjerstad (2007); Fehr and Schmidt (1999); Frohlich (1974); Ledyard (1995); and Rabin (1993).

7. The importance of trust has had a more central role in sociology. Zucker (1986) provides an excellent analysis of the multiple origins of trust. Deutsch (1973) and Sztompka (1999) also provide deep insights into the sociological theories of trust.

8. See figures 6.1 and 6.2 in chapter 6 as well as similar figures in many research articles.

9. Massive overfishing and deforestation tend to occur where microsituations within the broader context do not provide opportunities for harvesters to know each other well and gain trust that others are cooperating by reducing their harvesting levels.

10. Thaler and Sunstein (2003, 2008) refer to the importance of microsituational variables and public policy about choice-architecture. If regularities in human behavior are taken into account, microsituations can be designed in such a way that socially desired decisions are made by free choice. For example, having organ donation as the default choice substantially increases the number of organ donations (see also Levitt and List 2007).

11. In the field, researchers have to rely on indirect measures of trust such as (1) interviews with participants about their sense of trust and reciprocity in the field or surveys conducted after experiments and (2) observed behavior in the context of a collective-action problem. Further, as discussed below, researchers have no control over characteristics of the microsituation. The diversity of microsettings in the field means that it is practically impossible to isolate the effects of any single condition. In microsettings studied in the lab or agent-based models, the attributes of the situation are specified very clearly by the researcher.

12. When the impact of the broader context is examined in field research, however, considerable mobility of resource users may discourage development of trust and cooperation. In some settings, mobility may lead to "roving bandits" (Berkes et al. 2006).

13. Messick and Brewer (1983, 22) point to four ways that communication facilitates cooperation: (1) by eliciting information about the choices of others, (2) by enhancing trust in other group members, (3) by activating social values and responsibility, and (4) by creating a group identity (see also Ben-Ner and Putterman 2009).

14. One of the design principles discussed in chapter 4 relates the robustness of institutional arrangements to the proportional equivalence between benefits and costs of cooperation.

15. Simon overtly distinguished his concept of hierarchy from one involving human bosses at each level. "We shall want to consider systems in which the relations among subsystems are more complex than in the formal organizational hierarchy. . . . We shall want to include systems in which there is no relation of subordination among sub-systems" (Simon 1985, 197).

16. An example of the need for both levels to understand some outcomes is the long process of developing a successful policy for allocating fishing rights

to the groundfish off the coast of British Columbia described by Colin Clark (2006). After many years of increasing levels of overfishing off the coast, even after official quotas had been allocated, the government of British Columbia had to close the fishery in 1995 owing to noncompliance with the rules. After the fishery was permitted to recover for a few years, a new policy was implemented and the fishery was reopened. The new policy was that an official observer had to be on every boat to record all catches. Changing the microsituation on each boat led to much higher compliance and eventual development of a transferable quota system.

17. See, for example, Armitage, Berkes, and Doubleday (2007); Baland and Platteau ([1996] 2000); E. Ostrom (2001, 2009a); E. Ostrom, Gardner, and Walker (1994); Schlager (1990); Tang (1992); and Wade (1994).

18. In some settings, other variables will also be important, and some of those listed here will play no role. Given its likely importance in affecting the benefits and costs of collective action, however, we would argue that field researchers should try to obtain empirical measures for at least this set of variables to help explain successes and failures in collective action to overcome CPR dilemmas.

19. The speed of regeneration may also affect whether the users themselves can adequately manage a resource. Rodrigues et al. (2009) find that a slow regeneration rate of forest resources tends to increase the capability of local communities to self-manage, while a fast rate, as in the tropics, may exceed the capacity of self-organized groups to manage.

20. Basurto and Ostrom (2009) draw on this set of broader contextual variables affecting the cost-benefit calculation of local fishers to explain why two small-scale fishing communities on the Gulf of California in Mexico (Puerto Peñasco and the Seri village of Punta Chueca) were able to self-organize while a third, nearby fishing community (Kino Bay) was not. See also Cudney-Bueno and Basurto (2009).

21. In the analysis of the effect of multiple variables, developing simple mathematical models is difficult, while utilizing agent-based models becomes a powerful tool (see chapters 7 and 8).

22. As more researchers develop empirical studies involving observations for a large number of CPRs, it will be feasible to quantify many of the variables in the SES framework as recent studies drawing on the IFRI database have done (see Coleman 2009a; Coleman and Steed 2009).

23. The extensive work on multilevels and polycentricity is relevant to this question (see Armitage, Berkes, and Doubleday 2007; McGinnis 1999a, 1999b, 2000; V. Ostrom 2008a, 2008b; Young, King, and Schroeder 2008).

CHAPTER TEN   LEARNING FROM MULTIPLE METHODS

1. Other methods, such as GIS and remote sensing, also play an important role.

2. Further, many case studies of self-organized resource systems mentioned that resource users tended to monitor each other and use very small sanctions for the first infraction noticed by a user, and to gradually increase the severity of the punishment for subsequent offenses. The use of graduated sanctions was one

of the findings to grow out of the meta-analysis and became one of the design principles discussed in chapter 4.

3. The software of the laboratory experiments and the protocols of the field experiments can be found at http://commons.asu.edu.

4. For further information about the development of the Workshop, see Aligica and Boettke (2009).

5. It typically involves training in a suite of methods widely used in a given discipline as well.

6. Sigelman (2009) found that coauthored papers accounted for 45.1 percent of papers submitted to the *American Political Science Review* and 43.3 percent of the papers accepted between fall 2001 and summer 2007. These rates are somewhat lower than we found, but fairly high considering that one might expect fewer coauthored articles in disciplinary journals.

7. Restrictions on access to online databases and print libraries exist and can present a significant obstacle to scholars based at organizations that maintain subscriptions to few databases or print journals.

8. Between 2001 and 2007, only 3 percent of the articles published in the *American Political Science Review* had more than three authors (Sigelman 2009, 509).

9. To get a better sense of the criteria used to evaluate research, teaching, and service in tenure decisions, Rothgeb and Burger (2009, 516) conducted a survey of chairs of political science departments. Single-authored publications were identified as essential for tenure by chairs from 51 percent of the MA-granting departments and 72 percent of the departments with doctoral programs.

10. http://www.mad.zmaw.de/wdc-for-climate/ and http://www.ngdc.noaa.gov/wdc/.

11. http://www.ncbi.nlm.nih.gov/.

12. For example, Dataverse for sharing data (http://dvn.iq.harvard.edu/dvn/), OpenABM for sharing agent-based models (http://www.openabm.org/), and the Interuniversity Consortium for Political and Social Research (ICPSR).

13. The HSD program was a special NSF-initiative; 2008 was the last competition.

References

Abbott, Andrew. 1997. "On the Concept of Turning Point." *Comparative Social Research* 16:85–105.

Abel, N.O.J., and P. M. Blaikie. 1989. "Land Degradation, Stocking Rates and Conservation Policies in the Communal Rangelands of Botswana and Zimbabwe." *Land Degradation and Rehabilitation* 1:101–23.

Achen, Christopher H. 2002. "Toward a New Political Methodology: Microfoundations and ART." *Annual Review of Political Science* 5:423–50.

———. 2005. "Let's Put Garbage-Can Regressions and Garbage-Can Probits Where They Belong." *Conflict Management and Peace Science* 22(4) (January): 327–39.

Achen, Christopher H., and Duncan Snidal. 1989. "Rational Deterrence Theory and Comparative Case Studies." *World Politics* 41(2) (January): 143–69.

Acheson, James M. 2003. *Capturing the Commons: Devising Institutions to Manage the Maine Lobster Industry.* Hanover, NH: University Press of New England.

———. 2006. "Institutional Failure in Resource Management." *Annual Review of Anthropology* 33:117–34.

Adar, Eytan, and Bernardo Huberman. 2000. "Free Riding on Gnutella." *First Monday* 5(10), http://firstmonday.org/htbin/cgiwrap/bin/ojs/index.php/fm/issue/view/124.

Adhikari, Bhim, Salvatore Di Falco, and Jon C. Lovett. 2004. "Household Characteristics and Forest Dependency: Evidence from Common Property Forest Management in Nepal." *Ecological Economics* 48(2) (February): 245–57.

Adhikari, Bhim, and Jon C. Lovett. 2006. "Institutions and Collective Action: Does Heterogeneity Matter in Community-Based Resource Management." *Journal of Development Studies* 42(3):426–45.

Agrawal, Arun. 1999. *Greener Pastures: Politics, Markets, and Community among a Migrant Pastoral People.* Durham, NC: Duke University Press.

———. 2000. "Small Is Beautiful, but Is Larger Better? Forest-Management Institutions in the Kumaon Himalaya, India." In *People and Forests: Communities, Institutions, and Governance*, ed. Clark C. Gibson, Margaret A. McKean, and Elinor Ostrom, 57–85. Cambridge, MA: MIT Press.

———. 2001a. "State Formation in Community Spaces? Decentralization of Control over Forests in the Kumaon Himalaya, India." *Journal of Asian Studies* 60(1):9–40.

———. 2001b. "Common Property Institutions and Sustainable Governance of Resources." *World Development* 29(10) (October): 1623–48.

———. 2004. "Environmental Politics and Institutional Choices: Forestry and Wildlife Policies in the Developing World, 1980–2000." Presented at the CHAOS Seminar Series, University of Washington, Seattle, June 8–9, 2004.

———. 2005. *Environmentality: Technologies of Government and the Making of Subjects.* Durham, NC: Duke University Press.

———. 2007. "Forests, Governance and Sustainability: Common Property Theory and Its Contributions." *International Journal of the Commons* 1(1):111–36.

Agrawal, Arun, and Ashwini Chhatre. 2007. "Institutions, Co-Governance, and Forests in the Indian Himalaya." *Studies in Comparative International Development* 42(1/2) (Spring): 67–86.

Agrawal, Arun, and Clark C. Gibson. 1999. "Enchantment and Disenchantment: The Role of Community in Natural Resource Conservation." *World Development* 27(4):629–49.

———. 2001. *Communities and the Environment: Ethnicity, Gender, and the State in Community-Based Conservation.* New Brunswick, NJ: Rutgers University Press.

Agrawal, Arun, and Sanjeev Goyal. 2001. "Group Size and Collective Action: Third-Party Monitoring in Common-Pool Resources." *Comparative Political Studies* 34(1):63–93.

Agrawal, Arun, and Krishna Gupta. 2005. "Decentralization and Participation: The Governance of Common Pool Resources in Nepal's Terai." *World Development* 33(7) (July): 1101–14.

Agrawal, Arun, and Elinor Ostrom. 2001. "Collective Action, Property Rights, and Decentralization in Resource Use in India and Nepal." *Politics and Society* 29(4):485–514.

Agrawal, Arun, and Gautam N. Yadama. 1997. "How Do Local Institutions Mediate Market and Population Pressures on Resources? Forest Panchayats in Kumaon, India." *Development and Change* 28(3):435–65.

Ahn, T. K., Marco A. Janssen, and Elinor Ostrom. 2004. "Signals, Symbols, and Human Cooperation." In *The Origins and Nature of Sociality*, ed. Robert W. Sussman and Audrey R. Chapman, 122–39. New York: Aldine de Gruyter.

Ahn, T. K., Elinor Ostrom, and James Walker. 2009. "A Common-Pool Resource Experiment with Subjects from 41 Countries." Working Paper. Bloomington: Indiana University, Workshop in Political Theory and Policy Analysis.

Ainslie, Andrew. 1999. "When 'Community' Is Not Enough: Managing Common Property Natural Resources in Rural South Africa." *Development Southern Africa* 16(3) (Spring): 375–401.

Alchian, Armen. 1950. "Uncertainty, Evolution and Economic Theory." *Journal of Political Economy* 58(3) (June): 211–21.

Alchian, Armen, and Harold Demsetz. 1973. "The Property Rights Paradigm." *Journal of Economic History* 33(1):16–27.

Alexander, Richard D. 1987. *The Biology of Moral Systems.* New York: Aldine de Gruyter.

Aligica, Paul Dragos, and Peter J. Boettke. 2009. *Challenging Institutional Analysis and Development: The Bloomington School.* New York: Routledge.

Almond, Gabriel, and Stephen J. Genco. 1977. "Clouds, Clocks, and the Study of Politics." *World Politics* 2(4) (July): 489–522.

Altrichter, Mariana. 2008. "Assessing Potential for Community-Based Management of Peccaries through Common Pool Resource Theory in the Rural Area of the Argentine Chaco." *Ambio* 37(2):108–13.

Amenta, Edwin, Bruce G. Carruthers, and Yvonne Zylan. 1992. "A Hero for the Aged? The Townsend Movement, the Political Mediation Model, and US Old-Age Policy, 1934–1950." *American Journal of Sociology* 98(2):308–39.

Amenta, Edwin, and Jane D. Poulsen. 1996. "Social Politics in Context: The Institutional Politics Theory and Social Spending at the End of the New Deal." *Social Forces* 75(1):33–61.

Anderies, John M., Marco A. Janssen, and Elinor Ostrom. 2004. "A Framework to Analyze the Robustness of Social-Ecological Systems from an Institutional Perspective." *Ecology and Society* 9(1):18, http://www.ecologyandsociety. org/vol9/is1/art18.

Anderson, Terry L., and Peter J. Hill. [1977] 1990. "The Race for Property Rights." *Journal of Law and Economics* 33:117–97.

———. [1977] 1998. "From Free Grass to Fences: Transforming the Commons of the American West." In *Managing the Commons,* 2nd ed., ed. John A. Baden and Douglas S. Noonan, 119–34. Bloomington: Indiana University Press.

Anderson, Terry L., and Randy T. Simmons, eds. 1993. *The Political Economy of Customs and Culture: Informal Solutions to the Commons Problem.* Lanham, MD: Rowman and Littlefield.

Andersson, Krister P. 2002. "Can Decentralization Save Bolivia's Forests? An Institutional Analysis of Municipal Forest Governance." PhD diss., Indiana University.

———. 2004. "Who Talks with Whom? The Role of Repeated Interactions in Decentralized Forest Governance." *World Development* 32(2):233–50.

Andersson, Krister P., Clark C. Gibson, and Fabrice Lehoucq. 2006. "Municipal Politics and Forest Governance: Comparative Analysis of Decentralization in Bolivia and Guatemala." *World Development* 34(3):576–95.

Andersson, Krister, and Elinor Ostrom. 2008. "Analyzing Decentralized Resource Regimes from a Polycentric Perspective." *Policy Sciences* 41:71–93.

Andreoni, James. 1989. "Giving with Impure Altruism: Applications to Charity and Ricardian Equivalence." *Journal of Political Economy* 97(6) (December): 1447–58.

———. 1995. "Warm Glow vs. Cold Prickle: The Effect of Positive and Negative Framing on Cooperation in Experiments." *Quarterly Journal of Economics* 110(1):1–21.

Armitage, D., Fikret Berkes, and N. Doubleday, eds. 2007. *Adaptive Co-Management: Collaboration, Learning, and Multi-Level Governance.* Vancouver: University of British Columbia Press.

Arrow, Kenneth. 1974. *The Limits of Organization.* New York: Norton.

Ashlock, Dan, Mark D. Smucker, E. Ann Stanley, and Leigh Tesfatsion. 1996. "Preferential Partner Selection in an Evolutionary Study of the Prisoner's Dilemma." *BioSystems* 37:99–125.

Axelrod, Robert. 1984. *The Evolution of Cooperation.* New York: Basic Books.

———. 1986. "An Evolutionary Approach to Norms." *American Political Science Review* 80(4):1095–1111.

———. 1987. "The Evolution of Strategies in the Iterated Prisoner's Dilemma." In *Genetic Algorithms and Simulated Annealing,* ed. Lawrence Davis, 32–41. Los Altos, CA: Morgan Kaufman.

Axelrod, Robert, and William D. Hamilton. 1981. "The Evolution of Cooperation." *Science* 211(4489) (March): 1390–96.

Axtell, Robert L. 2001. "Zipf Distribution of U.S. Firm Sizes." *Science* 293:1818–20.

————. 2009. "The Emergence and Evolution of Institutions of Self-Governance on the Commons." Working Paper. Fairfax, VA: George Mason University, Department of Computational Social Science.

Bagnoli, Mark, Shaul Ben-David, and Michael McKee. 1992. "Voluntary Provision of Public Goods: The Multiple Unit Case." *Journal of Public Economics* 47:85–106.

Bagnoli, Mark, and B. Lipman. 1989. "Provision of Public Goods: Fully Implementing the Core through Private Provision." *Review of Economic Studies* 56(4) (October): 583–602.

Bagnoli, Mark, and Michael McKee. 1991. "Voluntary Contribution Games: Efficient Private Provision of Public Goods." *Economic Inquiry* 29(2):351–66.

Bainbridge, William S. 2007. "The Scientific Research Potential of Virtual Worlds." *Science* 317:472–76.

Baird, Ian G., and Philip Dearden. 2003. "Biodiversity Conservation and Resource Tenure Regimes: A Case Study from Northeast Cambodia." *Environmental Management* 32(5):541–50.

Baland, Jean-Marie, and Jean-Philippe Platteau. [1996] 2000. *Halting Degradation of Natural Resources: Is There a Role for Rural Communities?* New York: Oxford University Press.

Balasubramanian, R., and K. N. Selvaraj. 2003. "Poverty, Private Property and Common Pool Resource Management: The Case of Irrigation Tanks in South India." SANDEE Working Paper no. 2-03. Kathmandu, Nepal. http://www.esocialsciences.com/data/articles/Document117102008590.3419001.pdf.

Balmann, Alfons, Kathrin Happe, Konrad Kellermann, and Anne Kleingarn. 2002. "Adjustment Costs of Agri-Environmental Policy Switchings: An Agent-Based Analysis of the German Region Hohenlohe." In *Complexity and Ecosystem Management: The Theory and Practice of Multi-Agent Systems,* ed. Marco. A. Janssen, 127–57. Cheltenham, UK: Edward Elgar.

Banana, Abwoli Y., and William Gombya-Ssembajjwe. 2000. "Successful Forest Management: The Importance of Security of Tenure and Rule Enforcement in Ugandan Forests." In *People and Forests: Communities, Institutions, and Governance,* ed. Clark C. Gibson, Margaret A. McKean, and Elinor Ostrom, 87–98. Cambridge, MA: MIT Press.

Banana, Abwoli, William Gombya-Ssembajjwe, and Joseph Bahati. 2001. "Explaining Deforestation: The Role of Forest Institutions in Ugandan Forests—A Policy Brief." Kampala, Uganda: UFRIC, Makerere University.

Banana, Abwoli, Nathan Vogt, Joseph Bahati, and William Gombya-Ssembajjwe. 2007. "Decentralized Governance and Ecological Health: Why Local Institutions Fail to Moderate Deforestation in Mpigi District of Uganda." *Scientific Research and Essays* 2(10) (October): 434–45.

Bangert-Drowns, Robert L. 1995. "Misunderstanding Meta-Analysis." *Evaluation and the Health Professions* 18(3) (September): 304–14.

Barabási, Albert-László, and Réka Albert. 1999. "Emergence of Scaling in Random Networks." *Science* 286:509–12.

Bardhan, Pranab K. 2000. "Irrigation and Cooperation: An Empirical Analysis of 48 Irrigation Communities in South India." *Economic Development and Cultural Change* 48(4) (July): 847–65.

Bardhan, Pranab K., and Isha Ray, eds. 2008. *The Contested Commons: Conversations between Economists and Anthropologists.* Oxford: Blackwell.

Barreteau, Olivier. 2003. "Our Companion Modelling Approach." *Journal of Artificial Societies and Social Simulation* 6(1), http://jasss.soc.surrey.ac.uk/6/2/1.html.

Barreteau, Olivier, and François Bousquet. 2000. "SHADOC: A Multi-Agent Model to Tackle Viability of Irrigated Systems." *Annals of Operations Research* 94:139–62.

Barreteau, Olivier, François Bousquet, and Jean-Marie Attonaty. 2001. "Role-Playing Games for Opening the Black Box of Multi-Agent Systems: Method and Lessons of Its Application to Senegal River Valley Irrigated Systems." *Journal of Artificial Societies and Social Simulation* 4(2):5, http://www.soc.surrey.ac.uk/JASSS/4/2/5.html.

Barreteau, Olivier, Christophe Le Page, and Patrick D'Aquino. 2003. "Role-Playing Games, Models and Negotiation Processes." *Journal of Artificial Societies and Social Simulation* 6(2), http://jasss.soc.surrey.ac.uk/6/2/10.html.

Barrows, Richard, and Michael Roth. 1990. "Land Tenure and Investment in African Agriculture: Theory and Evidence." *Journal of Modern African Studies* 28(2) (June): 265–97.

Bassett, Thomas J. 1988. "The Political Ecology of Peasant-Herder Conflicts in the Northern Ivory Coast." *Annals of the Association of American Geographers* 78(3):453–72.

Basurto, Xavier. 2008. "Biological and Ecological Mechanisms Supporting Marine Self-Governance: The Seri Callo de Hacha Fishery." *Ecology and Society* 13(2):20, http://www.ecologyandsociety.org/vol13/iss2/art20/.

———. 2009. "The Role of Cross-Scale Linkages for Maintaining Local Autonomy: The Case of Costa Rica." Working Paper. Bloomington: Indiana University, Workshop in Political Theory and Policy Analysis.

Basurto, Xavier, and Elinor Ostrom. 2009. "Beyond the Tragedy of the Commons." *Economia delle fonti di energia e dell'ambiente* 52(1) (October): 35–60.

Bates, Robert H. 2007. "From Case Studies to Social Science: A Strategy for Political Research." In *The Oxford Handbook of Comparative Politics*, ed. Carles Boix and Susan C. Stokes, 172–85. Oxford: Oxford University Press.

———. 2008. *When Things Fell Apart: State Failure in Late-Century Africa.* New York: Cambridge University Press.

Bates, Robert H., Avner Greif, Margaret Levi, Jean-Laurent Rosenthal, and Barry R. Weingast, eds. 1998. *Analytical Narratives.* Princeton, NJ: Princeton University Press.

Beck, Nathaniel, and Jonathan N. Katz. 1996. "Nuisance vs. Substance: Specifying and Estimating Time-Series-Cross-Section Models." *Political Analysis* 6:1–36.

Beckenkamp, Martin. 2009. "Environmental Dilemmas Revisited: Structural Consequences from the Angle of Institutional Ergonomics." Preprint 2009/1. Bonn, Germany: Max Planck Institute for Research on Collective Goods.

Becker, C. Dustin. 1999. "Protecting a *Garua* Forest in Ecuador: The Role of Institutions and Ecosystem Valuation." *Ambio* 28(2) (March): 156–61.

————. 2003. "Grassroots to Grassroots: Why Forest Preservation Was Rapid at Loma Alta, Ecuador." *World Development* 31(1) (January): 163–76.

Becker, C. Dustin, and Rosario León. 2000. "Indigenous Forest Management in the Bolivian Amazon: Lessons from the Yuracaré People." In *People and Forests: Communities, Institutions, and Governance,* ed. Clark C. Gibson, Margaret A. McKean, and Elinor Ostrom, 163–91. Cambridge, MA: MIT Press.

Becker, Gary S. 1993. "Nobel Lecture: The Economic Way of Looking at Behavior." *Journal of Political Economy* 101(3):385–409.

Becker, Howard S. 1996. "The Epistemology of Qualitative Research." In *Ethnography and Human Development: Context and Meaning in Social Inquiry,* ed. Richard Jessor, Anne Colby, and Richard Schweder, 53–72. Chicago: University of Chicago Press.

Becu, N., P. Perez, A. Walker, O. Barreteau, and C. Le Page. 2003. "Agent Based Simulation of a Small Catchment Water Management in Northern Thailand: Description of the CATCHSCAPE Model." *Ecological Modelling* 170(2/3):319–31.

Bendor, Jonathan. 1988. "Review Article: Formal Models of Bureaucracy." *British Journal of Political Science* 18(3) (July): 353–95.

Benjamin, Charles E. 2004. "Livelihoods and Institutional Development in the Malian Sahel: A Political Economy of Decentralized Natural Resource Management." PhD diss., University of Michigan.

Benjamin, Paul, Wai Fung Lam, Elinor Ostrom, and Ganesh Shivakoti. 1994. *Institutions, Incentives, and Irrigation in Nepal.* Decentralization: Finance & Management Project Report. Burlington, VT: Associates in Rural Development.

Ben-Ner, Avner, and Louis Putterman. 2009. "Trust, Communication and Contracts: An Experiment." *Journal of Economic Behavior and Organization* 70(1–2):106–21.

Bennett, Andrew, Aharon Barth, and Kenneth R. Rutherford. 2003. "Do We Preach What We Practice? A Survey of Methods in Political Science Journals and Curricula." *PS: Political Science and Politics* 36(3) (July): 373–78.

Bennett, Andrew, and Colin Elman. 2006. "Complex Causal Relations and Case Study Methods: The Example of Path Dependence." *Political Analysis* 14(3) (Summer): 250–67.

Berger, Thomas. 2001. "Agent-Based Spatial Models Applied to Agriculture: A Simulation Tool for Technology Diffusion, Resource Use Changes and Policy Analysis." *Agricultural Economics* 25(2/3):245–60.

Berger, Thomas, and Pepijn Schreinemachers. 2006. "Creating Agents and Landscapes for Multiagent Systems from Random Samples." *Ecology and Society* 11(2):19, http://www.ecologyandsociety.org/vol11/iss2/art19/.

Bergstrom, Ted C. 2002. "Evolution of Social Behavior: Individual and Group Selection." *Journal of Economic Perspectives* 16(2):67–88.

Berkes, Fikret. 1985. "The Common Property Resource Problem and the Creation of Limited Property Rights." *Human Ecology* 13:187–208.

————. 1986a. "Local-Level Management and the Commons Problem: A Comparative Study of Turkish Coastal Fisheries." *Marine Policy* 10:215–29.

————. 1986b. "Marine Inshore Fishery Management in Turkey." In *Proceed-*

ings of the Conference on Common Property Resource Management, National Research Council, 63–84. Washington, DC: National Academies Press.

———. 1992. "Success and Failure in Marine Coastal Fisheries of Turkey." In *Making the Commons Work: Theory, Practice, and Policy,* ed. Daniel W. Bromley et al., 161–82. San Francisco, CA: ICS Press.

———. 2007. "Community-Based Conservation in a Globalized World." *Proceedings of the National Academy of Sciences* 104(39):15188–93.

Berkes, Fikret, David Feeny, Bonnie J. McCay, and James M. Acheson. 1989. "The Benefits of the Commons." *Nature* 340:91–93.

Berkes, Fikret, T. P. Hughes, R. S. Steneck, James A. Wilson, D. R. Bellwood, B. Crona, et al. 2006. "Globalization, Roving Bandits, and Marine Resources." *Science* 311:1557–58.

Berry, Sara. 1992. "Hegemony on a Shoestring: Indirect Rule and Access to Agricultural Land." *Africa* 62(3):327–55.

Bester, Helmut, and Werner Güth. 1998. "Is Altruism Evolutionarily Stable?" *Journal of Economic Behavior and Organization* 34(2):193–209.

Bharwani, Sukaina. 2006. "Understanding Complex Behavior and Decision Making Using Ethnographic Knowledge Elicitation Tools (KnETs)." *Social Science Computer Review* 24:78–105.

Bharwani, Sukaina, Mike Bithell, Thomas E. Downing, Mark New, Richard Washington, and Gina Ziervogel. 2005. "Multi-Agent Modelling of Climate Outlooks and Food Security on a Community Garden Scheme in Limpopo, South Africa." *Philosophical Transactions of the Royal Society B* 360:2183–94.

Bianco, W., M. Lynch, G. Miller, and I. Sened. 2006. "A Theory Waiting to be Discovered and Used: A Reanalysis of Canonical Experiments on Majority-Rule Decision Making." *Journal of Politics* 68(4):838–51.

Biel, Anders, and John Thøgersen. 2007. "Activation of Social Norms in Social Dilemmas: A Review of the Evidence and Reflections on the Implications for Environmental Behaviour." *Journal of Economic Psychology* 28:93–112.

Blomquist, William. 1992. *Dividing the Waters: Governing Groundwater in Southern California.* San Francisco, CA: ICS Press.

Blomquist, William, and Elinor Ostrom. 2008. "Deliberation, Learning, and Institutional Change: The Evolution of Institutions in Judicial Settings." *Constitutional Political Economy* 19(3) (September): 180–202.

Blount, S. 1995. "When Social Norms Are Not Fair: The Effect of Causal Attributions on Preferences." *Organizational Behavior and Human Decision Process* 63(2):131–44.

Bochet, Olivier, Talbot Page, and Louis Putterman. 2006. "Communication and Punishment in Voluntary Contribution Experiments." *Journal of Economic Behavior and Organization* 60(1):11–26.

Bolton, Gary E., and Axel Ockenfels. 2000. "ERC: A Theory of Equity, Reciprocity, and Competition." *American Economic Review* 90:166–93.

Boone, Catherine. 1998. "State Building in the African Countryside: Structure and Politics at the Grassroots." *Journal of Development Studies* 34(4):1–31.

———. 2003. *Political Topographies of the African State: Territorial Authority and Institutional Choice.* New York: Cambridge University Press.

———. 2007. "Property and Constitutional Order: Land Tenure Reform and the Future of the African State." *African Affairs* 106(425):557–86.

———. 2009. "Electoral Populism Where Property Rights Are Weak: Land Politics in Contemporary Sub-Saharan Africa." *Comparative Politics* 41(2) (January): 183–201.

Borgerhoff Mulder, Monique, and Peter Coppolillo. 2005. *Conservation: Linking Ecology, Economics, and Culture.* Princeton, NJ: Princeton University Press.

Bouchaud, Jean-Philippe. 2001. "Power-Laws in Economy and Finance: Some Ideas from Physics." *Quantitative Finance* 1:105–12.

Bousquet, François, Olivier Barreteau, P. d'Aquino, Michel Etienne, S. Boissau, S. Aubert, Christophe Le Page, D. Babin, and J.-C. Castella. 2002. "Multi-Agent Systems and Role Games: Collective Learning Processes for Ecosystem Management." In *Complexity and Ecosystem Management: The Theory and Practice of Multi-Agent Systems,* ed. Marco A. Janssen, 248–85. Cheltenham, UK: Edward Elgar.

Bower, John, and Derek W. Bunn. 2000. "Model-Based Comparisons of Pool and Bilateral Markets for Electricity." *Energy Journal* 21(3):1–29.

Bowles, Samuel. 2006. "Group Competition, Reproductive Leveling, and the Evolution of Human Altruism." *Science* 314:1569–72.

———. 2008. "Policies Designed for Self-Interested Citizens May Undermine 'The Moral Sentiments': Evidence from Economic Experiments." *Science* 320(5883):1605–9. Supporting Online Material, http://www.sciencemag.org/cgi/content/full/sci;320/5883/1605/DC1.

Boyd, Robert, Herbert Gintis, Samuel Bowles, and Peter J. Richerson. 2003. "The Evolution of Altruistic Punishment." *Proceedings of the National Academy of Sciences* 100(6):3531–35.

Boyd, Robert, and Peter J. Richerson. 1988. "The Evolution of Reciprocity in Sizable Groups." *Journal of Theoretical Biology* 132(3) (June): 337–56.

———. 1992. "Punishment Allows the Evolution of Cooperation (or Anything Else) in Sizable Groups." *Ethology and Sociobiology* 13:171–95.

Brady, Henry E. 2004. "Introduction, Symposium: Two Paths to a Science of Politics." *Perspectives on Politics* 2(2) (June): 295–300.

Brady, Henry E., and David Collier, eds. 2004. *Rethinking Social Inquiry: Diverse Tools, Shared Standards.* Lanham, MD: Rowman & Littlefield.

Brander, James A., and M. Scott Taylor. 1998. "The Simple Economics of Easter Island: A Ricardo-Malthus Model of Renewable Resource Use." *American Economic Review* 88(1):119–38.

Brandt, Hannelore, Christoph Hauert, and Karl Sigmund. 2003. "Punishment and Reputation in Spatial Public Goods Games." *Proceedings of the Royal Academy of Science: Biological Sciences* 270(1519):1099–1104.

Brass, Paul R. 2000. "Foucault Steals Political Science." *Annual Review of Political Science* 3:305–50.

Braude, Stanton, and Bobbi Low, eds. 2010. *An Introduction to Methods and Models in Ecology, Evolution, and Conservation Biology.* Princeton, NJ: Princeton University Press.

Braumoeller, Bear F. 2003. "Causal Complexity and the Study of Politics." *Political Analysis* 11(3):209–33.

———. 2004. "Hypothesis Testing and Multiplicative Interaction Terms." *International Organization* 58(4):807–20.

Bray, David Barton, Edward Ellis, Natalia Armijo-Canto, and Christopher Beck. 2004. "The Institutional Drivers of Sustainable Landscapes: A Case Study of the 'Mayan Zone' in Quintana Roo, Mexico." *Land Use Policy* 21:333–46.

Bray, David Barton, Leticia Merino-Pérez, Patricia Negreros-Castillo, Gerardo Segura-Warnholtz, Juan Manuel Torres-Rojo, and Hernicus F. M. Vester. 2003. "Mexico's Community-Managed Forests as a Global Model for Sustainable Landscapes." *Conservation Biology* 17(3):672–77.

Brennan, Geoffrey. 2008. "Homo Economicus and Homo Politicus: An Introduction." *Public Choice* 137(3–4):429–38.

Brock, William A., and Stephen R. Carpenter. 2007. "Panaceas and Diversification of Environmental Policy." *Proceedings of the National Academy of Sciences* 104(39):15206–11.

Bromley, Daniel W. 1986. "Closing Comments at the Conference on Common Property Resource Management." In *Proceedings of the Conference on Common Property Resource Management*, National Research Council, 591–98. Washington, DC: National Academies Press.

———. 1989. *Economic Interests and Institutions: The Conceptual Foundations of Public Policy*. Oxford: Basil Blackwell.

Bromley, Daniel W., David Feeny, Margaret McKean, Pauline Peters, Jere Gilles, Ronald Oakerson, C. Ford Runge, and James Thomson, eds. 1992. *Making the Commons Work: Theory, Practice, and Policy*. San Francisco, CA: ICS Press.

Brosig, Jeannette. 2002. "Identifying Cooperative Behavior: Some Experimental Results in a Prisoner's Dilemma Game." *Journal of Economic Behavior and Organization* 47:275–90.

Brown, Cliff, and Terry Boswell. 1995. "Strikebreaking or Solidarity in the Great Steel Strike of 1919: A Split Labor Market, Game-Theoretic and QCA Analysis." *American Journal of Sociology* 100(6):1479–1519.

Brown, Daniel G., Scott E. Page, Rick Riolo, Moira Zellner, and William Rand. 2005. "Path Dependence and the Validation of Agent-Based Spatial Models of Land Use." *International Journal of Geographical Information Science* 19(2):153–74.

Brown, Daniel, and Derek Robinson. 2006. "Effects of Heterogeneity in Residential Preferences on an Agent-Based Model of Urban Sprawl." *Ecology and Society* 11(1):46, http://www.ecologyandsociety.org/vol11/iss1/art46/main.html.

Brown, Katrina, and François Ekoko. 2001. "Forest Encounters: Synergy among Agents of Forest Change in Southern Cameroon." *Society and Natural Resources* 14(4) (April): 269–90.

Bruce, John W., and Shem E. Migot-Adholla, eds. 1994. *Searching for Land Tenure Security in Africa*. Dubuque, IA: Kendall/Hunt.

Brunckhorst, David J. 2000. *Bioregional Planning: Resource Management beyond the New Millennium*. Amsterdam: Harwood Academic.

Bryant, Raymond L. 1994. "The Rise and Fall of Taungya Forestry: Social Forestry in Defense of the Empire." *The Ecologist* 24(1):21–26.

———. 1996. "Romancing Colonial Forestry: The Discourse of 'Forestry as Progress' in British Burma." *Geographical Journal* 162(2) (July): 169–78.

Buchan, Nancy R., Eric J. Johnson, and Rachel T. A. Croson. 2006. "Let's Get Personal: An International Examination of the Influence of Communication, Culture and Social Distance on Other Regarding Preferences." *Journal of Economic Behavior and Organization* 60(3) (July): 373–98.

Buchanan, James. 1984. "Politics without Romance." *Zeitschrift des Instituts fur Hohere Studien* 3:1–11.

Buck [Cox], Susan J. 1988. "Interjurisdictional Management in Chesapeake Bay Fisheries." *Coastal Management* 16:151–86.

Buckley, Jack. 2004. "Simple Bayesian Inference for Qualitative Political Research." Special issue, *Political Analysis* 12(4) (Autumn): 386–99.

Burawoy, Michael. 1998. "The Extended Case Method." *Sociological Theory* 16(1) (March): 4–33.

Burger, Joanna, and Michael Gochfeld. 1998. "The Tragedy of the Commons 30 Years Later." *Environment* 40(10) (December): 4–13, 26–27.

Burtsev, Mikhail, and Peter Turchin. 2006. "Evolution of Cooperative Strategies from First Principles." *Nature* 440:1041–44.

Camerer, Colin F. 2003. *Behavioral Game Theory: Experiments in Strategic Interaction*. Princeton, NJ: Princeton University Press.

Camerer, Colin F., and T.-H. Ho. 1999. "Experience-Weighted Attraction Learning in Normal Form Games." *Econometrica* 67(4):827–74.

Campbell, Bruce, Iain Gordon, Martin Luckert, Lisa Petheram, and Susanne Vetter. 2006. "In Search of Optimal Stocking Regimes in Semi-Arid Grazing Lands: One Size Does Not Fit All." *Ecological Economics* 60(1):75–85.

Campbell, Bruce, Alois Mandondo, Nontokozo Nemarundwe, and Bevlyne Sithole. 2001. "Challenges to Proponents of Common Property Resource Systems: Despairing Voices from the Social Forests of Zimbabwe." *World Development* 29(4) (April): 589–600.

Campbell, Donald T. 1975. "'Degrees of Freedom' and the Case Study." *Comparative Political Studies* 8(2) (July): 178–93.

Campbell, Donald T., and Julian C. Stanley. 1966. *Experimental and Quasi-Experimental Designs for Research*. Chicago: Rand McNally.

Cant, Garth, Anake Goodall, and Justine Inns, eds. 2005. *Discourses and Silences: Indigenous Peoples, Risks and Resistance*. Christchurch, New Zealand: University of Canterbury Press.

Cardenas, Juan-Camilo. 2000. "How Do Groups Solve Local Commons Dilemmas? Lessons from Experimental Economics in the Field." *Environment, Development and Sustainability* 2(3–4):305–22.

———. 2003. "Real Wealth and Experimental Cooperation: Evidence from Field Experiments." *Journal of Development Economics* 70(2):263–89.

———. 2009. "Experiments in Environment and Development." Working Paper. Bogata: Universidad de los Andes, Economics Faculty.

Cardenas, Juan-Camilo, T. K. Ahn, and Elinor Ostrom. 2004. "Communication and Co-operation in a Common-Pool Resource Dilemma: A Field Experiment." In *Advances in Understanding Strategic Behaviour: Game Theory, Experiments and Bounded Rationality*, ed. Steffen Huck, 258–86. New York: Palgrave Macmillan.

Cardenas, Juan-Camilo, Marco A. Janssen, and François Bousquet. Forthcoming. "Dynamics of Rules and Resources: Three New Field Experiments on Water, Forests and Fisheries." In *Handbook on Experimental Economics and the Environment*, ed. John List and Michael Price. Cheltenham, UK: Edward Elgar.

Cardenas, Juan-Camilo, John K. Stranlund, and Cleve E. Willis. 2000. "Local Environmental Control and Institutional Crowding-Out." *World Development* 28(10):1719–33.

Carlson, Jean M., and John Doyle. 2002. "Complexity and Robustness." *Proceedings of the National Academy of Sciences* 9(suppl. 1) (February 19): 2499–2545.

Carney, Judith, and Michael Watts. 1990. "Manufacturing Dissent: Work, Gender and the Politics of Meaning in a Peasant Society." *Africa* 60(2):207–41.

Carpenter, Jeffrey P. 2007. "The Demand for Punishment." *Journal of Economic Behavior and Organization* 62:522–42.

Casari, Marco, and Luigi Luini. 2009. "Cooperation under Alternative Punishment Institutions: An Experiment." *Journal of Economic Behavior and Organization* 71(2):273–82.

Castella, Jean-Christophe, Tran Ngoc Trung, and Stanislas Boissau. 2005. "Participatory Simulation of Land-Use Changes in the Northern Mountains of Vietnam: The Combined Use of an Agent-Based Model, a Role-Playing Game, and a Geographic Information System." *Ecology and Society* 10(1):27, http://www.ecologyandsociety.org/vol10/iss1/art27/.

Castillo, Daniel, and Ali K. Saysel. 2005. "Simulation of Common Pool Resource Field Experiments: A Behavioral Model of Collective Action." *Ecological Economics* 55(3):420–36.

Castranova, Edward. 2005. *Synthetic Worlds: The Business and Culture of Online Games*. Chicago: University of Chicago Press.

Cederman, Lars K. 2002. "Modeling the Size of Wars: From Billiard Balls to Sandpiles." *American Political Science Review* 97(1):19–59.

Chambers, Elisha A. 2004. "An Introduction to Meta-Analysis with Articles from the *Journal of Educational Research* (1999–2002)." *Journal of Educational Research* 98(1) (September/October): 35–44.

Charness, Gary, and Matthew Rabin. 2002. "Understanding Social Preferences with Simple Tests." *Quarterly Journal of Economics* 117(3):817–69.

Chhatre, Ashwini, and Arun Agrawal. 2008. "Forest Commons and Local Enforcement." *Proceedings of the National Academy of Sciences* 105(36) (September 9): 13286–91.

Chhetri, Ram B., and T. R. Pandey. 1992. "User Group Forestry in the Far Western Region of Nepal." Kathmandu: ICIMOD.

Chhetri, Ram B., S. Tiwari, and H. Sigdel. 1998. "Situation Analysis Study: Commonalities and Variations of Situations in Selected Districts of Nepal." Working Paper. Kathmandu: EFEA Program.

Chibnik, Michael. 1985. "The Use of Statistics in Sociocultural Anthropology." *Annual Review of Anthropology* 14:135–57.

Cinyabuguma, Matthias, Talbot Page, and Louis Putterman. 2006. "Can Second-Order Punishment Deter Perverse Punishment?" *Experimental Economics* 9(3):265–79.

Ciriacy-Wantrup, S. V., and Richard C. Bishop. 1975. "'Common Property' as a Concept in Natural Resources Policy." *Natural Resources Journal* 15(4):713–27.

Clark, Colin W. 2006. *The Worldwide Crisis in Fisheries: Economic Models and Human Behavior.* New York: Cambridge University Press.

Clark, Robert S. 1977. *Fundamentals of Criminal Justice Research.* Lexington, MA: Lexington Books.

Clark, William Roberts, Michael J. Gilligan, and Matt Golder. 2006. "A Simple Multivariate Test for Asymmetric Hypotheses." *Political Analysis* 14(3) (Summer): 311–31.

Clarke, Kevin A., and David M. Primo. 2007. "Modernizing Political Science: A Model-Based Approach." *Perspectives on Politics* 5(4):741–54.

Clauset, Aaron, Cosma Rohilla Shalizi, and Mark E. J. Newman. 2009. "Power-Law Distributions in Empirical Data." *SIAM Review* 51(4):661–703.

Cohen, D., and Illan Eshel. 1976. "On the Founder Effect and the Evolution of Altruistic Traits." *Theoretical Population Biology* 10:276–302.

Coleman, Eric. 2009a. "Institutional Factors Affecting Ecological Outcomes in Forest Management." *Journal of Policy Analysis and Management* 28(1):122–46.

———. 2009b. "Essays on the Effects of Institutions and Trust on Collective Action." PhD diss., Indiana University.

Coleman, Eric, and Brian Steed. 2009. "Monitoring and Sanctioning in the Commons: An Application to Forestry." *Ecological Economics* 68(7) (May): 2106–13.

Collier, David, Henry E. Brady, and Jason Seawright. 2004. "Sources of Leverage in Causal Inference: Toward an Alternative View of Methodology." In *Rethinking Social Inquiry: Diverse Tools, Shared Standards,* ed. Henry E. Brady and David Collier, 229–66. Lanham, MD: Rowman & Littlefield.

Collier, David, and James Mahoney. 1996. "Insights and Pitfalls: Selection Bias in Qualitative Research." *World Politics* 49:56–91.

Commons, John R. [1924] 1968. *Legal Foundations of Capitalism.* Madison: University of Wisconsin Press.

Cookson, Richard. 2000. "Framing Effects in Public Goods Experiments." *Experimental Economics* 3(1):55–79.

Cooper, Harris, and Larry V. Hedges, eds. 1994. *The Handbook of Research Synthesis.* New York: Russell Sage Foundation.

Copeland, Brian R., and M. Scott Taylor. 2009. "Trade, Tragedy, and the Commons." *American Economic Review* 99(3):725–49.

Coppedge, Michael. 1999. "Thickening Thin Concepts and Theories: Combining Large N and Small in Comparative Politics." *Comparative Politics* 31(4) (July): 465–76.

Cordell, John, and Margaret A. McKean. 1992. "Sea Tenure in Bahia, Brazil." In *Making the Commons Work: Theory, Practice, and Policy,* ed. Daniel W. Bromley et al., 183–205. San Francisco, CA: ICS Press.

Cosmides, Leda, and John Tooby. 1992. "Cognitive Adaptations for Social Exchange." In *The Adapted Mind: Evolutionary Psychology and the Generation of Culture*, ed. Jerome H. Barkow, Leda Cosmides, and John Tooby, 163–228. New York: Oxford University Press.

———. 1994. "Better Than Rational: Evolutionary Psychology and the Invisible Hand." *American Economic Review* 84(2) (May): 327–32.

Coward, E. Walter. 1977. "Irrigation Management Alternatives: Themes from Indigenous Irrigation Systems." *Agricultural Administration* 4:223–37.

Cox, James. 2004. "How to Identify Trust and Reciprocity." *Games and Economic Behavior* 46:260–81.

Cox, James C., Daniel Friedman, and Steven Gjerstad. 2007. "A Tractable Model of Reciprocity and Fairness." *Games and Economic Behavior* 59:17–45.

Cox, James, Elinor Ostrom, James Walker, Antonio Jamie Castillo, Eric Coleman, Robert Holahan, Michael Schoon, and Brian Steed. 2009. "Trust in Private and Common Property Experiments." *Southern Economic Journal* 75(4) (April): 957–75.

Cox, James C., Klarita Sadiraj, and Vjollca Sadiraj. 2008. "Implications of Trust, Fear, and Reciprocity for Modeling Economic Behavior." *Experimental Economics* 11(1):1–24.

Cox, Michael, Gwendolyn Arnold, and Sergio Villamayor-Tomas. 2009. "Design Principles Are Not Blueprints, but Are They Robust?" Working Paper. Bloomington: Indiana University, Workshop in Political Theory and Policy Analysis.

Crawford, Sue E. S., and Elinor Ostrom. 2005. "A Grammar of Institutions." In Elinor Ostrom, *Understanding Institutional Diversity*, 137–74. Princeton, NJ: Princeton University Press. Originally published in *American Political Science Review* 89(3) (September 1995): 582–600.

Cress, Daniel M., and David A. Snow. 2000. "The Outcomes of Homeless Mobilization: The Influence of Organization, Disruption, Political Mediation, and Framing." *American Journal of Sociology* 105(4):1064–1104.

Crook, Darren S., and Anne M. Jones. 1999. "Design Principles from Traditional Mountain Irrigation Systems (Bisses) in the Valais, Switzerland." *Mountain Research and Development* 19(2):79–122.

Cudney-Bueno, Richard, and Xavier Basurto. 2009. "Lack of Cross-Scale Linkages Reduces Robustness of Community-Based Fisheries Management." *PLoS ONE* 4(7) (July): e6253.

Dafinger, Andreas, and Michaela Pelican. 2006. "Sharing or Dividing the Land? Land Rights and Farmer-Herder Relations in Burkina Faso and Northwest Cameroon." *Canadian Journal of African Studies/Revue Canadienne des Études Africaines* 40(1):127–51.

D'Aquino, Patrick, Christophe Le Page, François Bousquet, and Alassane Bah. 2003. "Using Self-Designed Role-Playing Games and a Multi-Agent System to Empower a Local Decision-Making Process for Land Use Management: The SelfCormas Experiment in Senegal." *Journal of Artificial Societies and Social Simulation* 6(3), http://jasss.soc.surrey.ac.uk/6/3/5.html.

Dasgupta, Partha S., and Geoffrey M. Heal. 1979. *Economic Theory and Exhaustible Resources*. Cambridge: Cambridge University Press.

Davis, Anthony. 1984. "Property Rights and Access Management in the Small Boat Fishery: A Case Study from Southwest Nova Scotia." In *Atlantic Fisheries and Coastal Communities: Fisheries Decision-Making Case Studies*, ed. Cynthia Lamson and Arthur J. Hanson, 133–64. Halifax: Dalhousie Ocean Studies Programme.

Dawes, Robyn M. 1973. "The Commons Dilemma Game: An N-Person Mixed-Motive Game with a Dominating Strategy for Defection." *Oregon Research Institute Research Bulletin* 13:1–12.

Dawes, Robyn M., John M. Orbell, Randy T. Simmons, and Alphons J. C. van der Kragt. 1986. "Organizing Groups for Collective Action." *American Political Science Review* 80(4):1171–85.

Dayton-Johnson, Jeff. 1999. "Irrigation Organization in Mexican *unidades de riego*: Results of a Field Study." *Irrigation and Drainage Systems* 13(1) (March): 55–74.

———. 2000. "Choosing Rules to Govern the Commons: A Model with Evidence from Mexico." *Journal of Economic Behavior and Organization* 42:19–41.

Deadman, Peter J. 1999. "Modelling Individual Behaviour and Group Performance in an Intelligent Agent-Based Simulation of the Tragedy of the Commons." *Journal of Environmental Management* 56:159–72.

Deadman, Peter J., Edella Schlager, and Randy H. Gimblett. 2000. "Simulating Common Pool Resource Management Experiments with Adaptive Agents Employing Alternate Communication Routines." *Journal of Artificial Societies and Social Simulation* 3(2), http://jasss.soc.surrey.ac.uk/JASSS.html.

Degnbol, Poul, Henrik Gislason, Susan Hanna, Svein Jentof, Jesper R. Nielsen, Sten Sverdrup-Jensen, and Douglas C. Wilson. 2006. "Painting the Floor with a Hammer: Technical Fixes in Fisheries Management." *Marine Policy* 30:534–43.

Degnbol, Poul, and Bonnie J. McCay. 2007. "Unintended and Perverse Consequences of Ignoring Linkages in Fisheries Systems." *ICES Journal of Marine Science: Journal du Conseil* 64(4):793–97.

De Moor, Martina. 2008. "Avoiding Tragedies: A Flemish Common and Its Commoners under the Pressure of Social and Economic Change during the Eighteenth Century." *Economic History Review* 62(1):1–22.

De Moor, Martina, Leigh Shaw-Taylor, and Paul Warde, eds. 2002. *The Management of Common Land in North West Europe, c. 1500–1850*. Turnhout, Belgium: Brepols.

Demsetz, Harold. 1967. "Toward a Theory of Property Rights." *American Economic Review* 57(2):347–59.

Denant-Boemont, Laurant, David Masclet, and Charles Noussair. 2007. "Punishment, Counter-Punishment and Sanction Enforcement in a Social Dilemma Experiment." *Economic Theory* 33(1):145–67.

de Oliveira, Angela C. M., Rachel T. A. Croson, and Catherine Eckel. 2009. "Are Preferences Stable across Domains? An Experimental Investigation of Social Preferences in the Field." CBEES Working Paper #2008–3. Dallas: University of Texas.

Derman, Bill, and Anne Hellum. 2002. "Neither Tragedy nor Enclosure: Are There Inherent Human Rights in Water Management in Zimbabwe's Communal Lands?" *European Journal of Development Research* 14(2):31–50.

Deutsch, Morton. 1973. *The Resolution of Conflict*. New Haven, CT: Yale University Press.

Dickersin, Kay. 1994. "Research Registers." In *The Handbook of Research Synthesis*, ed. Harris Cooper and Larry V. Hedges, 71–83. New York: Russell Sage Foundation.

Dietz, Thomas, Elinor Ostrom, and Paul Stern. 2003. "The Struggle to Govern the Commons." *Science* 302(5652):1907–12.

Dion, Douglas. 1998. "Evidence and Inference in the Comparative Case Study." *Comparative Politics* 30:127–45.

Dixon, Marc, Vincent J. Roscigno, and Randy Hodson. 2004. "Unions, Solidarity, and Striking." *Social Forces* 83(1):3–33.

Dodds, Peter S., Roby Muhamad, and Duncan Watts. 2003. "An Experimental Study of Search in Global Social Networks." *Science* 301:827–29.

Dogan, Mattei, and Dominique Pelassy. 1990. *How to Compare Nations: Strategies in Comparative Politics*. 2nd ed. Chatham, NJ: Chatham House.

Dorji, Lam, Edward Webb, and Ganesh Shivakoti. 2006. "Forest Property Rights under Nationalized Forest Management in Bhutan." *Sustainability: Science, Practice, and Policy* 2(1) (Spring): 25–35.

Dreyfus-Leon, Michel J. 1999. "Individual-Based Modelling of Fishermen Search Behaviour with Neural Networks and Reinforcement Learning." *Ecological Modelling* 120(2–3):287–97.

Dreyfus-Leon, Michel J., and Pierre Kleiber. 2001. "A Spatial Individual Behaviour-Based Model Approach of the Yellow Tuna Fishery in the Eastern Pacific Ocean." *Ecological Modelling* 146:47–56.

Ducourtieux, Olivier, Jean-Richard Laffort, and Silinthone Sacklokham. 2005. "Land Policy and Farming Practices in Laos." *Development and Change* 36(3) (May): 499–526.

Duffy, John. 2006. "Agent-Based Models and Human Subject Experiments." In *Handbook of Computational Economics: Agent-Based Computational Economics*, vol. 2, ed. Leigh Tesfatsion and Kenneth L. Judd, 949–1011. Oxford: Elsevier.

Duit, Andreas, and Victor Galaz. 2008. "Governance and Complexity—Emerging Issues for Governance Theory." *Governance: An International Journal of Policy, Administration, and Institutions* 21(3): 311–35.

Dyson-Hudson, Rada, and Eric Alden Smith. 1978. "Human Territoriality: An Ecological Reassessment." *American Anthropologist* 80:21–41.

Ebbinghaus, Bernhard, and Jelle Visser. 1999. "When Institutions Matter: Union Growth and Decline in Western Europe, 1950–1995." *European Sociological Review* 15(2):135–58.

Ebenhöh, Eva, and Claudia Pahl-Wostl. 2008. "Agent Behavior between Maximization and Cooperation." *Rationality and Society* 20:227–52.

EBSCOhost Research Databases. 2005. EBSCO*host* User Guide: Academic Search Databases. http://support.ebsco.com/knowledge_base/index.php?page_function=show_list&sid=1002&topic=957&document_type=Reference+%2F+User+Guide.

Eckel, Catherine, and Philip J. Grossman. 1996. "The Relative Price of Fairness:

Gender Difference in a Punishment Game." *Journal of Economic Behavior and Organization* 30:143–58.

Edney, Julian J., and Christopher S. Harper. 1978. "The Effects of Information in a Resource Management Problem: A Social Trap Analog." *Human Ecology* 6:387–95.

Edwards, Victoria M., and Nathalie A. Steins. 1998. "Developing an Analytical Framework for Multiple-Use Commons." *Journal of Theoretical Politics* 10(3):347–83.

Eerkens, Jelmer W. 1999. "Common Pool Resources, Buffer Zones, and Jointly Owned Territories: Hunter-Gatherer Land and Resource Tenure in Fort Irwin, Southeastern California." *Human Ecology* 27(2) (June): 297–318.

Elster, Jon. 1983. *Explaining Technical Change*. New York: Cambridge University Press.

———. 1989. *Solomonic Judgements: Studies in the Limitations of Rationality*. New York: Cambridge University Press.

———. 1998. "A Plea for Mechanisms." In *Social Mechanisms: An Analytical Approach to Social Theory*, ed. Peter Hedstroem and Richard Swedberg, 45–73. New York: Cambridge University Press.

Ensminger, Jean. 1990. "Co-Opting the Elders: The Political Economy of State Incorporation in Africa." *American Anthropologist* 92:662–75.

———. 1996. *Making a Market: The Institutional Transformation of an African Society*. New York: Cambridge University Press.

———. 2004. "Market Integration and Fairness: Evidence from Ultimatum, Dictator, and Public Goods Experiments in East Africa." In *Foundations of Human Sociality: Economic Experiments and Ethnographic Evidence in Fifteen Small-Scale Societies*, ed. Joseph Henrich, Robert Boyd, Samuel Bowles, Herbert Gintis, Ernst Fehr, and Colin Camerer, 356–81. Oxford: Oxford University Press.

Etienne, Michel. 2003. "SYLVOPAST: A Multiple Target Role-Playing Game to Assess Negotiation Processes in Sylvopastoral Management Planning." *Journal of Artificial Societies and Social Simulation* 6(2), http://jasss.soc.surrey.ac.uk/6/2/5.html.

Evans, Tom P., and Hugh Kelley. 2004. "Multi-Scale Analysis of a Household Level Agent-Based Model of Landcover Change." *Journal of Environmental Management* 72(1–2):57–72.

Fairhead, J., and Melissa Leach. 1996. *Misreading the African Landscape: Society and Ecology in a Forest-Savanna Mosaic*. New York: Cambridge University Press.

Falk, Armin, Ernst Fehr, and Urs Fischbacher. 2005. "Driving Forces behind Informal Sanctions." *Econometrica* 73(6):2017–30.

Farrelly, Daniel, and Nicola Turnbull. 2008. "The Role of Reasoning Domain on Face Recognition: Detecting Violations of Social Contract and Hazard Management Rules." *Evolutionary Psychology* 6(3):523–37.

Fearon, James D. 1991. "Counterfactuals and Hypothesis Testing in Political Science." *World Politics* 43(2) (January): 169–95.

Feeny, David. 1986. "Conference on Common Property Resource Management: An Introduction." In *Proceedings of the Conference on Common Property*

Resource Management, National Research Council, 7–12. Washington, DC: National Academies Press.

Feeny, David, Fikret Berkes, Bonnie J. McCay, and James M. Acheson. 1998. "The Tragedy of the Commons: Twenty-Two Years Later." In *Managing the Commons,* 2nd ed., ed. John A. Baden and Douglas S. Noonan, 76–94. Bloomington: Indiana University Press. Originally published in *Human Ecology* 18(1) (1990): 1–19.

Fehr, Ernst, and Simon Gächter. 2000a. "Cooperation and Punishment in Public Goods Experiments." *American Economic Review* 90(4):980–94.

———. 2000b. "Fairness and Retaliation: The Economics of Reciprocity." *Journal of Economic Perspectives* 14(3):159–81.

———. 2002. "Altruistic Punishment in Humans." *Nature* 415:137–40.

Fehr, Ernst, and Andreas Leibbrandt. 2008. "Cooperativeness and Impatience in the Tragedy of the Commons." IZA Discussion Paper no. 3625, University of Zurich.

Fehr, Ernst, and Klaus Schmidt. 1999. "A Theory of Fairness, Competition, and Cooperation." *Quarterly Journal of Economics* 114(3):817–68.

Fenno, Richard F., Jr. 1978. "Appendix: Notes on Method: Participant Observation." In *Home Style,* ed. Richard F. Fenno Jr., 249–95. Boston, MA: Little, Brown.

Fenoaltea, Stefano. 1988. "Transaction Costs, Whig History, and the Common Fields." *Politics and Society* 16(2–3) (June): 171–240.

Fleuret, Anne. 1988. "Some Consequences of Tenure and Agrarian Reform in Taita, Kenya." In *Land and Society in Contemporary Africa,* ed. R. E. Downs and S. P. Reyna, 136–58. Hanover, NH: University Press of New England.

Flyvbjerg, Bent. 2006. "Five Misunderstandings about Case-Study Research." *Qualitative Inquiry* 12(2):219–45.

Folke, Carl, Thomas Hahn, Per Olsson, and Jon Norberg. 2005. "Adaptive Governance of Social-Ecological Systems." *Annual Review of Environment and Resources* 30:441–73.

Frank, Robert H. 1987. "If *Homo Economicus* Could Choose His Own Utility Function, Would He Want One with a Conscience?" *American Economic Review* 77:593–604.

Freeman, Linton C. 2004. *The Development of Social Network Analysis: A Study in the Sociology of Science.* Vancouver: Empirical Press.

Frey, Bruno S., and Felix Oberholzer-Gee. 1997. "The Cost of Price Incentives: An Empirical Analysis of Motivation Crowding-Out." *American Economic Review* 87(4):746–55.

Frey, Bruno S., and Alois Stutzer. 2007. *Economics and Psychology: A Promising New Cross-Disciplinary Field.* Cambridge, MA: MIT Press.

Friedman, Daniel, and Shyam Sunder. 1994. *Experimental Methods: A Primer for Economists.* Cambridge: Cambridge University Press.

Friedmann, Johan, and Haripriya Rangan. 1993. *In Defense of Livelihood: Comparative Studies on Environmental Action.* West Harford, CT: Kumarian Press.

Frohlich, Norman. 1974. "Self-Interest or Altruism, What Difference?" *Journal of Conflict Resolution* 18(1):55–73.

Frohlich, Norman, and Joe A. Oppenheimer. 1992. *Choosing Justice: An Experimental Approach to Ethical Theory*. Berkeley and Los Angeles: University of California Press.

———. 2001. "Choosing: A Cognitive Model of Economic and Political Choice." Working Paper. Winnipeg: University of Manitoba, Faculty of Management.

Fudenberg, Drew, and Eric Maskin. 1986. "The Folk Theorem in Repeated Games with Discounting or with Incomplete Information." *Econometrica* 54(3):533–54.

Fukuyama, Francis. 1995. *Trust: The Social Virtues and the Creation of Prosperity*. New York: Free Press.

Futemma, Celia. 2000. "Collective Action and Assurance of Property Rights to Natural Resources: A Case Study from the Lower Amazon Region, Santarem, Brazil." PhD diss., Indiana University.

Gächter, Simon, Elke Renner, and Martin Sefton. 2008. "The Long-Run Benefits of Punishment." *Science* 322(5907):1510.

Gautam, A. P. 2002. "Forest Land Use Dynamics and Community-Based Institutions in a Mountain Watershed in Nepal: Implications for Forest Governance and Management." PhD diss., Asian Institute of Technology, Bangkok, Thailand.

Geddes, Barbara. 1990. "How the Cases You Choose Affect the Answers You Get: Selection Bias in Comparative Politics." *Political Analysis* 2:131–50.

———. 2003. *Paradigms and Sand Castles: Theory Building and Research Design in Comparative Politics*. Ann Arbor: University of Michigan Press.

Geist, Helmut J., and Eric F. Lambin. 2001. *What Drives Tropical Deforestation? A Meta-Analysis of Proximate and Underlying Causes of Deforestation Based on Subnational Case Study Evidence*. Louvain-la-Neuve (Belgium): LUCC International Project Office, LUCC Report Series no. 4.

———. 2002. "Proximate Causes and Underlying Driving Forces of Tropical Deforestation." *BioScience* 52(2) (February): 143–50.

George, Alexander L., and Andrew Bennett. 2005. *Case Studies and Theory Development in the Social Sciences*. Cambridge, MA: MIT Press.

George, Alexander L., and Timothy McKeown. 1985. "Case Studies and Theories of Organizational Decision-Making." In *Advances in Informational Processing in Organizations*, ed. R. Coulman and R. Smith, 21–58. Greenwich, CT: JAI Press.

Gerring, John. 2001. *Social Science Methodology: A Criterial Framework*. New York: Cambridge University Press.

———. 2004. "What Is a Case Study and What Is It Good For?" *American Political Science Review* 98(2) (May): 341–54.

———. 2007a. *Case Study Research: Principles and Practices*. New York: Cambridge University Press.

———. 2007b. "Is There a (Viable) Crucial-Case Method?" *Comparative Political Studies* 40(3) (March): 231–53.

Ghate, Rucha. 2004. *Uncommons in the Commons: Community Initiated Forest Resource Management*. New Delhi: Concept Publishing.

———. 2008. "A Tale of Three Villages: Practised Forestry in India." In *Promise, Trust, and Evolution: Managing the Commons of South Asia,* ed. Rucha Ghate, Narpat S. Jodha, and Pranab Mukhopadhyay, 122–43. Oxford: Oxford University Press.

Ghate, Rucha, and Harini Nagendra. 2005. "Role of Monitoring in Institutional Performance: Forest Management in Maharashtra, India." *Conservation and Society* 3(2) (December): 509–32.

Gibson, Clark C. 2001. "Forest Resources: Institutions for Local Governance in Guatemala." In *Protecting the Commons: A Framework for Resource Management in the Americas,* ed. Joanna Burger, Elinor Ostrom, Richard B. Norgaard, David Policansky, and Bernard D. Goldstein, 71–89. Washington, DC: Island Press.

Gibson, Clark C., and C. Dustin Becker. 2000. "A Lack of Institutional Demand: Why a Strong Local Community in Western Ecuador Fails to Protect Its Forest." In *People and Forests: Communities, Institutions, and Governance,* ed. Clark C. Gibson, Margaret A. McKean, and Elinor Ostrom, 135–61. Cambridge, MA: MIT Press.

Gibson, Clark C., and Tomas Koontz. 1998. "When 'Community' Is Not Enough: Institutions and Values in Community-Based Forest Management in Southern Indiana." *Human Ecology* 26(4):621–47.

Gibson, Clark C., Fabrice Lehoucq, and John Williams. 2002. "Does Privatization Protect Natural Resources? Property Rights and Forests in Guatemala." *Social Science Quarterly* 83(1) (March): 206–25.

Gibson, Clark C., Margaret A. McKean, and Elinor Ostrom, eds. 2000. *People and Forests: Communities, Institutions, and Governance.* Cambridge, MA: MIT Press.

Gibson, Clark C., Elinor Ostrom, and T. K. Ahn. 2000. "The Concept of Scale and the Human Dimensions of Global Change: A Survey." *Ecological Economics* 32(2) (February): 217–39.

Gibson, Clark C., John T. Williams, and Elinor Ostrom. 2005. "Local Enforcement and Better Forests." *World Development* 33(2):273–84.

Gigerenzer, Gerd, and Reinard Selten, eds. 2001. *Bounded Rationality: The Adaptive Toolbox.* Cambridge, MA: MIT Press.

Gigerenzer, Gerd, Peter M. Todd, and the ABC Research Group. 1999. *Simple Heuristics That Make Us Smart.* Oxford: Oxford University Press.

Gilbert, Nigel. 2007. *Agent-Based Models (Quantitative Applications in the Social Sciences Series).* Thousand Oaks, CA: Sage.

Gill, Jeff. 2004. "Introduction to the Special Issue." Special issue, *Political Analysis* 12(4) (Autumn): 323–37.

Gilles, Jere L., Abdellah Hammoudi, and Mohamed Mahdi. 1992. "Oukaimedene, Morocco: A High Mountain *Agdal.*" In *Making the Commons Work: Theory, Practice, and Policy,* ed. David Bromley et al., 229–46. San Francisco, CA: ICS Press.

Gilles, Jere L., and Keith Jamtgaard. 1981. "Overgrazing in Pastoral Areas: The Commons Reconsidered." *Sociologia Ruralis* 21:129–41.

Gillingham, Mary E. 1999. "Gaining Access to Water: Formal and Working

Rules of Indigenous Irrigation Management on Mount Kilimanjaro, Tanzania." *Natural Resources Journal* 39(3) (Summer): 419–41.

Gintis, Herbert, Eric Smith, and Samuel Bowles. 2001. "Costly Signaling and Cooperation." *Journal of Theoretical Biology* 213:103–19.

Glass, Gene V. 1976. "Primary, Secondary, and Meta-Analysis of Research." *Educational Researcher* 6(10) (November): 3–8.

Gleser, Leon J., and Ingram Olkin. 1994. "Stochastically Dependent Effect Sizes." In *The Handbook of Research Synthesis*, ed. Harris Cooper and Larry V. Hedges, 339–55. New York: Russell Sage Foundation.

Glimcher, Paul. 2003. *Decisions, Uncertainty, and the Brain: The Science of Neuroeconomics*. Cambridge, MA: MIT Press.

Goldstein, Daniel G., and Gerd Gigerenzer. 2002. "Models of Ecological Rationality: The Recognition Heuristics." *Psychological Review* 109:75–90.

Goldstone, Jack A. 1997. "Methodological Issues in Comparative Macrosociology." *Comparative Social Research* 16:107–20.

Goldstone, Robert L., and Ben C. Ashpole. 2004. "Human Foraging Behavior in a Virtual Environment." *Psychonomic Bulletin and Review* 11:508–14.

Goldthorpe, John H. 1997. "Current Issues in Comparative Macrosociology: A Debate on Methodological Issues." *Comparative Social Research* 16:1–26.

Gombya-Ssembajjwe, William. 1997. *Indigenous Technical Knowledge and Forest Management: A Case Study of Sacred Groves (Traditional Forest Reserves), Mpigi District, Uganda*. UFRIC Research Notes no. 1. Kampala, Uganda: Makerere University Printer.

Gooch, Margaret, and Jeni Warburton. 2009. "Building and Managing Resilience in Community-Based NRM Groups: An Australian Case Study." *Society and Natural Resources* 22(2):158–71.

Goodwin, Jeff, and Ruth Horowitz. 2002. "Introduction: The Methodological Strengths and Dilemmas of Qualitative Sociology." *Qualitative Sociology* 25(1) (Spring): 33–47.

Gordon, H. Scott. 1954. "The Economic Theory of a Common-Property Resource: The Fishery." *Journal of Political Economy* 62(2) (April): 124–42.

Gould, Roger V. 1993. "Collective Action and Network Structure." *American Sociological Review* 58(2):182–96.

Granato, Jim, Melody Lo, and Sunny M. C. Wong. 2010a. "The Empirical Implications of Theoretical Models (EITM): A Framework for Methodological Unification." *Política y Gobierno* 17(1):25–57.

———. 2010b. "A Framework for Unifying Formal and Empirical Analysis." *American Journal of Political Science* 54(3), forthcoming.

Granato, Jim, and Frank Scioli. 2004. "Puzzle, Proverbs, and Omega Matrices: The Scientific and Social Significance of Empirical Implications of Theoretical Models (EITM)." *Perspectives on Politics* 2(2) (June): 313–23.

Gray, Paul, John Williamson, David Karp, and John Dalphin. 2007. *The Research Imagination: An Introduction to Qualitative and Quantitative Methods*. New York: Cambridge University Press.

Green, Donald P., and Ian Shapiro. 1994. *Pathologies of Rational Choice Theory: A Critique of Applications in Political Science*. New Haven, CT: Yale University Press.

Grimm,Volker, Eloy Revilla, Uta Berger, Floran Jeltsch, Wolf M. Mooij, Steven F. Railsback, Hans-Hermann Thulke, Jacob Weiner, Thorsten Wiegand, and Donald DeAngelis. 2005. "Pattern-Oriented Modeling of Agent-Based Complex Systems: Lessons from Ecology." *Science* 310:987–91.

Grove, Allison. 1993. "Water Use by the Chagga on Kilimanjaro." *African Affairs* 92(368) (July): 431–48.

Guha, Ramachandra. 1989. *The Unquiet Woods: Ecological Change and Peasant Resistance in the Himalayas.* Berkeley and Los Angeles: University of California Press.

Guillet, David. 1992. *Covering Ground: Communal Water Management and the State in the Peruvian Highlands.* Ann Arbor: University of Michigan Press.

Gunawardena, Asha, and Paul Steele. 2008. "The Stake-Net Fishery Association of Negombo Lagoon, Sri Lanka: Why Has It Survived over 250 Years and Will It Survive Another 100 Years?" In *Promise, Trust, and Evolution: Managing the Commons of South Asia,* ed. Rucha Ghate, Narpat S. Jodha, and Pranab Mukhopadhyay, 144–64. Oxford: Oxford University Press.

Gürek, Özgür, Bernd Irlenbusch, and Bettina Rockenbach 2006. "The Competitive Advantage of Sanctioning Institutions." *Science* 312:60–61.

Gurung, T. R., François Bousquet, and Guy Trébuil. 2006. "Companion Modeling, Conflict Resolution, and Institution Building: Sharing Irrigation Water in the Lingmuteychu Watershed, Bhutan." *Ecology and Society* 11(2):36, http://www.ecologyandsociety.org/vol11/iss2/art36/.

Güth, Werner, and Hartmut Kliemt. 1995. "Competition or Co-Operation: On the Evolutionary Economics of Trust, Exploitation and Moral Attitudes." Working Paper. Berlin: Humboldt University.

———. 1998. "The Indirect Evolutionary Approach: Bridging the Gap between Rationality and Adaptation." *Rationality and Society* 10(3):377–99.

Guy, Mary E. 2003. "Ties That Bind: The Link between Public Administration and Political Science." *Journal of Politics* 63(3) (August): 641–55.

Guyot, Paul, and Shinichi Honiden. 2006. "Agent-Based Participatory Simulations: Merging Multi-Agent Systems and Role-Playing Games." *Journal of Artificial Societies and Social Simulation* 9(4), http://jasss.soc.surrey.ac.uk/9/4/8.html.

Hackett, Steven. 1992. "Heterogeneity and the Provision of Governance for Common-Pool Resources." *Journal of Theoretical Politics* 4(3):325–42.

Hackett, Steven, Edella Schlager, and James Walker. 1994. "The Role of Communication in Resolving Commons Dilemmas: Experimental Evidence with Heterogeneous Appropriators." *Journal of Environmental Economics and Management* 27:99–126.

Hales, David. 2001. "Tag-Based Cooperation in Artificial Societies." PhD thesis, Department of Computer Science, University of Essex, Essex, United Kingdom.

Hall, Peter. 2003. "Aligning Ontology and Methodology in Comparative Research." In *Comparative Historical Analysis in the Social Sciences,* ed. James Mahoney and Dietrich Rueschemeyer, 373–404. New York: Cambridge University Press.

Haller, Tobias, and Sonja Merten. 2008. "We Are Zambians—Don't Tell Us

How to Fish! Institutional Change, Power Relations and Conflicts in the Kafue Flats Fisheries in Zambia." *Human Ecology* 36(5) (October): 699–715.

Halstead, Paul, and John O'Shea. 1989. "Introduction: Cultural Responses to Risk and Uncertainty." In *Bad Year Economics: Cultural Responses to Risk and Uncertainty,* ed. Paul Halstead and John O'Shea, 1–7. New York: Cambridge University Press.

Happe, Kathrin, Konrad Kellermann, and Alfons Balmann. 2006. "Agent-Based Analysis of Agricultural Policies: An Illustration of the Agricultural Policy Simulator AgriPoliS, Its Adaptation and Behavior." *Ecology and Society* 11(1):46, http://www.ecologyandsociety.org/vol11/iss1/art49/.

Hardin, Garrett. 1968. "The Tragedy of the Commons." *Science* 162:1243–48.

Hardin, Russell. 1982. *Collective Action.* Baltimore, MD: Johns Hopkins University Press.

Hare, Matt P., and Claudia Pahl-Wostl. 2002. "Stakeholder Categorisation in Processes of Participatory Integrated Assessment." *Integrated Assessment* 3:50–62.

Harrison, Glenn W., and John A. List 2004. "Field Experiments." *Journal of Economic Literature* 42(4):1009–55.

Harrison, Paul. 1993. *The Third Revolution: Population, Environment, and a Sustainable World.* New York: Penguin.

Harsanyi, John C., and Reinhard Selten. 1988. *A General Theory of Equilibrium Selection in Games.* Cambridge, MA: MIT Press.

Hauert, Christoph, Silvia De Monte, Josef Hofbauer, and Karl Sigmund. 2002. "Volunteering as Red Queen Mechanism for Cooperation in Public Goods Games." *Science* 296(5570):1129–32.

Hauert, Christoph, and György Szabo. 2003. "Prisoner's Dilemma and Public Goods Games in Different Geometries: Compulsory versus Voluntary Interactions." *Complexity* 9(4):31–38.

Hauert, Christoph, Arne Traulsen, Hannelore Brandt, Martin A. Nowak, and Karl Sigmund. 2007. "Via Freedom to Coercion: The Emergence of Costly Punishment." *Science* 316:1905–7.

Hayes, Tanya. 2006. "Parks, People, and Forest Protection: An Institutional Assessment of the Effectiveness of Protected Areas." *World Development* 34(12) (December): 2064–75.

———. 2007. "Forest Governance in a Frontier: An Analysis of the Dynamic Interplay between Property Rights, Land-Use Norms, and Agricultural Expansion in the Mosquitia Forest Corridor of Honduras and Nicaragua." PhD diss., Indiana University.

Hayes, Tanya, and Elinor Ostrom. 2005. "Conserving the World's Forests: Are Protected Areas the Only Way?" *Indiana Law Review* 38(3):595–617.

Helbing, Dirk, and Wenjian Yu. 2009. "The Outbreak of Cooperation among Success-Driven Individuals under Noisy Conditions." *Proceedings of the National Academy of Sciences* 106:3680–85.

Hellström, Eeva. 1998. "Qualitative Comparative Analysis: A Useful Tool for Research into Forest Policy and Forestry Conflicts." *Forest Science* 44(2):254–65.

———. 2001. "Conflict Cultures: Qualitative Comparative Analysis of Environmental Conflicts in Forestry." *Silva Fennica* suppl. 2:2–109.

Henrich, Joseph, Robert Boyd, Samuel Bowles, Colin Camerer, Ernst Fehr, and Herbert Gintis, eds. 2004. *Foundations of Human Sociality: Economic Experiments and Ethnographic Evidence from Fifteen Small-Scale Societies*. Oxford: Oxford University Press.

Henrich, Joseph, Robert Boyd, Samuel Bowles, Colin Camerer, Ernst Fehr, Herbert Gintis, Richard McElreath, Michael Alvard, Abigail Barr, et al. 2005. "'Economic Man' in Cross-Cultural Perspective: Behavioral Experiments in 15 Small-Scale Societies." *Behavioral and Brain Sciences* 28(6):795–855.

Henrich, Joseph, Richard McElreath, Abigail Barr, Jean Ensminger, Clark Barrett, Alexander Bolyanatz, Juan-Camilo Cardenas, et al. 2006. "Costly Punishment across Human Societies." *Science* 312:1767–70.

Herr, Andrew, Roy Gardner, and James M. Walker 1997. "An Experimental Study of Time-Independent and Time-Dependent Externalities in the Commons." *Games and Economic Behavior* 19(1):77–96.

Hirshleifer, David, and Eric Rasmusen 1989. "Cooperation in a Repeated Prisoner's Dilemma with Ostracism." *Journal of Economic Behavior and Organization* 12:87–106.

Hitchcock, Robert K. 1980. "Tradition, Social Justice and Land Reform in Central Botswana." *Journal of African Law* 24(1) (Spring): 1–34.

Hoffmann, Irene. 2004. "Access to Land and Water in the Zamfara Reserve. A Case Study for the Management of Common Property Resources in Pastoral Areas of West Africa." *Human Ecology* 32(1) (February): 77–105.

Hoffmann, Robert. 2000. "Twenty Years on: The Evolution of Cooperation Revisited." *Journal of Artificial Societies and Social Simulation* 3(2), http://www.soc.surrey.ac.uk/JASSS/3/2/forum/1.html.

Holt, Charles A. 2007. *Markets, Games, and Strategic Behavior*. Boston, MA: Addison Wesley.

Holt, Flora Lu. 2005. "The Catch-22 of Conservation: Indigenous Peoples, Biologists, and Cultural Change." *Human Ecology* 33(2):199–215.

Homewood, K., E. F. Lambin, E. Coast, A. Kariuki, I. Kikula, J. Kivelia, M. Said, S. Serneels, and M. Thompson. 2001. "Long-Term Changes in Serengeti-Mara Wildebeest and Land Cover: Pastoralism, Population, or Policies." *Proceedings of the National Academy of Sciences* 98(22) (October): 12544–49.

Huberman, Bernardo A., and Natalie S. Glance. 1993. "Evolutionary Games and Computer Simulations." *Proceedings of the National Academy of Sciences* 90(16):7716–18.

Huberman, Bernardo A., and Rajan M. Lukose. 1997. "Social Dilemmas and Internet Congestion." *Science* 277:535–37.

Huigen, Marco G. A., K. P. Overmars, and W. T. de Groot. 2006. "Multiactor Modeling of Settling Decisions and Behavior in the San Mariano Watershed, the Philippines: A First Application with the MameLuke Framework." *Ecology and Society* 11(2):33, http://www.ecologyandsociety.org/vol11/iss2/art33/.

Hulme, David, and Mark Infield. 2001. "Community Conservation, Reciprocity and Park-People Relationships: Lake Mburo National Park, Uganda." In *African Wildlife and Livelihoods: The Promise and Performance of Community Conservation*, ed. David Hulme and Marshall Murphree, 106–30. Oxford: James Currey.

Hunter, John E., and Frank L. Schmidt. 1990. *Methods of Meta-Analysis: Correcting Error and Bias in Research Findings*. Newbury Park, CA: Sage.

Ingram, Helen, Anne L. Schneider, and Peter deLeon. 2007. "Social Construction and Policy Design." In *Theories of the Policy Process*, 2nd ed., ed. Paul A. Sabatier, 93–126. Boulder, CO: Westview Press.

Isaac, R. Mark, Deborah Mathieu, and Edward E. Zajac. 1991. "Institutional Framing and Perceptions of Fairness." *Constitutional Political Economy* 2(3) (Fall): 329–70.

Isaac, R. Mark, Kenneth F. McCue, and Charles R. Plott. 1985. "Public Goods Provision in an Experimental Environment." *Journal of Public Economics* 26:51–74.

Isaac, R. Mark, and James M. Walker. 1988a. "Group Size Effects in Public Goods Provision: The Voluntary Contributions Mechanism." *Quarterly Journal of Economics* 103 (February): 179–200.

———. 1988b. "Communication and Free-Riding Behavior: The Voluntary Contribution Mechanism." *Economic Inquiry* 26(4):585–608.

Isaac, R. Mark, James M. Walker, and Susan Thomas. 1984. "Divergent Evidence on Free Riding: An Experimental Examination of Possible Explanations." *Public Choice* 43:113–49.

Isaac, R. Mark, James M. Walker, and Arlington W. Williams. 1994. "Group Size and the Voluntary Provision of Public Goods: Experimental Evidence Utilizing Large Groups." *Journal of Public Economics* 54(1):1–36.

Jackman, Robert W. 1985. "Cross-National Statistical Research and the Study of Comparative Politics." *American Political Science Review* 29(1) (February): 161–82.

Jager, Wander, and Marco A. Janssen. 2002. "Using Artificial Agents to Understand Laboratory Experiments of Common-Pool Resources with Real Agents." In *Complexity and Ecosystem Management: The Theory and Practice of Multi-Agent Systems*, ed. Marco A. Janssen, 75–102. Cheltenham, UK: Edward Elgar.

Jagger, Pamela. 2009. "Can Forest Sector Devolution Improve Rural Livelihoods? An Analysis of Forest Income and Institutions in Western Uganda." PhD diss., Indiana University.

Jagger, Pamela, Marty Luckert, Abwoli Banana, and Joseph Bahati. 2009. "What Should We Be Asking? Aggregated vs. Disaggregated Responses to Household Livelihood Questionnaires." Working Paper. Bloomington: Indiana University, Workshop in Political Theory and Policy Analysis.

Janssen, Marco A. 2005a. "Agent-Based Modeling." In *Modelling in Ecological Economics*, ed. John Proops and Paul Safonov, 155–72. Cheltenham, UK: Edward Elgar.

———. 2005b. "Evolution of Institutional Rules: An Immune System Perspective." *Complexity* 11(1):16–23.

———. 2008. "Evolution of Cooperation in a One-Shot Prisoner's Dilemma Based on Recognition of Trustworthy and Untrustworthy Agents." *Journal of Economic Behavior and Organization* 65:458–71.

———. Forthcoming. "Introducing Ecological Dynamics in Common Pool Resource Experiments." *Ecology and Society*.

Janssen, Marco A., and T. K. Ahn. 2006. "Learning, Signaling, and Social Preferences in Public-Good Games." *Ecology and Society* 11(2):21, http://www.ecologyandsociety.org/vol11/iss2/art21/.

Janssen, Marco A., John M. Anderies, and Sanket R. Joshi. 2009. "Coordination and Cooperation in Asymmetric Commons Dilemmas." Submitted.

Janssen, Marco A., John M. Anderies, and Elinor Ostrom. 2007. "Robustness of Social-Ecological Systems to Spatial and Temporal Variability." *Society and Natural Resources* 20(4):307–22.

Janssen, Marco A., and Robert L. Goldstone. 2006. "Dynamic-Persistence of Cooperation in Public Good Games When Group Size Is Dynamic." *Journal of Theoretical Biology* 243(1):134–42.

Janssen, Marco A., Robert L. Goldstone, Filippo Menczer, and Elinor Ostrom. 2008. "Effect of Rule Choice in Dynamic Interactive Spatial Commons." *International Journal of the Commons* 2(2):288–312.

Janssen, Marco A., and Elinor Ostrom. 2006a. "Adoption of a New Regulation for the Governance of Common-Pool Resources by a Heterogeneous Population." In *Inequality, Cooperation, and Environmental Sustainability*, ed. Jean-Marie Baland, Pranab Bardhan, and Samuel Bowles, 60–96. Princeton, NJ: Princeton University Press.

———. 2006b. "Governing Social-Ecological Systems." In *Handbook of Computational Economics: Agent-Based Computational Economics*, vol. 2, ed. Leigh Tesfatsion and Kenneth L. Judd, 1465–509. Amsterdam: Elsevier.

———. 2006c. "Empirically Based, Agent-Based Models." *Ecology and Society* 11(2):37, http://www.ecologyandsociety.org/vol11/iss2/art37/.

———. 2008. "TURFs in the Lab: Institutional Innovation in Dynamic Interactive Spatial Commons." *Rationality and Society* 20:371–97.

Janssen, Marco A., Nicholas P. Radtke, and Allen Lee. 2009. "Pattern-Oriented Modeling of Commons Dilemma Experiments." *Adaptive Behavior* 17:508–29.

Janssen, Marco A., and Herbert J. M. de Vries. 1998. "The Battle of Perspectives: A Multi-Agent Model with Adaptive Responses to Climate Change." *Ecological Economics* 26(1):457–63.

Jodha, N. S. 1990. "Rural Common Property Resources: Contributions and Crisis." *Economic and Political Weekly* 25(26):A65–A78.

Johnson, Ronald N., and Gary D. Libecap. 1982. "Contracting Problems and Regulation: The Case of the Fishery." *American Economic Review* 72(5):1005–22.

Joireman, S. F. 2008. "The Mystery of Capital Formation in Sub-Saharan Africa: Women, Property Rights and Customary Law." *World Development* 36(7) (July): 1233–46.

Jones, Bryan D. 2001. *Politics and the Architecture of Choice: Bounded Rationality and Governance*. Chicago: University of Chicago Press.

Joshi, Neeraj N., Elinor Ostrom, Ganesh P. Shivakoti, and Wai Fung Lam. 2000. "Institutional Opportunities and Constraints in the Performance of Farmer-Managed Irrigation Systems in Nepal." *Asia-Pacific Journal of Rural Development* 10(2) (December): 67–92.

Kagel, John H., and Alvin E. Roth. 1995. *Handbook of Experimental Economics.* Princeton, NJ: Princeton University Press.

Kameda, Tatsuya, Masanori Takezawa, and Reid Hastle. 2003. "The Logic of Social Sharing: An Evolutionary Game Analysis of Adaptive Norm Development." *Personality and Social Psychology Review* 7(1):2–19.

Kanbur, Ravi. 1992. "Heterogeneity, Distribution and Cooperation in Common Property Resource Management." Policy Research Working Paper WPS 844. Washington, DC: The World Bank.

Keizer, Kees, Siegwart Lindenberg, and Linda Steg. 2008. "The Spreading of Disorder." *Science* 322 (December 12): 1681–85.

Kerr, Norbert L., and Cynthia M. Kaufman-Gilliland. 1994. "Communication, Commitment, and Cooperation in Social Dilemmas." *Journal of Personality and Social Psychology* 66:513–29.

Keser, Claudia, and Roy Gardner. 1999. "Strategic Behavior of Experienced Subjects in a Common Pool Resource Game." *International Journal of Game Theory* 28(2):241–52.

Killingback, Timothy, Jonas Bieri, and Thomas Flatt. 2006. "Evolution in Group-Structured Populations Can Resolve the Tragedy of the Commons." *Proceedings of the Royal Society B* 273:1477–81.

King, Gary, Robert Keohane, and Sidney Verba. 1994. *Designing Social Inquiry: Scientific Inference in Qualitative Research.* Princeton, NJ: Princeton University Press.

Kipuri, Naomi Ole. 1991. "Age, Gender and Class in the Scramble for Maasailand." *Nature and Resources: Managing Our Common Resources* 27(4):10–17.

Kiser, Larry L., and Elinor Ostrom. 1982. "The Three Worlds of Action: A Metatheoretical Synthesis of Institutional Approaches." In *Strategies of Political Inquiry,* ed. Elinor Ostrom, 179–222. Beverly Hills, CA: Sage.

Klooster, Daniel. 2000a. "Community Forestry and Tree Theft in Mexico: Resistance or Complicity in Conservation?" *Development and Change* 31(1) (January): 281–305.

———. 2000b. "Institutional Choice, Community, and Struggle: A Case Study of Forest Co-Management in Mexico." *World Development* 28(1) (January): 1–20.

Klopp, Jacqueline M. 2000. "Pilfering the Public: The Problem of Land Grabbing in Contemporary Kenya." *Africa Today* 47(1) (Winter): 6–26.

Knack, Stephen. 1992. "Civic Norms, Social Sanctions, and Voter Turnout." *Rationality and Society* 4 (April): 133–56.

Knight, Jack. 1992. *Institutions and Social Conflict.* New York: Cambridge University Press.

Kuhn, Thomas S. 1970. "Logic of Discovery or Psychology of Research." In *Criticism and the Growth of Knowledge,* Proceedings of the International Colloquium in the Philosophy of Science, London, 1965, ed. Imre Lakatos and Alan Musgrave, 1–23. New York: Cambridge University Press.

Kull, Christian A. 2002. "Empowering Pyromaniacs in Madagascar: Ideology and Legitimacy in Community-Based Natural Resource Management." *Development and Change* 33(1) (January): 57–78.

Kumar, Sanjay. 2002. "Does 'Participation' in Common Pool Resource Management Help the Poor? A Social Cost-Benefit Analysis of Joint Forest Management in Jharkhand, India." *World Development* 30(5) (May): 763–82.

Kurian, Mathew, and Ton Dietz. 2004. "Irrigation and Collective Action: A Study in Method with Reference to the Shiwalik Hills, Haryana." *Natural Resources Forum* 28(1) (February): 34–49.

Lahiff, Edward. 2000. "Land Tenure in South Africa's Communal Areas: A Case Study of the Arabie-Olifants Scheme." *African Studies* 59(1) (July): 45–69.

Laitin, David D. 2003. "The Perestroikan Challenge to Social Science." *Politics and Society* 31(1) (March): 163–84.

Lakatos, Imre. 1970. "Falsification and the Methodology of Scientific Research Programmes." In *Criticism and the Growth of Knowledge*, Proceedings of the International Colloquium in the Philosophy of Science, London, 1965, ed. Imre Lakatos and Alan Musgrave, 91–195. New York: Cambridge University Press.

Lam, Wai Fung. 1994. "Institutions, Engineering Infrastructure, and Performance in the Governance and Management of Irrigation Systems: The Case of Nepal." PhD diss., Indiana University.

———. 1996. "Improving the Performance of Small-Scale Irrigation Systems: The Effects of Technological Investments and Governance Structure on Irrigation Performance in Nepal." *World Development* 24(8) (August): 1301–15.

———. 1998. *Governing Irrigation Systems in Nepal: Institutions, Infrastructure, and Collective Action*. Oakland, CA: ICS Press.

Lam, Wai Fung, Myungsuk Lee, and Elinor Ostrom. 1997. "The Institutional Analysis and Development Framework: Application to Irrigation Policy in Nepal." In *Policy Studies and Developing Nations: An Institutional and Implementation Focus,* vol. 5, ed. Derick W. Brinkerhoff, 53–85. Greenwich, CT: JAI Press.

Lam, Wai Fung, and Elinor Ostrom. 2009. "Analyzing the Dynamic Complexity of Development Interventions: Lessons from an Irrigation Experiment in Nepal." *Policy Sciences*, OnlineFirst May 5, 2009, http://www.springerlink.com/content/l174382165v62868/.

Landry, Pierre F., and Mingming Shen. 2005. "Reaching Migrants in Survey Research: The Use of Global Positioning System to Reduce Coverage Bias in China." *Political Analysis* 13(1) (Winter): 1–22.

Lasswell, Harold D. 1951. "The Policy Orientation." In *The Policy Sciences: Recent Developments in Scope and Methods,* ed. Daniel Lerner and Harold D. Lasswell, 3–15. Stanford, CA: Stanford University Press.

Laury, Susan K., James M. Walker, and Arlington Williams. 1995. "Anonymity and the Voluntary Provision of Public Goods." *Journal of Economic Behavior and Organization* 27(3): 365–80.

Leal, Donald R. 1998. "Community-Run Fisheries: Avoiding the 'Tragedy of the Commons.'" *Population and Environment* 19(3) (January): 225–45.

LeBaron, Blake. 2001. "Stochastic Volatility as a Simple Generator of Power Laws and Long Memory." *Quantitative Finance* 1:621–31.

Ledyard, John O. 1995. "Public Goods: A Survey of Experimental Research." In *The Handbook of Experimental Economics,* J. Kagel and A. Roth, 111–94. Princeton, NJ: Princeton University Press.

Leimar, Olof, and Peter Hammerstein. 2001. "Evolution of Cooperation through Indirect Reciprocity." *Proceedings of the Royal Society London B* 268:745–53.

Levin, Simon A. 1999. *Fragile Dominion: Complexity and the Commons.* Reading, MA: Perseus Books.

Levine, Gilbert, Ko Hai Sheng, and Randolph Barker. 2000. "The Evolution of Taiwanese Irrigation: Implications for the Future." *International Journal of Water Resources Development* 16(4) (December): 497–510.

Levitt, Steven D., and John A. List. 2007. "What Do Laboratory Experiments Measuring Social Preferences Tell Us about the Real World?" *Journal of Economic Perspectives* 21(2):153–74.

Lewin, Kurt. 1946. "Action Research and Minority Problems." *Journal of Social Issues* 2(4):34–46.

Lian, Peng, and Charles R. Plott. 1998. "General Equilibrium, Markets, Macroeconomics and Money in a Laboratory Experimental Environment." *Economic Theory* 12(1):21–75.

Libecap, Gary D., and Steven N. Wiggins. 1984. "Contractual Responses to the Common Pool: Prorationing of Crude Oil Production." *American Economic Review* 74:87–98.

———. 1985. "The Influence of Private Contractual Failure on Regulation: The Case of Oil Field Unitization." *Journal of Political Economy* 93:690–714.

Liberman, Varda, Steven Samuels, and Lee Ross. 2007. "The Name of the Game: Predictive Power of Reputations versus Situational Labels in Determining Prisoner's Dilemma Game Moves." *Personality and Social Psychology Bulletin* 30:1175–85.

Lichbach, Mark Irving. 1996. *The Cooperator's Dilemma.* Ann Arbor: University of Michigan Press.

Lieber, Michael D., and Michael A. Rynkiewich. 2007. "Conclusion: Oceanic Conceptions of the Relationship between People and Property." *Human Organization* 66(1):90–97.

Lieberman, Evan S. 2005. "Nested Analysis as a Mixed-Method Strategy for Comparative Research." *American Political Science Review* 99(3) (August): 435–52.

Lieberson, Stanley. 1991. "Small N's and Big Conclusions: An Examination of the Reasoning in Comparative Studies Based on a Small Number of Cases." *Social Forces* 70(2) (December): 307–20.

Liebrand, W. B., D. M. Messick, and H.A.M. Wilke. 1992. *Social Dilemmas: Theoretical Issues and Research Findings.* Oxford: Pergamon Press.

Light, Richard J., and David B. Pillemer. 1984. *Summing Up: The Science of Reviewing Research.* Cambridge, MA: Harvard University Press.

Lijphart, Arend. 1971. "Comparative Politics and the Comparative Method." *American Political Science Review* 65(3) (September): 682–93.

Liljeros, Fredrik, Christofer R. Edling, Luis A. N. Amaral, H. Eugene Stanley, and Yvonne Aberg. 2001. "The Web of Human Sexual Contacts." *Nature* 411:907–8.

Lindgren, Kristian, and Mats G. Nordahl. 1994. "Artificial Food Webs." In *Artificial Life III,* ed. Chris G. Langton, 73–104. Reading. MA: Addison-Wesley.

Lipsey, Mark W., and David B. Wilson. 2001. *Practical Meta-Analysis.* Thousand Oaks, CA: Sage.

List, John. 2004. "Young, Selfish and Male: Field Evidence of Social Preferences." *Economic Journal* 114 (January): 121–49.

Little, Peter D., and David W. Brokensha. 1987. "Local Institutions, Tenure and Resource Management in East Africa." In *Conservation in Africa: People, Policies and Practice,* ed. David Anderson and Richard Grove, 193–206. New York: Cambridge University Press.

Liu, Jianguo, Marc Linderman, Zhiyun Ouyang, Li An, Jian Yang, and Hemin Zhang. 2001. "Ecological Degradation in Protected Areas: The Case of Wolong Nature Reserve for Giant Pandas." *Science* 292:98–101.

Lobe, Kenton, and Fikret Berkes. 2004. "The Padu System of Community-Based Fisheries Management: Change and Local Institutional Innovation in South India." *Marine Policy* 28:271–81.

Lohmann, Susanne. 2004. "Darwinian Medicine for the University." In *Governing Academia: Who Is in Charge at the Modern University?* ed. Ronald G. Ehrenberg, 71–90. Ithaca, NY: Cornell University Press.

———. 2007. "The Trouble with Multi-Methodism." *Qualitative Methods,* newsletter of the American Political Science Association organized section on qualitative methods 5(1) (Spring): 13–17.

Lopez, Maria Claudia, James J. Murphy, John M. Spraggon, and John K. Stranlund. Forthcoming. "Does Government Regulation Complement Existing Community Efforts to Support Cooperation? Evidence from Field Experiments in Colombia." In *Handbook on Experimental Economics and the Environment,* ed. John List and Michael Price. Cheltenham, UK: Edward Elgar.

Lotem, Arnon, Michael A. Fishman, and Lewi Stone. 1999. "Evolution of Cooperation between Individuals." *Nature* 400:226–27.

Lovett, Jon C., Stuart Stevenson, and Hilda Kiwasila. 2002. "Review of Common Pool Resource Management in Tanzania." Natural Resources Systems Programme, Final Technical Report. Department for International Development, Strategy for Research on Renewable Natural Resources. http://www.york.ac.uk/res/celp/webpages/projects/cpr/tanzania/pdf/final%20report.pdf.

Luce, R. Duncan, and Howard Raiffa. 1957. *Games and Decisions: Introduction and Critical Survey.* New York: Wiley.

Lund, Christian. 2006. "Twilight Institutions: Public Authority and Local Politics in Africa." *Development and Change* 37(4) (July): 685–705.

Lustick, Ian S. 1996. "History, Historiography, and Political Science: Multiple Historical Records and the Problem of Selection Bias." *American Political Science Review* 90(3) (September): 605–18.

MacMillan, Katie, and Thomas Koenig. 2004. "The Wow Factor: Preconceptions and Expectations for Data Analysis Software in Qualitative Research." *Social Science Computer Review* 22(2) (Summer): 179–86.

Macy, Michael, and John Skvoretz. 1998. "The Evolution of Trust and Cooperation between Strangers: A Computational Model." *American Sociological Review* 63:638–60.

Madin, Joshua S., Shawn Bowers, Mark P. Schildhauer, and Matthew B. Jones. 2007. "Advancing Ecological Research with Ontologies." *Trends in Ecology and Evolution* 23(3):159–68.

Mahoney, James. 2003. "Strategies of Causal Assessment in Comparative Historical Analysis." In *Comparative Historical Analysis in the Social Sciences,* ed. James Mahoney and Dietrich Rueschemeyer, 337–72. New York: Cambridge University Press.

Mahoney, James, and Gary Goertz. 2006. "A Tale of Two Cultures: Contrasting Quantitative and Qualitative Research." *Political Analysis* 14(3) (Summer): 227–49.

Mahoney, James, and Dietrich Rueschemeyer, eds. 2003. *Comparative Historical Analysis in the Social Sciences.* New York: Cambridge University Press.

Makombe, Godswill, Ruth Meinzen-Dick, Stephen P. Davies, and R. K. Sampath. 2001. "An Evaluation of Bani (Dambo) Systems as a Smallholder Irrigation Development Strategy in Zimbabwe." *Canadian Journal of Agricultural Economics* 49(2) (July): 203–16.

Malayang, Ben S., III. 1991. "Tenure Rights and Exclusion in the Philippines." *Nature and Resources: Managing Our Common Resources* 27:18–23.

Manson, Stephen M., and Tom P. Evans. 2007. "Agent-Based Modeling of Deforestation in Southern Yucatán, Mexico, and Reforestation in the Midwest United States." *Proceedings of the National Academy of Sciences* 104:20678–83.

March, James G., and Johan P. Olsen. 1984. "The New Institutionalism: Organizational Factors in Political Life." *American Political Science Review* 78(3) (September): 734–49.

March, James G., Martin Schulz, and Xueguang Zhou. 2000. *The Dynamics of Rules: Change in Written Organizational Codes.* Stanford, CA: Stanford University Press.

Marshall, Graham R. 2004. "Farmers Cooperating in the Commons? A Study of Collective Action in Salinity Management." *Ecological Economics* 51:271–86.

———. 2008. "Nesting, Subsidiarity, and Community-Based Environmental Governance beyond the Local Level." *International Journal of the Commons* 2(1):75–97.

Martin, Adrian, and Mark Lemon. 2001. "Challenges for Participatory Institutions: The Case of Village Forest Committees in Karnataka, South India." *Society and Natural Resources* 14(7) (August): 585–97.

Martin, Fenton. 1985. *Common Pool Resources: A Preliminary Bibliography.* Bloomington: Indiana University, Workshop in Political Theory and Policy Analysis.

Marwell, Gerald, and Ruth E. Ames. 1979. "Experiments on the Provision of Public Goods I: Resources, Interest, Group Size, and the Free Rider Problem." *American Journal of Sociology* 84:1335–60.

———. 1980. "Experiments on the Provision of Public Goods II: Provision Points, Stakes, Experience and the Free Rider Problem." *American Journal of Sociology* 85:926–37.

Marwell, Gerald, and Ruth E. Ames. 1981. "Economists Free Ride, Does Anyone Else?" *Journal of Public Economics* 15:295–310.

Maynard Smith, John. 1964. "Group Selection and Kin Selection." *Nature* 201:1145–47.

McAdam, Doug, Sidney Tarrow, and Charles Tilly. 2001. *Dynamics of Contention*. New York: Cambridge University Press.

McCarthy, Nancy, Brent Swallow, Michael Kirk, and Peter Hazell, eds. 2000. *Property Rights, Risk, and Livestock Development in Africa*. Nairobi, Kenya, and Washington, DC: International Livestock Research Institute and International Food Policy Research Institute.

McCarthy, Nancy, and Jean-Paul Vanderlinden. 2004. "Resource Management under Climatic Risk: A Case Study from Niger." *Journal of Development Studies* 40(5) (June): 120–42.

McCay, Bonnie J., and James M. Acheson. 1987. *The Question of the Commons: The Culture and Ecology of Communal Resources*. Tucson: University of Arizona Press.

McCloskey, D. N. 1976. "English Open Fields as Behavior toward Risk." In *Research in Economic History: An Annual Compilation*, vol. 1, ed. P. Uselding, 124–70. Greenwich, CT: JAI Press.

McDermott Hughes, David. 2001. "Cadastral Politics: The Making of Community-Based Resource Management in Zimbabwe and Mozambique." *Development and Change* 32(4) (September): 741–68.

McGinnis, Michael, ed. 1999a. *Polycentric Governance and Development: Readings from the Workshop in Political Theory and Policy Analysis*. Ann Arbor: University of Michigan Press.

———, ed. 1999b. *Polycentricity and Local Public Economies: Readings from the Workshop in Political Theory and Policy Analysis*. Ann Arbor: University of Michigan Press.

———, ed. 2000. *Polycentric Games and Institutions: Readings from the Workshop in Political Theory and Policy Analysis*. Ann Arbor: University of Michigan Press.

McGrath, David G., Oriana T. Almeida, and Frank D. Merry. 2007. "The Influence of Community Management Agreements on Household Economic Strategies: Cattle Grazing and Fishing Agreements on the Lower Amazon Floodplain." *International Journal of the Commons* 1(1):67–87.

McKean, Margaret A. 1982. "The Japanese Experience with Scarcity: Management of Traditional Common Lands." *Environmental Review* 6:63–88.

———. 1986. "Management of Traditional Common Lands (*Iriaichi*) in Japan." In *Proceedings of the Conference on Common Property Resource Management*, ed. National Research Council, 533–90. Washington, DC: National Academies Press.

———. 2000. "Common Property: What Is It, What Is It Good For, and What Makes It Work?" In *People and Forests: Communities, Institutions, and Governance*, ed. Clark C. Gibson, Margaret A. McKean, and Elinor Ostrom, 27–55. Cambridge, MA: MIT Press.

McKean, Margaret A., and Elinor Ostrom. 1995. "Common Property Regimes in the Forest: Just a Relic from the Past?" *Unasylva* 46(180):3–15.

McKeown, Timothy J. 2004. "Case Studies and the Limits of the Quantitative Worldview." In *Rethinking Social Inquiry: Diverse Tools, Shared Standards,* ed. Henry E. Brady and David Collier, 139–67. Lanham, MD: Rowman & Littlefield.

Mearns, Robin. 1996. "Community, Collective Action, and Common Grazing: The Case of Post-Socialist Mongolia." *Journal of Development Studies* 32(3) (February): 297–339.

Meinzen-Dick, Ruth. 2007. "Beyond Panaceas in Water Institutions." *Proceedings of the National Academy of Sciences* 104(39):15200–15205.

Meinzen-Dick, Ruth, K. V. Raju, and Ashok Gulati. 2002. "What Affects Organization and Collective Action for Managing Resources? Evidence from Canal Irrigation Systems in India." *World Development* 30(4) (April): 649–66.

Merino Pérez, Leticia, and Mariana Hernández Apolinar. 2004. "Destruccion de Instituciones Comunitarias y Deterioro de los Bosques en la Reserva de la Biosfera Mariposa Monarca, Michoacán, México." *Revista Mexicana de Sociologia* 66(2) (April–June): 261–309.

Messick, David M., and Marilyn Brewer. 1983. "Solving Social Dilemmas: A Review." *Review of Personality and Social Psychology* 4:11–44.

Milinski, Manfred, Dirk Semmann, and Hans-Jürgen Krambeck. 2002. "Reputation Helps Solve the 'Tragedy of the Commons.'" *Nature* 415 (January 24): 424–26.

Miller, John H., and Scott E. Page. 2007. *Complex Adaptive Systems: An Introduction to Computational Models of Social Life.* Princeton, NJ: Princeton University Press.

Mitchell, Melanie 1998. *An Introduction to Genetic Algorithms.* Cambridge, MA: MIT Press.

Monroe, Kristen Renwick. 2005. *Perestroika! The Raucous Revolution in Political Science.* New Haven, CT: Yale University Press.

Morikawa, Tomonori, John M. Orbell, and Audun S. Runde. 1995. "The Advantage of Being Moderately Cooperative." *American Political Science Review* 89(3):601–11.

Morrow, C. E., and R. W. Hull. 1996. "Donor-Initiated Common Pool Resource Institutions: The Case of the Yanesha Forestry Cooperative." *World Development* 24(10):1641–57.

Moses, Jonathon W., and Torbjørn L. Knutsen. 2007. *Ways of Knowing: Competing Methodologies in Social and Political Research.* New York: Palgrave Macmillan.

Moxnes, Erling. 1998. "Not Only the Tragedy of the Commons: Misperceptions of Bioeconomics." *Management Science* 44(9):1234–48.

Munck, Gerardo L. 2004. "Tools for Qualitative Research." In *Rethinking Social Inquiry: Diverse Tools, Shared Standards,* ed. Henry E. Brady and David Collier, 105–21. Lanham, MD: Rowman & Littlefield.

Munck, Gerardo L., and Richard Snyder. 2007. "Debating the Direction of Comparative Politics: An Analysis of Leading Journals." *Comparative Political Studies* 40(1) (January): 5–31.

Mwangi, Esther. 2007a. "Subdividing the Commons: Distributional Conflict in the Transition from Collective to Individual Property Rights in Kenya's Maasailand." *World Development* 35(5) (May): 815–34.

———. 2007b. *Socioeconomic Change and Land Use in Africa: The Transformation of Property Rights in Maasailand*. New York: Palgrave Macmillan.

Nagendra, Harini. 2007. "Drivers of Reforestation in Human-Dominated Forests." *Proceedings of the National Academy of Sciences* 104(39):15218–23.

———. 2008. "Do Parks Work? Impact of Protected Areas on Land Cover Clearing." *Ambio* 37(5):330–33.

Nagendra, Harini, Mukunda Karmacharya, and Birendra Karna. 2005. "Evaluating Forest Management in Nepal: Views across Space and Time." *Ecology and Society* 10(1), http://www.ecologyandsociety.org/vol10/iss1/art24/.

Nagendra, Harini, Sajid Pareeth, Bhawna Sharma, Charles Schweik, and Keshav Adhikari. 2007. "Forest Fragmentation and Regrowth in an Institutional Mosaic of Community, Government and Private Ownership in Nepal." *Landscape Ecology* 23(1) (January): 41–54.

Namara, Agrippinah. 2006. "From Paternalism to Real Partnership with Local Communities? Experiences from Bwindi Impenetrable National Park (Uganda)." *Africa Development* 31(2):39–68.

Namubiru, Evelyn Lwanga. 2008. "Coping with Top-Down Institutional Changes in Forestry." PhD diss., Indiana University.

Neiland, Arthur E., S. Jaffry, B.M.B. Ladu, M. T. Sarch, and S. P. Madakan. 2000. "Inland Fisheries of North East Nigeria Including the Upper River Benue, Lake Chad and the Nguru-Gashua Wetlands I: Characterisation and Analysis of Planning Suppositions." *Fisheries Research* 48(3) (October): 229–43.

Neiland, Arthur E., Sunday P. Madakan, and Christopher Béné. 2005. "Traditional Management Systems, Poverty and Change in the Arid Zone Fisheries of Northern Nigeria." *Journal of Agrarian Change* 5(1) (January): 117–48.

Neiland, Arthur E., J. Weeks, S. P. Madakan, and B.M.B. Ladu. 2000. "Inland Fisheries of North East Nigeria Including the Upper River Benue, Lake Chad and the Nguru-Gashua Wetlands II: Fisheries Management at Village Level." *Fisheries Research* 48(3) (October): 245–61.

Netting, Robert McC. 1972. "Of Men and Meadows: Strategies of Alpine Land Use." *Anthropological Quarterly* 45:132–44.

———. 1981. *Balancing on an Alp: Ecological Change and Continuity in a Swiss Mountain Community*. New York: Cambridge University Press.

Nikiforakis, Nikos. 2008. "Punishment and Counter-Punishment in Public Good Games: Can We Really Govern Ourselves?" *Journal of Public Economics* 92(1–2):91–112.

Nikiforakis, Nikos, and Hans-Theo Normann. 2008. "A Comparative Statics Analysis of Punishment in Public-Good Experiments." *Experimental Economics* 11:358–69.

North, Douglass C. 1990. *Institutions, Institutional Change, and Economic Performance*. New York: Cambridge University Press.

North, Douglass C., and Robert P. Thomas. 1973. *The Rise of the Western World: A New Economic History*. New York: Cambridge University Press.

Nowak, Martin A. 2006. "Five Rules for the Evolution of Cooperation." *Science* 314:1560–63.

Nowak, Martin A., Sebastian Bonhoeffer, and Robert M. May. 1994. "Spatial Games and the Maintenance of Cooperation." *Proceedings of the National Academy of Sciences* 91(11):4877–81.

Nowak, Martin A., and Robert M. May. 1992. "Evolutionary Games and Spatial Chaos." *Nature* 359(6398):826–29.

Nowak, Martin A., and Karl Sigmund. 1998. "Evolution of Indirect Reciprocity by Image Scoring." *Nature* 393(6685):573–77.

NRC (National Research Council) 1986. *Proceedings of the Conference on Common Property Resource Management.* Washington, DC: National Academies Press.

———. 2002. *The Drama of the Commons.* Committee on the Human Dimensions of Global Change. Elinor Ostrom, Thomas Dietz, Nives Dolšak, Paul Stern, Susan Stonich, and Elke Weber, eds. Washington, DC: National Academies Press.

Nugent, Jeffrey B., and Nicholas Sanchez. 1999. "The Local Variability of Rainfall and Tribal Institutions: The Case of Sudan." *Journal of Economic Behavior and Organization* 39:263–91.

Oakerson, Ronald. 1986. "A Model for the Analysis of Common Property Problems." In *Proceedings of the Conference on Common Property Resource Management,* National Research Council, 13–30. Washington, DC: National Academies Press.

Oerlemans, Natasia, and Gerald Assouline. 2004. "Enhancing Farmers' Networking Strategies for Sustainable Development." *Journal of Cleaner Production* 12(5) (June): 469–78.

O'Hara, Sarah L., and Tim Hannan. 1999. "Irrigation and Water Management in Turkmenistan: Past Systems, Present Problems and Future Scenarios." *Europe-Asia Studies* 51(1) (January): 21–41.

Ohtsuki Hisashi, Christoph Hauert, Erez Lieberman, and Martin A. Nowak. 2006. "A Simple Rule for the Evolution of Cooperation on Graphs and Social Networks." *Nature* 441(7092):502–5.

Oliver, Pamela. 1980. "Rewards and Punishments as Selective Incentives for Collective Action: Theoretical Investigations." *American Journal of Sociology* 85(6):1356–75.

Olson, Mancur. 1965. *The Logic of Collective Action: Public Goods and the Theory of Groups.* Cambridge, MA: Harvard University Press.

———. 2000. *Power and Prosperity: Outgrowing Communist and Capitalist Dictatorships.* New York: Basic Books.

Orbell, John M., Tomonori Morikawa, Jason Hartwig, James Hanley, and Nicholas Allen. 2004. "'Machiavellian' Intelligence as a Basis for the Evolution of Cooperative Dispositions." *American Political Science Review* 98(1):1–15.

Orbell, John M., Alphons J. C. van de Kragt, and Robin M. Dawes. 1988. "Explaining Discussion-Induced Cooperation." *Journal of Personality and Social Psychology* 54:811–19.

Ortmann, Andrea, Gerd Gigerenzer, Bernhard Borges, and Daniel G. Goodstein. 2008. "The Recognition Heuristic: A Fast and Frugal Way to Investment Choice?" In *Handbook of Experimental Economics Results,* vol. 1, ed. Charles L. Plott and Vernon L. Smith, 993–1003. Amsterdam: North Holland.

O'Shea, J. M. 1989. "The Role of Wild Resources in Small-Scale Agricultural Systems: Tales from the Lakes and the Plains." In *Bad Year Economics: Cultural Responses to Risk and Uncertainty*, ed. Paul Halsted and John O'Shea, 57–67. New York: Cambridge University Press.

Ostrom, Elinor. 1986. "Issues of Definition and Theory: Some Conclusions and Hypotheses." In *Proceedings of the Conference on Common Property Resource Management*, ed. National Research Council, 599–615. Washington, DC: National Academies Press.

———. 1990. *Governing the Commons: The Evolution of Institutions for Collective Action.* New York: Cambridge University Press.

———. 1992. "The Rudiments of a Theory of the Origins, Survival, and Performance of Common-Property Institutions." In *Making the Commons Work: Theory, Practice, and Policy*, ed. Daniel W. Bromley et al., 293–318. San Francisco, CA: ICS Press.

———. 1996. "Incentives, Rules of the Game, and Development." In *Proceedings of the Annual World Bank Conference on Development Economics 1995*, 207–34. Washington, DC: The World Bank.

———. 1998. "A Behavioral Approach to the Rational Choice Theory of Collective Action." *American Political Science Review* 92(1) (March): 1–22.

———. 1999. "Self-Governance and Forest Resources." CIFOR Occasional Paper no. 20. Bogor, Indonesia: Center for International Forestry Research.

———. 2000. "Collective Action and the Evolution of Social Norms." *Journal of Economic Perspectives* 14(3) (Summer): 137–58.

———. 2001. "Reformulating the Commons." In *Protecting the Commons: A Framework for Resource Management in the Americas*, ed. Joanna Burger, Elinor Ostrom, Richard Norgaard, David Policansky, and Bernard Goldstein, 17–41. Washington, DC: Island Press.

———. 2005. *Understanding Institutional Diversity.* Princeton, NJ: Princeton University Press.

———. 2006. "Converting Threats into Opportunities." *PS: Political Science and Politics* 39(1) (January): 3–12.

———. 2007. "A Diagnostic Approach for Going beyond Panaceas." *Proceedings of the National Academy of Sciences* 104:15181–87.

———. 2009a. "Design Principles of Robust Property Rights Institutions: What Have We Learned?" In *Property Rights and Land Policies*, ed. Gregory K. Ingram and Yu-Hung Hong, 25–51. Cambridge, MA: Lincoln Institute of Land Policy.

———. 2009b. "A General Framework for Analyzing Sustainability of Social-Ecological Systems." *Science* 325(5939) (24 July): 419–22.

Ostrom, Elinor, Arun Agrawal, William Blomquist, Edella Schlager, and Shui Yan Tang. 1989. *CPR Coding Manual.* Bloomington: Indiana University, Workshop in Political Theory and Policy Analysis.

Ostrom, Elinor, Paul Benjamin, and Ganesh Shivakoti. 1994. "Use of Case Studies and Structural Coding in a Relational Database for Storage and Analysis of Irrigation Institutions and Systems in Nepal." In *From Farmers' Fields to Data Fields and Back: A Synthesis of Participatory Information Systems for Irrigation and Other Resources,* ed. Jennifer Sowerwine, Ganesh Shivakoti,

Ujjwal Pradhan, Ashutosh Shukla, and Elinor Ostrom, 49–68. Proceedings of an International Workshop held at the Institute of Agriculture and Animal Science (IAAS), Rampur, Nepal, March 21–26, 1993. Colombo, Sri Lanka: International Irrigation Management Institute (IIMI), and Rampur, Nepal: IAAS.

Ostrom, Elinor, and Roy Gardner. 1993. "Coping with Asymmetries in the Commons: Self-Governing Irrigation Systems Can Work." *Journal of Economic Perspectives* 7(4) (Fall): 93–112.

Ostrom, Elinor, Roy Gardner, and James Walker. 1994. *Rules, Games, and Common-Pool Resources*. Ann Arbor: University of Michigan Press.

Ostrom, Elinor, and Marco A. Janssen. 2004. "Multi-Level Governance and Resilience of Social-Ecological Systems." In *Globalisation, Poverty and Conflict: A Critical 'Development' Reader,* ed. M. Spoor, 239–59. Dordrecht, the Netherlands: Kluwer.

Ostrom, Elinor, and Harini Nagendra. 2006. "Insights on Linking Forests, Trees, and People from the Air, on the Ground, and in the Laboratory." *Proceedings of the National Academy of Sciences* 13(51) (December): 19224–31.

———. 2007. "Tenure Alone Is Not Sufficient: Monitoring Is Essential." *Environmental Economics and Policy Studies* 8(3):175–99.

Ostrom, Elinor, Larry Schroeder, and Susan Wynne. 1993. *Institutional Incentives and Sustainable Development: Infrastructure Policies in Perspective*. Boulder, CO: Westview Press.

Ostrom, Elinor, and James M. Walker. 1991. "Communication in a Commons: Cooperation without External Enforcement." In *Laboratory Research in Political Economy,* ed. Thomas R. Palfrey, 287–322. Ann Arbor: University of Michigan Press.

Ostrom Elinor, James M. Walker, and Roy Gardner. 1992. "Covenants with and without a Sword: Self-Governance Is Possible." *American Political Science Review* 86(2):404–17.

Ostrom, Vincent. 2008a. *The Intellectual Crisis in American Public Administration*. 3rd ed. Tuscaloosa: University of Alabama Press.

———. 2008b. *The Political Theory of a Compound Republic: Designing the American Experiment*. 3rd ed. Lanham, MD: Lexington Books.

Ostrom, Vincent, and Elinor Ostrom. 1977. "Public Goods and Public Choices." In *Alternatives for Delivering Public Services: Toward Improved Performance,* ed. E. S. Savas, 7–49. Boulder, CO: Westview Press.

Oyono, Phil René. 2004a. "The Social and Organisational Roots of Ecological Uncertainties in Cameroon's Forest Management Decentralisation Model." *European Journal of Development Research* 16(1) (March): 174–91.

———. 2004b. "One Step Forward, Two Steps Back? Paradoxes of Natural Resources Management Decentralisation in Cameroon." *Journal of Modern African Studies* 42(1):91–111.

Paavola, Jouni, and W. Neil Adger. 2005. "Institutional Ecological Economics." *Ecological Economics* 53(3):353–68.

Pacheco, Diego. 2007. "An Institutional Analysis of Decentralization and Indigenous Timber Management in Common-Property Forests of Bolivia's Lowlands." PhD diss., Indiana University.

Pacheco, Pablo. 2004. "What Lies behind Decentralisation? Forest, Powers and Actors in Lowland Bolivia." *European Journal of Development Research* 16(1) (March): 90–109.

Pagdee, Adcharaporn, Yeon-Su Kim, and P. J. Daugherty. 2006. "What Makes Community Forest Management Successful: A Meta-Study from Community Forests throughout the World." *Society and Natural Resources* 19(1) (January): 33–52.

Page, Scott. 2007. *The Difference: How The Power of Diversity Creates Better Groups, Firms, Schools, and Societies.* Princeton, NJ: Princeton University Press.

Pahl-Wostl, Claudia. 2002. "Participative and Stakeholder-Based Policy Design, Evaluation and Modeling Processes." *Integrated Assessment* 3:3–14.

Palfrey, Thomas R., and Howard Rosenthal. 1988. "Private Incentives in Social Dilemmas: The Effects of Incomplete Information and Altruism." *Journal of Public Economics* 35:309–32.

Parayil, Govindan, and Florence Tong. 1998. "Pasture-Led to Logging-Led Deforestation in the Brazilian Amazon: The Dynamics of Socio-Environmental Change." *Global Environmental Change* 8(1) (April): 63–79.

Parker, Dawn C., Stephen M. Manson, Marco A. Janssen, Matthew J. Hoffmann, and Peter J. Deadman. 2003. "Multi-Agent Systems for the Simulation of Land-Use and Land-Cover Change: A Review." *Annals of the Association of American Geographers* 93(2):313–37.

Peluso, Nancy L., and Peter Vandergeest. 1995. "Social Aspects of Forestry in Southeast Asia: A Review of Postwar Trends in the Scholarly Literature." *Journal of Southeast Asian Studies* 26(1) (March): 196–218.

Pender, John, Pamela Jagger, Ephraim Nkonya, and Dick Sserunkuuma. 2004. "Development Pathways and Land Management in Uganda." *World Development* 32(5) (May): 767–92.

Pierson, Paul. 2003. "Big, Slow-Moving, and . . . Invisible: Macrosocial Processes in the Study of Comparative Politics." In *Comparative Historical Analysis in the Social Sciences,* ed. James Mahoney and Dietrich Rueschemeyer, 177–207. New York: Cambridge University Press.

Pinckney, Thomas C., and Peter K. Kimuyu. 1994. "Land Tenure Reform in East Africa: Good, Bad or Unimportant?" *Journal of African Economies* 3(1) (April): 1–28.

Pitt, Mark A., In Jae Myung, and Shaobo Zhang. 2002. "Toward a Method of Selecting among Computational Models of Cognition." *Psychological Review* 109(3):472–91.

Platt, Jennifer. 1986. *A History of Sociological Research Methods in America, 1920–1960.* New York: Cambridge University Press.

Platteau, Jean-Philippe. 2003. "Community-Based Development in the Context of Within Group Heterogeneity. " Paper presented at the Annual Bank Conference on Development Economics, Bangalore, India.

Plott, Charles R., and David P. Porter. 1996. "Market Architectures and Institutional Testbedding: An Experiment with Space Station Pricing Policies." *Journal of Economic Behavior and Organization* 31(2):237–72.

Pokorny, Benno, and Heiner Schanz. 2003. "Empirical Determination of Political Cultures as a Basis for Effective Coordination of Forest Management Systems." *Society and Natural Resources* 16(10) (November): 887–908.

Pontusson, Jonas. 2007. "Methods in Comparative Political Economy." *Comparative Social Research* 24:325–33.

Posner, Richard. 1975. *Economic Analysis of Law*. Boston, MA: Little, Brown.

Poteete, Amy R. 2001. "The International Forestry Resources and Institutions (IFRI) Research Program and the Search for Communal Management of Forest Resources." Special issue on Non-Timber Forest Products, *EFTRN (European Tropical Forestry Research Network) News* 32 (Winter): 73–75.

————. 2002. "Exclusion as a Strategy for Regulating the Use of Forest Resources." In *Institutions for Sustainable Management,* ed. Paul O. Ongugo, Jane W. Njuguna, and Serah W. Mwanyiky, 52–72. Proceedings of the 2nd Biennial Meeting of the International Forestry Resources and Institutions (IFRI) Research Network held at Kenya Forestry Research Institute (KEFRI), Nairobi, Kenya, June 23–28, 2002. Nairobi: KEFRI.

————. 2003a. "Ideas, Interests, and Institutions: Challenging the Property Rights Paradigm in Botswana." *Governance* 16(4) (October): 527–57.

————. 2003b. "When Professionalism Clashes with Local Particularities: Ecology, Elections and Procedural Arrangements in Botswana." *Journal of Southern African Studies* 29(2) (June): 461–85.

————. 2009. "Defining Political Community and Rights to Natural Resources in Botswana." *Development and Change* 40(2) (March): 281–305.

Poteete, Amy R., and Elinor Ostrom. 2004a. "Heterogeneity, Group Size and Collective Action: The Role of Institutions in Forest Management." *Development and Change* 35(3) (June): 437–61.

————. 2004b. "In Pursuit of Comparable Concepts and Data about Collective Action." *Agricultural Systems* 82(3) (December): 215–32.

————. 2008. "Fifteen Years of Empirical Research on Collective Action in Natural Resource Management: Struggling to Build Large-N Databases Based on Qualitative Research." *World Development* 36(1) (January): 176–95.

Poteete, Amy R., and David Welch. 2004. "Institutional Development in the Face of Complexity: Constructing Systems for Managing Forest Resources." *Human Ecology* 32(3) (June): 279–311.

Przeworski, Adam, and Henry Teune. 1970. *The Logic of Comparative Social Inquiry*. New York: Wiley.

Quinn, Claire H. 2001. "Review of Common Pool Resources in Semi-Arid Tanzania." Common Pool Resources Project, Centre for Law and Policy, University of York. http://www.york.ac.uk/res/celp/webpages/projects/cpr/tanzania/tanzania.htm.

Quinn, Claire H., Meg Huby, Hilda Kiwasila, and Jon C. Lovett. 2003. "Local Perceptions of Risk to Livelihood in Semi-Arid Tanzania." *Journal of Environmental Management* 68(2) (June): 111–19.

————. 2007. "Design Principles and Common-Pool Resource Management: An Institutional Approach to Evaluating Community Management in Semi-Arid Tanzania." *Journal of Environmental Management* 84:100–13.

Rabin, Matthew. 1993. "Incorporating Fairness in Game Theory and Economics." *American Economic Review* 83:1281–1302.

Ragin, Charles C. 1987. *The Comparative Method: Moving beyond Qualitative and Quantitative Strategies*. Berkeley and Los Angeles: University of California Press.

———. 1992. "Introduction: Cases of 'What Is a Case'?" In *What Is a Case? Exploring the Foundations of Social Inquiry,* ed. Charles C. Ragin and Howard S. Becker, 1–17. New York: Cambridge University Press.

———. 2000. *Fuzzy-Set Social Science*. Chicago: University of Chicago Press.

Ragin, Charles C., and Howard S. Becker. 1992. *What Is a Case? Exploring the Foundations of Social Inquiry*. New York: Cambridge University Press.

Ramnath, Madhu. 2001. "Conflicting Perspectives of Forest Management in Bastar, Central India." *Natural Resources Forum* 25(3) (August): 245–56.

Rangan, Haripriya. 1997. "Property vs. Control: The State and Forest Management in the Indian Himalaya." *Development and Change* 28(1) (January): 71–94.

Rapoport, Anatol, and A. M. Chammah. 1965. *Prisoner's Dilemma: A Study in Conflict and Cooperation*. Ann Arbor: University of Michigan Press.

Rawls, John. 1971. *A Theory of Justice*. Cambridge, MA: Harvard University Press.

Reed, Jeffrey G., and Pam M. Baxter. 1994. "Using Reference Databases." In *The Handbook of Research Synthesis,* ed. Harris Cooper and Larry V. Hedges, 57–70. New York: Russell Sage Foundation.

Reeson, Andrew F., and John G. Tisdell. 2008. "Institutions, Motivations and Public Goods: An Experimental Test of Motivational Crowding." *Journal of Economic Behavior and Organization* 68(1) (October): 273–81.

Regmi, Ashok. 2007. "The Role of Group Heterogeneity in Collective Action: A Look at the Intertie between Irrigation and Forests. Case Studies from Chitwan, Nepal." PhD diss., Indiana University.

Resnick, Paul, Richard Zeckhauser, John Swanson, and Kate Lockwood. 2006. "The Value of Reputation on eBay: A Controlled Experiment." *Experimental Economics* 9(2):79–101.

Resosudarmo, Ida Aju Pradnja. 2004. "Closer to People and Trees: Will Decentralisation Work for the People and the Forests of Indonesia?" *European Journal of Development Research* 16(1) (March): 110–33.

Ribot, Jesse, Arun Agrawal, and Anne Larson. 2006. "Recentralizing While Decentralizing: How National Governments Reappropriate Forest Resources." *World Development* 34(11) (November): 1864–86.

Ribot, Jesse, Ashwini Chhatre, and Tomila Lankina. 2008. "Introduction: Institutional Choice and Recognition in the Formation and Consolidation of Local Democracy." *Conservation and Society* 6(1):1–11.

Ribot, Jesse C., and Nancy Peluso. 2003. "A Theory of Access." *Rural Sociology* 68(2) (June): 153–81.

Richards, Diana. 2001. "Reciprocity and Shared Knowledge Structures in a Prisoner's Dilemma Game." *Journal of Conflict Resolution* 45:621–35.

Richards, Michael. 1997. "Common Property Resource Institutions and Forest

Management in Latin America." *Development and Change* 28 (January): 95–117.

Richerson, Peter J., and Robert Boyd. 2005. *Not by Genes Alone: How Culture Transformed Human Evolution.* Chicago: University of Chicago Press.

Ridley, M. 1998. *The Origins of Virtue: Human Instincts and the Evolution of Cooperation.* New York: Penguin Books.

Riolo, Rick L., Michael D. Cohen, and Robert Axelrod 2001. "Evolution of Cooperation without Reciprocity." *Nature* 414:441–43.

Riseth, Jan Åge. 2007. "An Indigenous Perspective on National Parks and Sámi Reindeer Management in Norway." *Geographical Research* 45(2):177–95.

Robbins, Paul F., Anil K. Chhangani, Jennifer Rice, Erika Trigosa, and S. M. Mohnot. 2007. "Enforcement Authority and Vegetation Change at Kumbhalgarh Wildlife Sanctuary, Rajasthan, India." *Environmental Management* 40:365–78.

Rocheleau, Dianne. 1995. "Maps, Numbers, Text, and Context: Mixing Methods in Feminist Political Ecology." *Professional Geographer* 47(4) (November): 458–66.

Rodrigues, António, Heinz Koeppl, Hisashi Ohtsuki, and Akiko Satake. 2009. "A Game Theoretical Model of Deforestation in Human Environment Relationships." *Journal of Theoretical Biology* 258:127–34.

Rogowski, Ronald. 2004. "How Inference in the Social (but Not the Physical) Sciences Neglects Theoretical Anomaly." In *Rethinking Social Inquiry: Diverse Tools, Shared Standards,* ed. Henry E. Brady and David Collier, 75–83. Lanham, MD: Rowman & Littlefield.

Röling, Niels. 1996. "Towards an Interactive Agricultural Science." *European Journal of Agricultural Education and Extension* 2(4):35–48.

Rosenthal, David A., William T. Hoyt, James M. Ferrin, Susan Miller, and Nicholas D. Cohen. 2006. "Advanced Methods in Meta-Analytic Research: Applications and Implications for Rehabilitation Counseling Research." *Rehabilitation Counseling Bulletin* 49(4) (Summer): 234–46.

Rosenthal, MaryLu C. 1994. "The Fugitive Literature." In *The Handbook of Research Synthesis,* ed. Harris Cooper and Larry V. Hedges, 85–94. New York: Russell Sage Foundation.

Rosenthal, R., and M. R. DiMatteo. 2001. "Meta-Analysis: Recent Developments in Quantitative Methods for Literature Reviews." *Annual Review of Psychology* 52:59–82.

Rothgeb, John, and Betsy Burger. 2009. "Tenure Standards in Political Science Departments: Results from a Survey of Department Chairs." *PS: Political Science and Politics* 42(3) (July): 513–35.

Rothstein, Bo. 2005. *Social Traps and the Problem of Trust: Theories of Institutional Design.* Cambridge: Cambridge University Press.

Rudel, Thomas K. 2005. *Tropical Forests: Regional Paths of Destruction and Regeneration in the Late Twentieth Century.* New York: Columbia University Press.

———. 2008. "Meta-Analyses of Case Studies: A Method for Studying Regional and Global Environmental Change." *Global Environmental Change* 18(1) (February): 18–25.

Rudel, Thomas K., and Jill Roper. 1996. "Regional Patterns and Historical Trends in Tropical Deforestation, 1976–1990: A Qualitative Comparative Analysis." *Ambio* 5(3):160–66.

Rudolph, Susanne Hoeber. 1996. "The Role of Theory in Comparative Politics: A Symposium." *World Politics* 48(1):21–28.

Rueschemeyer, Dietrich. 2003. "Can One or a Few Cases Yield Theoretical Gains?" In *Comparative Historical Analysis in the Social Sciences*, ed. James Mahoney and Dietrich Rueschemeyer, 305–36. New York: Cambridge University Press.

Ruttan, Lore M. 2006. "Sociocultural Heterogeneity and the Commons." *Current Anthropology* 47(5) (October): 843–53.

———. 2008. "Economic Heterogeneity and the Commons: Effects on Collective Action and Collective Goods Provisioning." *World Development* 36(5) (May): 969–85.

Saijo, Tatsuyoshi, and Hideki Nakamura. 1995. "The 'Spite' Dilemma in Voluntary Contribution Mechanism Experiments." *Journal of Conflict Resolution* 39:535–60.

Salafsky, Nick, Daniel Salzer, Alison Stattersfield, Craig Hilton-Taylor, Rachel Neugarten, Stuart Butchart, Ben Collen, Neil Cox, Lawrence Master, Sheila O'Connor, and David Wilkie. 2008. "A Standard Lexicon for Biodiversity Conservation: Unified Classifications of Threats and Actions." *Conservation Biology* 22(4):897–911.

Sally, David. 1995. "Conservation and Cooperation in Social Dilemmas: A Meta-Analysis of Experiments from 1958 to 1992." *Rationality and Society* 7:58–92.

Salmon, Timothy C. 2001. "An Evaluation of Econometric Models of Adaptive Learning." *Econometrica* 69(6):1597–1628.

Samad, M., and Douglas Vermillion. 1999. "An Assessment of the Impact of Participatory Irrigation Management in Sri Lanka." *International Journal of Water Resources Development* 15(1/2) (March): 219–40.

Sampson, Robert J., Stephen W. Raudenbush, and Felton Earls. 1997. "Neighborhoods and Violent Crime: A Multilevel Study of Collective Efficacy." *Science* 277:918–24.

Sánchez, Angel, and José A. Cuesta. 2005. "Altruism May Arise from Individual Selection." *Journal of Theoretical Biology* 235(2):233–40.

Sandberg, Audun. 2008. "Collective Rights in a Modernizing North: On Institutionalizing Sámi and Local Rights to Land and Water in Northern Norway." *International Journal of the Commons* 2(2):269–87.

Sandler, Todd. 1992. *Collective Action: Theory and Applications*. Ann Arbor: University of Michigan Press.

Santos, Francisco C., and Jorge M. Pacheco. 2005. "Scale-Free Networks Provide a Unifying Framework for the Emergence of Cooperation." *Physical Review Letters* 95, http://jorgem.pacheco.googlepages.com/055.pdf.

Sarch, Marie-Thérèse. 1996. "Fishing and Farming at Lake Chad: Overcapitalisation, Opportunities, and Fisheries Management." *Journal of Environmental Management* 48(4) (December): 305–20.

Sarch, Marie-Thérèse, Arthur E. Neiland, Sunday P. Madakan, and Bernard

Ladu. 1996. "Traditional Management of Artisanal Fisheries in North East Nigeria: A Research Framework." CEMARE Research Paper 100. University of Portsmouth, UK: Centre for the Economics and Management of Aquatic Resources.

Sartori, Giovanni. 1991. "Comparing and Miscomparing." *Journal of Theoretical Politics* 3(3) (July): 243–57.

Satz, D., and J. Ferejohn. 1994. "Rational Choice and Social Theory." *Journal of Philosophy* 91(2):71–87.

Saunders, Carol D. 2003. "The Emerging Field of Conservation Psychology." *Human Ecology Review* 10(2):137–49.

Scharpf, Fritz W. 2000. "Institutions in Comparative Policy Research." *Comparative Political Studies* 33(6–7) (September): 762–90.

Scheffer, Marten, Stephen A. Carpenter, Jonathan A. Foley, Carl Folke, and Brian Walker. 2001. "Catastrophic Shifts in Ecosystems." *Nature* 413:591–96.

Schelling, Thomas C. 1960. *The Strategy of Conflict.* Cambridge, MA: Harvard University Press.

———. 1978. *Micromotives and Macrobehavior.* New York: Norton.

Schlager, Edella. 1990. "Model Specification and Policy Analysis: The Governance of Coastal Fisheries." PhD diss., Indiana University.

———. 1994. "Fishers' Institutional Responses to Common-Pool Resource Dilemmas." In *Rules, Games, and Common-Pool Resources,* ed. Elinor Ostrom, Roy Gardner, and James M. Walker, 247–66. Ann Arbor: University of Michigan Press.

———. 2007. "A Comparison of Frameworks, Theories, and Models of Policy Processes." In *Theories of the Policy Process*, 2nd ed., ed. Paul A. Sabatier, 293–319. Boulder, CO: Westview Press.

Schlager, Edella, William Blomquist, and Shui Yan Tang. 1994. "Mobile Flows, Storage, and Self-Organized Institutions for Governing Common-Pool Resources." *Land Economics* 70(3) (August): 294–317.

Schlager, Edella, and Elinor Ostrom. 1992. "Property-Rights Regimes and Natural Resources: A Conceptual Analysis." *Land Economics* 68(3) (August): 249–69.

Schluessler, Rudolf. 1989. "Exit Threats and Cooperation under Anonymity." *Journal of Conflict Resolution* 33:728–49.

Schoonmaker Freudenberger, Mark. 1993. "Regenerating the Gum Arabic Economy: Local-Level Resource Management in Northern Senegal." In *In Defense of Livelihood: Comparative Studies on Environmental Action,* ed. John Friedmann and Haripriya Rangan, 52–78. West Hartford, CT: Kumarian Press.

Schweik, Charles M. 1998. "The Spatial and Temporal Analysis of Forest Resources and Institutions." PhD diss., Indiana University.

———. 2000. "Optimal Foraging, Institutions, and Forest Change: A Case from Nepal." In *People and Forests: Communities, Institutions, and Governance,* ed. Clark C. Gibson, Margaret A. McKean, and Elinor Ostrom, 99–134. Cambridge, MA: MIT Press.

Schweik, Charles M., and Robert English. 2007. "Tragedy of the FOSS Commons? Investigating the Institutional Designs of Free/Libre and Open Source

Software Projects." *First Monday* 12(2), http://firstmonday.org/htbin/cgiwrap/bin/ojs/index.php/fm/issue/view/224.

Scott, Anthony D. 1955. "The Fishery: The Objectives of Sole Ownership." *Journal of Political Economy* 63:116–24.

Scott, James C. 1976. *The Moral Economy of the Peasant: Rebellion and Subsistence in Southeast Asia.* New Haven, CT: Yale University Press.

Scott, Penny. 1998. *From Conflict to Collaboration: People and Forests at Mount Elgon, Uganda.* Gland, Switzerland, and Cambridge, UK: IUCN.

Scruggs, Lyle. 2007. "What's Multiple Regression Got to Do with It?" *Comparative Social Research* 24:309–23.

Sefton, Martin, Robert Shupp, and James M. Walker. 2007. "The Effect of Rewards and Sanctions in Provision of Public Goods." *Economic Inquiry* 45(4):671–90.

Selten, Reinhard, Michael Mitzkewitz, and Gerald R. Uhlich. 1997. "Duopoly Strategies Programmed by Experienced Players." *Econometrica* 65:517–55.

Sen, Amartya. 1977. "Rational Fools: A Critique of the Behavioral Foundations of Economic Theory." *Philosophy and Public Affairs* 6(4):317–44.

Sengupta, Nirmal. 1991. *Managing Common Property: Irrigation in India and the Philippines.* New Delhi: Sage.

Shalev, Michael. 2007. "Limits and Alternatives to Multiple Regression in Comparative Research." *Comparative Social Research* 24:261–308.

Shankar, Anisha, and Charles Pavitt. 2002. "Resource and Public Goods Dilemmas: A New Issue for Communication Research." *Review of Communication* 2(3):251–72.

Shelby, Lori B., and Jerry J. Vaske. 2008. "Understanding Meta-Analysis: A Review of the Methodological Literature." *Leisure Sciences: An Interdisciplinary Journal* 30(2) (March): 96–110.

Shepsle, Kenneth A. 1989. "Studying Institutions: Some Lessons from the Rational Choice Approach." *Journal of Theoretical Politics* 1:131–49.

Shipton, Parker. 1988. "The Kenyan Land Tenure Reform: Misunderstandings in the Public Creation of Private Property." In *Land and Society in Contemporary Africa,* ed. R. E. Downs and S. P. Reyna, 91–135. Hanover, NH: University Press of New England.

Shivakoti, Ganesh P., and Elinor Ostrom, eds. 2002. *Improving Irrigation Governance and Management in Nepal.* Oakland, CA: ICS Press.

Siegel, Scott, with Ariel Ahram, Julia Azari, Ashwini Chhatre, Bridget Coggins, Jana Grittersova, Matthew Ingram, Matthew Lieber, Claire Metelits, Tom Pepkinksy, Andrew Pieper, Karthika Sasikumar, and Prerna Singh. 2007. "Trends in Multi-Method Research: Sailing Ahead, Reckoning with Old Risks and New." *Qualitative Methods* 5(1) (Spring): 24–28.

Sigelman, Lee. 2009. "Are Two (or Three or Four . . . or Nine) Heads Better Than One? Collaboration, Multidisciplinarity, and Publishability." *PS: Political Science and Politics* 42(3) (July): 507–12.

Signorino, Curtis S. 1999. "Strategic Interaction and the Statistical Analysis of International Conflict." *American Political Science Review* 93(2) (June): 279–97.

Sikor, Thomas, and Christian Lund. 2009. "Access and Property: A Question of Power and Authority." *Development and Change* 40(1) (January): 1–22.

Silva-Forsberg, Maria Clara. 1999. "Protecting an Urban Forest Reserve in the Amazon: A Multi-Scale Analysis of Edge Effects, Population Pressure, and Institutions." PhD diss., Indiana University.

Simon, Herbert A. 1955. "A Behavioural Model of Rational Choice." *Quarterly Journal of Economics* 69:99–188.

———. 1957. *Models of Man*. New York: Wiley.

———. 1985. *The Sciences of the Artificial*. Cambridge, MA: MIT Press.

———. 1999. "The Potlatch between Political Science and Economics." In *Competition and Cooperation: Conversations with Nobelists about Economics and Political Science*, ed. James Alt, Margaret Levi, and Elinor Ostrom, 112–19. New York: Russell Sage Foundation.

Singleton, Sara. 1999. "Commons Problems, Collective Action and Efficiency: Past and Present Institutions of Governance in Pacific Northwest Salmon Fisheries." *Journal of Theoretical Politics* 11(3):367–91.

Sjaastad, Espen, and Daniel W. Bromley. 1997. "Indigenous Land Rights in Sub-Saharan Africa: Appropriation, Security and Investment Demand." *World Development* 25(4) (April): 549–62.

Skocpol, Theda, and Margaret Somers. 1980. "The Uses of Comparative History in Macrosocial Inquiry." *Comparative Studies in Society and History* 22(2) (April): 174–97.

Slavin, Robert E. 1986. "Best-Evidence Synthesis: An Alternative to Meta-Analytic and Traditional Reviews." *Educational Researcher* 15 (November): 5–11.

Smajgl, Alex, Luis R. Izquierdo, and Marco Huigen. 2008. "Modeling Endogenous Rule Changes in an Institutional Context: The ADICO Sequence." *Advances in Complex Systems* 11(2):199–215.

Smajgl, Alex, Anne Leitch, and Tim Lynam. 2009. *Outback Institutions: An Application of the Institutional Analysis and Development (IAD) Framework to Four Case Studies in Australia's Outback*. Alice Springs, Australia: Desert Knowledge Cooperative Research Centre, DKCRC Report 31.

Smith, Rogers M. 2004. "Identities, Interests, and the Future of Political Science." *Perspectives on Politics* 2(2) (June): 301–12.

Smith, Vernon L. 1962. "An Experimental Study of Competitive Market Behavior." *Journal of Political Economy* 70:111–37.

———. 1982. "Microeconomic Systems as an Experimental Science." *American Economic Review* 72 (December): 923–55.

———. 2009. "Theory and Experiment: What Are the Questions?" *Journal of Economic Behavior and Organization*, doi:10.1016/j.jebo.2009.02.008.

Smith, Vernon L., and James M. Walker. 1993. "Monetary Rewards and Decision Cost in Experimental Economics." *Economic Inquiry* 31:245–61.

Snyder, Richard. 2001. "Scaling Down: The Subnational Comparative Method." *Studies in Comparative International Development* 36(1) (Spring): 93–110.

Somanathan, E., R. Prabhakar, and B. S. Mehta. 2002. "'Collective Action for Forest Conservation: Does Heterogeneity Matter?" New Delhi: Indian Statistical Institute. http://www.isid.ac.in/~planning/workingpapers/dp02-01.pdf.

Spoehr, A., ed. 1980. *Maritime Adaptations: Essays on Contemporary Fishing Communities*. Pittsburgh: University of Pittsburgh Press.

Stanley, E. Ann, Dan Ashlock, and Leigh Tesfatsion. 1994. "Iterated Prisoner's Dilemma with Choice and Refusal of Partners." In *Artificial Life III*, ed. Chris G. Langton, 131–76. Reading, MA: Addison-Wesley.

Stern, Paul C., Thomas Dietz, Nives Dolšak, Elinor Ostrom, and Susan Stonich. 2002. "Knowledge and Questions after 15 Years of Research." In *The Drama of the Commons*, National Research Council, ed. Committee on the Human Dimensions of Global Change, ed. Elinor Ostrom, Thomas Dietz, Nives Dolšak, Paul C. Stern, Susan Stonich, and Elke U. Weber, 445–86. Washington, DC: National Academies Press.

Sudtongkong, Chanyut, and Edward L. Webb. 2008. "Outcomes of State vs. Community-Based Mangrove Management in Southern Thailand." *Ecology and Society* 13(2):27, http://www.ecologyandsociety.org/vol13/iss2/art27/.

Sundar, Nandini. 2001. "Is Devolution Democratization?" *World Development* 29(12) (December): 2007–23.

Sutton, Alexander J., Fujian Song, Simon M. Gilbody, and Keith R. Abrams. 2000. "Modelling Publication Bias in Meta-Analysis: A Review." *Statistical Methods in Medical Research* 9:421–45.

Sztompka, P. 1999. *Trust: A Sociological Theory*. Cambridge: Cambridge University Press.

Tang, Shui Yan. 1992. *Institutions and Collective Action: Self-Governance in Irrigation*. San Francisco, CA: ICS Press.

———. 1994. "Institutions and Performance in Irrigation Systems." In *Rules, Games, and Common-Pool Resources,* ed. Elinor Ostrom, Roy Gardner, and James Walker, 225–45. Ann Arbor: University of Michigan Press.

Tarrow, Sidney. 2004. "Bridging the Quantitative-Qualitative Divide." In *Rethinking Social Inquiry: Diverse Tools, Shared Standards,* ed. Henry E. Brady and David Collier, 171–79. Lanham, MD: Rowman & Littlefield.

———. 2008. "Paired Comparison: Towards a Theory of Practice." Working Paper. Ithaca, NY: Cornell University.

Terborgh, John. 1999. *A Requiem for Nature*. Washington, DC: Island Press.

Tesfatsion, Leigh, and Kenneth L. Judd, eds. 2006. *Handbook of Computational Economics II: Agent-Based Computational Economics*. Oxford: Elsevier.

Thaler, Richard H., and Cass R. Sunstein. 2003. "Libertarian Paternalism." *American Economic Review* 93(2):175–79.

———. 2008. *Nudge*. New Haven, CT: Yale University Press.

Theesfeld, Insa. 2004. "Constraints on Collective Action in a Transitional Economy: The Case of Bulgaria's Irrigation Sector." *World Development* 32(2):251–71.

Thelen, Kathleen. 2003. "How Institutions Evolve: Insights from Comparative Historical Analysis." In *Comparative Historical Analysis in the Social Sciences,* ed. James Mahoney and Dietrich Rueschemeyer, 208–40. New York: Cambridge University Press.

Thompson, L. L., E. A. Mannix, and M. H. Bazerman. 1988. "Negotiation in Small Groups: Effects of Decision Rule, Agendas and Aspirations." *Journal of Personality and Social Psychology* 54:86–95.

Thompson, Paul M., Parvin Sultana, and Nurul Islam. 2003. "Lessons from Community Based Management of Floodplain Fisheries in Bangladesh." *Journal of Environmental Management* 69(3) (November): 307–21.

Thoms, Christopher A. 2004. "Self-Mediated Interactions among Community Forestry Actors in Nepal: A Political Ecology of the UK's Livelihoods and Forestry Programme." PhD diss., University of Michigan.

Thoms, Christopher A., Birendra K. Karna, and Mukunda B. Karmacharya. 2006. "Limitations of Leasehold Forestry for Poverty Alleviation in Nepal." *Society and Natural Resources* 19(10):931–38.

Thomson, James T., David Feeny, and Ronald J. Oakerson. 1992. "Institutional Dynamics: The Evolution and Dissolution of Common-Property Resource Management." In *Making the Commons Work: Theory, Practice, and Policy*, ed. Daniel W. Bromley et al., 129–60. San Francisco, CA: ICS Press.

Torgerson, Douglas. 1986. "Between Knowledge and Politics: Three Faces of Policy Analysis." *Policy Sciences* 19(1) (March): 33–59.

Trawick, Paul. 2001a. "The Moral Economy of Water: Equity and Antiquity in the Andean Commons." *American Anthropologist* 103(2) (June): 361–79.

———. 2001b. "Successfully Governing the Commons: Principles of Social Organization in an Andean Irrigation System." *Human Ecology* 29(1):1–25.

———. 2003. "Against the Privatization of Water: An Indigenous Model for Improving Existing Laws and Successfully Governing the Commons." *World Development* 31(6) (June): 977–96.

Tropp, Jacob. 2003. "Displaced People, Replaced Narratives: Forest Conflicts and Historical Perspectives in the Tsolo District, Transkei." *Journal of Southern African Studies* 29(1) (March): 207–33.

Tsebelis, George. 1989. "The Abuse of Probability in Political Analysis: The Robinson Crusoe Fallacy." *American Political Science Review* 83(1):77–91.

Tucker, Catherine M. 1999. "Private versus Common Property Forests: Forest Conditions and Tenure in a Honduran Community." *Human Ecology* 27(2):201–30.

———. 2004. "Community Institutions and Forest Management in Mexico's Monarch Butterfly Reserve." *Society and Natural Resources* 17(7) (August): 569–87.

Tucker, Catherine M., Darla Munroe, Harini Nagendra, and Jane Southworth. 2005. "Comparative Spatial Analyses of Forest Conservation and Change in Honduras and Guatemala." *Conservation and Society* 3(1):72–91.

Tucker, Catherine M., and Elinor Ostrom. 2005. "Multidisciplinary Research Relating Institutions and Forests." In *Seeing the Forests and the Trees: Human-Environment Interactions in Forest Ecosystems*, ed. Emilio F. Moran and Elinor Ostrom, 81–104. Cambridge, MA: MIT Press.

Tucker, Catherine M., J. C. Randolph, Tom Evans, Krister P. Andersson, Lauren Persha, and Glen M. Green. 2008. "An Approach to Assess Relative Degradation in Dissimilar Forests: Toward a Comparative Assessment of Institutional Outcomes." *Ecology and Society* 13(1):4, http://www.ecologyandsociety.org/vol13/iss1/art4/.

Turing, Alan. 1950. "Computing Machinery and Intelligence." *Mind* 59:433–60.

Turner, Matthew D. 1999. "Conflict, Environmental Change, and Social Institutions in Dryland Africa: Limitations of the Community Resource Management Approach." *Society and Natural Resources* 12(7) (October–November): 643–57.

Tvedten, Inge. 2002. "'If You Don't Fish, You Are Not a Caprivian': Freshwater Fisheries in Caprivi, Namibia." *Journal of Southern African Studies* 28(2) (June): 421–39.

Tversky, Amos, and Daniel Kahneman. 1981. "The Framing of Decisions and the Psychology of Choice." *Science* 211:453–58.

Twyman, Chasca. 2001. "Natural Resource Use and Livelihoods in Botswana's Wildlife Management Areas." *Applied Geography* 21(1) (January): 45–68.

Tyler, Tom. 2008. "Psychology and Institutional Design." *Review of Law and Economics* 4(3):801–87.

Vanberg, Viktor J., and Roger D. Congelton. 1992. "Rationality, Morality and Exit." *American Political Science Review* 86:418–31.

van Laerhoven, Frank. 2008. "Local Governance and the Challenge of Solving Collective Action Dilemmas." PhD diss., Indiana University.

van Steenbergen, Frank. 1995. "The Frontier Problem in Incipient Groundwater Management Regimes in Bolchistan (Pakistan)." *Human Ecology* 23(1) (March): 53–74.

Varughese, George. 1999. "Villagers, Bureaucrats, and Forests in Nepal: Designing Governance for a Complex Resource." PhD diss., Indiana University.

Varughese, George, and Elinor Ostrom. 2001. "The Contested Role of Heterogeneity in Collective Action: Some Evidence from Community Forestry in Nepal." *World Development* 29(5):747–65.

Vatn, Arild. 2005. *Institutions and the Environment.* Cheltenham, UK: Edward Elgar.

———. 2009. "Cooperative Behavior and Institutions." *Journal of Socio-Economics* 38:188–96.

Velez, Maria Alejandra, John K. Stranlund, and James J. Murphy. 2009. "What Motivates Common Pool Resource Users? Experimental Evidence from the Field." *Journal of Economic Behavior and Organization* 70:485–97.

Verplaetse, Jan, Sven Vanneste, and Johan Braeckman. 2007. "You Can Judge a Book by Its Cover: The Sequel. A Kernel of Truth in Predicting Cheating Detection." *Evolution and Human Behavior* 28:260–71.

Vogt, Nathan, Joseph Bahati, Jon Unruh, Glen Green, Abwoli Banana, William Gombya-Ssembajjwe, and Sean Sweeney. 2006. "Integrating Remote Sensing Data and Rapid Appraisals for Land-Cover Change Analyses in Uganda." *Land Degradation and Development* 17(1) (January/February): 31–43.

Vollan, Bjørn. 2008. "Socio-Ecological Explanations for Crowding-Out Effects from Economic Experiments in Southern Africa." *Ecological Economics* 67(4):560–73.

von Neumann, John, and Arthur W. Burks. 1966. *Theory of Self-Reproducing Automata.* Urbana: University of Illinois Press.

Wade, Michael J. 1977. "An Experimental Study of Group Selection." *Evolution* 31:134–53.

———. 1978. "A Critical Review of the Models of Group Selection." *Quarterly Review of Biology* 53:101–14.

Wade, Robert. 1994. *Village Republics: Economic Conditions for Collective Action in South India.* San Francisco, CA: ICS Press.

Wagner, John, and MaliaTalakai. 2007. "Customs, Commons, Property, and Ecology: Case Studies from Oceania." *Human Organization* 66(1):1–10.

Waichmann, Israel, and Till Requate. 2008. "Do Personality Traits Matter in Oligopoly Experiments?" Working Paper. Kiel, Germany: University of Kiel, Department of Economics.

Walker, James M., and Roy Gardner 1992. "Rent Dissipation and Probabilistic Destruction of Common-Pool Resource Environments: Experimental Evidence." *Economic Journal* 102:1149–61.

Walker, Kendra L. 2009. "Protected-Area Monitoring Dilemmas: A New Tool to Assess Success." *Conservation Biology* 23(5):1294–303.

Watts, Duncan J., and Steven H. Strogatz. 1998. "Collective Dynamics of 'Small-World' Networks." *Nature* 393:440–42.

Webb, Edward, and Lam Dorji. 2008. "Efficiency and Low Costs under Non-Limiting Supply." In *Promise, Trust, and Evolution: Managing the Commons of South Asia,* ed. Rucha Ghate, Narpat S. Jodha, and Pranab Mukhopadhyay, 352–69. Oxford: Oxford University Press.

Webb, Edward, and Ganesh P. Shivakoti, eds. 2008. *Decentralization, Forests and Rural Communities: Policy Outcomes in South and Southeast Asia.* New Delhi: Sage India.

Wedekind, Claus, and Manfred Milinski. 2000. "Cooperation through Image Scoring in Humans." *Science* 288:850–52.

Weinstein, Martin S. 2000. "Pieces of the Puzzle: Solutions for Community-Based Fisheries Management from Native Canadians, Japanese Cooperatives, and Common Property Researchers." *Georgetown International Environmental Law Review* 12(2):375–412.

Weissing, Franz, and Elinor Ostrom. 1993. "Irrigation Institutions and the Games Irrigators Play: Rule Enforcement on Government- and Farmer-Managed Systems." In *Games in Hierarchies and Networks: Analytical and Empirical Approaches to the Study of Governance Institutions,* ed. Fritz W. Scharpf, 387–428. Frankfurt: Campus Verlag; Boulder, CO: Westview Press. Reprinted in Michael McGinnis, *Polycentric Games and Institutions: Readings from the Workshop in Political Theory and Policy Analysis* (Ann Arbor: University of Michigan Press, 2000), pp. 366–98.

Wertime, Mary Beth, Elinor Ostrom, Clark Gibson, and Fabrice Lehoucq. 2007. "Field Manual, Version 13." International Forestry Resources and Institutions (IFRI) research program. http://sitemaker.umich.edu/ifri/files/ifri_manual.pdf.

Western, David. 1982. "The Environment and Ecology of Pastoralists in Arid Savannas." *Development and Change* 13(2) (April):183–211.

White, Howard D. 1994. "Scientific Communication and Literature Retrieval." In *The Handbook of Research Synthesis,* ed. Harris Cooper and Larry V. Hedges, 41–55. New York: Russell Sage Foundation.

Wiggins, Steven N., and Gary D. Libecap. 1987. "Firm Heterogeneities and Cartelization Efforts in Domestic Crude Oil." *Journal of Law, Economics, and Organization* 3:1–25.

Wilcox, Nathaniel T. 2006. "Theories of Learning in Games and Heterogeneity Bias." *Econometrica* 74(5):1271–92.

Wilke, H.A.M., David M. Messick, and Christel G. Rutte. 1986. *Experimental Social Dilemmas*. Frankfurt am Main: Peter Lang.

Wilmsen, Edwin N. 1989. *Land Filled with Flies: A Political Economy of the Kalahari*. Chicago: University of Chicago Press.

Wilson, David S. 1975. "A Theory of Group Selection." *Proceedings of the National Academy of Sciences* 72:143–46.

———. 1983. "The Group Selection Controversy: History and Current Status." *Annual Review of Ecology and Systematics* 14:159–87.

Wilson, Douglas C., Modesta Medard, Craig K. Harris, and David S. Wiley. 1999. "The Implications for Participatory Fisheries Management of Intensified Commercialization on Lake Victoria." *Rural Sociology* 64(4):554–72.

Wilson, James. 2002. "Scientific Uncertainty, Complex Systems, and the Design of Common-Pool Institutions." In *The Drama of the Commons*, National Research Council, ed. Committee on the Human Dimensions of Global Change, ed. Elinor Ostrom, Thomas Dietz, Nives Dolšak, Paul C. Stern, Susan Stonich, and Elke U. Weber, 327–59. Washington, DC: National Academies Press.

———. 2007. "Scale and Costs of Fishery Conservation." *International Journal of the Commons* 1(1):29–42.

Wilson, James, Liying Yan, and Carl Wilson. 2007. "The Precursors of Governance in the Maine Lobster Fishery." *Proceedings of the National Academy of Sciences* 104(39):15212–17.

Wilson, Paul N., and Gary D. Thompson. 1993. "Common Property and Uncertainty: Compensating Coalitions by Mexico's Pastoral *Ejidatarios*." *Economic Development and Cultural Change* 41(2):299–318.

Wolf, Eric R. 1957. "Closed Corporate Communities in Meso-America and Java." *Southwestern Journal of Anthropology* 13:1–18.

Woodhouse, Philip. 1995. "Water Rights and Rural Restructuring in South Africa: A Case Study from Eastern Transvaal." *International Journal of Water Resources Development* 11(4) (December): 527–44.

Wright, Sewall. 1945. "Tempo and Mode in Evolution: A Critical Review." *Ecology* 26:415–19.

Yamagishi, Toshio. 1986. "The Provision of a Sanctioning System as a Public Good." *Journal of Personality and Social Psychology* 51(1):110–16.

Yang, Baiyin. 2002. "Meta-Analysis Research and Theory-Building." *Advances in Developing Human Resources* 4(3) (August): 296–316.

Yin, R. K. 2002. *Case Study Research: Design and Methods*. Newbury Park, CA: Sage.

Yoder, Robert D. 1994. *Locally Managed Irrigation Systems*. Colombo, Sri Lanka: International Irrigation Management Institute.

Young, Emily. 2001. "State Intervention and Abuse of the Commons: Fisheries Development in Baja California Sur, Mexico." *Annals of the Association of American Geographers* 91(2) (June): 283–306.

Young, Oran. 2002. *The Institutional Dimensions of Environmental Change: Fit, Interplay and Scale.* Cambridge, MA: MIT Press.

———. 2006. "Vertical Interplay among Scale-Dependent Environmental and Resource Regimes." *Ecology and Society* 11(1): 27, http://www.ecologyand society.org/vol11/iss1/art27/.

Young, Oran, Frans Berkhout, Gilberto Gallopin, Marco A. Janssen, Elinor Ostrom, and Sander van der Leeuw. 2006. "The Globalization of Socio-Ecological Systems: An Agenda for Scientific Research." *Global Environmental Change* 16(3):304–16.

Young, Oran, L. A. King, and H. Schroeder, eds. 2008. *Institutions and Environmental Change.* Cambridge, MA: MIT Press.

Zahavi, Amotz. 1977. "The Cost of Honesty (Further Remarks on the Handicap Principle)." *Journal of Theoretical Biology* 67:603–5.

Zucker, Lynne G. 1986. "Production of Trust: Institutional Sources of Economic Structure, 1840–1920." In *Research in Organizational Behavior,* ed. Barry M. Staw and L. L. Cummings, 53–111. Greenwich, CT: JAI Press.

Index

and indigenous rights, 49; innovation of, 164–65; origin of, 189, 191–92; in use, 98. *See also* design principles
Runde, Audun, 226
Ruttan, Lore, 97–98

Sahel, 48
salience, 143
Sally, David, 109–10
Salmon, Timothy, 203
Sámi, 49
sample: bias, 77, 83–84; nonindependence of observations in, 83–85; quota, 77; random, 76–77; representative, 26, 74, 76–77, 85–87, 90, 104, 113, 115; size, 36, 110. *See also* large-N research
Sánchez, Angel, 109
sanctioning, 158–59, 230; evolution of, 186–87; in experiments, 162, 253; graduated, 100–101; and overharvest, 145
Santos, Francisco, 181
Sarch, Marie-Thérèse, 122
satellite imagery, 34, 53
satisficing, 200, 202
Saysel, Ali, 200–202
scarcity, 239. *See also* natural resources
Schelling, Thomas, 182
Schlager, Edella, 95–98, 156–57, 200
Schluessler, Rudolf, 185
Schmidt, Klaus, 224
Schreinemachers, Pepijn, 210
Scott, Anthony, 31
security: of returns, 229; of tenure, 45
self-governance, 43, 106, 171, 243
self-interest, 22. *See also* rational choice
self-organization, 236, 238, 243, 246–47
Selvaraj, K. N., 55
Senegal, 48, 205–6
sensitivity, 144
Shankar, Anisha, 155
Shepsle, Kenneth, 99
Shivakoti, Ganesh, 103
Sigmund, Karl, 183–84
signaling, 150, 183–84
Simon, Herbert, 233–34, 286n10.15
Skvoretz, John, 184
Smajgl, Alex, 208
small-N research: benefits of, 11–12; problems of, 36, 78
Smith, John, 182

Smith, Vernon, 143
social dilemmas, 32, 217–18, 109–10, 236; in experiments, 142; models of, 145, 222; second-order, 185–86; third-order, 253
social-ecological systems: analytical frameworks of, 234–35, 277n2.13; research on, 244
socioeconomic variables, 238, 240
Somanathan, E., 55
spatial data, 208
spatial games, 180–82
specialization: and disciplinary divides, 4, 39, 82; drawbacks of, 258, 261–62; and methodologies, 20–21; of researchers, 265
standardization: of concepts, 133; of research instruments, 128
Stanley, E. Ann, 185
statistical fixes, 13, 86
statistical significance, 84
Steed, Brian, 131, 254
Steele, Paul, 59
Stranlund, John, 161, 163
strategies: in agent-based models, 172; communal sharing, 188; conditional cooperation, 153; grim trigger, 185; and heterogeneity, 82–83; and heuristics, 225; imitation of, 200; participatory, 202–3; of sampling, 134; social comparison, 200; Tit-for-Tat, 178–79; types of, 284n7.1
stylized facts, 196
subtractability, 42
suckers, 150, 183, 229
sufficiency, 222
survey research, 209–10; data in, 25, 37, 65, 210, 254; household, 67, 72–74, 119, 121–22, 137, 209–10; opinion, 7, 168
Sutton, Alexander, 86
symbols, 184. *See also* signaling
syntax, 189–90
synthetic research, 39–45, 64, 87, 89, 107–10, 277n2.12; challenges of, 38–39, 61–62, 87, 113–14; narrative, 111–13. *See also* meta-analysis
Szabo, György, 182

Takezawa, Masanori, 188
Talakai, Malia, 267–68